'A striking despatch from the epistemological coalface, providing a truly fasci-nating insight into the nuts and bolts of how the "first draft of history" is pre-pared. Compelling and immediate, this is a priceless addition to the story of Nigeria.'

Paddy Docherty, author of *Blood and Bronze*

'A timely account of the civil war, whose shadow still falls on a dysfunctional Nigeria, and another Federal commander's term in the presidency is ending. Derrick's vantage point at *West Africa*, then the authoritative London weekly, is strengthened by research since, and detailed, argued analysis.'

Richard Bourne OBE, Senior Research Fellow, Institute of Commonwealth Studies, University of London

'Derrick offers a unique perspective on the Biafra war, reflecting on both the successes and short-comings of contemporary British news coverage. His even-handed account, based on personal experience and subsequent research, is an impressive addition to the literature on this often-forgotten war.'

S. Elizabeth Bird, Professor Emerita of Anthropology, University of South Florida and author of *Surviving Biafra*

'With this clear-eyed and timely examination of what the international media got wrong, and what they got right, Derrick has fashioned an engaging history of the war for Biafra, a conflict many still struggle to understand.'

Andrew Walker, journalist and author of *'Eat the Heart of the Infidel'*

'The Biafra war is still a deep wound in the hearts of many Nigerians. This careful, balanced exploration of the events that led to this tragedy may provide some relief for those in the Igbo community still struggling with the memories of the atrocities committed against them.'

Martin Plaut, Senior Research Fellow, Institute of Commonwealth Studies, University of London

'Combines the immediacy and detail of great journalism with the thoughtful analysis and broad perspectives of great historical writing. Perhaps uniquely for books about this war, it is neither dominated by re-visited obsessions of the past nor filtered through the selective vision of the present; I found so much here that other accounts have ignored or forgotten.'

Oliver Owen, Departmental Lecturer in Social Anthropology, University of Oxford

T0333537

BIAFRA IN THE NEWS

JONATHAN DERRICK

Biafra in the News

The Nigerian Civil War Seen from a London News Desk

HURST & COMPANY, LONDON

First published in the United Kingdom in 2022 by
C. Hurst & Co. (Publishers) Ltd.,
New Wing, Somerset House, Strand, London, WC2R 1LA
© Jonathan Derrick, 2022
All rights reserved.

Distributed in the United States, Canada and Latin America by
Oxford University Press, 198 Madison Avenue, New York, NY 10016,
United States of America.

The right of Jonathan Derrick to be identified as the author
of this publication is asserted by him in accordance with the
Copyright, Designs and Patents Act, 1988.

A Cataloguing-in-Publication data record for this book
is available from the British Library.

ISBN: 9781787386860

This book is printed using paper from registered sustainable
and managed sources.

www.hurstpublishers.com

Printed in Great Britain by Bell and Bain Ltd, Glasgow

CONTENTS

LIST OF ABBREVIATIONS

ACB	African Continental Bank
AEF	French Equatorial Guinea
AFP	Agence France-Presse
AG	Action Group
AOF	French West Africa
BBA	Britain–Biafra Association
BBC	British Broadcasting Corporation
BOFF	Biafran Organisation of Freedom Fighters
BP	British Petroleum
CCN	Christian Council of Nigeria
CD&W	Colonial Development and Welfare
CMS	Church Missionary Society
CND	Campaign for Nuclear Disarmament
COR	Calabar, Ogoja and Rivers Provinces
CRO	Commonwealth Relations Office
DM	Deutschmark
EEC	European Economic Community
ENBS	Eastern Nigeria Broadcasting Service
FCO	Foreign and Commonwealth Office
FMG	Federal Military Government
GOC	general officer commanding
ICRC	International Committee of the Red Cross
ICSA	Interim Common Services Agency
IPC	International Publishing Corporation
IPOB	Indigenous People of Biafra

LIST OF ABBREVIATIONS

JCA	Joint Church Aid
LBA	licensed buying agent
LGO	Lagos Garrison Organisation
LSE	London School of Economics
MASSOB	Movement for the Actualisation of the Sovereign State of Biafra
MCF	Movement for Colonial Freedom
NA	Native Authority
NAF	Nigerian Air Force
NCNC	National Council of Nigerian Citizens
NEPU	Northern Elements Progressive Union
NLC	National Liberation Council
NNDP	Nigerian National Democratic Party
NPC	Northern People's Congress
NPN	National Party of Nigeria
OAS	Organisation Armée Secrète
OAU	Organisation of African Unity
SAC	Service d'Action Civique
SAS	Special Air Service
SDECE	Service de Documentation Extérieure et de Contre-Espionnage
SIS	(British) Secret Intelligence Service
SMC	Supreme Military Council
SOAS	School of Oriental and African Studies
SWAFP	Socialist Workers and Farmers Party
UAC	United Africa Company
UDI	Unilateral Declaration of Independence
UMBC	United Middle Belt Congress
UNICEF	United Nations Children's Fund
UPE	universal primary education
UPGA	United Progressive Grand Alliance
UPI	United Press International
WCC	World Council of Churches

LIST OF ILLUSTRATIONS

1. Nigerian Head of State Yakubu Gowon © Keystone Press/Alamy Stock Photo
2. Lt. Col. Odumegwu Ojukwu © Keystone Pictures USA/ZUMAPRESS.com/Alamy Live News
3. The changing boundaries of Biafra, 1967–69, as the territory shrank from the entire former Eastern Region into a small enclave in the Igbo heartland. Cartography by Bill Nelson.
4. Biafran soldiers carrying a wounded comrade. Credit: Al J. Venter.
5. Biafran recruits under training towards the end of the war. Credit: Al J. Venter.
6. Two of the child victims of the conflict, near Uli. Credit: Al J. Venter.
7. A Biafran propaganda poster. Credit: Al J. Venter.
8. A rural scene in Biafran territory in the war. Credit: Al J. Venter.

PREFACE

Fifty years have passed since the war fought by Nigeria to prevent the secession of the country's Eastern Region as the Republic of Biafra. This book is my contribution to the commemoration of the semi-centenary, based on my work recording the Nigerian crisis and war almost from beginning to end, on the staff of the London weekly *West Africa*, where I worked from April 1966 to August 1970. I worked particularly on the news pages, writing probably well over half of the news of events in Nigeria. I never visited the war zone. However, in later years I worked for six years in Nigeria—at the Institute for Agricultural Research, Ahmadu Bello University, Zaria, and then at the University of Ilorin—and got to know the country much better, visiting many parts of it, including the former Biafran war zone. I also worked for many years, in Paris and London, for the magazine and book companies run by the late Raph Uwechue.

After all this, the contribution I can make to commemoration of the Biafra war is still limited. I cannot think of competing with the eyewitness accounts by several other journalists of the war and the hideous famine that accompanied it. Nor can I take on the immense task of a full, definitive account of the whole conflict—readers should not expect that from this work. I believe such an account still remains to be written, though I must add straight away that, although I have read many of the books published on the conflict, I may have missed many. There are several books covering the whole of the conflict, notably John de St Jorre, *The Nigerian Civil War* (1972); Zdenek Červenka, *A History of the Nigerian War 1967–1970* (1971); and

Michael Gould, *The Struggle for Modern Nigeria: The Biafran War 1967–1970* (2012). The first, in my view the best, includes many eyewitness accounts of events covered by the author as a reporter. Gould's book is the fruit of thorough research, including many interviews with participants, as are some of the numerous books covering particular aspects—the military operations, the related politics, the international involvement, the famine and relief efforts. Obviously some books on the war are partisan, but all are useful contributions. Still, in my view, an adequate full history of the crisis and war, using archives (now open for the period concerned in Britain) and reminiscences while people are still around to give them, and the plentiful other material, remains to be written. I, however, cannot take it on.

What I offer instead is a reminiscence of the crisis and war as seen from a London editorial desk. I was far from the scene of action in miles, but with colleagues often travelling to the scene, and constant attention to the topic every week, I can claim to have followed the conflict with unusual continued attention. It was from a distance, certainly, and I cannot compare my position with those of reporters and others who were on the spot, still less with those of Nigerians who lived and died through it all. But I hope readers will consider an account from my vantage point useful.

I record the main events of the crisis and war as the magazine reported and analysed them, and our reaction at the time. Many episodes described fully in other works will only be described briefly here. About some of them I will, after recalling without hindsight what we wrote and thought at the time, flash forward to examine facts revealed in the following fifty years and some interpretations of those facts. It would be absurd to try to write as I would have done in 1970, ignoring all that had been published since then. I ask readers to be patient with repeated phrases such as "at the time" and "it was later confirmed".

On certain topics arousing particular controversy at the time and later. I have broken from the narrative to give an updated assessment. These are the famine and the reporting of it; the worldwide popular sympathy for Biafran war victims; the relief airlift to Biafran territory; and the propaganda by the warring parties and their foreign supporters—something I was well placed to observe. On all these topics which have aroused heated debate, subsequent writing has added little of significance to the facts known to us on *West Africa* at the time; this book has no major revelations. However, on one infamous episode which was known at the time to some others besides the people involved, the massacre at Asaba, recent research has led to full details being published, and this I refer to. One other matter—French arms supplies to Biafra—remains mysterious and I have to say that the full truth about that, so far as I know, remains to be told. There are some other matters on which I have to say the same.

Passionate feelings were aroused in Britain and many other countries about this war, and with good reason. These were essentially moral feelings, and no account of the war has been, or could be, without moral comments: who could write such a dry, unfeeling account? This book is full of words of praise and blame. In fact moral feeling is part of the story. No accurate account of this conflict can show it as just a clash of selfish interests; the moral aspect was an essential one, especially in the worldwide reactions of sympathy for Biafra, in which there was no hidden agenda of self-interest.

Nigerians with strong retrospective partisan feelings for either side in the war will disagree with some of my judgements, but I give good reasons for them. I hope that they will not suggest that there is something wrong with my making criticisms after enjoying Nigeria's hospitality for six years. If anyone does suggest this, I have three answers. First, when in Nigeria, I talked only rarely with Nigerians about the civil war, and did not seek to gather information about it. Secondly, I never had any grudges against anyone I encountered in Nigeria, or its government at the time—there is nothing personal behind what I have written. Lastly, I readily agree that any Nigerian living in Britain can say what he or she likes about any British government and its actions.

Whatever I say in these pages about my former colleagues on the *West Africa* magazine, or other journalists that I met, or any other named individuals known to me personally, relates only to their work; there is nothing personal about anyone, certainly no fifty-year-old office tittle-tattle. Regarding my *West Africa* colleagues, I must express here my great thanks for helping me on my first job, to start my career, and I pay tribute to all their work. I particularly salute the

memory of two people who would have been very interested to see
this book but who both passed away in 2014: Kaye Whiteman, one
of the work colleagues, and Raph Uwechue. And I thank all who
helped or encouraged me in the preparation of this book.

1

NIGERIA

BUILD-UP TO THE CRISIS

Biafra. There is no country of that name on a map of Africa. But the name lives on in the memories of millions of Africans who attempted, fifty years ago, to break away from the Nigerian Federation and create an independent Republic of Biafra. The Biafrans, mostly of the Igbo[1] people, fought hard in a brutal war aggravated by a terrible famine. They lost, and then resumed life in Nigeria in a splendid reconciliation. But they did not forget their struggle and suffering; nobody in their place could.

Among other Nigerians, too, the civil war in their country is well remembered, at least among the over-sixties. But in the West, far from the equatorial forest region where the war was fought, does the name of Biafra still ring a bell?

Among many British people who were of secondary school age or older in 1967–70, it surely does. During those years, the newspapers proclaimed that name constantly. The breakaway state, while it held out, was better known to the British public than Nigeria had been before. It was a household word, and was linked closely with images that must remain in many minds: images of starving skin-and-bone children. People who lived through the war, of course, remember the reality of those children, among many thousands of war victims.

No event in newly independent Africa hit the European and North American headlines as Biafra did—not even the first Congo crisis, the years of chaos, conflict and destruction that followed the Belgians' departure in 1960. The coming of independence in other parts of sub-Saharan Africa, peaceful in almost all cases, was followed in the British press, but with limited interest where many of the new countries were concerned. However, there was considerably more interest in eastern and southern African countries where British settlers had migrated since the 19th century and were still powerful for a time. And in West Africa, Ghana had a high profile as the first black African colony of Britain to become independent, in 1957, under a famous leader, Kwame Nkrumah, who aroused admiration around Africa and considerable interest, often unfriendly, in the Western media.

Nigeria, the most populous country of Africa, became independent on 1 October 1960, as a Federation (from 1963 a Federal Republic) of three regions—Northern, Western and Eastern—plus the Federal Capital Territory of Lagos. It enjoyed good relations with Western countries and a generally "good press" there. British firms did good business with Nigeria, an important trade partner for the UK, and investors flocked to a country with obvious good prospects. Thousands of British people lived and worked in the country, never as settlers, but as business staff, teachers, lecturers, technical staff, and so on. For them, and for home-based officials, academics and others interested in Nigeria, the sporadic coverage of the country in the British press was supplemented by a specialist weekly magazine, *West Africa*, founded back in 1917; this magazine, while published in London and British-owned, was by the 1960s read mainly by Nigerians and other West Africans.

Nigeria's federal government was called, in the common Western language of the time, a "moderate" one. That meant that it was different from the governments of President Nkrumah of Ghana, President Nyerere of Tanzania, and some other African leaders who promoted economic nationalism and socialism and were strongly and vocally committed to the liberation of Africans still under colonial or white settler rule in South Africa, Rhodesia and the Portuguese colonies; in Britain and the US these were often portrayed as on the Communist side in the Cold War paranoia of that time.

There was in fact a division among African states over foreign relations, though it was not dictated by the Cold War. It was shown in the creation of two blocs of states in 1961, the Casablanca group (in which Nkrumah and President Nasser of Egypt were prominent) and the Monrovia group, which included Nigeria. In 1965 the division was sharply revealed over the question of Rhodesia. That was a major African preoccupation, and also the number-one African issue in Britain in the year before Nigeria fell into a disaster attracting all the world's attention.

After Northern Rhodesia became independent under African rule, headed by President Kenneth Kaunda, in 1964 the white settler leaders in Southern Rhodesia, now renamed as simply Rhodesia, resolved under the leadership of their prime minister, Ian Smith, to avoid having to hand power to Africans there. After months of negotiation and tension with the British government—now the first Labour government of Harold Wilson, whose policies towards Africa were almost identical with those of the Conservatives, who had presided over decolonisation—Ian Smith's government made a Unilateral Declaration of Independence (UDI) on 11 November 1965. In response, the Organisation of African Unity (OAU), the continental inter-government body created in 1963, called on all members to break off diplomatic relations with Britain for its failure to suppress Smith's rebellion. Ghana, Tanzania and seven other countries carried out the resolution. Nigeria's prime minister did not, choosing rather to travel to London to suggest a special Commonwealth summit to discuss the Rhodesia question.

This federal prime minister, Sir Abubakar Tafawa Balewa, had since independence been head of the federal government, which had been a series of coalitions dominated by his party, the Northern People's Congress (NPC), the ruling party in the Northern Region, which covered 80 per cent of the country's area. The head of that party and the real ruler of the whole country was the premier of the Northern Region, Sir Ahmadu Bello, Sardauna of Sokoto.[2] Both men had been knighted by Queen Elizabeth, but it was Sir Abubakar who was best known to the British and the rest of the world, where he was much respected as a peaceable, diplomatic character. The "distinguished Prime Minister of Nigeria", as Wilson called him, was as well

3

fitted as anyone to attempt the task of resolving the Rhodesia stand-off. But that task was in fact impossible for anyone then, as Britain refused to use force to end Rhodesian UDI, depending instead on international sanctions which came into force but which the white settler regime was well able to withstand with help from South Africa, Portugal and some less public friends. Nevertheless, the special Commonwealth summit met in Lagos and passed resolutions in January 1966.

As it did so, just a short distance away there was serious political violence in the Western Region. The democratic system installed at Nigeria's independence had never functioned like a proper democracy, and was undermined by ruthless power seeking and blatant corruption among political leaders. The Yoruba people, who formed most of the population of the Western Region and Lagos, were divided politically from 1962; their main party, the Action Group (AG), split and lost power over the regional government. The new party ruling in the West, the Nigerian National Democratic Party (NNDP) under Samuel Akintola, was allied to the NPC. When it secured re-election by flagrant rigging of regional elections in October 1965, violent protests broke out and there was soon something like a low-intensity civil war. There was no danger to the Commonwealth leaders in Lagos, but their host had deep trouble on his doorstep.

After seeing off the Commonwealth delegates, Sir Abubakar Tafawa Balewa received the commercial editor of *West Africa*, Bridget Bloom, for an interview at his official residence in Lagos in the evening of 14 January 1966.[3] A few hours later, soldiers commanded by Major Emmanuel Ifeajuna arrested him and took him away to be shot dead and buried by a roadside.

The coup of 15 January 1966

This action was part of an attempted coup d'état by a group of junior army officers. Their leader, Major Chukwuma Nzeogwu, struck at the heart of the NPC-dominated government, in Kaduna, capital of the Northern Region, killing Sir Ahmadu Bello. Other conspirators killed S.L. Akintola in Ibadan, capital of the Western Region. The plotters also killed the federal minister of finance, Chief Festus Okotie-Eboh, and seven senior army officers: six from the Northern and Western Regions (Brigadier S. Ademulegun, Brigadier Zakariya Maimalari and four others) and one Easterner, Lt Colonel Arthur Unegbe.

The shocking violent events of 15 January 1966—remembered by Nigerians simply as "January the Fifteenth"—have been repeatedly studied and described, by some of the men responsible and many other writers, ever since.[4] Here only the essential facts need be recalled. The conspirators sought to take power and end the multiple criminal activities linked with the politicians who had ruled the country. Nzeogwu, in a broadcast, declared,

> Our enemies are political profiteers, swindlers, the men in high places that seek bribes and demand ten percent, those that seek to keep the country divided permanently so that they can remain in office as ministers and VPs of ease, the tribalists, the nepotists, those that make the country big for nothing before international circles ...[5]

In the event they failed to take power, but the Federal Government that Tafawa Balewa had headed was unable to retain power and handed over full authority to the head of the army, Major General Johnson Aguiyi-Ironsi. A military regime took over, not including the officers who had carried out the attacks—these were in fact arrested—but including new military governors of the regions (which now numbered four, as explained below). The country was now ruled by a Supreme Military Council, under Ironsi as supreme commander of the armed forces, and a Federal Executive Council. All the federal and regional civilian governments were abolished, as was the office of the titular president, Nnamdi Azikiwe, who had been in Britain when the coup occurred; all the political parties were outlawed.

Very many Nigerians celebrated the prospect of an end to the evils the coup promised to end. Nigerian politicians had aroused public contempt not only because of their self-enrichment but also because their political manoeuvres exploited and aggravated the ethnic divisions in the country. They, however, did not invent or monopolise what was then generally called "tribalism". The peoples of Nigeria were then always described in English as "tribes", and the word is still common among Nigerians, although many of them dislike it as it is redolent of colonial attitudes (after all, who calls the Welsh and the Scots "tribes"?).

Whatever word is used, the importance of belonging to one of Nigeria's constituent peoples is a key factor that every account of the Biafran conflict necessarily has to consider at the outset.

Peoples, regions and politics

In each of Nigeria's three regions at independence there was a predominant ethnic group. In the Western Region it was the Yorubas, in the Eastern Region the Igbos. In the Northern Region it was the Hausa–Fulani people, commonly so called because the Habe people, called "Hausa" by others and speaking the Hausa language, had for some centuries mingled with the separate Fulani people, whose Islamic reformist leaders had in the 19th century conquered the Hausa emirates. The emirs and other urban Fulani people speak Hausa and the Hausa–Fulani people are often called simply "Hausas" by other Nigerians. The Hausa language is widely spoken or understood by non-Hausas, and is the common language of the Nigerian army.

The Hausas, Igbos and Yorubas are the most numerous and best-known peoples of Nigeria; there have been suggestions of changing the country's name to Wazobia, from the three main languages' words for "come": *wa* (Yoruba), *zo* (Hausa), *bia* (Igbo). But millions of Nigerians belong to other tribes, which by the 1960s were commonly called "minorities", and their position was a very important part of the background to the civil war. In the Northern Region at independence, the Hausa–Fulani emirates and their allied party, the NPC, held hegemony that went beyond the areas where the emirs— the emirs of Kano, Zaria, Bauchi and Katsina, and several other greater and lesser emirs, with the sultan of Sokoto at their head— actually reigned. The emirate system, traditional but fostered by the British, also included non-Hausa states of the Kanuri people (Borno) and the Nupe people (Bida). In addition, much of the North's vast area was peopled by dozens of tribes in what was called the Middle Belt of Nigeria, such as the Tiv people along the Benue River and the cluster of tribes on the Plateau. These were mostly non-Muslim, unlike the majority in the emirates; at first called Pagans by the British, by the 1960s they were increasingly Christian.

There were also important "minorities" in the South, notably the Ijaw people in the Niger Delta and the Ibibios in the south-east corner of the Eastern Region. As party politics developed in the run-up to independence, there were demands on behalf of the minorities which caused concern to the British, who therefore set up in 1958 the Willink Commission to inquire into "the fears of minorities and the means of allaying them". Why was this thought necessary? What did those people fear?

The explanation of this goes to the root of Nigerian politics as it developed to decide who would occupy the widening government positions open to Nigerians under the constitutions enacted by Britain in 1947, 1951 and 1954. To simplify a complex and varying picture: Nigerians, not only their political leaders, consider politics and government from the perspective of representation or non-representation of the community to which they feel they belong. And usually this community is, to use the word still commonly used by Nigerians, the tribe. The question about federal, regional, state or local government is: do those in power represent the tribe I belong to, or at least treat it favourably? Or are they of a different tribe or group of tribes and likely to ignore, neglect or even mistreat my people?

The writer Elechi Amadi wrote after the civil war, "Ours was, and still is, a tribal society. The herd instinct is strong, and most people feel far more at home among members of their own tribe than in any other community." He added,

> Poverty, with its concomitant low standard of living, lends strength to this herd instinct. People see the tribe as an island of survival in a seething, unstable socio-economic sea. Who else would give you a job, if not your brother? How could a policeman caution you for a minor offence and let you go if he was not your tribesman? How could a scholarship board know the needs of your community if your son was not a member of the board? Red tape was cut, all formalities brushed aside, if your man was at the top ... It is wrong to think that only the poorly educated have these notions.[6]

Tribal identity can be fluid, or vague, or even contrived. Amadi's Ikwerre people, very much under Igbo cultural influence, are sometimes considered an Igbo subgroup, sometimes not. The Igbos living west of the lower Niger are sometimes considered distinct from the mass of Igbos living east of the river, and are called Anioma, but they speak Igbo and are widely described as Western Igbos. And identifying with a community below the level of a major ethnic group can be important, as with the Ijebu, Egba and other sections of the Yorubas. But with variations, a feeling that ethnic identification is very important is general.

When it comes to political attitudes and activity, it is easy to arouse feelings that "our people" ought if possible to be in power, and if others are in fact in power, these are likely to favour their own at the expense of "our people" and exert what is commonly described as "domination"—a constantly recurring word in Nigeria in the years leading up to the civil war, and indeed later. Whether correctly alleged or not, it means treating a certain region or ethnic group with neglect, disregard or discrimination in such matters as provision of services, economic development, and especially employment. The group feeling disfavoured can see the party or government run by the other group as alien and ill-intentioned.

Such situations recur in other parts of Africa and, indeed, around the world. While free elections can voice or incite divisive feelings, and Africans establishing one-party regimes gave that as a reason, that did not in fact avoid such problems. Under both democracy and dictatorship, people of a certain region in any country can come to feel in a particularly acute way that the government in power does not represent them, is remote from them and simply gives them orders. In Britain that feeling has recently existed in Scotland, the North of England, and Wales under prolonged Conservative government. There, resentment remained peaceful, but across the Irish Sea it was very different. In the Northern Ireland troubles which started at the very time of the Nigerian civil war (but went on for much longer), the basic grievance—exclusion and discrimination—of the Nationalist/Republican/Catholic community resembled that of many peoples in Nigeria who saw themselves as disadvantaged.

But there was a big difference. In Northern Ireland, people of the disadvantaged community still enjoyed the modern amenities of the West and all the benefits of the British welfare state. In Nigeria, such benefits did not exist and modern amenities were thinly spread for a population of over 50 million, most of whom earned low incomes, mainly from smallholder farming, whether they grew food for themselves or for trade within Nigeria, or crops for export or industrial use. An increasing number lived in cities and towns where better incomes could be had by some, but many had no jobs and there was no unemployment benefit. Great numbers of people lived by trading but did not usually make big money. Health services were scarce and could be of poor quality when provided by the state, or of good quality but costly when provided by the churches and other private agencies.

Description of the deprived lives of the majority in Nigeria then, and still today, could go on. The facts are well known and explain—to enlarge on Elechi Amadi's point—why it matters so much whether people can expect their government to provide more clinics, schools, tarred roads, piped water, electricity, and above all jobs for their district, or alternatively are convinced that these things will be denied them by an alien government exercising "domination".

It is irrelevant that their ancestors had lived without those amenities of life for centuries. Now that they were possible, people obviously needed them—this was the "revolution of rising expectations". The government was expected to provide them, especially as in fact, on a very inadequate scale, it did. The British, in the latter part of their rule, had seen the need to provide some improvements in Africans' daily lives through Colonial Development and Welfare (CD&W). When Nigerian governments were elected to power in the regions in 1951, they expanded state health services, built better roads, and notably provided more education, that being seen by everyone as the way for every man and woman to get ahead. For example, the Western Region government of the AG under Chief Obafemi Awolowo introduced universal primary education. However, resources were limited; not every part of the country could be satisfied even if all governments had the best intentions, and that is what governments were commonly perceived not to have.

These sentiments lay behind the political calls for separation, or devolution, to bring the government nearer to one's home area. They were often made in the name not of an individual tribe (of which Nigeria has 200 or more) but of a wider group of several tribes. An example was the movement on behalf of peoples of the Middle Belt, who widely felt alienated from the party which controlled the whole region. The Middle Belt campaigners against the Northern regime had their own party, the United Middle Belt Congress (UMBC), led by Joseph Tarka. His people, the Tivs, were at the forefront of the campaign, and there were two localised but serious uprisings among them, in 1960 and 1964.

Although Nigerians have commonly spoken of "the North" as if it were one solid mass, even within the Hausa–Fulani emirates the traditional class system, admired and maintained for decades by the British, was not unopposed. The Northern Elements Progressive Union (NEPU) headed by Aminu Kano opposed the traditional Hausa–Fulani local government system and the NPC, proclaiming a "class struggle" to liberate the *talakawa* ("commoners" in Hausa). It did not shake the NPC's power, and this example of socially based politics was not widely followed in Nigeria. Anyway, the Hausa–Fulani class structure and the elaborate traditional local government system of the "Native Authorities", or NAs (that term was still used after independence), with their efficient tax collection and their own police (*dogarai* in Hausa) were fairly unique.

Elsewhere there were traditional distinctions of rank and status, though the Igbos have always been an unusually egalitarian people; and, more important, modern development created a new class, a minority of wealthy people—businesspeople, politicians, senior civil servants, and some others. By the 1960s the gap between those few and the poor majority was blatant, especially in Lagos. This gap was of course noticed and denounced, but left-wing politics concentrating on the needs of the underprivileged regardless of tribe or region did not succeed well. Nigeria did have a vigorous trade union movement, which organised a successful two-week general strike in 1964; and, as in Western countries, that movement had its links with political parties. There were left-wing intellectuals among the Southern Nigerian peoples, and a small far-left Socialist Workers and Farmers Party (SWAFP). But their impact was very small, and it was noted, all over Africa, that trade unions represented wage workers, who were relatively better off than the great majority. Politicians were better able to appeal to the underprivileged not by calling on all of them, of all tribes, to unite to fight the fat cats, but by urging each ethnic group against a rival one: "Your hardships will not end as long as you are dominated by those—s, get out from under them, demand your own separate state."

In the Eastern Region, the ruling party from 1951 was the National Council of Nigerian Citizens (NCNC), founded by Nnamdi Azikiwe (always called Zik) as a pan-Nigerian party. The first head of the regional government in Enugu, Eyo Ita, was an Efik of Calabar, but after his early removal in 1953 the NCNC came to be seen as a party of Igbo supremacy—though it had plenty of support in Lagos and the Western Region—and the Eastern government, headed first by Azikiwe and from 1960 by Michael Okpara, as an Igbo supremacy government. In the East, the various peoples, Igbos and minority peoples, had many different languages but a good deal in common culturally, as they had been converted to Christianity on a large scale over the previous century and the churches were a part of life for them. As such, there were schools, which missionaries had started first, though government schools had been added later. Even so, there were minority grievances and calls for separation.

In 1961, when British Southern Cameroons, a UN Trust Territory legally separate from Nigeria but for all practical purposes part of the Eastern Region, had a referendum to choose between union with Nigeria or with ex-French Cameroun, the decisive vote against Nigeria was very much an anti-Igbo vote. There remained many non-Igbo peoples in the region, in Calabar, Ogoja and Rivers Provinces, and among them a movement for a separate COR (Calabar, Ogoja and Rivers Provinces) State developed (the word "state" was the one chosen by such movements from an early date). The Willink Commission report rejected this and all other proposals for splitting the regions.

After independence, the Western Region was the first to have a portion separated from it in response to minorities' demands. The Mid-West Region was created in 1963, out of Benin and Delta Provinces, with a number of peoples including the Bini or Edo people of the historic kingdom of Benin and the Urhobos, the Itsekiris, the Western Igbos, and some of the Ijaws (others of whom lived in Rivers Province of the Eastern Region). Its creation was approved by 80 per cent of voters in a referendum, and was followed by elections which brought the NCNC to power under Dennis Osadebay as premier in February 1964.

Thus there were four regions at the time of the military takeover in January 1966, when military governors (all indigenes of the respective regions) were appointed for them: Lt Colonel Odumegwu Ojukwu in the East, Lt Colonel Hassan Katsina (son of the reigning emir of Katsina) in the North, Lt Colonel Adekunle Fajuyi in the West and Lt Colonel David Ejoor in the Mid-West; meanwhile, Major Mobolaji Johnson was appointed military administrator of Lagos.

In celebrating the fall of the civilian governments in January 1966, Nigerians seemed often to put all the blame on the fallen politicians. But although unscrupulous power-mongering, corruption and other abuse of office had been blatant among them, politicians had not been an alien occupying force. They might seem to live in another world in their comfortable "Senior Service" quarters and their Mercedes, but they remained attached to their home villages and extended families, as all Nigerians did and still do. Many other Nigerians were accomplices in abuse of power.

Some British experts on Africa started writing from the inter-war period about "de-tribalisation" of people moving to towns or into modern sorts of employment, but this was nonsense. Leaving aside the doubts about the word "tribe", people with secondary and higher education, employees of the government and business, and people who spent much of their time in the cities did not abandon family ties among the majority living and farming in villages. On the contrary, they actively formed or joined associations of people from a particular town or area, whose aim was not just to respect tradition, but to help migrants and others adapt to Westernised life and work for defence of a home area's interests and improvement of its situation: these included the Ijesha Patriotic Association in the West, the Urhobo Progress Union in the Mid-West, the Tiv Progressive Association in the North, and countless others. Such positive efforts helped very many people—villagers could be helped with school fees by "sons abroad", for example. But there was another side to this interaction between the modern sector and the village. When someone with a senior position and a good income visited the home village, he would be offered yams, mangoes, and demands: "What are you doing to give jobs to our people?"

When senior people in all areas, not just politicians, were suspected of nepotism and favouritism, doubtless it was often true, but not always. The worst aspect of ethnic feeling was hasty judgement and suspicion. People could suspect someone had got a job because of where he came from when in fact he had been the best-qualified applicant. If a government was accused of ethnic favouritism in the granting of scholarships (one complaint of Rivers people against the Eastern Region government), how often was it true? Could it not have been an excuse for an individual's failure to get a scholarship? A stitch-up among Igbos or Ijebus in a government office in Nigeria might occur, or might be imagined (like a stitch-up among Old Etonians in a British government office, or among Freemasons in a French one). People can give mistaken ethnic labels to others. It may not have mattered much in ordinary life, but hasty ethnic-based judgements did great harm in the national crisis.

During that crisis, and later, Nigerians sometimes accused foreign commentators of exaggerating tribalism. In fact those commentators were probably reflecting what Nigerians told them, but they may not always have kept things in proportion. Nigerians were not squabbling the whole time. People of many tribes worked well together in government service and state corporations, on the Nigerian Railway, in the police, in other employment. The University College of Ibadan, founded in 1948 to award University of London degrees and turned into an independent university in 1962, was well known as a place where students from around the country studied together under multinational and multi-ethnic teaching staff.

The fact that Nigerians speak scores of different languages, and many are able to read and write those languages in which there are countless publications and recordings, has not been given as a reason for civil strife, and cannot be. Diversity of mother tongues is accepted, many people speak several of the Nigerian languages, and English and Pidgin are common languages. Religion is not a reason for strife either, despite what was often said during the civil war, and despite the recent phenomena among Muslims (or pseudo-Muslims) in Nigeria, which were undreamed of in the 1960s. Religion could come into ethnic or regional discord then, as when the Sardauna of Sokoto used his position as Northern Region premier to lead Islamic conversion campaigns around the region; and Southern Nigerian Christians utter a good deal of "Islamophobia" (to use a recently adopted term). But tribe or region is what counts; millions of Yorubas are Muslim, and in the 1960s it was estimated that the population of Lagos was half Muslim, but in ethnic politics these Muslims have limited affinity with their Hausa co-religionists. The teachings of both Islam and Christianity are opposed to racism, tribalism and any failure to recognise the equal worth of all human beings; in the crisis and civil war, prominent Nigerian Christians spoke out against these things. During the war Christians in Nigeria in fact fired on fellow Christians as readily as those in Europe did in wars over several centuries; but, to anticipate later chapters in this book, the war was not about religion.

Where religion is concerned, one must not forget that millions in the 1960s still followed the traditional religions of Nigeria. These had differing local roots, but belief in invisible forces and witchcraft was and remains general, with variations, all over Nigeria and other African countries. There were also sinister semi-secret cults—traditional, modern or both together—which have continued and sometimes make the news. Normally these things were little talked of in the media in the 1960s, though everyone knew about them—it was well known, for example, that soldiers wore protective amulets in the war. But adherence to the universal religions was very public, and religion had a place in life in Nigeria which it was already fast losing in Britain in the 1960s. During the crisis the country's leading daily paper, the *Daily Times*, at one Christmas time had a front-page headline, "Hail the Prince of Peace": that would not have been seen in the mainstream British press at that time.

Some basic things of life are similar all over the country. Most of the population in the 1960s were small farmers (only recently has the urban population possibly exceeded half), and many of the food crops are grown all over the country: yams and cassava, the main tuber crops, and maize, a major cereal. Some other crops are grown only in the forest belt, notably the oil palm with all its useful products, or principally in the savanna further north: groundnuts, millet, sorghum; but distribution around the country is assured by the large-scale internal food trade, which also includes the trade in cattle, reared by nomadic Fulani herdsmen and taken south to provide beef for areas where cattle cannot be reared. Although cuisine obviously varies by locality, the basic dish everywhere is the same, a sort of starch paste or dough made of cereals or tubers, with a stew or "soup" including meat and herbs. All this is in common with other parts of West Africa also.

There is, indeed, much in common among Nigerians, much to unite them. Nobody outside ever forced them to fight each other. Yet they did so, terribly, for two and a half years. And every account of the war, by Nigerians and others, agrees on the reason, one simple reason: collective distrust, fear and resentment among the peoples of the country.

This chapter has left until the last the worst and most damaging of these collective hostile sentiments: the one between North and South, due to the North–South gap that developed during the British colonial era. Northern Nigeria and Southern Nigeria, originally separate, were amalgamated under Governor General Sir Frederick (later Lord) Lugard in 1914. Christian missions made progress in the South, starting with the Anglican Church Missionary Society (CMS) in the Egba Yoruba kingdom and the Church of Scotland in Calabar in the 1840s, and spread Western education, use of English, and literacy in both Nigerian languages and English. All this continued to expand in the 20th century under British rule, with government schools added to the mission schools; the Catholic missions won converts in many areas, with mass conversion among the Igbos, and spread their schools at the same time. But in what became the Northern Region, the British, while encouraging missions in the Middle Belt where they won many converts, banned them almost completely in the Hausa–Fulani emirates and Borno, the "true North" as it was sometimes called. Government schools were also excluded from that area almost completely, to help preserve the traditional hierarchical Islamic society on which the British built their Indirect Rule system. Whether this effort at preservation was desired by the emirs, as the British said, or imposed by the British, as Nigerians including Northerners came increasingly to suggest, it had effects that caused immense problems when self-government, which the British rulers had not expected to see for a very long time, came into view from the 1940s.

Around Africa, Western education was eagerly sought after, more of it was wanted, and those who received it did all sorts of work, initially subordinate, for the government and business firms, as clerks, teachers, telegraphists, railwaymen, and such like. Eventually

Africans entered higher salaried positions, and when nationalist politics began, it was those Western-cultured people who formed parties and sought political power, which eventually came their way. Hence the populous region of the Northern Nigeria emirates, with very little Western education, was at a disadvantage. Within that region Southern Nigerians—Yorubas, Igbos and others—took the jobs requiring modern skills or qualifications, on the Nigerian Railway for example. Many also started all sorts of small businesses in the North, though the Hausas are themselves great traders. In big Northern cities like Kano, Zaria and Sokoto, these Southern Nigerian migrants had their own districts, called Sabon Gari.[7] There was not complete segregation from the Hausa–Fulani and Kanuri people, but there was considerable separation. Igbos in particular aroused the hostility commonly shown towards an enterprising minority seen as alien, like Jews and Armenians in other countries. On their side Igbos came often to express disdain for "illiterate Northerners" (that this region had had scholars writing in Arabic or Arabic-script Hausa for centuries did not matter—Western education was what counted now).

Once the British began gradually to hand over power, people of the Muslim emirates of the North began to fear that Southern Nigerians would not only hold more and more administrative and technical positions at ever-higher levels, but also exert political power over the emirates. The Northern People's Congress was set up in 1951 to defend the Muslim Northern heartland against this danger. Thus the greatest of all the Nigerian "domination" phobias developed, the phobia about "Southern domination" in the North. That phobia was shared by many British officials in the North who liked the emirates' traditional order.

The political developments in the 1950s, when under successive constitutions negotiated between the British and the Nigerian parties increasing power was placed in Nigerian hands through regional and federal elections, cannot be recalled in detail here. All the main parties—the NPC, AG and NCNC (ruling parties in the North, West and East respectively from 1951)—worked together to secure constitutional progress towards independence, but not all had the same ideas. In March 1953, in the federal parliament, Anthony Enahoro of the AG proposed a resolution calling on Britain to give independence in 1956. There was strong opposition to this among Northern leaders, not in a hurry to see the British go, and when an AG delegation went to hold a meeting in Kano on 16 May 1953, there were violent attacks in the city against Southern Nigerians, especially Igbos; at least 36 people, including Northerners, were killed. The attacks were not due solely to Hausa public feeling: there was incitement and preparation behind them. They sent a message to Southern Nigerians and the British: "Watch out! See what we can do if our interests are ignored." Thus Nigerian politics, at that early stage, descended to despicable organised violence. Much more was to come later, but for the time being the violence was or seemed isolated, and the parties still worked together and with the British. At that time there was talk of separating the North from the rest of Nigeria. In view of things said during the civil war, it may be noted that while Britain could in theory have partitioned Nigeria then, it was never likely to do so; the NPC leaders preferred to rule over the whole of Nigeria, and before long they did.

The Eastern and Western Regions obtained self-government in 1957, the Northern in 1959, and after federal elections the country became independent on 1 October 1960, with the North in a dominant position because of its size and its control of about half the seats in the federal parliament. But to ensure control, the NPC had to seek an alliance with one part of the South, which was not difficult as there was political disunity there. Nigeria became independent under a coalition of the NPC and NCNC. Dr Nnamdi Azikiwe became governor general and, later, president, but this was a titular post and power was in the hands of the NPC and its leader, the Northern Region premier, Sir Ahmadu Bello, with the federal prime minister, Tafawa Balewa, the head of government as seen by the rest of the world. So the North ruled: the response to fear of "Southern domination" was to create what other Nigerians called "Northern domination". Northern leaders set out to provide more Western education for their people—for example at Ahmadu Bello University, set up in 1962 and called after the premier whose name it still bears today, where positive discrimination was instituted to help Northerners. But this could not end the Southerners' advantage or the perceived danger of their "domination", as they continued to advance even further in Western education and the resulting opportunities, and so Northern leaders wanted to ensure that they had the last word where power was concerned.

The Western Region was excluded from power at the centre. It was made to feel its inferior position in 1962–3; when the AG split, Awolowo lost power, the NNDP under Akintola took over in Ibadan, and Awolowo was tried for a botched plot and gaoled. Other AG leaders were tried with him, including Chief Enahoro, who was extradited from Britain under the Fugitive Offenders Act in 1963 after a court case that made British headlines. This was a rare occasion (at that time) for Nigeria to make those headlines, but there was only limited criticism of the Nigerian government, as the trials of AG leaders were properly conducted.

The federal and regional governments of the newly independent country were not paralysed by the political bickering and tension. They scored many positive achievements in the early 1960s, including carrying on the administration of a vast country; expanding education, including universities such as the University of Nigeria, established at Nsukka in the Eastern Region in 1960; establishing new industries, while private investment added more; extending the railway to Maiduguri; building a big bridge over the lower Niger at Onitsha; and much else. The economy was doing well in many respects, and the start of oil production from 1958 in the Eastern and Mid-Western Regions, with oil exports and local refining, promised well for the future. But many of the government's economic ventures were tainted with corruption, and all the development took place against a background of uncertainty.

A crisis in 1962–4 over the holding of a census revealed the unresolved political problems: as the census would be used to delimit electoral constituencies, politicians, fearing that they might lose some representation, organised cheating—people were widely transported from one place to another to be counted in each—and so the results were quite unreliable. The basic North–South divide lay behind everything. Before the federal elections of late 1964 the NPC–NCNC coalition broke down and the Northern party was allied to the NNDP in the West, while the NCNC joined the AG, led by Dauda Adegbenro in place of the imprisoned Awolowo, in the United Progressive Grand Alliance (UPGA). The UPGA called for a boycott of the elections because of interference with its campaigning, no polling took place in the Eastern Region, and in the resulting tense situation talk of secession of the East was heard; the elections were then run in the East and the tension subsided, but now that region was excluded from power at the centre. However, Igbos and other Easterners still did well in business, employment up to the top levels, and education all over the country.

A worse crisis, already mentioned, followed a few months later. In response to the rigged elections in the West in October 1965, and the violent protests and near-guerrilla activity that followed, it was rumoured that the ruling federal coalition (NPC and NNDP) planned to use the army to restore order (or its control). At any rate it is commonly believed that such a plan involving the army—which had just 9,000 men, amazingly few for such a big country, and which had so far been kept out of the political struggles except for a minor role in suppressing the Tiv unrest—led certain junior officers to devise, or accelerate, plans for a military coup. The story of what lay behind the attacks on 15 January 1966 and what happened then has been analysed in many accounts. Some were examined in *West Africa* as they gradually came out; the official report by the Nigeria Police Force Special Branch did not become public knowledge in Britain until 1969,[8] but several official (and one-sided) accounts were published earlier, with several accounts in published books.

One thing that stood out from the beginning, and is still obvious in impartial accounts, is that Nzeogwu and other plotters believed in the unity of Nigeria and wanted to start reform of the whole country; they were not responding to Eastern Region grievances or Igbo ethnic chauvinism—the aim, Nzeogwu declared, was to "establish a strong, united and progressive nation free from corruption and internal strife".[9] But the principal coup plotters were Igbos; this is certain even if there are conflicting figures given for the hard core of plotters and other officers who collaborated with them.[10] It was as Igbos that other Nigerians came to view them: they could have been admired as idealists with a vision for much-needed reform for the whole country, or condemned with good reason as cold-blooded assassins, but, in fact, what mattered was that they were *Igbos*.

The immediate effect of their action, however, was the fall of the civilian governments, a new military regime with promises of better governance, and widespread public approval for this. There was some mourning for Tafawa Balewa, but it was "good riddance" for the regional governments, which had turned into near dictatorships; the fighting in the West came to an end. There were celebrations around the country. But the party did not last long. "They are ringing their bells now, they will be wringing their hands soon."

2

1966

THE YEAR OF SELF-DESTRUCTION

A London eye on West Africa

When I joined the editorial staff of *West Africa* in April 1966, the
weekly was in its fiftieth year. Originally started by the West Coast
trading firms and intended mainly for a British readership—officials,
businesspeople, residents doing various work in West Africa—it was
also read by Africans from the start. It was taken over by the Mirror
Group in London in 1947, just as nationalism was gathering pace in
Africa with popular new parties. The new owners and the editor
appointed in January 1949, David Morgan Williams, seized the
opportunity to broaden the magazine's appeal and raise the circulation from a low level. Encouraged personally by Cecil King, the
Mirror Group chairman from 1951, the magazine was run by
Overseas Newspapers (Agencies) Ltd, which under a reorganisation
in 1963 became a subsidiary of Daily Mirror Newspapers, itself a
subsidiary of the International Publishing Corporation (IPC). The
offices in 1966 were at Orbit House, New Fetter Lane, just across the
road from the IPC's multi-storey block. The magazine was quite
separate editorially from the *Daily Mirror* and *Sunday Mirror*, though
there was plenty of contact and cooperation.

The magazine had news, features and editorials. At this time, unlike some periods before and later, it provided regular coverage of major news in and relating to West Africa, especially Nigeria, Ghana, Sierra Leone and the Gambia. Features, often published without their authors' names like The news pages, were written in-house or contributed from outside; they covered politics, business, the arts and much else. There were regular "Portraits" of prominent people, African and non-African, many of them in academia or the arts rather than politics; and weekly book reviews. The editor wrote, besides front-page editorials, the regular "Matchet's Diary" column combining news and comment. There were always several pages of commercial news, and there was the readers' letters page which interested African readers—now the great majority.

Besides the editor, David Williams, the editorial staff in 1966 consisted of Kaye Whiteman, the deputy editor, and Bridget Bloom, the commercial editor, with me added from April (there was no list of staff on the masthead at that time). Williams, a stout red-faced Welshman, was a hyperactive character who usually came to the office before the rest of us and left after the rest of us. He expected hard work from us, of course, but was a considerate boss. West Africa and *West Africa* were his life (other interests being rugby and cricket). His knowledge of Commonwealth West Africa was exceptional, and his African contacts and friends innumerable. The younger Kaye and Bridget were similarly devoted to West Africa and well in with many people there; it was they in particular who took a close interest in the ex-French countries, and they usually wrote the regular column signed Griot[1] (commonly but not always dealing with francophone countries). There had been no Africans on the editorial staff and would not be for another few years, but I would say definitely that the focus of the British staff was on Africa more than Britain.

The magazine served and reflected a region transformed in the previous twenty years, and not just by nationalism and the transition to independent states—politics was not everything. There was an explosion of African activity in all domains, in Nigeria as in other countries. There was expansion of Nigerian-run trade and business; big businessmen emerged, such as the millionaire Igbo lorry transport operator Sir Louis Ojukwu; Festus Okotie-Eboh of the Mid-West, another millionaire, a successful businessman as well as a politician; the Lagosian businessmen Sir Mobolaji Bank Anthony and S.L. Edu; and the prominent Dantata business dynasty of Kano. Education expanded rapidly, including local universities and a big increase in students going overseas. Writing by Nigerians flourished, including historical and other academic writing—for example, by the eminent historian Kenneth Dike, who became the first vice chancellor of Ibadan in 1962—and also the work of novelists such as Chinua Achebe, Cyprian Ekwensi and Amos Tutuola, and the playwright Wole Soyinka. Some such as Tutuola portrayed traditional rural life (among the Yorubas in his case); Ekwensi depicted above all the lively but harsh life of fast-growing cities like Lagos (but also diversified to portray Fulani cattle herders' life in *Burning Grass*); Achebe (Igbo like Ekwensi) portrayed both old and new. They and others wrote in English, but the popular travelling musical theatre troupe of Hubert Ogunde, which visited Britain, performed in Yoruba, and West African popular music used African languages mainly.

The popular high-life musical genre is seen as typical of this period of expansion and optimism; its most famous exponents initially were Ghanaians such as E.T. Mensah, but many Nigerian artists performed it, such as Bobby Benson and Victor Uwaifo. *West Africa* published a good deal about these artists, entertainers and writers, in whom Kaye Whiteman had a particular interest (he reported on the Black and African Arts Festival in Dakar in Senegal in April 1966).

That twenty-year burst of activity affected the Nigerian press also, and especially the *West Africa* magazine's stablemate, the *Daily Times* of Lagos. It had been published since 1926, initially as the *Nigerian Daily Times*. In 1936 it had been taken over by West African Newspapers, then owners of both *West Africa* and the successful monthly *West African Review*. Hence, when the Mirror Group bought up West African Newspapers in 1947, it took over the *Daily Times* and made it the nucleus of a West African newspaper empire developed under Cecil King. The other two papers that came under Overseas Newspapers Ltd, the *Daily Graphic* of Ghana and the *Daily Mail* of Sierra Leone, were sold to local ownership after independence. But in the 1960s the *Daily Times* was still more than half owned by

Overseas Newspapers, which in February 1967 held 74.3 per cent of ordinary shares and 3.7 per cent of debenture stock. And it was a flourishing concern, whose success owed very much to the energy and dynamism of Alhaji Babatunde Jose, who eventually became chairman and managing director in 1968. He was a close colleague and friend of the *West Africa* staff, often visiting them in London or welcoming them in Lagos at his home or at the well-known offices at 3 Kakawa Street on Lagos Island.

There were close relations also with many of the staff of the Daily Times of Nigeria Ltd, the publishing company, including notably a famous editor of the *Daily Times* itself from 1962 to 1966, Peter Enahoro, a lively and vigorous writer who became well known by the pen name on his regular column, Peter Pan; coming from the Ishan people of the Mid-West, he was a brother of the Action Group (AG) politician Anthony Enahoro. Several journalists of the group successively spent a few months at the Overseas Newspapers office, for work and training supervised by the editorial manager, Ted Carey. The *Daily Times* was by the 1960s Nigeria's leading daily; other group publications included the *Sunday Times*, the magazine *Spear*, and *Lagos Weekend*, which was Nigeria's *News of the World*, salacious and crude and often entertaining, attracting frequent criticism but also big sales. At the *West Africa* office we saw all these papers regularly, and also several other Nigerian newspapers which presumably the *Daily Times* sent us: the *Daily Sketch* of Ibadan, the Federal Government-owned *Morning Post* of Lagos, Awolowo's *Nigerian Tribune*, and the *West African Pilot*, the historically famous paper started by Azikiwe in 1937, now a poorly produced shadow of its former self.

African newspapers, including those regularly sent from Ghana and Sierra Leone, were among our sources for copy on *West Africa*. Others included news agency dispatches, company reports, official publications by West African governments, United Nations and World Bank information, and—a most useful source—the BBC Monitoring Service's regular *Summary of World Broadcasts*, which reproduced excerpts from the broadcasts of several radio stations in Africa. In Nigeria there were by the early 1960s the federal Nigerian Broadcasting Corporation and the radio authorities of the Northern, Eastern and Western Regions (the West also ran Nigeria's first television service). Besides these local stations Nigerians also listened in large numbers to the BBC World Service. The *West Africa* staff knew well the journalists of that service dealing with broadcasts to Africa, and quite often contributed to those broadcasts.

Production of *West Africa* was often a frantic effort to get a new issue finished between Monday and Thursday, in an atmosphere of creative chaos; after that we relaxed a little each Friday. Sometimes the editorial staff on duty were down to two, often to three, as people travelled on the magazine's business or went on holiday. Those travelling for business of course produced copy on their return or sent it by cable. This was the age of the telegram and the typewriter; computers were known only as big machines found in a few other offices. The staff, however, travelled by air, as the great age of the steamer had ended. Elder Dempster, the famous shipping line serving West Africa, still advertised in the magazine as it had done since 1917, and Nigerians returning home still went by sea sometimes, but it was the twilight of the era of sailing from Liverpool to Lagos. The aeroplane had reduced the distance between West Africa and Europe greatly, but communication by telephone was still a problem; telephone calls to Nigeria were made but were often difficult.

Relations among the staff of all departments—advertising and circulation as well as editorial—were generally relaxed, though there were of course disagreements; Williams said the advertising rates were "philanthropic". As a junior staff member I knew little about boardroom disputes or top-level decisions. I heard something about the Overseas Newspapers (or IPC) decision to close down five Caribbean newspapers under its control in 1966, and the very hostile reactions it aroused in the countries concerned. Following this there was talk of redundancies, but there were none in *West Africa* editorial. I sometimes heard hints that the company was not flush with money, but there were no clear signs of financial trouble when I was there; contributors were paid fairly promptly and quite well. There was satisfaction with the circulation of *West Africa*, but if I heard any figures I do not recall them, except for a figure of 6,000 sales every week in Ghana in 1966.

There was never a dull moment. The unboring work extended out of office hours, with receptions at embassies and High Commissions, for example, and the organised events and permanent sociability of the Africa Centre in Covent Garden, recently opened and popular among Africans and the Africa-oriented. Many of these called at the office also. Among frequent visitors I remember Bankole Timothy, the Sierra Leonean journalist, working close to Orbit House at the Diamond Corporation of West Africa, and a long-time friend of David Williams; Ben Enwonwu, the famous Igbo Nigerian sculptor; Michael Crowder, the historian; Anthony Kirk-Greene, a former colonial official in Northern Nigeria, now an Oxford don and prolific writer; and Basil Davidson, the well-known writer on Africa, then writing often, in *West Africa* and elsewhere, on the wars for independence in the Portuguese colonies of Angola, Mozambique and Portuguese Guinea (Guinea-Bissau). In the office or outside we often met other journalists specialising in Africa, such as Colin Legum of *The Observer*, Roy Lewis of *The Times* and Walter Schwarz (a former *West Africa* staff member) of *The Guardian*.

Africans were constantly dropping in at the office, and often invited us to their meetings, dances and parties. Like my colleagues, I got to know something of the life of what was now a large West African community in Britain. Many were students, often on scholarships; these were mostly men, but there were many women, and the settled West African communities of today had begun to develop by then—I saw many families at social occasions. People remained very attached to their home countries, reading *West Africa* and any of the home newspapers they could get, organising meetings of ethnic unions and broader organisations like the Nigeria Union of Great Britain and Ireland, listening and dancing to the home countries' highlife, juju and other African popular music—and other world music too, of course, especially soul. The classified advertisements in *West Africa* at that time illustrated all this well, including adverts of meetings and the regular advert of Stern's Radio, "London's West African Record Centre", in Tottenham Court Road.

West Africans in Britain probably wrote most of the readers' letters sent to the magazine; but many came from Africans in other countries, especially the US, and a large number from within West African countries. Throughout my time on *West Africa* I was in charge of the readers' letters page. Only a small proportion of the letters sent for publication could fit onto that page, which was quite often less than a full page for lack of space. But I read many of the others too, and got an insight into what African readers were thinking about many subjects. I think I was too harsh in cutting and editing letters that were published, but I did make sure always that both sides' points of view in any conflict within African states were represented; that of course included the Nigerian crisis and civil war.

Soon after I joined the staff Bridget Bloom went to Nigeria for three months' leave of absence, for a research project connected with Nigeria's negotiations with the European Economic Community (EEC), as it was then. I then took over as commercial editor, and continued as such for some time after she returned.

The commercial pages covered many aspects of the economies of West African states, which were also dealt with in many features (on budgets, development plans and foreign aid, for example) in the magazine. The region had been mainly a supplier of raw materials to industrialised countries for over a century, and still was. The raw materials included solid minerals—gold in Ghana, diamonds in Sierra Leone and Ghana, tin in Nigeria—and by the mid-1960s oil in Nigeria was a very important new element. By 1966 oil was being produced by Shell-BP (the biggest producer), which also opened a refinery at Port Harcourt in 1965, and the French firm Safrap (subsidiary of Elf) in the Eastern Region, and Gulf Oil (now Chevron, of the US) off the coast of the Mid-West; Agip of Italy was to start production later. Oil production rose from 9,921,938 barrels in May to 11,302,418 in June 1966.[2]

The leading exports had for generations been agricultural and forest produce: mainly cocoa from Ghana and Nigeria, groundnuts from Northern Nigeria and The Gambia, palm oil and palm kernels from Nigeria (especially the East) and Sierra Leone among other countries, and cotton from Nigeria. This category of exports still dominated Ghana's and The Gambia's export earnings in the mid-1960s, but diamonds dominated Sierra Leone's. In Nigeria, oil, already providing a quarter of export earnings in 1965, was soon to provide much more. Big merchant firms such as John Holt and the numerous firms that had merged into the United Africa Company (UAC) had handled the agricultural and forest produce exports and imports of manufactures into West Africa for decades, but from the late 1940s official marketing boards handled the produce trade, though the big firms were their licensed buying agents (LBAs) for some time. Those firms were still doing well in the 1960s, some with many varied activities—the UAC had its own ocean shipping line (Palm Line), its river boats along the Niger and Benue, its stakes in several industries such as Nigerian Breweries, and its well-known Kingsway Stores, one of the two main department store chains in Nigeria (the other being operated by the Greek-Cypriot Leventis family).

The giant UAC had been an object of African suspicion, resentment and even attack in the era of nationalism, but it had changed and adapted. It withdrew from produce-buying altogether; it gave up the buying of palm products in Eastern Nigeria in the early 1960s, except for the output of its own plantations, always very small compared with purchases from smallholders' trees and village groves. It was still a power in the region, and none of us on *West Africa*, nor anybody else, could have imagined that in twenty years the UAC would vanish from the business scene.

Sir Frederick Pedler, deputy chairman of the UAC from 1965 to 1968, was well known to Williams, and the *West Africa* staff were on familiar terms with the UAC's public relations staff in London. David Williams was a good friend of the chairman of Ashanti Goldfields, the biggest gold mine operator in Ghana; this was General Sir Edward Spears, who retained his post when the firm was taken over by Lonrho in 1968. Lonrho was then a newcomer in West Africa, but it took over the historic merchant firm of John Holt in 1969. I did not hear of any contact between the magazine's staff and Lonrho's "Tiny" Rowland at that time. I think there was not much with the staff of Shell-BP.

Good everyday relations with businesspeople are normal for a publication dealing with commercial affairs. We on the editorial staff were not hostile to private enterprise, and neither, I believe, were most of the African readers, for trading is a part of life for Nigeria and all West Africa; where state socialism has happened in Africa, it has had to be imposed oppressively, as in Nyerere's Tanzania and Guinea under President Sékou Touré, or else it has hardly existed in reality despite proclamations, as in Nkrumah's Ghana. That said, *West Africa*'s economic conservatism was contrary to a section of African and international opinion that highlighted and condemned "neo-colonialism"—a term often used then, and meaning among other things the power exercised by Western big business in Africa and other parts of the Third World. The word could also mean the hegemony that the West generally exercised simply because of the gross economic inequality in the world, accumulated over five centuries and due in the past to aggression and exploitation. The big Western firms did not exploit Africa on their own; they were agents of a wider exploitation by the whole industrialised world.

Over the previous twenty years there had been much recognition in the world of the gross global inequality, which meant that trade between Africa and Europe could not be on equal terms. *West Africa* recorded and supported African states' efforts to improve the continent's poor trading position, mainly by two means—industrialisation, to reduce the dependence on raw material exports, and worldwide commodity agreements to end the constant and often very damaging fluctuations in raw material exports. Many new industries were established after independence, such as cotton textile and groundnut oil mills in Nigeria, while on the commodity trading side the International Coffee Agreement was successfully concluded in 1962. For Ghana and Nigeria a similar agreement on cocoa could be useful, but this was not to come until 1976. No such agreement was possible for vegetable oils, whose tropical producers were also increasingly threatened at this time by the EEC and its Common Agricultural Policy. *West Africa* closely followed EEC–Africa trade negotiations and their consequences for years. In the end, all the EEC/EU agreements, all the commodity agreements (many of which eventually broke down), and all the industrialisation schemes failed to alter significantly Africa's position in the world economy. The global economic inequality remains as it was in the 1960s.

Besides the economic inequality on the world scale, there was (and is) enormous inequality within Nigeria and other African countries; besides the West's exploitation of Africa, there was and still is exploitation within African states, with Africans commonly the exploiters by the 1960s—especially Nigeria's marketing boards, originally intended to guarantee fair prices to farmers, but ending up by profiting at farmers' expense, in close collaboration with political leaders. Rural incomes were very low, and were a major reason for the "drift to the towns" much debated by Africa experts. But urban life was very hard too, in cities where the wealth of some—sometimes extreme wealth—was often displayed next to dismal slums, in contrasts recalling descriptions of London or New York at the turn of the century. This was probably worst in Lagos, where for example (not an extreme example) the *Daily Times* offices in Kakawa Street had on one side a pleasant bar, the Can-Can, where the journalists often went, and on the other side slum dwellings. There were more attractive cities in Nigeria, like Enugu, Abeokuta and Calabar.

For all the growing urban problems, the general rural deprivation was the biggest problem all over the Third World. Village poverty was general. Even when African countries did not have actual famines such as those publicised in appeals by NGOs like Oxfam, every year the months before harvest were a lean time for millions, and deficient diets were common, especially protein deficiency. When some commentators on the famine caused by war and blockade in the Nigerian civil war said that extreme protein deficiency, producing a terrible condition called by the Ghanaian (Akan) name *kwashiorkor*, occurred even in peacetime, they were not wrong about Africa in general. However—to anticipate the later chapters in this book—the Eastern Region of Nigeria, which became the war and famine zone, did not experience anything like those conditions before the war. The fact that most Africans live near the margin even in peacetime has made the continent's persistent civil wars all the more disastrous.

Nigeria's basic economic problems were as great as ever in 1966 but were not getting worse. On the contrary, oil seemed to offer many possibilities for the future. Nigerians were concerned about the skewed world economic order, and had mixed feelings about expatriate West Coast big business; but this was not a big issue in the country. It was a very big country and no company dominated it or influenced its politics—there were no parallels with the Union Minière in the Congo[3] or Bookers in Guyana. Radical, left-wing and "Third Worldist" writing by Africans, Europeans and Americans was plentiful at the time, and was right to highlight constantly the vast economic power of the West over the rest of the world, but it had a flaw. The

West's power was often over-emphasised so as to suggest that Africans were totally helpless, just clay in white people's hands. In fact, African governments did have room for manoeuvre and power to make avoidable decisions, good or less good; the word "puppet" was much over-used. Radical writers were not alone in this; American Cold Warriors readily accused some African leaders such as Nkrumah of being puppets of Moscow, and the francophone African leaders who were very close to France were often thought to be its obedient slaves. When such views were applied to Nigeria, they were way off beam. Anyone who looks for external factors, economic or political, to help explain the immediate background to the great Nigerian crisis will not find any. Nigerians caused their own crisis, on their own.

Ironsi's military regime

The general peace that came to Nigeria for several months after the military takeover in January 1966 was hardly disturbed except by attacks in Rivers Province in February by a group of activists led by Isaac Boro, who damaged an oil pipeline in the cause of a Niger Delta Republic. It was a small amateurish effort, called "nutty" (off the record) by a *West Africa* journalist, but it lasted for two weeks and was a sign of things to come. The grievances of minority peoples like the Ijaws had not disappeared with the military regime's ban on ethnic associations with a political nature, and oil was to fuel local grievances in the Niger Delta for decades until today. At the time Boro's action, for which he was arrested and charged, was seen as a minor interruption in a promising new era.

During those few months of hope or complacency in Nigeria there was an important event in a nearby part of Africa, the overthrow of President Nkrumah of Ghana on 24 February 1966, by army officers who installed a National Liberation Council (NLC) headed by Lt General Joseph Ankrah. The editor of *West Africa* welcomed and praised the coup, and so did I at the time, though I now think it did not deserve such vocal support, even though the economic situation had declined in Ghana and Nkrumah had lost his earlier popularity. Another event during those early months of 1966 was a British general election on 31 March, which confirmed Wilson's Labour government in power with a much-increased majority. Its main African preoccupation remained Rhodesia; Wilson had forecast that the Smith regime would succumb to sanctions in "weeks rather than months", but months passed and it was still there. While the new Ghana regime hastened to restore relations with Britain, African states continued to demand an end to Smith's UDI, and *West Africa* readers' letters continued to voice concern over Rhodesia. But African states had their own houses to keep in order.

In Nigeria, after all the positive reactions to the 15 January coup, there was some rethinking as the actions of Nzeogwu and his comrades were examined and analysed. Their coldly planned, targeted killings were something new in Nigerian politics, though there had been other political violence before. As those killings were re-examined, ethnic suspicion set in with a vengeance. The plotters were not all Igbos, but most were. Nigerians noted that the Northern and Western regional premiers had been assassinated but not the Eastern and Mid-Western ones, both Igbo. One account said that the plotters had decided not to attack Okpara in Enugu because one of the visiting Commonwealth heads of government, President Makarios of Cyprus, was his guest that night; that would not convince the conspiracy theorists. Some accounts suggested that the death of the Igbo victim, Colonel Unegbe, had not been intended; in fact it turned out that he had been on the list of those to be killed, but that did not fit in with the mounting suspicions of a big Igbo plot to give the Igbos power over Nigeria.

The conspiracy theorists went further and suggested that General Ironsi had been involved in the coup. In fact, the reliable accounts examined by the *West Africa* staff showed that he was not involved and may even have been on the list of those to die. The Igbo plot story also brought in Colonel Ojukwu, who at the time was in command of the Fifth Battalion in Kano. Chukwuemeka Odumegwu Ojukwu was then in his ninth year of service in the army, which he had joined after years of private education in Britain financed by his father, Sir Louis Ojukwu. Now for the first time he was in the news, where he was soon to be every day. In Kano he played a decisive role in persuading Nzeogwu in Kaduna to give up his temporary power there and hand over to Ironsi.[4] But the conspiracy theorists quickly assumed that, on the contrary, Ironsi and Ojukwu had been in the thick of the plot with Nzeogwu—because they were Igbos. They also fastened onto the fact that Nzeogwu and his comrades had only been arrested, not charged.

The conspiracy muttering became uglier when it became known that a change in the country's constitution was being actively discussed and might even be imposed by the regime's authority (an anomaly for a military regime supposed to be temporary), and that this could mean an end to the federal system installed in 1947; the unification of the civil services, which were divided between the federal and regional services, was planned. *West Africa*, in an editorial on 23 April 1966 entitled "Ironsi's 100 Days", praised the regime for the commissions of inquiry and prosecutions for corruption. It rashly said, "By now those who saw in the army's intervention in politics only an assertion of Ibo aspirations should have been silenced" (they had not!). On the ideas for replacing the federal system, the magazine said that the regime, far from imposing its own ideas on a future constitution, "has not even laid it down that Nigeria is to be a unitary state". That must have been the information the editor had at that time. But he added that senior civil servants, especially in the North, "are unenthusiastic about the proposal for unifying Nigeria's civil service", and the North's affairs needed to be handled delicately.

Indeed, that idea was seen as a major threat by many Northerners. It could mean that civil servants promoted within the North according to a policy of "Northernisation" might face competition from better-qualified Southern Nigerians, and that Northern civil servants could be posted to other parts of the country and non-Northerners to the North. The abolition of the federal system, making Nigeria a unitary state, would be even worse for the North, reviving all the fears of "Southern domination". Yet many Nigerians hoping to see a new start thought that ending the self-governing regions would promote loyalty to the country and not to regions or tribes. This group of enthusiasts had its way. By Decree no. 34 of the military government on 24 May 1966, Nigeria would be a unitary state and the regions would be abolished, though "groups of provinces" covering the areas of the regions would be units for decentralisation for the time being. Besides formally banning political parties, the regime said it would retain power for another three years.

In the editorial, entitled "No-Party State", of its issue of 28 May, *West Africa* said there would be some misgivings about this change, for example among regional civil servants, but the change would be "widely popular". It added that "the military regime, which has the right and the power—some would say the duty—to give a lead of this kind, has already made the major decision about the future constitution". It had certainly done so, and it was not a duty, in fact not a sane decision at all. It was bound to be seen as a blow against the Northerners' position in the country. The *West Africa* staff came to regret this editorial. It came from listening too much to a particular group of Nigerians with particular ideas, and that was not the only occasion. The British-owned magazine, far from seeking to impose British views and policies on Africa as some might have suspected, in fact listened and reacted to African views, which could be the views of one group of Africans only, maybe a powerful or even governing group but not speaking for everyone.

On 29 and 30 May 1966, and for some days afterwards, there were violent attacks on Igbos in Northern cities—Kano, Kaduna, Sokoto, Gusau—in which 92 were killed and 506 wounded, according to an official statement. Ordinary men, women and children were attacked, and thousands of others escaped to get back to the East. *West Africa* asked on 18 June 1966, "After months of excited talk of 'one country, one people', is Nigeria really back to 1953?" Now, as then, these large-scale killings in the North were not just mob outbreaks, but they were instigated and organised. In all such cases, things may well go further than the original instigators wanted, but that does not excuse them. The word "riot" is often misleading, suggesting a mob out of control, whereas in the US "race riots" by whites against blacks were commonly organised pogroms; I regret that *West Africa*, following normal custom, referred to the "Northern riots" of May 1966. But it did not question the general assumption that the murderous attacks were organised; it said the organisers were generally thought to be "politicians disappointed in their hopes of an early return to civilian rule, or fearing an end to Northern preponderance".[5] The attacks were a reaction to the new Federal Government policy; as in 1953, the message was "Don't mess with the North". Igbos were targeted because the Igbo people were blamed for the unitary government policy, and those Igbos living in the North were sitting targets for the cowardly thugs—other Igbos, especially Ironsi, were warned that they had hostages living unprotected in Kano, Zaria and Sokoto.

Igbos were attacked because of Ironsi, but in addition much was made, later and perhaps at the time also, of the commissioner for special duties charged with reorganisation of the civil service, who was a prominent Igbo civil servant, Francis Nwokedi. His ability and experience were undoubted, but it was strange at least to appoint him to examine major questions relating to the entire future government of the country in a few weeks, after tours which were far from a proper public consultation. But what mattered to many Nigerians was not such reasonable criticism, but the simple fact that Nwokedi was Igbo. He was fitted with Ironsi into the myth of a giant Igbo scheme to dominate Nigeria. In fact, Ironsi and the whole Supreme Military Council, with multi-ethnic membership, were responsible for the unitary government plan, not Nwokedi. But the runaway myth was on its way. Instead of attacking Igbos, Northerners and other Nigerians could have argued that the whole unitary state idea was highly impracticable for a large and diverse country—most of the world's biggest and most populous countries have federal or at least decentralised government, including some with better internal communications than Nigeria had then—as well as being bound to seem a threat to at least one region (what would be the reaction in Scotland if the British government decided to end devolution?).

The idea was indeed a crass one, devised by people who, like Communists, wanted a dictatorship to impose what they thought best for the country. Did those people not realise how far the paranoid Igbophobia had already gone? Who knows whether it might have been kept in check, even then, by more intelligent policies?

After the May massacres, and the worse ones to follow a few months later, many commentators spoke of a triumphant and insensitive attitude shown by Igbos in the North after the 15 January events. Some also spoke of dislike and distrust of Igbos going back a long time and not based only on politics. This has been a theme of writing about the Nigerian crisis, and some of what was said is justified. Igbos generally are well known to be enterprising people with a strong work ethic who readily migrate far and wide to trade and seek work, besides striving to educate themselves and get better jobs in all domains. Migrants like that have often attracted hostility, which is unreasonable unless hard work and success lead them to put on airs of superiority. Unfortunately, the accounts of Igbos doing just that have been common—despising Hausas as "cattle drivers", for example. But however foolish and deplorable such behaviour is, not only does it not excuse massacre—that is obvious—but one may wonder how widespread it was. Hausas and Southern Nigerian migrants in the North did not live totally apart; they worked together; migrants' children learned to speak Hausa fluently. One thing is certain—what happened in May 1966 and again later was not a spontaneous outbreak by people angered at being called "cattle drivers" or concerned that so many Igbos and so few Hausas worked on the railway in the North. It was a deliberate murderous attack, not at all inevitable, totally criminal and evil, led by political thugs ready to kill the innocent for what they thought to be the interests of the North.

It achieved its purpose; the message "Don't mess with the North" was heard. After a two-day meeting of the Supreme Military Council discussing the riots and a message from a meeting of emirs at Kaduna, it was announced that Decree no. 34 had "in no way affected the territorial divisions of the country" and there would be a referendum on the territorial structure and public service changes.[6] Ironsi had in fact said weeks earlier that there would be a referendum, but had then, absurdly, issued a decree on ending federalism. Now he backtracked, but not completely, as the decree was not abrogated. Calm returned to the North, and an inquiry into the attacks was ordered. Colonel Ojukwu, the military governor of the East, urged Easterners who had fled from the North to return, and many did.

Soon afterwards the emir of Kano was installed as chancellor of the University of Nigeria, at a ceremony attended by Ojukwu—a very good sign, Nigerians must have thought. Indeed, normal life did seem to be resuming. Nigeria's negotiators, led by the distinguished economist Dr Pius Okigbo (an Igbo, incidentally), concluded an Association Treaty with the EEC and it was signed at a ceremony in Lagos on 16 July, attended among others by Brigadier Babafemi Ogundipe, chief of staff at the Supreme Headquarters.[7] Yet such things went on against a background of threats and fear. There was overt opposition to Ironsi in the North, and rumours flew around about further trouble to come. One rumour was that the 15 January plotters (who were in prison) or their supporters were planning to complete the "unfinished job" of the January coup. Was this really planned, or was it suspected or imagined by people making other plots? In fact, there was at least one real military plot, as the country was soon to find out.

The coup of 29 July 1966

On 29 July, a Friday, David Williams held a party at the very pleasant home he and his wife Penelope had by the Thames at Richmond. The guest list included, besides me and others of the company staff, a good many Africans and others known to the editor. One was Colonel Robert Adebayo, who had been in London in recent months, on one of the short officers' training courses which many Africans took. Shortly before the party he rang to say he could not be there as he had to go back to Nigeria. Had he been summoned back by the supreme commander because of fear of some trouble?

In fact, that supreme commander, General Ironsi, went on a tour around the country in late July, ending up in Ibadan on 28 July. Whilst there, soldiers came to arrest him during the night of 28–29 July as he stayed with Colonel Fajuyi, the military governor of the West. Fajuyi refused to hand his guest over to mutineers, who therefore arrested both of them, took them to a spot outside the city, and shot them both dead.[8] This was part of a new attempt at a coup d'état, which also involved attacks and killings by troops in Lagos. At first it was not clear, even in Nigeria, just what was happening. At the *West Africa* editor's party people passed round the scattered news that had come in, but from London everything seemed uncertain then and during the weekend, though it was known that Ironsi was "missing". On the Monday, at the office, we pieced together more news that was coming in. When it became clear that Ironsi must have been murdered, one work colleague said, "It's getting like Russia."[9]

On Monday, 1 August, the situation became a little clearer, and *West Africa* described it in detail in the issue of 6 August, in the normal news pages ("Dateline Africa") and a special report by Bridget Bloom in Lagos, "What Happened in Nigeria". It was clear now that this was a Northern coup. Its leaders struck in Lagos and Abeokuta as well as Ibadan, and soon began a fearful slaughter of Igbo officers at the Ikeja barracks just outside Lagos, whose full details were not immediately known outside the scene of crime. While the killing was mainly confined to the army, some civilians were killed in Lagos. The leader of the coup was apparently Colonel Murtala Muhammed from Kano, but he made no broadcast and in fact did not take power; instead there was no military government, no government at all in Lagos for three days after Ironsi went officially "missing". In Lagos, several military officers and senior civilians—the chairman of the Public Service Commission, Alhaji Sule Katagum (a Northerner), and federal permanent secretaries, among others—met to decide what to do. The senior officer in the army after Ironsi, Brigadier Ogundipe, made two broadcasts and tried to assert authority. Lt Colonel Yakubu Gowon, who had returned from a course overseas just before the January coup (in which, according to one account, he was marked down to be killed, but was in fact not attacked) and had then become army chief of staff, was said in Bridget's report to have "apparently been negotiating on behalf of the rebels". At one point Ogundipe, a Yoruba, gave up trying to take on the leadership; he then went into hiding. On 1 August it was announced that Gowon had become supreme commander and thus head of the military regime. He set up his headquarters at Dodan Barracks in Lagos.

During those days of extreme tension it became known that some Northerners were calling for independence for the Northern Region, which may in fact have been the original purpose of the coup; there had already been calls for this in May. We later heard from an eyewitness that people had paraded in the North with NPC flags. And the three days of crisis in Lagos nearly led to acceptance of Northern secession. That this had been actively discussed was made clear in the report from Lagos in *West Africa* of 6 August, and the editorial in that issue, headed "The Worst Crisis", conceded that there could be a case for separating Nigeria into several states, but went on to argue strongly against doing so.

However, Bridget Bloom's report, while quoting Gowon's broadcast of 1 August, did not refer to the part of it which apparently showed that he had been about to declare an end to the Nigerian federation but had been persuaded not to do so. I myself was not aware of this until it was pointed out in Frederick Forsyth's book published in 1969,[10] though in fact Walter Schwarz had highlighted it in his book published in 1968.[11] One phrase Gowon uttered in that broadcast, "the basis for unity is not there", has often been quoted. If one reads all the latter part of the broadcast,[12] it is hard to doubt the interpretation that the wording had been altered hastily—and care-lessly, leaving the alteration obvious—to remove an intended announcement about Northern Nigerian independence.

During those three days, Gowon had had talks with the British high commissioner, Sir Francis Cumming-Bruce, and the American ambas-sador, Elbert G. Matthews. One or both of them apparently helped to persuade Gowon not to agree to Northern independence. Later, during the civil war, there was much criticism of the two envoys' advice, suggesting that they had thwarted an opportunity to end an unworkable political union which was breaking down.[13] I do not share this opinion, because in that situation of tension, murder, mayhem and chaos, a break-up of Nigeria would not have been an amicable, easy separation at all. It would have led to more bloodshed, in which the Eastern Nigerians in the North could have been the first victims. In fact they were to face mass murder two months later, but this was not inevitable, and the British and US diplomats were not wrong if they hoped that something could be saved from the wreck.

In any case, they were not alone in opposing Northern indepen-dence. The senior Nigerians in the crisis talks argued against it too, and it is possible that there was decisive opposition in the army. In the weeks following the violent events of 29 July we heard often of Captain Paul Dickson taking control of Ikeja Airport, the Lagos inter-national airport, and throwing his weight around there unhindered for months at least. Forty years later, *West Africa*'s Kaye Whiteman, in his book about the city of Lagos, recalled that Dickson had voiced the preference of Middle Belt men of the rank and file for Gowon as military chief, while Murtala Muhammed deferred to Gowon's higher rank.[14] Gowon comes from a small Middle Belt people, the Angas of the Plateau, though he was brought up among the Anglican Church Missionary Society (CMS) community in Wusasa outside Zaria; the fact that he was a Christian Northerner and not a Muslim was to prove important later, but for now what mattered was that Northerners in the army accepted him. However, besides preferring Gowon as military leader, Middle Belt soldiers also preferred continued Nigerian unity to Northern secession, which could mean their indefinite subjection to the Hausa–Fulani part of the region; and yet Gowon, after being accepted by fellow officers as leader, was apparently close to declaring Northern secession.

Forty years later, Whiteman interviewed Cumming-Bruce, now Lord Thurlow after succeeding to a family title, in advanced old age (he died a few years later at 101); and the former high commissioner said, "I sometimes wonder whether I did the right thing in keeping Nigeria together."[15] The old man's thoughts took him quite far here—he had not had the power to keep Nigeria together single-handedly; he was a diplomatic representative to an independent state, not a colonial governor. But his arguments may perhaps have tipped the scales, however important the top Nigerian civil servants and the army certainly were.

Instead of announcing the break-up of Nigeria, Gowon announced on 8 August a three-stage plan for a return to civilian rule, and the immediate repeal of Decree no. 34 (this was formally carried out on 31 August). Constitutional talks on the country's future were also announced. And one early step, on 2 August, was the release of Chief Obafemi Awolowo, in Calabar prison, and his fellow AG leaders. It was no doubt hoped that this popular move would take some minds off the recent violence and win Gowon some civilian support among Yorubas at least. But for some time people of the West and Lagos continued to demand withdrawal of Northern troops from their area, as well they might; those troops were a menace, as the army had largely destroyed itself in a few days. The divisions among the Yorubas seemed to be buried; Awolowo was proclaimed by eminent personalities among them to be "Leader of the Yorubas". This was not a democratic process, but Awolowo was widely considered to have such a position in the coming years. At the same time as Awolowo was released, Colonel Adebayo was appointed military governor of the West.

Any of the mutinous troops and officers who had wanted Northern Nigeria to be independent were disappointed, but they were able to carry on with another plan: fearful revenge against Eastern and especially Igbo officers for the killing of officers of Northern and Western origin in the January coup. The final death toll was not known quickly at the time, but in time the sickening truth came out and was described in a publication of the Eastern government, which gave a list of 213 officers, NCOs and privates murdered, 186 of them Eastern.[16] They included a few of the 15 January plotters, but not Nzeogwu and Ifeajuna, who were detained in the East.

It should have been utterly predictable that many army officers would want to avenge the killings of seven of their number in January. When details of the revenge killing in July came in, at first very incomplete, we at *West Africa* thought back with horror to those young officers of the January plot, calmly sitting down with a list of their fellow officers, ticking off who should live and who should die. It is a chilling and horrible picture; some of those plotters had attended a party given by Brigadier Maimalari the day before murdering him. There was no possible justification for killing those officers (some later accounts said the plan was to arrest them—but to shoot them if they resisted arrest). According to the study by N.J. Miners,[17] they were killed because they were potential obstacles to the planned coup—that is, just because they were in the way! The officers had committed no crimes; if the aim was to stop them carrying out the suspected plan for military repression in the West,[18] the removal of the political masters planning that operation would have stopped it anyway.

And in truth Sir Ahmadu Bello and S.L. Akintola, too, did not need to be killed to end their misrule; still less Tafawa Balewa. Nigeria had several bloodless coups d'état later and could have had one that time. The two regional premiers could have been arrested and put on trial for many abuses of power. Of course the plotters would have to take over the country first, and a coup by junior officers presents problems, which those ones sought to avoid by killing senior officers; as they did not in fact take power, they might as well have tried to do so bloodlessly. Did those assassins really think the officers they killed would not be missed? The only thing that could have prevented retaliation would have been courts martial of the January conspirators. But Ironsi did not take that step—because they were widely seen as heroes? Nobody should ever have seen those men as heroes. They were men of blood, who bear a good deal of responsibility for other violence that followed.

But they should not be blamed for all of that. Those other people who committed large-scale murder later in 1966 were not obliged to do so; they were responsible for their actions, including the hideous mass retaliation on 28–29 July (213 dead to avenge 7). Instead of that murderous rampage, officers angered by the January killings and Ironsi's policies could have deposed and arrested Ironsi, installed a new military regime with representatives from many parts of the country (like Ironsi's), repealed Decree no. 34, and arrested the men of 15 January for court martial, while leaving alone officers and soldiers who had committed no crime apart from being Igbo. Even if they had shot the January plotters (and them alone) out of hand, that would have been better understood, even in the East, than what actually happened. That slaughter removed Eastern Nigerian officers from the army where they had played a prominent role for years. It shattered the army for a time and, above all, it thrust Eastern Nigeria down into a position of subjection. As the army ruled the country, driving Easterners out of the officer corps ended participation (*not* domination) of their region in the government of the country. Easterners, especially Igbos, already had good cause to feel violently cast down.

From the time Gowon became supreme commander, Ojukwu refused to recognise him as such. The reason he gave was that nothing had been stated officially about the fate of the supreme commander Ironsi, but he cannot have doubted that Ironsi was dead, and Ojukwu's real reason was probably the hideous bloodletting in the coup which led to Gowon's assumption of power. He said in a broadcast that the "brutal and planned annihilation of officers of Eastern Nigerian origin" cast serious doubts about whether Nigerians "could ever sincerely live together as members of the same nation".[19] He declared that he could not travel to Lagos without risk to his life, and with troops barely under any sort of control roaming the federal capital, he had cause.

The fatal blow

In principle, a return to civilian rule under a satisfactory new constitution could have done something to undo the harm done to Eastern

Nigerians in particular, and Ojukwu was put under strong pressure to allow Eastern participation in the constitutional talks arranged in Lagos. Talks by an Ad Hoc Commission on Constitutional Proposals began on 12 September and an Eastern delegation under Professor Eni Njoku, former vice chancellor of the University of Lagos, did go, after some hesitation. Sir Louis Ojukwu, the military governor's father, urged them to go to Lagos just before he died on 12 September;[20] we at *West Africa* probably did not hear about that at the time, but of course we recorded the tycoon's death and (in the issue of 24 September) his funeral, where all the regional governments were represented, while the other three military governors and Gowon sent condolences.

Before those talks there had been many other initiatives to discuss a way out of the crisis, and these continued. In some regions prominent and respected people held "Leaders of Thought" meetings; in the East the governor convened a Consultative Assembly.[21] The Lagos constitutional talks progressed for a time, with the Easterners calling for a loose confederation in which the central government would have very limited powers. Meanwhile, the reality on the ground was becoming even looser. The Eastern Region and the rest of the country were turning rapidly into two hostile camps, with mutual distrust and fear accumulating. There was plenty of talk of Eastern secession now; Ojukwu rejected the idea, but he told British and US diplomats in late September, "If, however, circumstances place us outside what is now known as Nigeria, you may be certain then that we should have been forced out."[22]

West Africa had an editorial on 20 August entitled "Bastions of Unity", lamenting that two such bastions had now "succumbed": the army and the University of Ibadan. That university went through several months of internal discord, with Igbo staff and students driven out, including the vice chancellor, Kenneth Dike, though it was some time before his departure was confirmed. They joined the mass migration which steadily reinforced the rift between the East and the rest. Everyday contact continued for a time, however. Nigerians showed their capacity for getting on with normal life despite crises; even during the weekend of the coup ordinary life had largely continued in Lagos despite an "intangible tenseness", said *West Africa*'s report on 6 August; later, normal administration and trade went on for some weeks. So did contact between the two military leaders, Gowon and Ojukwu; as a result, the surviving Eastern Nigerian troops were withdrawn from other parts of the country back to the East, and non-Eastern troops left the East. But in their shock at what had happened in July, Eastern Nigerians expressed feelings of growing alienation from the rest of the country, and from the North especially; they were already worried that the Northerners might attack their region.

During the days of fear after 29 July, Peter Enahoro of the *Daily Times* realised that the change of regime put him in danger, and managed to leave the country and reach London. I heard later, from a *Daily Times* journalist, that he had been arrested or threatened with arrest because of certain documents in his possession (not explained), and Alhaji Jose in Lagos and Overseas Newspapers in London had arranged for him to be allowed to leave Nigeria for London. I do not know what really happened; that source was an unfriendly one, and Enahoro himself, in an article published in 1968 on "Why I Left Nigeria", only said why, not how (I did not see that article at the time; it was in the respected journal *Transition* published in Uganda, which the *West Africa* office did not receive). Anyway he was soon coming to the office at Orbit House regularly, doing some work but not on *West Africa*.

We on the *West Africa* staff recorded all the grim events in Nigeria, as a major source of information on the developing crisis. There was one change for the magazine which by chance came in the midst of crisis: the start of regular printing in Lagos of copies for sale to Nigeria, Ghana and Liberia, while other copies would still be printed in London. On 3 September 1966 an editorial entitled "Coming Home" explained this innovation, taking effect from that issue; it did not affect the editorial side of production, which remained in London. The editor took the occasion to say this about the magazine's role: "Dealing from outside with the affairs of a score of countries we cannot be the conscience of any particular one. This is and must be the function of the National Press. Even when that Press is shackled or is unequal to the task we cannot play its role." Unfortunately, the African newspapers were commonly unable to speak out freely on any major domestic matter, being under constant government pressure, open or implicit. And *West Africa* was under that pressure too. Its staff could not be arrested by order of an African government in London, but the paper could be banned. The Lagos printing made the publishers of *West Africa* even more vulnerable than they already were.

For a Commonwealth Heads of Government Meeting in London in September 1966, the Nigerian delegation was headed by Brigadier Ogundipe. He then stayed in London as high commissioner, in place of the man appointed to the post earlier, Lawrence Anionwu (an Igbo).[23] He had no training, experience or skill in diplomacy, as was soon to become very apparent.

On 12 September there were two bomb explosions in Lagos, one (with no casualties) at the Federal Palace Hotel, the other in the high-class residential district of Ikoyi; the second killed the bomber himself. He was an Igbo, but no organisation claimed responsibility and the full story was never revealed then or later. Terrorist bomb outrages intended to kill indiscriminately were well known in Europe and North Africa by then, but almost unknown in sub-Saharan Africa. There were allegations of other terrorist attacks or plans for them, but it seems nothing is known precisely about any of them. Ojukwu condemned all lawlessness and sabotage from whatever quarter.[24]

Large-scale violence began against Easterners in several cities of the North again during September, from the 18th according to some accounts. First there were attacks at Makurdi, Boko and Minna, and some Eastern Nigerian railwaymen stopped work in the North. Then a dreadful climax came on 29 and 30 September when Easterners in many Northern cities—Kaduna, Kano, Zaria, Jos, and others—were attacked on a massive scale. Thousands were murdered and hundreds of thousands fled to head for the East.[25] In the most publicised atrocity, at Kano airport, mutinous soldiers of the Fourth Battalion attacked and killed Igbo refugees about to board a flight to safety.

These massacres came to be called "pogroms", and the comparison with Tsarist Russia is accurate. The Tsarist regime was not like the Nazis later; its aim with the pogroms was to kill a number of Jews, terrorise the rest, and force a large number of them to emigrate; and it was the same with Igbos and other Easterners in Northern Nigeria now. As Colin Legum wrote in a detailed, horrific account of the pogroms, published in *The Observer* of 16 October 1966, "There is not the least doubt that the Hausas of the North decided to rid their region for ever of the Ibos", but the Hausas did not kill them all: instead "they sanctioned enough thuggery to start a panic among the Ibos", who naturally then fled. There was no systematic plan to kill all of them; when many were killed, others were able to reach railway stations to escape, and that was obviously the plan.

During several days of mass murder it may well have happened that gangs of killers on one side rushed to attack on hearing of killing of their people by the other side. This had happened in the India–Pakistan Partition massacres, and it could have happened in Northern Nigeria and also in the East. It was reported at the time that a false report of killings of Northerners in the East was heard over Radio Cotonou in Dahomey and re-broadcast over Radio Kaduna, and set off reprisals in the North.[26] In fact, killing of Northerners in the East did happen, at least on one occasion at Port Harcourt; however, from later accounts the date seems uncertain, and they could have been an enraged response to what was happening in the North. And it was very obvious at the time that there was planning and organisation behind the slaughter in the North.

Besides Legum in *The Observer*, Walter Schwarz in his book published in 1968 also gave sickening details of the killings; he said "ex-politicians, civil servants, local government officials and former party stalwarts stage-managed the pogroms", mentioning people travelling around to incite mobs.[27] A similar mention was made by Frederick Forsyth in his book first published in 1969.[28] John de St Jorre, in his book published in 1972, wrote, "As in the May troubles, students, civil servants and local politicians led demonstrations and helped to get the mobs out on to the streets. Once again the killings were organised though the form of planning is obscure"; while noting that the motives were hard to fathom, he suggested that "In many ways, the October holocaust was a continuation, a crescendo to the Northerners' vengeance for their humiliations, real and imagined, under Ironsi's government."[29] It should be noted that while Schwarz and Forsyth showed strong sympathies for Biafra during the war, Legum supported the Federal Government and de St Jorre's book is impressively impartial.

One distinguished historian of Nigeria, Elizabeth Isichei, has cast doubt on the normal assumption about the pogroms, saying, "It is difficult to think of a convincing political motive, and the riots seem too widespread and ferocious to have resulted simply from manipulation."[30] With all respect to her, I do not accept her view on this point. From the start, as I recall, Nigerians—and not only Easterners— assumed that a deliberate political mass crime had taken place in the North in September–October 1966. Babatunde Jose, who as head of the biggest Nigerian newspaper publishing group knew better than anyone what was happening, talked about the pogroms at a cocktail party at the Overseas Newspapers office in London in December 1966, and said firmly, "This was genocide!"

During the war, when Biafrans naturally repeated how that crime had driven them out of Nigeria, supporters and spokesmen of the Nigerian Federal Government did not deny that it had happened, or that it had been a deliberate crime; rather, they did not want the subject mentioned at all. Years later, at the University of Ilorin, when I presented a seminar paper about clerks in colonial West Africa, I suggested that ethnic resentment against Igbos in clerical positions in Northern Nigeria might have been part of the background to the pogroms; but my colleagues (all Yorubas) firmly rejected any such idea—"politics is politics" was their explanation of that event.

Isichei does, however, raise a good question: what possible gain could anyone have expected by driving a million Easterners out of the North? Predictably, the whole Northern Region lost overnight countless skilled workers such as railwaymen, as well as countless traders and small businesspeople who had been useful to the whole community. It seems like madness, and in fact the consequences were felt acutely by Northerners. And in contrast to the May massacres, there was no political event that could have been used as a pretext for murder. Now all those who had fumed over the actions of "the Igbos" had seen the Eastern Region totally defeated and thrust down in May and July; was the thirst for revenge not satisfied? Kaye Whiteman, who went to Nigeria to report for *West Africa* on the pogroms and their impact, met one man in Enugu who said, "We were prepared to swallow the May killings in the North, and July 29 was a part of the power struggle, but why did they have to do this?"[31]

But although the massacres of September and October seem like lunacy, that does not mean there was not planning and organisation.

There was, and a possible motive is suggested in a scholarly work which Elizabeth Isichei cites but does not agree with. Professor James O'Connell, an Irish priest and political science professor who worked in Nigeria for years and certainly had no anti-Northern bias, wrote that "This time not only did the Hausa–Fulani participate but many Middle-Belt peoples (spurred on, it is true, by rumours assiduously sown by Hausa–Fulani provocateurs) were active in the massacres", and then suggested what lay behind this Hausa–Fulani action: "The violence was one of the last gestures of a dying order (the organizational element was provided by a combination of traditionalists and former NPC politicians) that disliked the shape of change but had no positive policy for the future."[32] This suggests that the local authority system of the emirates and the power of their political arm, the NPC, had been damaged beyond possibility of repair, and this enraged their supporters. In fact the emirates' local authority system was to be greatly reformed in the coming years, on lines long demanded by NEPU under Aminu Kano (who was to join the Federal Government); and during 1966 the power of the Hausa–Fulani "True North" was undermined by the self-assertion of the Middle Belt peoples, a defeat symbolised by the failure to achieve Northern secession. O'Connell does not suggest that the civilian Northerners calling for secession went on to organise the pogroms, but it seems quite possible. However, O'Connell's interpretation was stated only very briefly then. I do not know if there has been any research since then into what lay behind the pogroms; there probably has, in Nigeria or elsewhere.

The impression is of ferocious, unthinking lashing out at sitting targets, expressing a sort of chauvinism verging on fascism. Kaye Whiteman's reports for *West Africa* from the North at the time included some suggestions of this. He heard Northerners expressing a sort of nationalism, using such words as "self-help", and quoted one as saying it was necessary to "refute the false propaganda that Northerners are lazy and not prepared to take up hard jobs".[33] In that spirit, Northerners worked hard for the next months to learn the jobs Easterners had done. They did so, but Kaye's report said in an understatement, "This simple nationalism may have its horrifying and ugly side …" Reporters found no regrets in the North for what had been done to Easterners.

When we discussed the pogroms in the office later, the name of one possible suspect for the person behind them was mentioned: Inuwa Wada, an NPC politician of Kano, prominent in the emirate government there and for a time a federal minister. According to an official report of the colonial government inquiry into the 1953 Kano disturbances, he made a highly inflammatory speech in the lead-up to the attacks, talking of assembling a thousand men.[34] I do not know whether there was evidence of him instigating the 1966 attacks, or whether he was suspected simply because of his past record. There was certainly not enough proof for us to publish anything.

The gangsters behind the pogroms did not represent all Northerners. Many were shocked by the violence and saved people's lives. The Northern Region government itself organised shelter and evacuation for thousands of people, and its head, the military governor Colonel Hassan Katsina, put down the Fourth Battalion mutiny. Three months after the slaughter, *West Africa* published a letter from Miss H.M. Burness of the Church Missionary Society. She wrote of a retired civil servant who sheltered the families of men being hunted by soldiers, a Hausa teacher who took Igbos into his own house, and officers in the North who said, "Before you kill them, you must kill me"; also of Igbo policemen killed while defending Hausas from lynching.[35] A few years later I met Miss Burness at Wusasa (one CMS mission that had been allowed to function in the North under British rule, and the one where Yakubu Gowon had been brought up), and she told me that Alhaji Isa Wali, the Nigerian high commissioner to Ghana, had saved people from death in the North. Isa Wali had died at a young age a few months after his brave action, in February 1967.

When in Northern Nigeria in the 1970s I also heard of one emir who proclaimed, "Those who kill will be killed," and so ensured that Eastern Nigerians in his emirate were spared. And I heard of a police officer who allowed the local Eastern Nigerians to take shelter in his police station from the lynch mob, and kept them safe until they could leave. Foreigners helped threatened people also. The United Africa Company flew its Igbo staff to safety. I heard later that European senior staff at Ahmadu Bello University (ABU) at Zaria had driven Easterners to safety in their cars, which the thugs did not attack. This is worth noting because in the earlier violence in May

1966 Easterners had accused the British high commissioner, who toured the North about then, and British staff at ABU of some involvement in the attacks. This was sheer nonsense; the British people I met at that university were incapable of such an improbable crime. Eastern Nigerians, and later Biafrans, often harped on the common pro-Hausa sympathies of British people working in Northern Nigeria, in the colonial era and even later; such sympathies were indeed common, as I noticed in the 1970s, but that was not a reason to accuse British people of major crimes.[36] There were to be more such wild accusations in the coming years.

While some people saved victims of the pogroms, many soldiers joined in the killing, and the police did not all do their duty, though some helped their own colleagues to escape and they were very thin on the ground anyway. Some courts martial of soldiers involved in the killings were reported, but otherwise the killers were unchecked, for several days, and unpunished.

The worst killings began just after the Constitutional Conference adjourned for Nigeria's independence day on 1 October. Horrified at the way some Nigerians had chosen to celebrate the anniversary, Gowon met the leaders of delegations to the conference on Monday, 3 October, to talk about the killings. He said, "There has been a damage and I am very, very sorry about it", and went on to make a pathetic plea: "Gentlemen, I will ask you, when you go back home, particularly those of us from the North, to waste no effort in going to each and every man, each and every village, and speak to the people … We have seen enough of bloodshed. For God's sake, let us try to stop all this. We can only do this if we are able to convince the local people … To our Eastern friends, for God's sake, please don't lose hope."[37] This would have been fine coming from a churchman, but here was the head of a country's government pleading with people to persuade murderers to desist! This showed how the central government was quite helpless. But the Eastern Region government, though still a relatively effective government, was overwhelmed also; Ojukwu reluctantly ordered non-Easterners to leave the region temporarily as he could not guarantee their safety.

In late October a statement by the Supreme Military Council on the events of 1966 promised aid to victims of violence and declared,

"Foremost, the Government condemn unreservedly all recent outrages and acts of violence and lawlessness in the country and would
like to express its deep sympathy for the victims and their relatives."[38]
Feeble words from a feeble government; no wonder Easterners/
Biafrans constantly said that Northerners had been allowed to get
away with murder.

Not surprisingly, there were more calls than ever for secession of
the East from Nigeria. There had been suggestions of this before—
some Igbo dons at Ibadan apparently discussed the idea earlier in
1966. But those Nigerians who said later that "the Igbos" had been
plotting secession for years, or that they had first wanted to dominate
Nigeria and, when that failed, had decided to secede, were people
who did not comprehend the enormity of what had been done to the
Easterners. It was, as many accounts agree, because of the pogroms
that the idea of secession, now forgotten in the North, where there
had been little cause for it anyway, spread in the East. For some time
Ojukwu continued to reject it.

In the pogroms, Eastern Nigerians of all ethnic groups were
attacked indiscriminately. The new defiant stance in Enugu was in the
name of both Igbos and minority peoples; one poster depicted various
Easterners with labels showing them to be Ijaw, Ibibio, Igbo, etc.,
pursuing a white-robed Hausa, with the slogan "This is your region,
defend it". Many minority people served the regional government—
such as the new Ibibio secretary to the government, Ntieyong Udo
Akpan[39]—or supported it. But even though minority Easterners had
suffered with the Igbos in the pogroms, many of them continued to
support the movement for separation from the region.

It is widely accepted that 10,000 people were probably killed in the
pogroms; the Eastern/Biafran leaders spoke of 30,000, but even if
"only" 10,000 were killed, the effect of the attacks also included individual, family and collective traumas and the hurried flight of hundreds
of thousands of survivors into an already densely populated region. For
a traumatic few weeks refugees from the North staggered into the
Eastern Region, many mutilated or badly injured. Their families and
home communities of course rushed to help them, but a major effort
was needed by the regional government. It coped well with the massive task, as *West Africa*'s Kaye Whiteman described in a report from

the region, interviewing Felix Ihenacho, who headed a new committee to assist the refugees.[40] Kaye also reported on the effects of the massacres and forced flight of Easterners on the North, mentioning that "In Kano the largest Sabon Gari in the North is now a ghost town" and that over the whole Federation possibly three-quarters of Nigerian skilled railway staff had been lost; the railway was operating at 46 per cent capacity.[41] After returning from this reporting tour, Kaye wrote, "Anyone who has visited the North and the East must pass the judgment that *nothing* can justify what happened."[42]

Eastern Nigerians' shock and fury at the wanton killing was combined with fear of further violence by "the Hausas", even an attack on their region. In fact the Nigerian army was for a time incapable of such an operation, but gradually it was brought back to some order and discipline, and meanwhile the Eastern Region had hardly any troops or weapons to resist an attack. In October 1966 an aircraft crashed in Cameroon and was found to be carrying arms for Eastern Nigeria. This showed that the Easterners were actively preparing to resist attack—"They'd be fools not to," Kaye said in the office.

At the same time as they were being violently driven out of the Northern Region, Igbos were also forced by various pressures to leave the West and Lagos. This process had in fact begun in the North and elsewhere in August 1966; many civil servants were among those who, even if not threatened directly with violence, realised that they were no longer wanted and left for the East. In effect Igbos found that the whole country, except for the Mid-West Region, which remained an oasis of calm and harmony for the time being, was turning against them. Normal relations between different parts of the country were being eroded by the end of 1966; the Eastern railway line between Port Harcourt and the North was virtually closed because of the hostility between the two regional governments.[43]

After the pogroms the Constitutional Conference in Lagos met without the Eastern delegation. It had become irrelevant as the rift between the East and the rest widened, and eventually it was adjourned by Gowon on 17 November. Although it had got nowhere, the conference had revealed some regional political attitudes. The Eastern delegates favoured a confederation with very limited powers at the centre, and the Northern delegates at first called for this also but then changed their view to support a continued federal system. This was probably linked to the movement for new states in the North, as that movement's supporters did not want to see an almost totally independent Northern Region continuing to rule over them. Certainly there was widespread talk of the creation of new states in the constant discussions of the country's future in the latter months of 1966.

On 30 November Gowon declared that a committee would work out a new draft constitution and then there would be a representative Constituent Assembly; but in advance of such steps he rejected the idea of confederation.[44] This put him more than ever at odds with the Eastern leaders. Efforts to ease the hostility between the East and the rest did not let up, including special efforts to find a way for all the military leaders, including Ojukwu, to meet. *West Africa* expressed understanding of Ojukwu's refusal to go to Lagos while Northern troops were there, and the editor said in the issue of 19 November (in Matchet's Diary) and in an editorial of 3 December that military rule should end as soon as possible. There was little prospect of this, and removal of Northern troops from the West and Lagos was held up because few Yorubas were serving in the army; however, recruiting began in the West, Lagos and the Mid-West in December.[45] Meanwhile, there was no sign of the promised new constitutional committee, which in any case would have been a waste of breath as the country was ever more divided into two parts exchanging virulent propaganda attacks and preparing for more violence.

Not all Nigerians joined in such attacks; not all accepted the worst-ever surge of tribalism. Prominent Christians tried to urge calm, understanding and sense. Several articles in this tenor appeared in the *Nigerian Christian*, a periodical we did not receive in the *West Africa* office; they were collected together in a short book published in 1969, *Christian Concern in the Nigerian Civil War* (I believe I bought it in Nigeria later). Regrettably the articles are reproduced without dates, but their quiet protests at the country's downhill descent are valid for the whole crisis period and, indeed, later. In a two-part article headed "Let Us Face This Tribalism", possibly in 1966 or 1967, the leading Nigerian historian Obaro Ikime, then lecturing at Ibadan, analysed the common ethnic stereotypes that inflamed hostility:

To many a southern Nigerian, the Northerner is summed up in the word *Gambari*—by which we mean not just the herdsman we see driving his cows along our roads but a complete nincompoop ... We thus brand a whole people FOOLS, for this is what we mean when we speak of the *Gambari* ... The situation in which we find ourselves today is, to a large extent, the outcome of the determination of the Northerner to be more than *Gambari* in the national setting.

To many a Nigerian the Ibo is selfish, grasping, ubiquitous, always seeking a place for his brother Ibo. All Ibos are avaricious, fiercely and unscrupulously competitive; determined to get to the top and to fill the bottom with yet more Ibos ... When we complain about the "omnipresence" of the Ibo men, do we stop to remind ourselves that if the Ibo gets on, it is partly at least because he is prepared to do the jobs which the average Yoruba and Mid-Westerner would dismiss as mean and dirty? As with the Northerner so with the Ibo, their virtues are deliberately and cruelly discountenanced ...

As for the Yoruba, he is cowardly, untrustworthy, lazy, cunning, "diplomatic", essentially dirty in his habits. It is impossible, we say, to trust a Yoruba. Behind his outward smoothness and refinery there lurks a basically self-seeking, dirty nature ...[46]

In the North, what was often said about contemptuous attitudes among Easterners there had some truth—after the war and the reconciliation, when I met a group of Igbos in Kano one of them mentioned the pogroms and said with regret and without prompting, "We called them cattle drivers." But to stress these things too much can lead to blaming of the victims. All over the world systematic contempt for a whole community can breed deadly resentment, as in Northern Ireland; but the Igbos in Kano were not like Orangemen in Belfast. And of course nothing can excuse mass murder. After July 1966 it was Easterners, especially Igbos, who suffered most from ethnic hatred. They certainly returned it in words—in venomous propaganda by the Eastern government's newspaper, the *Nigerian Outlook*, and the Eastern Nigeria Broadcasting Service (ENBS) for example—but in actions, they were the main victims. They were especially victims of the tendency to blame an entire nation for the real or supposed actions of some of its members. Throughout the crisis and war, opponents of the Eastern Nigerian/Biafran leaders constantly talked of what "the Igbos" had done in 1966—"the Igbos", a nation of perhaps ten million people.

Anti-Igbo sentiment was more understandable within the Eastern Region, ruled for 15 years by a party that was predominantly Igbo in that region. Igbos' migration, spurred on by their dynamism, started in the neighbouring Niger Delta area, where the great seaport city of Port Harcourt became a largely Igbo city. Before the modern city was founded in 1912 and named after an otherwise forgotten British colonial secretary, there was an Ikwerre settlement, Diobu; and Ikwerres claimed that the city, mainly Igbo in population, was built on their land. During the civil war this issue was debated in *West Africa*'s correspondence columns. Land issues are not to be taken lightly in Africa, and Rivers people's anti-Igbo sentiment had some reason, though it was eventually taken to extreme and indefensible lengths. But it was not the same with the prejudice against Igbo migrants to the North and to many big Southern cities like Ibadan—often said to be the biggest city in Nigeria at that time, though it is not clear when Lagos overtook it—and the federal capital. Igbos moving there did not take over or dominate those cities, though there was a concentration of Igbos in the Lagos district of Ajegunle (as there was a concentration of Irish people in north-west London). They did not stop other Nigerians getting jobs or succeeding in trade; if they preferred to give jobs to their own people, Yorubas and others did the same.

Irrational Igbophobia was fuelled by politics. Nigerians tracing the country's political history since the 1940s, as several writers of letters to the editor of *West Africa* did at this time, sometimes spoke of a longstanding Igbo domination plan, linked in some minds with the Igbo State Union, a cultural organisation which may have played some role in politics but probably never had the power behind the scenes that was imagined—any more than the similar Yoruba organisation, Egbe Omo Oduduwa, founded by Chief Awolowo. Paranoia was fed by the events of 1966, so that the year ended with widespread suspicion of what "the Igbos" had been doing and might do next.

The feud between the East and the rest extended to the Nigerian community in Britain. Back in August 1966 the regular congress and summer school of the Nigeria Union, still displaying pan-Nigerian sentiment under its Igbo president, Alex Orakwusi, had been addressed by Lt Colonel David Okafor, an Igbo officer who was still military adviser at the High Commission in London; he said, "I wish that we back home could emulate you people."[47] But the reverse happened: in the next few months the Nigeria Union split up, with a new leadership rejecting Orakwusi's, in a reflection of the worsening division back home. There, however, peace efforts went on; just before Christmas the advisers to the four military governors (who were the former civilian titular governors of the regions) had talks with Gowon in Lagos.[48]

3

THE BREAK-UP

The Aburi meeting

On 4 and 5 January 1967 Colonel Gowon and the four military governors met in Ghana, at Peduase Lodge at Aburi, north of Accra, built under Nkrumah as a country house for the head of state. The talks had been arranged in cooperation with the head of Ghana's new military regime, General Ankrah, as a way to bring all the Nigerian governors together, including Colonel Ojukwu, who feared to go anywhere in Nigeria outside the East. Aided by Ankrah, who could speak to them as a superior officer, the governors and Gowon were able to reach an agreement, because of an extraordinarily friendly spirit—they talked as old messmates, calling each other by familiar names (Jack for Gowon, Emeka for Ojukwu). A full transcript was published a few weeks later,[1] but the outlines of what was agreed were of course known straight away.[2]

It was agreed that the country would for now be ruled by the Supreme Military Council (SMC), which would henceforth meet within Nigeria, and its approval would be needed for all major decisions, including "appointments to senior ranks in the Police, Diplomatic and Consular Services as well as appointments to superscale posts in the Federal Civil Service and the equivalent posts in Statutory Corporations". An important provision was that where it

57

was not possible for the SMC to meet, "the matter requiring determination must be referred to Military Governors for their comment
and concurrence". This seemed to confirm Ojukwu's view that una-
nimity would be required for SMC decisions. That would mean that
any of the four governors could veto any major decision; and why
would the SMC ever be unable to meet unless one member (that is,
Ojukwu) could not attend because of danger to his life? Hence the
Aburi agreement provided for a very loose grouping, though the
word "confederation" was not used. Ojukwu was clearly right to say
that there was unanimous agreement that "the regions should move
slightly further apart than before."

There was agreement on reorganisation of the army, with new
area commands. The whole meeting expressed "profound regret for
the bloodshed which has engulfed the region for the past year" and
agreed on rehabilitation of victims and recovery of displaced people's
property. The meeting also declared that force must not be used to
solve the country's problems, and that the Ad Hoc Constitutional
Committee should resume sessions as soon as practicable. This last
was an important provision, or could have been—it could have
encouraged anyone not happy with the agreement to accept that this
was a temporary measure by a military regime supposed to be temporary, and everything could be reconsidered in talks on a new constitution for civilian rule; Gowon said the Aburi talks had not been to
draw up a constitution.

At Aburi, Gowon told the others, away from the tape recorder,
about what had happened to General Ironsi and Colonel Fajuyi, and
afterwards their deaths were officially announced and funerals with
full honours promised. On 15 January 1967, the anniversary of the
first coup, there was two minutes' silence in memory of those killed
in the coups of 1966. But the Federal Military Government (FMG)
saw fit to issue at that time its booklet *Nigeria 1966*, giving its version
of the events, which could only revive the bitter quarrels about them.[3]
West Africa said later (18 March) that this was a mistake, and Ojukwu
said he was "extremely upset" by it.[4] What may have upset him particularly was that the official list of those murdered included only ten
senior officers killed in the July coup. This was one of several publications recording the shocking events of 1966. Besides *Nigeria 1966*, a

non-official publication by diehard defenders of the North, *The Nigerian Situation: Facts and Background* by the Current Issues Society of Kaduna, and the Eastern Region's official *Nigeria Crisis 1966* were reviewed by Kaye Whiteman in *West Africa* of 21 January. The Eastern publication was in four volumes: (1) *Eastern Nigeria Viewpoint*, (2) *The Problem of Eastern Nigeria: The Case of Eastern Nigeria*, (3) *Pogrom*, (4) *The Ad Hoc Conference on the Nigerian Constitution*. Volume 3 was the most important for the mass of Eastern Nigerians, and in late January an official inquiry into the killings in May, July and October 1966 started work in the East, headed by Gabriel Onyiuke, who had been federal attorney general under Ironsi.[5] This showed that Ojukwu, too, thought it a good idea to revive dreadful memories; no other purpose could be served by that inquiry in the East, which was not likely to be able to call Northern witnesses to testify about the organisation of the crimes or official Northern reactions to them.

However, the funerals of Johnson Aguiyi-Ironsi and Francis Adekunle Fajuyi were a welcome and promising gesture. Commodore Joseph Wey, head of the navy and a Calabar Easterner, led an FMG delegation accompanying Ironsi's body to the East, for burial at Umuahia-Ibeku.[6] For months before the reburials, a song in memory of Fajuyi, sung by I.K. Dairo, Nigeria's leading popular musician in the juju genre, had been a hit, top of the Stern's weekly list published in *West Africa*. This could only have expressed and encouraged Yorubas' sympathy for the Easterners, which was clearly visible at this time, when the repeated calls in the West for withdrawal of Northern troops were ignored, though they were backed by Governor Adebayo. Because of widespread attitudes in the West and Mid-West, the rift between the East and the rest of Nigeria was not 100 per cent.

For a month after Aburi there was an uneasy calm as no decisive action was taken either to implement the agreement or to renounce it. There were disagreements about interpretation of the agreement, and it had left a lot still to be decided—*West Africa* pointed out, for example, that it had not addressed the vital problem of revenue for the central government and the regions. But in Lagos there was opposition to the whole basic concept behind the agreement.

At *West Africa* we did not know—or if anyone knew of it unofficially, we did not publish it—about a meeting on 20 January of federal permanent secretaries, who adopted a resolution strongly opposed to the Aburi agreement, saying it would effectively create a "confederation" with almost all powers held by the regions.[7] Those permanent secretaries were prominent in the crisis years, including Allison Ayida, a Mid-Westerner, permanent secretary of the Ministry of Economic Affairs. By all accounts they did a remarkable job keeping administration going in a crisis-ridden country, and they could well think they understood the country's problems better than the men in uniform. Their resolution at that meeting was of course simply advice, which civil servants are supposed to give. But what sort of advice was it? It seems to have been advice based on an inability to think outside established routine even amidst crisis, and if their views were decisive in undermining the Aburi agreement, they had a heavy responsibility for the new disasters that followed. But they were not alone; we heard very reliably, later on, that the federal attorney general, T.O. Elias, had opposed the Aburi provisions, and other leading figures in Lagos probably did also.

Later it was alleged by some that the British government advised the FMG not to implement the Aburi agreement. This is most improbable, especially as a British roving ambassador, Malcolm MacDonald (former British colonial secretary and governor of Kenya), had helped pave the way for the Aburi talks. Britain had no reason to oppose an amicable agreement on a looser political grouping. As it happened, Sir Francis Cumming-Bruce left Nigeria about a month after Aburi; in late February his successor, Sir David Hunt, took up the post.

In the weeks of indecision at the top after Aburi, the campaigners for new states—or new regions, as some said—were not idle. The Aburi meeting had ignored the issue of new states and the agreement was bad news for those campaigners; it would mean that any region's government could stop division of the region as long as it liked. In the East there were riots at Okrika and Abonnema in Rivers Province around the time of Aburi, with the slogan "No state, no tax",[8] and peaceful activity in support of state creation went on amid surveillance and harassment by the regional authorities. The Enugu government had earlier divided the region into 20 new provinces, with some devolved powers, and it said this would deal with the minority grievances. Ojukwu made this comment when interviewed by *West Africa*'s Bridget Bloom in his capital. On the general situation of Nigeria, the governor, who had earlier stated that "the East believes in confederation",[9] now said that confederation was not ideal but should be an interim solution because of the violence inflicted on Eastern Nigerians.[10]

Bridget went to conduct that interview after being arrested for some hours at Port Harcourt. She was treated courteously while all documents she had were examined, and then released without being told any reason for the arrest.[11] Probably the police were on special alert in that area of minority state agitation where Isaac Boro had staged his attack a year earlier—also the area of oil production. On the road between Port Harcourt and Enugu there were six road-blocks, four police and two army.

On 3 February 1967 the publishers of *West Africa* organised a reception to celebrate the magazine's 50th birthday, on an upper floor in the *Daily Mirror* building. A special issue was published, dated 4 February and including many special features recalling the history of the weekly. I took a great interest in that issue, and later, having moved on to become a historian (while also remaining a journalist), I was to revive my interest in the founding editor, Albert Cartwright.[12] That was not the best time for a party, with a major crisis following recent massacres in the main country covered by the magazine. But by chance there seemed to be some hope for Nigeria at the time the special issue and the reception were being prepared.

The loss of hope

However, the 50th anniversary issue of the magazine included, besides the Ojukwu interview, a report of a press conference by Gowon on 26 January in which he said, "Without an effective central authority to hold the country together, the minorities in each region will definitely assert their right to self-determination." This must have confirmed the Eastern view that the Eastern minority movements were being used as a threat to dissuade Ojukwu from secession. But Gowon's words could be taken as indicating reluctance to implement the Aburi agreement, which would leave the regions with almost unlimited powers and the minority movements frustrated, at least until the promised new constitution. About a month later, Eastern minority leaders held a press conference in Lagos, saying that if the Eastern Region seceded, the minority areas would break away from the region; they called on Gowon to decree new regions.[13]

Gowon did not do so then, and no decisive steps had been taken two months after Aburi, but with the impasse hopes were dashed, as *West Africa* said in an editorial on 11 March. Unless a political arrangement on the lines of Aburi was decreed and accepted by all, it was expected that the East would secede, and also that the Federal Government would take action against it. Gowon had indicated that he was ready to do this back in November, and on 1 March he told diplomats that the Aburi decision not to use force to resolve the crisis was only valid "so long as there is no attempt anywhere on the part of anyone to disintegrate this country".[14] The question was whether the Nigerian army, after all its self-inflicted ordeal, would be capable of action against a secessionist East. But secretly, behind barrack gates, efforts were certainly being made to improve its capability.

On 17 March the long uncertainty ended with a decree, Decree no. 8, which went far to implement the Aburi decisions. It is remarkable that despite all the doubts in the East, despite pressures by top civil servants and minority leaders to abandon or greatly alter the agreement, much of it was confirmed. The SMC was given full executive and legislative powers, and the concurrence of the head of the FMG and all the military governors was required for many matters, including trade, industry, transport, and the armed forces and police.[15] Earlier *West Africa* editorials on 11 and 18 March had said the point of dispute between Enugu and Lagos was the powers of the SMC, but on this the decree agreed with the Eastern view and confirmed Aburi. However, there were parts of the decree that the East did not accept. These stated that the military governors could not exercise their powers "so as to impede or prejudice the executive authority of the Federation, or endanger the continuance of Federal Government"; and that the SMC could take over the executive and legislative functions of a regional government during a period of emergency declared for the region, for which the consent of three governors would suffice, and take measures against a region attempting to secede or contravening section 86 of the Constitution. (The Constitution was deemed to be still in force, with the military authority having assumed powers of the former civilian governments.)

These provisions were seen by the Eastern leaders as directed against them, and as contrary to the Aburi agreement. They rejected the decree; the aroused population of the East chanted "On Aburi we stand"; and the slide towards secession proceeded. Ever since, there have been arguments about who was responsible for wrecking the possibility of peace after Aburi. In truth, both sides can be blamed. One must ask why Gowon so often repeated that there must be no confederation, and yet agreed at Aburi and, to a great extent, in Decree no. 8 on something close to confederation; his words seem to show that he did not really want any major reduction of the central government's powers. Yet a confederation, as a temporary measure pending a new constitution and return to civilian rule, could have led not to secession but gradually, over time, to a resumption of closer relations, getting back eventually to a federal system. On his side, Ojukwu did not respond to clear signs of support for the East's views in the West and Mid-West. There was a good possibility that the leaders of those regions would prevent any provisions of Decree no. 8 being used against the East as feared, if the Eastern leaders worked within new arrangements under the decree. And Ojukwu, who certainly had a "just fear" (as *West Africa* said on 14 January) of travelling outside the East, could have made an exception for Benin, close by in the friendly Mid-West; yet he refused even to go to an SMC meeting in Benin in March, as well as all other meetings of the council after Aburi.

On balance, I would say that the confederation solution should have been given a try. Gowon and his advisers should have thought "outside the box" and agreed to this solution more readily and wholeheartedly, and the Eastern leaders should have accepted all of Decree no. 8 despite limited risks from parts of it. The minority peoples' advocates had waited for years and could have waited a little longer, until a new constitution.

After the decree was rejected, it was widely expected that Ojukwu would declare the East's secession on 31 March, but on that day he instead ordered that some revenue collected in the East, but for the federal treasury, should now be paid to the Eastern Region. This was followed by the East's appropriation of earnings in the East from federal statutory bodies or institutions, and later, on 19 April, the takeover of the operations in the East of ten Federal statutory corporations (the Nigerian Broadcasting Corporation, the Nigerian Railway, the Nigerian Ports Authority, and others).[16] These limited measures were all easily revocable, as were the federal sanctions imposed in response, at first mainly restrictions on air services, though suspension of postal services followed and was more serious. But what mattered was the spirit behind these measures. The Eastern government wanted to draw apart from the rest of Nigeria, as promised by Aburi, while the Federal Government would not offer more than Decree no. 8. Noting this impasse, *West Africa* said on 8 April, "At this stage compromise looks impossible. Is the only question then, whether the present Federation will end with a bang or with a whimper?"

What was bringing the Federation to an end was the mass crime of September and October 1966 in the North, as *West Africa*'s Matchet's Diary noted on 15 April: there was a "complete lack of understanding between the North and the East", since the pogroms were "slaughter so brutal and massive that it cannot be forgiven for many years" and yet, in the North, they "now seem to be regarded as a thing of the past". Hence the diarist wrote, "After visiting all four Regions of Nigeria I feel little hope for the survival of the Federation." In the East, besides the traumatic memories there was the immense burden caused by the influx of so many refugees and returnees. The official figure of these was 1.8 million; in an article in *West Africa* the Nigerian (Yoruba) economist Professor Sam Aluko estimated 1.58 million displaced persons from the North, 100,000 from Lagos, 40,000 from the West, 20,000 from the East, and 13,000 from the Mid-West.[17]

Things fall apart

Whatever was alleged later, it seems clear that Ojukwu did not make a final decision to secede until very near the time it happened. However, well before then the mood in the East was insurgent and warlike, reflected in constant propaganda, sometimes reasoned and sometimes virulent. It was conducted in Enugu by the Ministry of Information, whose director was Cyprian Ekwensi, previously director of Federal Information Services, and there were now organised efforts to spread the Eastern Nigerian message in Britain and the US. On the other side, the Northern view was also belligerent, as expressed by Radio Kaduna, and the North, where in March Gowon made his first visit since taking power, was sure to back strong action against the East. But in early May 1967 this was still not true of the West and the Mid-West.

I recall that the name "Biafra" for the proposed secessionist state was circulating in the early months of 1967, possibly earlier (later accounts said it was being talked of in the East as early as mid-1966, but I do not recall hearing of this). It was called after the Bight of Biafra, but some scholars might have thought also of a country that had given its name to the Bight; however, nothing is known about the state in an area marked as Biafra on 18th-century maps, which was not in what later became Eastern Nigeria but seems to have been quite nearby to the East.

On 22 April the SMC announced a staged return to civilian rule, to be completed "early in 1969", and also agreed on the creation of new states.[18] However, there was not yet a decree to create the new states. It is clear that Gowon was keeping this as one option, just as Ojukwu was keeping secession as one option. Gowon said in late April that if the East seceded, the Federal Government would have a clear signal to create a COR (Calabar, Ogoja and Rivers Provinces) State, and this would be backed by force if necessary;[19] but he still said this would happen *after* secession.

Early in May, Chief Awolowo resigned as head of the Western delegation to the Ad Hoc Constitutional Conference, due to start on 5 May, and when heads of other delegations did the same, the conference was adjourned. Probably the conference was seen as irrelevant as war seemed to be approaching. More significant was a speech by Awolowo to Western Region Leaders of Thought on 1 May, in which he said: "If the Eastern Region is allowed by acts of omission or commission to secede from or opt out of Nigeria, then the Western Region and Lagos must also stay out of the Federation."[20] As a lawyer, Awolowo chose his words carefully, but as a politician he would have known how they would be taken. They were widely seen as a declaration of support for the East in the crisis. In fact, they were not: if looked at closely, he was actually encouraging the FMG to send in the troops quickly if the East seceded, but it was reasonable to see them that way in the context of Western attitudes at that time. The Leaders of Thought said that all peaceful means must be tried to keep the East in the Federation even if it meant "a constitutional arrangement that is looser than hitherto". On 7 May Awolowo led a delegation to Enugu for talks with Ojukwu.

Those talks led nowhere, and Ojukwu later criticised the delegation. Igbos had a long-standing political quarrel with Awolowo, going back to the early days of nationalist politics, but in that time of great danger this should have been forgotten, to take advantage of the very obvious signs of Western and Mid-Western sympathy for the East. Ojukwu and his colleagues should at least have explored the possibility of working with those states' military and civilian leaders, under the provisions of Decree no. 8, in an alliance to stand up to the North; that might have led to talks on the return of Igbos who had left the West and Lagos. Instead they showed contempt for those willing to meet them halfway. For example, they made the absurd accusation that the military governor David Ejoor had asked for British troops to be sent to the Mid-West.[21] Yet this did not stop Ejoor promising that his state would not be used for any military action.

Nigerians and others tried for weeks to avert war. Ghana made new efforts to mediate, Ojukwu going to Accra in late March.[22] During March, the new British high commissioner, Sir David Hunt, called on Ojukwu.[23] It seems that he and Ojukwu did not get on well, and such things matter in diplomacy; but although Hunt became well known during the war for his pro-federal attitude, at that stage it was reasonable to advise Ojukwu of the dangers involved in secession, as he apparently did—even people sympathetic to the Eastern side could give such advice, simply to avoid war. The United Africa Company (UAC) tried to persuade Ojukwu against secession; this was made public much later.[24] But although I do not recall our hearing of it from the company at the time, it was very obvious then that the big firms in Nigeria wanted to avoid war; our commercial news pages were now regularly reporting losses suffered by several firms because of the

1966 events, such as John Holt.[25] The firms could press Ojukwu not out of love for the FMG, but just for the sake of peace. Amid widespread expectations that the East would secede, and doubts about whether the federal armed forces could prevent it, we heard rumours of leading Western businesses in Nigeria making contingency plans to operate in an independent Eastern Nigeria. "Saboteurs!" commented Bridget Bloom in the office. While many rumours were flying around then, this one was probably well founded.

Reports from the East suggested that by April it would not have been easy for Ojukwu to go on resisting calls for secession for long. While the Eastern minorities were an unknown quantity, as noted in *West Africa*[26]—how many of them did their activists in Lagos represent?—there was no doubt about the mood among very many Igbos, spoiling for a fight with "the Hausas". However, there were people stirring up those feelings, and others who tried to urge caution. These differences were described later by Raph Uwechue, a diplomat who had by then left the federal diplomatic service after opening the Nigerian embassy in Paris as chargé d'affaires, and N.U. Akpan, secretary to the government in Enugu. Uwechue mentions briefly, in his book published during the war,[27] the clash of opinions for and against secession, the opponents being "mainly from the business community"—unsurprisingly, since trade was already badly disrupted. Akpan, in his book published not long after the war, reproduces a memorandum he sent to the governor urging him not to declare secession.[28] It became known that Sir Louis Mbanefo, the chief justice of Eastern Nigeria, was also against it: an eminent Igbo, a highly respected jurist who had served as an ad hoc judge of the International Court of Justice, and a prominent lay Anglican leader, chancellor of the Diocese on the Niger. These men were to stand by their people in the hour of need after their good advice was ignored. Ojukwu was being pulled in different directions by this time, in March, April and May 1967. So was Gowon on the other side—the weeks of indecision after Aburi showed this, and afterwards it seems there were conflicting arguments at the top in Lagos as well as Enugu, though there was considerable secrecy on both sides.

For several months after he took power, Yakubu Gowon remained with an Igbo girlfriend, Edith Ike, who lived with him in Dodan

Barracks. As he was in a highly precarious position at a time when other Nigerians saw Igbos as the enemy, this showed great devotion on his part, as well as hers. The affair must have been known among the public in Lagos, and among journalists going there, even if nothing could be published. I remember hearing about it in the *West Africa* office later, at the time when Gowon married his wife, Victoria Zakari, in April 1969; David Williams mentioned in conversation something about "the Igbo girl" but would not say anything more. Later still, when the Biafrans had surrendered and there was a clamour for urgent relief supplies to be sent, Edith Ike publicly called on Gowon to let supplies be flown in, as reported in *The Times*; Williams then said something about Gowon's letters to her, but refused to say more. The full story came out in Nigeria much later.[29] Edith Ike, by then pregnant, left Gowon and Nigeria, apparently about the time of the secession and war—her position must have become very uncomfortable by then—and went initially to West Germany. She bore a son, who later lived in the US and spent a long time in prison there for drugs offences. Pardoned by President Obama, he went early in 2016 to Nigeria, where Yakubu Gowon recognised Musa Gowon as his son; indeed he looks identical to the former Nigerian head of state. Edith Ike had returned to Nigeria earlier but was dead by the time her son went there.

Back in 1967, Kaye Whiteman went to the Eastern Region in early May and reported on the mood there: "It is a strange and somewhat exhilarating atmosphere. You can see why it captivates Israelis and American Negroes so completely. It is the comradeship of the siege mentality, of 'We shall overcome' and 'Keep the faith, baby' … public opinion is mobilised to an extent rare in Africa."[30] Kaye added that there was also "a kind of police state", and hoped it would be temporary. It was not—this was the ugly other side of the determined rallying of a much-wronged people: suspicious enthusiasts for the cause watching out for any dissent or disloyalty. It was to continue into the coming war, even though the cause of Eastern defiance really was popular among Igbos. Kaye's article poured scorn on Federal Government hopes of splitting the East. Those hopes were probably concentrated on the minorities, where Ojukwu knew he had a problem; in early May, *West Africa* reported a meeting at Uyo, an important

Ibibio town, addressed by Ojukwu, who admitted inequities affecting the minorities, and asked for time to put them right—he even said Igbos and Ibibios were like a husband and wife who quarrel but stay together (an unfortunate comparison, as many couples separate permanently). Among Igbos there was great unity. Kaye Whiteman's report said, "I fear a machine is in motion that it will be difficult to stop ... it seems clear that the frightful experience of massacre and pogrom is only now beginning to work its psychological toll."

In the same issue *West Africa* reported a development that may have brought a major confrontation decisively closer: Northern Region Leaders of Thought and emirs agreed to support the creation of new states. It would have been very difficult to justify splitting the East while leaving the enormous North, with most of Nigeria's ethnic groups, undivided. Now both could be split together. Besides weakening the East, this could have the advantage of arousing satisfaction and support for the Federal Government among Middle Belt peoples (including Gowon's own people), who accounted for a good deal of the army's strength. Although Ojukwu could still say that "a confederation of sorts" could hold Nigeria together,[31] he must have quickly realised that the way was now open for Gowon to take a decisive step that would mean an open clash. And on 25 May it was announced that federal troops would be withdrawn from the Ibadan and Abeokuta bases in the West, a belated concession to a constantly repeated demand—was this clearing the decks?

I do not recall that we on *West Africa* had any sense that the crunch was imminent when we completed on 25 May the issue dated the 27th. That issue included a report of an interview given to the monthly magazine *Africa and the World* by Chukwuma Nzeogwu, the originator of the crisis, who had been freed from detention in the Eastern Region. He had stood for the unity of Nigeria in January 1966 and said he still believed in it, opposing secession. He said that a confederation could lead, after ten or fifteen years, to a return to closer union. This was a reasonable idea, though someone with Nzeogwu's record had no right to give advice to anyone. But the time for considering such ideas, from any source, had passed.

On 26–27 May 1967 the Eastern Region Consultative Assembly met and gave the governor, in a resolution of 27 May, authority to declare the region an independent country. It was not a democratic body, but there were no democratic bodies at federal or regional level anywhere in Nigeria then, and this gathering certainly reflected a widespread popular desire to end the Nigerian connection. In Lagos a decree was passed the same day, announced by Gowon in a broadcast at 9.11 p.m., which ended the division into regions and re-divided Nigeria into 12 states. The Northern Region was divided into 6 states: North Western, West Central, North Central, Kano, North Eastern and Benue-Plateau. The Lagos Federal Capital Territory became Lagos State, taking some territory from the Western Region. Apart from that, the Western Region was simply turned into the Western State, and the Mid-Western Region became the Mid-Western State. The Eastern Region became three states, East Central State (capital Enugu) peopled by Igbos, and two states for the minority peoples, Rivers State (capital Port Harcourt) and South-Eastern State (capital Calabar). Military governors were named the next day for all the states, including Ojukwu as governor of East Central State. In his broadcast on 27 May, Gowon said he was assuming full powers as commander-in-chief and head of the FMG.

On 30 May 1967, at 5 a.m., Ojukwu announced in a broadcast that the Eastern Region of Nigeria had become the Republic of Biafra. *West Africa* published the broadcast speech in full. The basic reason given for secession was that "you, the people of Eastern Nigeria" were "aware that you cannot be protected in your lives and in your property by any government based outside Eastern Nigeria".[32] What lay behind this was illustrated in the new country's flag, with three horizontal stripes, red for blood, black for mourning, and just a green one suggesting life, with half of a rising sun in the black stripe.[33] In truth, it was the organisers of the Northern Nigeria pogroms who destroyed Nigerian unity, not Ojukwu. *West Africa*'s editorial on 3 June was headed "Things Fall Apart", from the title (taken from the famous poem by W.B. Yeats) of Chinua Achebe's best known novel; it said secession now seemed to have been inevitable since October 1966, and many would agree with that, though some might say it was inevitable from 29 July 1966.

I heard later that there had been severe annoyance with this editorial in Lagos. That may have been because it said that military action, if taken, might lead to a stalemate; Gowon had swiftly declared he would "crush the rebellion", and the spirit of a country at war, likely to be hostile to any suggestion that victory was not certain, was already aroused. Or perhaps the editorial was seen as suggesting that the end of the Federation was final (Achebe's novel is about the disintegration of the old African order). In a way it was, for it could not be like it was before if it could be restored only by force. But restoring it by force was what was promised in Lagos, and what eventually happened. That, however, did not seem inevitable to everyone at the time.

4

THE FIRST SIX MONTHS OF WAR
(JULY–DECEMBER 1967)

The territory covered by the newly proclaimed Republic of Biafra had an area of 29,484 square miles, making it bigger than the newly independent Lesotho and The Gambia; the population was estimated at 14 million, more than that of almost any independent African state at that time. It continued functioning much as the Eastern Region of Nigeria had done, with the British-founded administration and courts operating much as before; in fact they were to continue operating, remarkably, throughout the coming war and suffering. There was nothing like a revolutionary regime. But among the Igbos, at least, there was immense enthusiasm for the secessionist state. Names were changed with zealous speed, with the East Nigeria Broadcasting Service becoming the Broadcasting Corporation of Biafra, the *Nigerian Outlook* newspaper renamed the *Biafra Sun*, and the University of Nigeria at Nsukka becoming the University of Biafra. Eastern Nigerians around the world eagerly declared that they were now Biafrans; a Biafra Union of Great Britain and Ireland was quickly set up, and the Igbo boxing champion Dick Tiger (world middleweight champion 1966; real name Richard Ihetu) declared, "I am a Biafran and will die a Biafran."[1]

At the same time, everyone knew that all this was under threat, and the new state was likely to be attacked. Preparations to resist, already begun, were stepped up, despite a critical shortage of arms, with air raid precautions in Enugu for example. Later accounts confirm that men and boys rushed eagerly to join the Biafran army but at first had hardly any weapons to train with. The creation of a Biafran army had begun before secession with some experienced officers, the battered remnants who had escaped the slaughter in July 1966, notably Lt Colonel Hilary Njoku, the senior surviving Igbo officer, who had been at Ibadan with General Ironsi and Colonel Fajuyi in July 1966 and had narrowly escaped death. Others included Major Chukwuma Nzeogwu, even though he had publicly opposed secession and was on poor terms with Ojukwu. Njoku, but not Nzeogwu, was appointed to the Executive Council for Biafra created on 6 June 1967, and promoted to brigadier.

For six weeks after secession there was no fighting. The border on the Niger Bridge between Biafra and the Mid-Western State of Nigeria was closed by the Federal Government on 1 June, but it was easy to cross the Niger away from the bridge, as the Mid-West retained a sort of neutrality tolerated by the Lagos government, and was a route for both traders and journalists to enter Biafran territory. Apart from this loophole, the sanctions ordered by the Federal Military Government (FMG) were applied thoroughly, including a ban on all foreign currency transactions with the Enugu government or its agencies, and a ban on shipping calling at Eastern Nigerian/ Biafran ports.[2] On a visit to London, Philip Asiodu, permanent secretary of the Federal Ministry of Industries, said on 12 June that these were "total sanctions", unlike the Rhodesia sanctions.[3] However, for the moment the border between Biafra and Cameroon remained open and much used. An agreement between the two governments to restrict movement across the border was announced on 7 June, after the Biafran leaders Sir Louis Mbanefo, C.C. Mojekwu and Pius Okigbo crossed it, but it seems not to have been enforced; *West Africa*'s Griot columnist, reporting from Mamfe in West Cameroon in the issue of 8 July, spoke also of telephone links to Biafra still open and trade continuing. Such trade could only make a small difference to the economic blockade of Biafra.

During those weeks, we recorded no negotiations to avoid war— though the secretaries general of the Organisation of African Unity

(OAU) and the Commonwealth, Diallo Telli and Arnold Smith, visited Lagos at this time—and there was little chance that it would be avoided. There were suggestions later that Gowon—who soon after the declaration of Biafra was promoted to major general—wanted to avoid war, but if he did, it would have been in the hope that Ojukwu would renounce the secession. The Federal Government, by creating the twelve states including Rivers and South-Eastern, had taken a step from which it would have been difficult if not impossible to retreat. A federal spokesman said on 1 July that the secessionists must accept the 12 new states, as well as renouncing secession and recognising the FMG's authority;[4] these were the basic federal demands which were never to change. On 17 June a government spokesman said there were plans for military operations soon to remove the Ojukwu regime;[5] thousands of reservists were called up, troops were readied for war; on 1 July Ojukwu was dismissed with ignominy from the armed forces and sacked as governor of East Central State; and Gowon issued a Code of Conduct for the troops to follow when war came.[6] It laid down, among other provisions, that children and pregnant women must not be harmed, hospitals must be left alone, there must be no looting, prisoners of war must be properly treated, and the Geneva Convention must be observed (Nigeria had adhered to the 1949 Geneva Conventions in 1961).

During this "phoney war" period, attention was focused on the oil industry, which was supposed to be Biafra's main asset—in news agency language it was always to be the "oil-rich secessionist state". For a time the Federal Government exempted oil exports from the blockade of what was now proclaimed as Biafra's sea coast. But legally, the oil was supposed to be an export of Nigeria, and any attempt to pay Biafra for it would have been impossible legally and difficult in practice. However, attention was concentrated not on payment for exports, but on the tax obligations of the oil companies headed by Shell-BP. These consisted of the petroleum profits tax, paid to the Federal Government and retained by it in full, and other liabilities—income tax, capital gains tax, other direct taxation, income from oil pipelines, licensing fees, rent on oil licences and leases, royalties on oil and gas, and premiums on oil licences and leases—of which the Federal Government took 15 per cent and the region of oil production 50 per cent, with the rest divided among all regions of Nigeria.[7]

The Biafrans, as the effective authority in the oil-producing area (except for the Mid-Western fields), demanded payment of the revenue legally owing to the Federal Government, and the issue could not be evaded, as a payment of £7 million was believed to be due (later it appeared that there was not so much urgency, as payment could be delayed until the following February). By late June it was learned that Shell-BP intended to make a "token" payment of £250,000 to Biafra. This was condemned by the Federal Government, which was backed by an angry roar from the Nigerian press. The maritime blockade was promptly extended to oil shipments. This affected the Mid-West's oil production as well as the East's, because the Mid-West's was pumped by pipeline for shipment from Bonny. Now the oil could still be pumped, but not exported.

From that moment, the Biafrans could no longer place any hopes in the oil industry under their control. The Federal Government was able to declare and, if necessary, enforce the blockade. It was the legal government and all shipping was obliged by law to comply with its orders—so long, that is, as it could enforce those orders. It soon proved well able to do so. The Biafrans were up against the basic reality that their adversaries both ruled legally and controlled in practice the whole area of the Federation apart from the former Eastern Region. Biafrans and their supporters sometimes protested against the acceptance of the Gowon government as legal; recalling the 29 July 1966 coup, they asked "Who are the rebels?" It was right to recall with utter disgust the murderous coup which had led to Gowon taking power, but it was quite irrelevant to the question of legality. Many governments around the world had come to power by violence, and were treated as legal governments. The Lagos government effectively controlled the country apart from Biafra: that was what mattered to the rest of the world.

If the Biafrans hoped that the Gowon government's control of the rest of Nigeria would break down, they deluded themselves. That government's shaky position in its early months was forgotten amid the rallying of support against "the rebels". On 12 June 1967 a new Federal Executive Council was sworn in, with Gowon as chairman and as vice chairman Chief Obafemi Awolowo, who was also commissioner for finance (ministers were still called "commissioners", to indicate that this was supposed to be a temporary regime—the Supreme Military Council remained as the ultimate centre of power). Other members included the Tiv leader Joseph Tarka, commissioner for transport, and Anthony Enahoro, commissioner for information. They, like Gowon himself, were from minority peoples, and in fact there was now a regime of the minorities: their day had come. Of course the Yorubas and Hausa–Fulanis were represented, the former by the senior political figure in the country; but the Muslim Northerners included notably Aminu Kano, a Hausa but also the veteran leader of the Hausa–Fulani opposition to the former NPC regime, who became commissioner for communications. If he is considered also, the government can be seen as one of the former "outs". This gave it a solid base that endured through the war and beyond, all the more solid because so many of the army rank and file came from the minority areas. And this new regime of the former "outs" included commissioners from the Eastern minority states: Wenike Briggs (a former Action Group politician) from Rivers State, and Okoi Arikpo from South-Eastern State. Arikpo, an Ekoi from Ogoja Province, was an anthropologist and teacher before entering politics in the 1950s; a few months later he was appointed Nigeria's commissioner for external affairs, and he and Enahoro, in particular, were to be constantly seen defending the federal cause around the world.

"That traitor Arikpo", as Biafra Radio called him because he was an Easterner who chose the federal side, was one of many people of the Eastern minorities who chose that side. Others, however, chose the Biafran side and stuck to it. Among officers, Lt Colonel George Kurubo, from Rivers State, who, after a short spell as head of the Nigerian Air Force, had fled with other Eastern officers to escape the slaughter of July 1966, was with the Biafrans initially, and was even appointed to the Biafran Executive Council, and promoted to brigadier soon afterwards.[8] Kurubo then defected to the federal side, which, however, did not give him a command in the war but packed him off to Moscow as ambassador. In contrast, Lt Colonel Philip Effiong, from the area of South-Eastern State, who also joined the

Executive Council and became a brigadier, served the Biafrans until the end. The Executive Council included Igbos such as the economic adviser to the governor, Pius Okigbo, and minority people such as the secretary to the government, N.U. Akpan, and Matthew Mbu, a politician who later, in an enlarged Executive Council in September, became Biafra's commissioner for external affairs. As for the ordinary inhabitants of the areas supposed to be covered by Rivers and South-Eastern States, one may assume that most of them kept quiet and waited to see which side won, but showed less of the great enthusiasm for the war seen in Enugu.

Biafrans, whether Igbos or minority people, had to face the fact that their enemies had wide support among many of the Nigerian peoples. Biafrans spoke of their foes as "the Hausas", but this did not recognise the true situation. It is true that soldiers from the Middle Belt had always been called Northerners, and they spoke Hausa, as it was the common language of the army. But probably only a minority of Nigerian officers and men came from the Hausa emirates (the actual ethnic breakdown of the army was probably not published; at least it did not appear in *West Africa*). This would not have mattered if the political authority had been Hausa-dominated, but it was not.

In late June the Biafrans seized a river steamer on the Niger, belonging to a UAC subsidiary, at Onitsha. Much more serious were two bomb outrages in Lagos on 2 July, one at a filling station, the other aimed at a police station but in fact killing four people in a house. This led, as the Biafrans should have expected, to renewed hostility to the Igbos still in Lagos, and measures against them.[9]

Fighting broke out on 6 July on the northern border between secessionist and federal territory, north from Nsukka. Whoever fired the first shots—Olusegun Obasanjo, at the time in command of 2 Area Command based at Ibadan and later general officer commanding of the federal Third Division, wrote later that it was the federal side[10]—troops of 1 Area Command of the Nigerian army then pushed south to pursue the government's aim to end the secession. They followed the road to Nsukka, which they reached on 14 July, and also advanced further east into the former Ogoja Province; Ogoja town was taken on 11 July. *West Africa* was soon reporting from this first war front,[11] which came under the command of the First Division under Colonel Muhammadu Shuwa. While Brigadier Hassan Katsina's boast that the federal forces could achieve victory in 48 hours was ridiculous, Obasanjo admitted later, "The Federal side prepared and planned for an operation lasting days rather than weeks."[12]

While initially very short of infantry weapons, the Biafrans had a rudimentary air force which they started to use from an early stage. It included a B-26 adapted as a fighter-bomber (the US embassy in Lagos had to issue a statement that this US-built aircraft had been sold as surplus by the French air force), and some helicopters taken from the oil companies. In all, the Biafrans had at various times, in the earlier part of the war, two B-25s, two B-26s, two DH Doves, and a Fokker Friendship formerly belonging to Nigeria Airways, hijacked by the Easterners before secession.[13] They carried out a number of air raids, over a wide area; one on 20 August hit the small arms factory at Kaduna and killed one of the West German air force personnel working there. These air raids brought no military gain, but they were a shock to ordinary Nigerian people who were affected, and were to be recalled, as a sort of excuse, when the Nigerian Air Force carried out air raids a hundred times worse on the Biafrans later. On 7 October the Fokker Friendship was used as a bomber over Lagos and was blown up over the capital's upper-class residential area of Ikoyi.[14]

In the first days of fighting, Chukwuma Nzeogwu was killed in action on 26 July, fighting for a cause he did not really believe in. There were various stories told about his death, but one certain thing is that his body was found by federal troops and buried with full honours. Another prominent casualty on the Biafran side in the early phase of the war was the poet Christopher Okigbo (Pius's brother); a major in the Biafran army, he fell during August on the northern front near Nsukka.[15]

On 26 July the Nigerian Navy and troops of the Lagos Garrison Organisation under Lt Colonel Benjamin Adekunle captured Bonny, the historic seaport town now most important for its oil tanker terminal. If the Biafrans had clung to hope that they could resume oil exports, that hope was now gone. Thus the role played by the small Nigerian Navy (one frigate and some smaller craft, also making use of merchant vessels of the Nigerian National Shipping Line) was decisive. With Bonny captured, and the nearby coastline patrolled, there was no way in which tankers could sail to and from Biafran territory. We did not hear about any efforts to smuggle oil out aboard small craft, as was done on a large scale by Iraq during the years of sanctions some decades later. The Biafrans had oil but could not export it—though the refinery was very useful. Shell-BP could do nothing about this turn of events, which proved to any doubters that it was not in fact in command of the situation. "Big Oil" has great power in the world, but it is limited in wartime because transport of crude oil is so very vulnerable—one small warship can set a big tanker ablaze easily with one torpedo. Shell-BP had to submit to the situation after being condemned by both sides; at the end of July, all its installations in Biafra were taken over and its manager there, Stanley Gray, was arrested. He later left Biafra with all remaining expatriate staff of the company there.[16]

Most British and other Westerners working in Biafra left in the first few weeks. The British government advised its subjects to leave, a common procedure in times of crisis in any country. Many did not leave willingly, and when they did it was not because of lack of support for Biafra. On the contrary, some returned to proclaim loudly their sympathy for the Biafrans. They and others were called "white Biafrans" (not in derision) by the *West Africa* staff. The hideous sufferings and defiant response of the Eastern Nigerians had won wide support or sympathy from foreigners among them; the British deputy high commissioner in Enugu, Jim Parker, did his duty by reporting objectively on the mass support for Ojukwu and his government, but he also had definite sympathy for their cause. However, there were as many or more British people who strongly supported the Nigerian side as the war progressed. They included the high commissioner in Lagos, Sir David Hunt, and the editor of *West Africa*, David Williams.

In Biafra as war set in, one early step was the closure of all schools, which was hard for people with such a high rate of education. I do not recall reading, and have not read since, the reason for this step. Older schoolchildren may have been needed for war work, even in the army as time went on, but why were even primary schools closed? In the event, millions of young Igbos lost years of education.

THE FIRST SIX MONTHS OF WAR (JULY–DECEMBER 1967)

The Mid-West venture and disaster

A small Biafran force crossed the Niger Bridge to invade the Mid-Western State on 9 August 1967, and quickly occupied the whole state with no resistance; some even entered a part of West Central State to the north. Several Igbo officers serving with the small federal force stationed in the Mid-West cooperated with the invasion. It was announced that the commander of the Biafran invasion force was Colonel Victor Banjo, a Yoruba officer who had joined the Biafrans after being detained for 14 months following the January 1966 coup. It was quickly apparent that he was pursuing a plan to use his force, called a "Liberation Army", to go beyond the occupation of the Mid-West and promote a revolt against Gowon's regime by Yorubas and other Southern Nigerians. The hopes in Enugu of Yoruba support against the Northerners persisted, and there were some grounds for them. Yorubas still resented Northern domination and the Northern troops enforcing it; and Obasanjo recalled extreme tension between Yoruba and Northern soldiers in the West.[17] It was reasonable to hope that some leading Yorubas who for the moment supported Awolowo and the government to which he belonged might be ready to change sides. Ojukwu obviously approved of the idea of seeking Yoruba support, but *West Africa* reported on 19 August that in a broadcast on 14 August Banjo said, "I am a Nigerian, I believe in the Nigerian nation."[18] Did Ojukwu approve such language as a way to seek support for the removal of Gowon, or did Banjo go further than the Biafran leader had intended? The full facts were not clear at the time; nor were they about some other developments in the Biafran-occupied Mid-West, including a meeting between Banjo and the British deputy high commissioner in Benin, and the raiding of bank vaults by the Biafrans.

It became clear later that there was a plan for some sort of revolution in Southern Nigeria, perhaps socialist or egalitarian in aim, definitely aimed at ending Northern domination.[19] This involved Banjo and the 15 January 1966 assassin of Tafawa Balewa, Emmanuel Ifeajuna, who, like Nzeogwu, was a "one Nigeria" revolutionary, not an Igbo chauvinist; also Philip Alele, a non-Igbo Mid-Westerner, described as a "superb socialist agitator" who had rallied support for

81

secession among Biafrans,[20] and Sam Agbam, an Igbo ex-diplomat. All four were to be executed in Biafra soon after the collapse of whatever plans they had been pursuing in the Mid-West.[21]

Also involved in Banjo's plan (or dream) was Wole Soyinka, the already famous Yoruba dramatist (later to win a Nobel Prize). He was already noted as a political activist for democracy and against dictatorship, especially in the opposition to Akintola in the West in 1965; he had helped Eastern officers to escape death after the July 1966 coup, and early in the war was in Britain, seeking support for an international arms embargo and a search for a new way forward, a "Third Force", in Nigeria. None of this was reported in *West Africa* at the time. He visited Ojukwu in Enugu and soon afterwards, at the time of the Mid-West invasion, contacted Obasanjo on behalf of Banjo, to ask him to give Banjo's force unhindered access to Lagos and Ibadan; Obasanjo refused. *West Africa* of 2 September reported the arrest of Soyinka, with no details of his activities leading to it. Many years later, Obasanjo mentioned his encounter with Soyinka but without giving his name.[22] The playwright was detained for two years without trial, despite worldwide protests. His fiercely damning account of his time in gaol, published in 1972, had only a few scattered references to his actions before his arrest;[23] much later he provided a fuller account for Gould's 2012 book.[24]

From the Mid-West, Banjo's force entered the Western State and advanced as far as Ore. This was only about 150 miles from Lagos, and there were very few troops to resist their advance to the capital. It was like the Young Pretender's advance to Derby in 1745; now, as then, panic hit the capital, which seemed to lie open to attack. But the outcome was the same as then. The "Liberation Army" halted for days, giving time for the federal forces to destroy bridges on the road ahead and prepare for a counterattack, which soon came. After fighting in the area of the state border and the recapture of Ore, announced by the federal side on 23 August,[25] the attacking force retreated into the Mid-West. In Lagos, many of the Igbos who had stayed there were lynched. The others were told to register from 9 August, and about a thousand were rounded up and taken to Apapa Barracks on 11 August, most being freed the next day.[26]

Some prominent Yoruba people might have been interested in Banjo's idea if his forces had managed to push further ahead, but on

12 August, when the counterattack had not yet started, Chief Awolowo called on all Yorubas to support the Federal Government. Soon afterwards he made another appeal to "all Yoruba people" to "lose no time and spare no efforts in giving every conceivable support to the Federal troops in defence of their homeland, and of the fatherland".[27] The Mid-West invasion helped rally support for the Federal Government among Yorubas and others.

On the same day as the Biafrans entered the Mid-West, it became known that the British government had overcome its hesitation about authorising arms sales to the Federal Government.[28] The arguments about this were to some extent public knowledge in London, and had gone on for some weeks. The present work cannot throw much new light on the British arms sales, which was the aspect of the war most debated at the time in Britain;[29] it was only briefly covered in *West Africa*. In the weeks after secession, the British government agreed to the delivery of naval patrol boats already ordered by the FMG, and to the supply of anti-aircraft defences, but refused to supply aircraft or bombs for air attack. The Federal Government may have expected arms supplies simply to continue as before, with much bigger amounts, but in Britain—as in most or all arms-exporting countries—the government was entitled to refuse licences for arms exports, and this meant that the issue was discussed at the highest political level. While it seems that some arms supplies never stopped, the attitude of London showed hesitation and unease, and that, added to the apparent hesitation to back Lagos over the Shell payments, caused strong anti-British feeling among Nigerians on the federal side.

The British public in 1967 may not have known that the government considered the possibility of intervening in another way, to try to bring about peace—and rejected it.[30] The British government soon gave in to the Nigerian demand, though still not for military aircraft. Nigeria then turned to the Soviet Union for those. Ten days after the Mid-West invasion, Soviet transport planes landed aircraft and other military supplies at Kano.[31] MiG-17s and Il-28s were soon being used in the war, as well as L-29s from Czechoslovakia, with Egyptian and other foreign pilots. For infantry weapons, the decision to license sales, taken before the invasion of the Mid-West, came at just the right time for the FMG.

Much has been made of the British government's concern over Nigerian oil supplies at that time, when the closure of the Suez Canal, following the Six Day War, made oil imports from Nigeria noticeably cheaper than those from the Middle East. It did have that concern, and would surely have wanted to prevent a halt to oil exports if possible, but it could not. For about a year Britain supplied arms to Nigeria without getting any oil from it. The oil could not flow again until there was either a peace settlement or a military victory, which most probably would mean a federal victory; and Britain made no effort to secure the former. So the British government must have thought the only way to get Nigerian oil again was to help the Federal Government win as quickly as possible, though that would no longer help with the immediate oil supply and price problem unless Nigeria won a quick or easy victory—as the British government in London may have expected even though, contrary to a common belief, the high commissioner in Lagos did not. That reason for supplying arms was never declared. Other reasons were given by the minister of state for Commonwealth affairs to his cabinet colleagues on 7 September 1967:

> Our policy on arms was to supply the Federal Government with reasonable quantities of types similar to those supplied in the past (e.g., rifles) but to refuse sophisticated weapons (e.g., aircraft, rockets, etc.). When the Mid-Western Region was occupied by forces of the Eastern Region on 9th August, this policy had been reviewed. It had been decided not to stop supplies to the Federal Government; since they were the legitimate Government and there were some 17,000 British lives at stake in Federal controlled territory.[32]

The first of the two reasons given was to be the main one restated in the next two and a half years. The second was also stated in public, though it was completely unjustified. "Some 17,000 British lives at stake"? Who was threatening them? Nigerians and Biafrans treated British residents correctly and well, then and before and after, as I and many others can testify. It was grotesque to suggest that the Federal Government would make ordinary British people suffer because of anger at their home government. Or did British ministers think that a successful Biafran secession would at once cause the Federation to collapse in chaos? Quite probably there were such ideas in Europe, inspired by recent memories of the attacks on and rescue of white people in Stanleyville in the Congo in 1964, but Nigeria was not the Congo.

In Biafra, Sir Francis Ibiam, former Governor of the Eastern Region and now an adviser to Ojukwu, gave up his knighthood in protest at the British government decision; other Biafrans took similar action.[33] In Britain, there was a protest by prominent leaders of the Church Missionary Society, the Church of Scotland Foreign Missionary Society and the Methodist Missionary Society, in a joint statement opposing any British arms sales to Nigeria. This protest, which Ogundipe called "prejudiced and one-sided",[34] was the beginning of a strong campaign in Britain against the arms sales to Nigeria. For some months the campaign had limited impact, but it continued, with members of both Houses of Parliament supporting it.

Troops of a federal Second Division advanced against the Biafrans in September,[35] under the command of Colonel Murtala Muhammed, one of the main authors of the second coup of 1966. Later reports said that division, or part of it, was hastily assembled with press-ganged men or released prisoners, given very little training. Even such poor-quality troops were able, though rather slowly, to drive back the Biafrans in the Mid-West, who were few in number and surrounded by an unfriendly population. The Biafran occupation, at first light-handed except for reported attacks on Hausa residents (many of whom were evacuated, with Europeans, from Sapele to Lagos), became harsher after the first weeks.

On 29 August a Biafran White Paper, circulated in London and elsewhere, set out a detailed plan for cooperation between an independent Biafra and the remainder of Nigeria, including a joint services authority. A *West Africa* editorial noted that the Biafrans still insisted that their state should include all the former Eastern Region, but suggested that the Federal Government could agree to an independent state covering East Central State alone and agree to cooperation on the lines suggested by Enugu.[36] *West Africa* repeated this suggestion in another editorial on 16 September. Unfortunately for that idea, the Biafrans would not agree to give up the Eastern minority areas, which would mean giving up their oil industry and their sea coast. The timing of the White Paper may indicate that Ojukwu, if he had ever agreed fully to Banjo's scheme (which seemed to envisage Biafra returning to a reformed Nigeria), now knew it could never succeed and wanted to re-emphasise Biafran independence. The document was followed by a "peace offensive" in which, for example, Dr Michael Okpara, former premier of the Eastern Region and a frequent travelling representative of Biafra, visited East Africa. Other Biafran representatives had been constantly visiting the West to explain the Biafran case, including Chinua Achebe, Mbanefo, and Eni Njoku.

While the Second Division moved on Benin, on the Mid-West coast men of the Lagos Garrison Organisation (LGO) captured Sapele and Warri[37] and moved inland; the LGO was then renamed the Third Infantry Division and then the Third Marine Commando Division, a name which did not denote highly trained special forces but troops operating in rivers and creeks. As they retreated, the Biafrans left the local Igbo population exposed to vicious revenge and arbitrary killing. It was estimated that mob violence killed several thousand Igbo people, with the Nigerian troops intervening very late or not at all to save them. Worse was to follow.

The Nigerian Second Division advance was accompanied by a group of foreign journalists, for now the war had aroused the interest of the Western media. Some reporters had begun covering the war quite early, such as John de St Jorre of *The Observer*, who crossed the Niger from the Mid-West into Biafra before fighting began. Some reporters went straight into Biafran territory; there were two good airports there, at Enugu and Port Harcourt, but it seems that at this time people travelling into or out of Biafra commonly went across the land border with Cameroon, until September when the federal forces captured Ikom and the main border crossing nearby. Now the reporters flying into the Nigerian side and following the Nigerian Second Division included Kaye Whiteman of *West Africa*.

The Biafran occupiers made a pathetic last-ditch declaration of the Mid-West as the "Republic of Benin" before retreating from Benin City on 20 September. *West Africa*'s correspondent sent a long report from Benin published in the issue of 30 September. From there the Nigerians advanced down the road to Asaba, on the west bank of the Niger facing Onitsha on the east bank. The Nigerian government saw the world's press recording its victories, but the reporters, though under tight control by the military, were bound to hear something of the large-scale killing of Igbo civilians. After an appeal by church leaders, Gowon ordered army commanders to stop those killings;[38] the Code of Conduct was supposed to make such a specific order unnecessary. *West Africa*'s columnist Griot (on that occasion Kaye Whiteman) said on 21 October, "Nobody would now want to be an Ibo in the Mid-West, I was told," and mentioned how two Igbos, caught stealing a cow, had been saved from lynching by the presence of foreign journalists.

After retreating across the Niger bridge, the Biafran troops blew up two of its eight sections, enough to make it unusable. Murtala Muhammed then tried to launch an assault across the river but failed three times, starting on 12 October, with the loss of hundreds of his men;[39] the Nigerians did not capture Onitsha then, but they destroyed its famous market. But although the Biafrans halted the Nigerian advance at the natural barrier of the Niger, the outcome of their invasion of the Mid-West was an utter disaster for them. Thousands of their people in the Mid-West had been murdered and other Mid-Westerners, previously content with the state's non-combatant position, were now strongly committed to the federal war effort.

Federal forces in Asaba killed several hundred unarmed Igbo civilians on 7 October; more were killed in the following days, to make probably at least a thousand dead in all, mostly men and boys. The foreign journalists following the federal forces a few miles away may have heard something of this major war crime for which Murtala Muhammed was responsible; *West Africa*'s correspondent went into Asaba and seemingly did hear something, perhaps not enough to be sure—he wrote, "I saw no people in Asaba," adding that while some people there and in some surrounding areas had fled across the Niger or into the bush, "the rest must be dead".[40] The foreign journalists were under close supervision, and any Nigerian journalists who heard what had happened would have been unable to publish anything. Anyway, there was limited interest in the Nigerian war in the West at that time. The war which hit the headlines then was the Vietnam War, which was televised and reported around the world and aroused increasing protests within the US and beyond.

But there was already some unease about the Nigerian war. In *The Times* of 31 October a letter was published by Dame Margery Perham, the famous Africanist scholar who in the colonial era had published the classic *Native Administration in Nigeria* in 1937. She wrote, "An Ibo clergyman brought me a letter today from his sister describing how in their family town, where there was no fighting, the government troops collected all the men including her young brother and used a machine gun upon them." In response, Ogundipe, in his choleric style which was soon to become renowned in his press conferences, wrote, "No iota of truth can be found in Dame Margery Perham's allegations …"[41] In fact, what Perham had said was true, and although she did not name the town, she was referring to the Asaba massacre. Here I leave the chronology of the war for a moment and flash forward many decades, to the revelation of the full hideous story about Asaba.

Eventually the facts were freely published in Nigeria, when the post-war reconciliation made uncensored writing about the Biafran war possible, though many years passed before some facts came out. Obasanjo, who was Nigeria's military head of state from 1976 to 1979, later, as the elected head of state, in 1999 ordered an inquiry headed by Mr Justice Oputa to examine human rights violations in Nigeria from January 1966 onwards; and evidence of the Asaba crime was given. This commission followed the example of the famous Truth and Reconciliation Commission after the end of the apartheid regime in South Africa; such initiatives were unheard of in the 1960s. However, the full report of the Oputa Commission was never published.[42] Then, in 2017, the full story of Asaba[43] was told by Elizabeth Bird and Fraser Ottanelli, who conducted many interviews in Nigeria, with Gowon and other retired senior officers as well as survivors of the massacre. Gowon had already said in 2002 that he had not ordered the massacre (which can be accepted as true) and had not heard about it until several years later (which is hard to believe).[44] In fact, the truth had been known at the top level of the Nigerian government within weeks in 1967. On 21 January 1968 Colin Legum in *The Observer* wrote an account of the Asaba massacre, generally close to the facts except for saying that it was a response to a Biafran attack, which was not the case.

A few months later, when everything had changed in British public opinion and Biafra was in the headlines, I paid a private visit to Oxford during the summer of 1968 and by chance met a Western Igbo

Catholic priest from Asaba, Father Patrick Isichei (Elizabeth Isichei's brother-in-law). He told me how federal troops had murdered large numbers of men and boys at Asaba. Patrick became a friend and for a time a work colleague in later years, but I do not recall discussing the war with him. It was only through the research of Bird and Ottanelli that I learned how Patrick, at Oxford, was the clergyman who had received news of the crime from his sister, who had managed to get a federal soldier to post a letter for her, and how he had shown it to Margery Perham and inspired her letter to *The Times*. At the time I did not feel able to do anything with the information Patrick gave to me a few months after that. My editor would not have made use of it; although pro-Nigerian, he was ready to acknowledge proven facts, as he showed over the Nigerian air raids, but I am fairly sure he would not have published second- or third-hand information from a Biafran source. But what I should have done was pass on the information to people who could have checked it up and published something. I greatly regret I did not do so.

Biafran defeats at Enugu and Calabar

Back in October 1967, the Asaba killing, which was concealed from the outside world, came three days after an event which the Nigerian government proudly proclaimed to the outside world: the capture of Enugu, the Biafrans' capital, on 4 October.[45] Reporters followed the First Division troops into the city later, finding that all the inhabitants had left before it fell (I heard later that Ojukwu was the last man to leave). Kaye Whiteman wrote, as *West Africa*'s columnist Griot, a report headed "The Empty City", saying the deserted city with all its empty homes and offices seemed "strange and frightening".[46]

After the capture of Enugu, Anthony Ukpabi Asika was appointed administrator of East Central State; four months later, in February 1968, he set up his offices in Enugu.[47] He was a lecturer at Ibadan, one of the few Igbo dons who had not left that university. He had a particular sort of academic personality, tending to sound remote, and was not a good communicator. But nobody in his position could have avoided being condemned by the Biafrans as a collaborator. There were some other well-known Igbos on the federal side, but not many, and they had little chance of winning over their people. Asika kept on trying. At an early stage he made an appeal to Igbos in which he faced the facts of the pogroms in the North and said, "Your other Nigerian brothers were sorry and are sorry, very sorry."[48] Were they? Many may have been in private conversation, but I found that the normal reaction of Nigerians backing the government during the war, when the pogroms were mentioned, was to bluster and change the subject.

The Biafrans, showing their adaptability and efficiency, which were widely admired, moved their capital to Umuahia, with some admin-istration conducted from Aba, and continued to organise resistance to the federal advance, which did not go far beyond Enugu at that time. Indeed, Biafran forces continued to control areas very near the city and even re-entered the city itself, if only for short periods, for some months. When the Biafran Consultative Assembly met at Umuahia soon after the fall of Enugu, on 11 October, Ojukwu spoke of treachery within as the cause of Biafran defeats at Enugu and else-where; this represented a permanent ugly obsession among the Biafrans. Later, at the same assembly on 27 January 1968, he said the "disaster of our withdrawal from the capital city of Enugu" was directly due to subversion organised by Nigeria.[49] Despite that admis-sion, Biafran propagandists continually told the world that Enugu was still the Biafran capital. Biafra Radio, still operating after losing the former Eastern Nigeria Broadcasting Service studios, claimed that it was still broadcasting from Enugu. Few people, however, can have taken that radio seriously, apart from the Biafran population to whom its broadcasts were primarily directed. One does not expect a broad-caster in wartime to be objective and temperate about the enemy; Lagos Radio was not, Kaduna Radio still less; but Biafra Radio was in a class by itself, with vehement propaganda filled not only with false-hoods, but with the wildest and weirdest falsehoods. It sounded absolutely crazed at times, but there was an intelligible aim: to keep the Biafran population mobilised and committed to the struggle.

What kept them mobilised and committed most of all was a fear that defeat would be followed by the mass murder of all of them, or at least all Igbos. From an early date, Biafrans talked of "geno-cide" as the likely result of a federal victory. Obviously Igbos, and maybe many minority Easterners too, feared that "the Hausas" who had carried out the pogroms in the North were now coming to complete the job of extermination in the homeland of former Eastern Nigeria. A *West Africa* editorial on 7 October 1967 recalled the pogroms and said, "There is no doubt that it is fear of a similar massacre which sustains Ibo resistance to the Federal Government." And the killings in the Mid-West must have reinforced the fear enormously. The Asaba massacre must have been known very quickly to the population in Biafran territory, and other war crimes were to follow in the Mid-West.

At any rate, the Biafrans' common determination to fight on was not diminished by the successive defeats. At the same time, all that we on *West Africa* heard about the other side indicated a similar popular determination to fight on to victory. We heard of no peace movement in Nigeria such as that which Wole Soyinka tried to start. As I handled the readers' letters page on the magazine, I saw numerous letters from Nigerians every week, most of which could not be published for lack of space. If I recall rightly, there were very few letters from Yorubas or other non-Eastern Nigerians opposing the war. I believe this is significant because if there was serious opposition to the war among non-Eastern Nigerians, while those with such views could have been forced to keep quiet about them within Nigeria, among the thousands of Nigerians living freely in Europe and America there would have been some signs of those views. One very well-known non-Eastern Nigerian who opposed the war was the Mid-Westerner Peter Enahoro, already mentioned. He made his views clear, in conversation, while working at the Overseas Newspapers office in London, before going off, I believe in 1968, to work with the West German overseas radio service, Deutsche Welle. He and Wole Soyinka did not agree with the Biafrans completely; they regretted the secession, but they opposed a military solution. This stand was highly exceptional among Nigerians, who saw it as being effectively pro-Biafran. The impression we had throughout was of solid support among non-Eastern Nigerians for the official slogan "To keep Nigeria one is a task that must be done".

What inspired the general enthusiasm for the war among other Nigerians? Among other things, the ill feeling towards the Igbo people, which had been swelling since the events of 1966; officially the adversary was "the rebels" or Ojukwu personally, but for many ordinary Nigerians it was "the Igbos". People of the Eastern minorities, headed by their governors based for the moment in Lagos,[50] spread their resentment at Igbo domination and Biafran state oppression among other Nigerians. But besides ethnic hostility there was a genuine patriotic feeling that the country should not be broken up (though some might say it already had been in 1966). It was believed that a successful secession by Biafra might lead to other groups of Nigerians planning to break away, and that the same might happen in other African countries, nearly all multi-ethnic.

That was an argument which led other African governments to back the Nigerian government from the start—all of them initially, though some probably had misgivings. Many Africans were influenced by the recent memory of the secession of Katanga from the Congo in 1960–3, headed by Moïse Tshombe. There were in fact many big differences between Katanga and Biafra. Tshombe's Lunda people had had no reason to rebel against the other Congolese, who had not oppressed them—rather, all Congolese had been oppressed by the Belgians. Lunda chauvinism was used as a tool by the giant mining company Union Minière, other Belgian interests, and the white Rhodesian settlers to run a vital portion of the Congo as they wished. But Biafra was very clearly a genuine, spontaneous African initiative, with many well-educated leaders and at first massive support from the grassroots, against extreme ill-treatment in Nigeria; while the mining company there, Shell-BP, had no power over events, as was shown in mid-1967, and became the (self-interested) ally of the federal side.

The difference between the two secessions was pointed out by President Mobutu of the Congo,[51] and by the Irish diplomat Conor Cruise O'Brien, who, as UN representative in Katanga during the United Nations Operation in the Congo, had attempted to end Tshombe's secession in 1961 (it had eventually been ended in early 1963); he could speak with authority about Katanga and Tshombe, and after visiting Biafra in the first months of the war, he declared that its case was totally different. Writing in *The Observer*, he said Biafra's war was "a popular and patriotic war" and "a nation has been born".[52] But Tshombe's name was still widely reviled, even though he had later become prime minister of the whole Congo in 1964–5 and other African rulers had accepted him as one of their number then. Nigerians knew a lot about the earlier Congo crisis, in which many Nigerian officers and men now engaged in their country's civil war had served as UN peacekeepers. By coincidence, Tshombe, by then in exile in Spain, was kidnapped and taken to Algeria soon after Biafra's secession, on 30 June. Even without headlines reporting this, Africans would have instantly recalled Tshombe and Katanga when the word "secession" was heard again.

As it happened, the next scheduled summit meeting of the OAU after the Biafran declaration of secession was in Kinshasa, capital of the Congo. Even with a different venue, that meeting of African governments in September 1967 would have resolved to back Nigeria, whose delegation was headed by Awolowo, against the secession. It declared that the assembly of heads of state, "reiterating their condemnation of secession in any member state", was "concerned at the tragic and serious situation in Nigeria". It agreed to set up a Consultative Committee of six states which would go to Nigeria, but this would be to assure the Federal Government of "the assembly's desire for the territorial integrity, unity and peace of Nigeria".[53]

There was unease among Africans about the civil war that had hit the most populous country of the continent; in late August, 24 senior Ghanaians, headed by the Chief Justice, called for African mediation in Nigeria.[54] But African governments, with wide backing among Africans, believed the Nigerian government must be supported, being acutely aware that in other countries leaders of some ethnic or other group with grievances could think of breaking away if Biafra succeeded in providing a precedent, perhaps with the backing of interfering Westerners, as in Katanga.

Representatives of the OAU Consultative Committee travelled to Lagos on 22 November 1967 to discuss the war with the Gowon government. Four were heads of state—Emperor Haile Selassie of Ethiopia, the Ghanaian military ruler General Ankrah, and Presidents Diori of Niger and Ahidjo of Cameroon; the other states were the Congo and Liberia. There had been opposition to the mission in Nigeria, whose government made clear that it was not for the purpose of mediation. Behind closed doors the heads of state were said to have subjected Gowon to some questioning; but their overall conclusion was that he must be supported.

The OAU mission cannot be called a peace initiative. There were no serious peace initiatives for many months after the war began. The Vatican sent two representatives, Monsignor Dominic Conway and Monsignor Georges Rochcau, to Lagos to urge efforts to make peace; they went to Biafra afterwards, and were politely received on both sides, but did not succeed in their aim. There was already some international concern about the war and the food shortages setting in among the more crowded population of shrinking Biafran territory (more on this in later chapters). But on the diplomatic front, all countries at this early stage recognised the government in Lagos as the rightful government of all Nigeria, with the right to suppress a rebellion.

The British press was reporting on the war more by then, and reflecting public unease about it; in September a *West Africa* editorial could already say, "Hardly a day goes by without a letter in the London *Times* calling for a stop to the Nigerian war."[55] Among those writing to the press and otherwise showing concern were former British colonial government officials. Many of these had worked in the North, helping run the Indirect Rule system which they admired, and greatly liked the Hausa–Fulani social order headed by the emirs; now they commonly spoke out in defence of the Federal Government. One egregious example was the former governor of Northern Nigeria Sir Bryan Sharwood Smith, who wrote a letter to *The Times* of 2 November 1967 defending Gowon and criticising Margery Perham's letter mentioned earlier, saying reports of massacres should not be credited "until vouched for by reasonable, independent witnesses": as if an eminent scholar like Dame Margery (incidentally a champion of the Northern Nigeria Indirect Rule system for decades) could not be trusted to assess the credibility of information she received, which was in fact completely true. Biafrans noted the common pro-Northern bias of British people who had worked or were still working in Nigeria; but there were many such people ready to defend the Biafrans also. As regards the editorial policies of British newspapers, they may have shown some sympathy for the Biafrans, but at that stage were far from giving them full support.

Among the British media, the BBC World Service was particularly important for Africans, as they listened to it for news in great numbers. The *West Africa* staff was in regular contact with the BBC Africa specialists, but I never listened to the BBC World Service at that time; it was from Biafran complaints that I learned that the BBC was regularly accused of pro-Lagos bias. Some truth in these accusations was discovered by Frederick Forsyth, a journalist who had joined the BBC after several years with Reuters and who was sent to Biafra soon after the war began; in Enugu, Jim Parker told him that his briefing at the BBC before leaving, highly slanted on the federal side, had echoed the views of Parker's superior, the high commissioner in Lagos, and had been far from the reality of what was going on.[56] Other reports have confirmed this about the two diplomats: Hunt reported correctly what the Nigerian government and public thought, Parker reported correctly what the Eastern Nigerian and then Biafran government and public thought, which was part of their duty as diplomats; and each was sympathetic to the viewpoint he reported (are diplomats supposed to avoid this, and how many do?). Parker very soon left Enugu, but Hunt stayed in Lagos and continued to express unshakeable belief in the federal cause. This was to become notorious when the war became front-page news later. As for the BBC World Service, it was then funded by a grant-in-aid from the Commonwealth Relations Office and must certainly have been influenced by the High Commission in Lagos. But controversy over the roles of the BBC and the British government itself was still limited in the first six months of the war.

Much more will be said in later chapters about these matters. But a point about the media coverage can be made straight away. Journalists covering wars in other countries properly aim at objectivity, but we are soon made aware that the people involved in the fighting are not always interested in that. Their main concern is often "Whose side are you on?" If a foreign journalist reports something discreditable to one side, even if it is based on certain fact, he is thought to be biased in favour of the other side or even in its pay. If he or his editor shows signs of sympathy for one side, the other side will reject what they say even if it is undoubted fact. In the Nigerian war, Biafrans accused the BBC of reporting Nigerian successes wrongly and saw this not as a genuine mistake, but as a sign of underlying bias. While Forsyth's account shows clearly that there was editorial sympathy for the federal side in the BBC, and there are other indications of it, I cannot say—not having listened personally to any of its broadcasts at that time—whether that sympathy really did distort BBC reporting. I can say that there were Nigerians who accused the BBC of being pro-Biafran.

Diplomats and politicians faced the same response as journalists. Hunt was accused of letting his confident belief in the rightness of Nigeria's war effort colour his appreciation of the facts; but his critics were supporters of the cause of Biafra. On the other side, those who said confidently that Biafra could not be defeated were accused of being, and in fact often were, people who did not want it to be defeated. In recalling attitudes to the war, I am struck by the way in which partisans of Nigeria or Biafra, whose real concern was the moral rightness of one side, argued strongly about something different: the facts of who was winning and who losing. When predictions of Biafra's early defeat were proved wrong, Biafrans and their supporters mocked them and felt they had scored a point. This of course can happen in any war.

Certainly the Biafrans defied many predictions of their early defeat. After the disaster in the Mid-West and the fall of Enugu, they defeated Murtala Muhammed's initial Niger crossings and held their own for several months in the north-west and the south; they were not finally driven away from Enugu fully until January 1968, and they attacked the federal forces at Bonny several times, before being driven from there in January 1968. A federal advance on Port Harcourt, announced by Arikpo as having started on 3 December, did not succeed.[57] But while failing to advance in those sectors for some months, the federal forces scored a major victory, to pave the way for more, with the capture of Calabar by the Third Division in a seaborne operation on 18 October 1967.

During the fierce fighting for Calabar, hundreds were killed by the federal forces in a prison and a police barracks; Adekunle, GOC of the Third Division, said they had refused to surrender.[58] But for at least some of the Efik and Ibibio people of Calabar and the surrounding area, the federal occupation was what Nigerians called it, "liberation". One cannot be sure how many had wanted it before the day the Nigerian side won and became the side that it was wise to cheer on.

But there had certainly been opposition to Biafran rule there and in the area scheduled for the Rivers State. *West Africa* carried few reports of the situation in those areas, but there certainly was repression there, fuelled by suspicion of the people's true loyalties. However, among the people of the area where the South-Eastern State was now (gradually) to be established, some remained in prominent positions in Biafra. Besides the secretary to the government in Umuahia, N.U. Akpan, they included James Udo-Affia, Biafran commissioner for health, who defended Biafra at the House of Commons in London with Kenneth Dike on 7 November 1967; and, very prominently, Okokon Ndem, a well-known voice on Biafra Radio.

It took time for normal life to resume in Calabar, and the Biafrans still held the west bank of the Cross River estuary opposite Calabar for some months, preventing federal forces from advancing in that direction. But the Nigerian forces could advance northwards and eastwards, and thus were able to cut Biafran territory off completely from Cameroon, taking the border crossing point at Ekang in December and joining up with First Division forces coming from the north.[59] This was a blow for the Biafrans; their trade across the lines might still have been able to reach into Cameroon, but with much more difficulty now. In all parts of the war zone, federal troops, whose numbers were growing but still limited, could not enforce dense occupation and constant control over all areas they overran.

In fighting in the Calabar sector, the Biafrans employed some of the white mercenaries who were to fascinate the Nigerian and the Western media throughout the war. From the very beginning, each side claimed that the other was employing large cohorts of mercenaries in its ground forces also, and indeed depended on them. This was largely nonsense, but there were a few foreign military personnel on both sides. The term "mercenary" may not apply properly to all of them, as it suggests an individual soldier of fortune, and the Nigerian Air Force's Egyptian pilots, for example, were presumably recruited under an agreement with President Nasser's government. Also, some who seemed to be true soldiers of fortune were in fact recruited with the connivance of Western government agencies or at their instigation. This was true of the group of about 40 soldiers headed by Roger Faulques, a former Katanga mercenary, who joined the Biafrans in late 1967 through a semi-secret French agency (of which more later). The Federal Government showed journalists the captured passports and travel documents of three mercenaries in the Calabar sector.[60] Those mercenaries achieved very little and by early 1968 had all left except for four, including two who fought well for Biafra, the Welsh-South African Taffy Williams and the German ex-Legionnaire Rolf Steiner.[61]

The Biafrans lost a good deal of money on mercenaries, but probably much more on arms purchases. They tried to buy arms on the black market from well before the war but were inevitably overcharged or cheated. Ibiam said Biafra had to pay five times the retail price for arms bought on the European black market.[62] After the war, a novel by an ex-Biafran writer, S. Okechukwu Mezu, presented a dismal story of Biafran representatives being massively swindled in arms deals. It is fiction but seems clearly to be based on fact, with some real people easily identifiable under false names; Biafran arms-buying representatives in the novel have false names, but it may well be that the real-life ones, like those in the novel, were academics and others with no experience of business, least of all under-the-counter business (maybe experienced Igbo businesspeople helped in reality). The novel is vague about dates, but the story seems probably related to the first months of war. It rings true and descriptions of the swindles are excruciating.[63] Factual accounts published later support this fictional one, though the full facts about this clandestine activity are hard to discern. It is obvious what problems the Biafrans had in the face of an enemy able to buy all the arms it needed legally and openly.

The Biafrans had foreign exchange at their disposal before losing a good deal of it. The Eastern Region government had had its funds in Europe, which would have been inherited by the Biafran government unless the Federal Government sought to prevent this by some legal means. One estimate was of at least £7 million, including £6 million transferred by the African Continental Bank (ACB) just before the Federal Government prohibited such transfers by that bank—founded by Azikiwe and later owned by two Eastern Region state corporations—in April 1967.[64] At that time the Nigerian pound could initially be exchanged for sterling and hence other hard currencies, though it was not actually tied to sterling (when the British pound was devalued in November 1967, the Nigerian pound did not follow suit).[65] But, as noted earlier, many economic and financial enactments by the FMG before and after secession were designed to starve the Easterners/Biafrans of money, especially foreign exchange, and supplies. Any money which was already held in hard currency in the West could be used, though Britain had its fairly severe exchange controls. It was reported that the fortune inherited by Ojukwu from his late father was used to help the Biafran cause.

A good deal of Biafran activity concerning arms and money took place in France, and the French government probably turned a blind eye to it; how much of the semi-secret French aid to Biafra had begun before mid-1968 is unclear, but one part of it—the dispatch of mercenaries already mentioned—began in late 1967. In August 1967 the Nigerian press headlined the discovery of a Biafran document setting out an agreement with the distinguished Rothschild Bank of Paris, granting the bank exclusive rights to Biafra's oil and other minerals. A government spokesman handed the press a photocopy of a document giving Nwokedi power to conclude the deal. There were some doubts about whether these documents were genuine, but from later accounts it is clear that they were. Obviously the Biafrans signed the agreement in the hope of money paid up front. Whether they would have tried to wriggle out of the agreement if they won the war one cannot tell; anyway it remained a scrap of paper.

In other ways the Biafrans did get money and did succeed in having arms supplied and shipped. At this stage they were shipped mainly from Portugal. In late October the *Jozina*, a Dutch ship sailing from Lisbon, was seized off the Nigerian coast and found to have a huge cargo of arms.[66] Somehow the crew had hoped to evade the blockade and land the cargo—among the creeks and inlets of the coast where the Biafrans' writ still ran, it might have been possible—but they failed and Biafra suffered one more defeat. However, the Biafrans had a good working airport at Port Harcourt, which was used for arms shipments. From some point in 1967 flights from Portugal delivered arms to the Biafrans, largely or entirely run by Hank (Henry) Wharton, the American pilot whose arms flight heading for the then Eastern Nigeria had crashed in Cameroon a year earlier; released after a short spell in prison in Cameroon, he now piloted or arranged flights to Port Harcourt from Lisbon. *West Africa* of 18 November 1967 quoted a report of at least eight aircraft on this arms run to Biafra "regularly for several months".

That report also mentioned one plane, a Super Constellation, returning to Lisbon with 32 bullet holes. At that time there were federal air raids on Port Harcourt for several weeks.[67] The Biafrans' air raids had not yet ceased by then—their B-52 dropped two bombs on Calabar while journalists were there as guests of the federal army,[68] and the oil terminal at Bonny was hit, causing damage worth £5.5 million according to Adekunle[69]—but soon reports of such raids ceased, while the Nigerian Air Force was increasingly active. One of its raids damaged the Alesa-Eleme oil refinery near Port Harcourt but left it still able to serve the Biafrans for a while.[70] Raids on such targets affect ordinary civilian life but can be considered militarily justified. However, the Nigerian Air Force rapidly turned to indiscriminate air raids on towns and villages, hitting markets and hospitals. This was blamed at the time, and later, on Egyptian pilots bombing from a great height, regardless of what lay below.

In mid-November there was a 24-hour pause in federal bombing to allow a DC-4 of the International Committee of the Red Cross (ICRC) to land at Port Harcourt with medical supplies and personnel for the Red Cross Centre at Achi in Biafran territory. This aircraft had landed at Lagos earlier,[71] but later reports suggested that other Red Cross flights went to Biafra from Fernando Po, the conveniently situated nearby island in Spanish Guinea, with Federal Nigerian representatives inspecting the humanitarian cargo. This continued airlift was little publicised at the time, but it took place, and was accepted by the Federal Government; however, one report said there was a halt for some time after November 1967. The ICRC was already providing some help on both sides by late 1967, and a Red Cross spokesman said in Geneva that half a million people were "in distress".[72] Food shortages on the Biafran side were worsening and this was already widely known.

West Africa expressed concern at the consequences of further federal advances into the densely populated Igbo heartland, and said the logical course was for Ojukwu to seek a ceasefire, but acknowledged that Biafrans expressed fear of extermination and believed that only sovereignty could keep them safe.[73] This was indeed the fixed Biafran position. Among the Igbos there was no sign of any opposition to the Biafran war effort, except for the Banjo–Ifeajuna plot—and that plot's aim had not been to come to terms with the Gowon government, but to defeat it in another way. In December 1967 Cecil King, chairman of the International Publishing Corporation and ultimate boss of *West Africa* and the *Daily Times*, paid a visit to Lagos and, in a meeting with Gowon recorded with a photo in the *Daily Times*, mentioned that Mbanefo and Eni Njoku had approached him for mediation, saying there was not absolute insistence on Biafran independence.[74] How King thought it helpful to say this in public is hard to tell; Mbanefo and Njoku in fact stayed loyal to Ojukwu throughout, but if they had deviated from his policy it would have been worse than useless for King to mention it publicly. However, the FMG—which at that time said there could be negotiations with "the rebels" but not with Ojukwu himself—went even further than King and issued a statement in January 1968 listing many prominent people of the former Eastern Region with whom it would be willing to talk, including Nnamdi Azikiwe, Pius Okigbo and Louis Mbanefo.[75] This must have removed any chance of the people concerned breaking ranks and contacting Lagos; however, some unofficial contacts between the two sides probably went on. Anyway, the year 1967 ended with no sign of any resolution of the conflict either on the battlefield or through negotiations.

5

RETREAT AND RECOGNITION
(JANUARY–JUNE 1968)

Hunger, relief and blockade running

The territory covered by the Republic of Biafra at its declaration was densely populated but had abundant food resources. Its people were still largely agricultural and grew yams, cassava, cocoyams, maize and other starch food staples, and many sorts of fruit such as bananas and pineapples; the oil palm, on individual and village plantations, produced palm oil and kernels, and palm wine; there were also coconut palms, and cocoa was grown, though on a much smaller scale than in Western Nigeria. Villages had chickens and small livestock; the rivers and the Delta and the coast produced fish. Equally important, incomes for at least a considerable number were enough for gaps in the daily diet to be filled by imports into the region. The problem was that those gaps were quite big. The region had only one area suitable for cattle rearing, in the former Ogoja Province, and most beef had to come from cattle brought, by road or rail or on the hoof, from the North. Another source of protein was dried cod or stockfish, which came from far-off Norway and Iceland but had been a staple of diet in that region of Africa for centuries.

When a trade embargo was placed on the Eastern Region before secession, and the seaports were blockaded, it was very easy to stop delivery of stockfish and other food imports; cattle supplies could also be halted easily. While some trade across the lines was to go on throughout the war—the front line did not have trenches and barbed wire, and it was always easy to cross—shortages set in from an early stage in Biafra. Most important, protein began to disappear from daily diets, though starch food remained adequate for some time; a review in *West Africa* of the book *Yams*, by D.G. Coursey, said the Igbos were "the most enthusiastic yam cultivators in the world".[1] While people suffered increasingly within their home villages, there were by early 1968 many refugee camps for displaced people.

On the federal side, the Federal Rehabilitation Commission was established in March 1968, while the International Committee for the Red Cross (ICRC) had a coordinating role for relief and aid for the restoration of normal life in areas occupied by federal forces. Much of the actual work of relief, which was well below the need, was done by voluntary agencies. The Christian Council of Nigeria (CCN) organised an Emergency Relief Collection on 3 September 1967 and collected £911 5s. 3d.[2]—not much, but this was just the start of plenty of activity for relief in the war zone by the Protestant churches in Nigeria. A report in the *Nigerian Christian*, seemingly towards the end of 1967,[3] said that at Calabar "food will be extremely scarce, at least for a time" and conditions were bad at Asaba, which "is still largely a deserted city as far as civilians are concerned" (no hint as to the reason for this). It mentioned the work of the Nigerian Red Cross, the ICRC, the CCN and the Catholic Secretariat; these agencies had started distribution of food, clothing and medicines among other forms of relief in Asaba, where people were destitute.

In *West Africa* of 3 February 1968, Matchet's Diary quoted a CCN warning that "endemic diseases have increased unchecked" in Biafran territory, but added that other reports spoke only of shortages of antibiotics and anaesthetics. Shortages of those were bad enough, and the blockade was bound to affect medicine supplies. That diary report said markets in food and other local produce "appear to flourish". But the correspondent's report a week later (cited below) said—quoting Pius Okigbo—that while more yams and cassava had been planted, milk and sugar were very short, and meat was 50 per cent more expensive than before secession. Things were to get steadily worse.

Shortages were relieved to a small extent by the trade across the lines, the "attack trade" as it was called, but the Federal Government took drastic action to stop this by issuing new currency notes and declaring that the old ones would all cease to be legal tender from 22 January 1968.[4] Biafran currency was issued later in the month—a Biafran pound—but it was of limited use for the "attack trade". While the old Nigerian currency notes were demonetised and became useless pieces of paper, the old Nigerian coins remained in circulation. This allowed some trade across the lines to continue, and resourceful Biafrans were sometimes able to obtain hard currency for trading. But overall, the Nigerian currency change was a very severe blow to the Biafrans. Besides traders, the Biafran state itself was hard hit. Its representatives made desperate efforts, following the announcement of the coming currency change, to take suitcases and bags full of the old notes to Europe to get them changed. Where they succeeded, they got only a fraction of the nominal value of the notes.

On 20 January a DC-7 made an emergency landing at Lomé in Togo, filled with Nigerian currency notes to the estimated value of £7.4 million, from the African Continental Bank in Port Harcourt and Onitsha, which were being taken to Nigeria, seemingly in a last desperate effort by the Biafrans to get some value for them before the deadline. The notes were quickly handed over to the Nigerian government,[5] which President Eyadéma of Togo supported throughout, and eight people on the plane, including the Rhodesian mercenary Alastair Wicks, spent some months in gaol in Togo. How they had planned to change the notes in Nigeria is hard to imagine; where would they have landed, under what identities, and what story could they have told about all that money? In any case, the Biafrans lost again, badly.

No full study of the Biafran "attack trade" has been published to my knowledge, and one can only guess how much was able to continue after January 1968 and how far its curbing added to the shortages of food and medical supplies. As noted earlier, the situation had become serious enough, months before, to attract the concern of the ICRC, which began flights to deliver relief supplies into Biafran territory in November 1967; apparently halted for some time, they had resumed by April 1968.[6] Those who said later that starvation in the Biafran enclave was suddenly sprung on the outside world in June 1968—usually meaning, or actually saying, that it was sprung by an efficient propaganda machine—were people who had not read closely reports coming from the area for several months before then.

From the first, the Catholic missionaries and other priests knew all about the daily plight of civilians in the war zone. The Catholic Church had won mass conversion among the Igbos in particular since the 1930s. Many of the minority peoples were Catholic, but the Church was a particularly important part of the scene among the Igbos. There were churches in hundreds of villages, seminaries training very many Igbo priests, convents with both missionary and African nuns, Catholic hospitals, and notably scores of Catholic schools. Besides primary schools there were prominent Church secondary schools, including Christ the King College at Onitsha and Bishop Shanahan College at Orlu, and seminaries producing Igbo priests from the 1930s and, later, bishops. The Diocese of Enugu had an Igbo bishop, John Cross Anyogu, from 1963 until he died, two days before the war began, on 4 July 1967; Francis Arinze became archbishop of Onitsha on the eve of war in June 1967 (he is now a senior cardinal in Rome). But the missionaries were still vital. Most were of the Irish province of the Holy Ghost Fathers, while many Irish Kiltegan Fathers were also present. Although there were rapidly increasing numbers of indigenous clergy, in countless Igbo parishes the Irish missionary was a prominent, much-respected local figure.

The Igbos were and still are seen as a predominantly Catholic people. It is difficult to measure religious allegiance exactly, but although Catholics may not have been a majority of the Igbo population in the 1960s,[7] their presence was predominant because of the great numbers educated at Catholic schools. Over much of Africa, Western education is the way for an individual's progress and gives status, and this has been especially true among the Igbos, who have no traditional upper class (with the minor exception of some rulers in Onitsha and among the Western Igbos) and have impelled each new generation to seek progress through commerce or education, or both. In scores of Igbo villages in the 1960s the Catholic church and school, with Catholic statues and crucifixes, had a prominent position, even if there were traditional religious rites in the forest which some Catholics attended on the quiet (as in medieval Europe). That was how the Catholic Church became predominant in the area that became Biafra. It is hardly necessary to add that the Biafrans, of all faiths, acted for their own reasons, and showed an independent determination that was much admired; they were not manipulated by Catholic priests or anyone else.

There were hundreds of thousands of Catholics among the other Nigerian peoples—among the numerous Mid-Western peoples, the Yorubas, and the Northern minorities—and many served in the Nigerian army. And among the Igbos the Catholic Church did not have a monopoly. The Anglican Church had a long history among them, with its base at Onitsha, since the days of the 19th-century Yoruba bishop on the Niger, Samuel Ajayi Crowther. The Presbyterian Church, which had a pre-eminent position at Calabar, had expanded inland from there into Igbo country. Among prominent Biafran leaders, Sir Louis Mbanefo was a leading Anglican layman, chancellor of the Diocese on the Niger, and Sir Francis Ibiam (Dr Akanu Ibiam after he renounced his British honour), adviser to the governor, a prominent Presbyterian, was the first lay chairman of the CCN and one of six vice presidents of the World Council of Churches. Most of the Biafran leaders had a Catholic background or education, including Odumegwu Ojukwu, though he went to secular secondary schools in Nigeria and Britain.

When war came, the Catholic Church and its hospitals, its convents and all its institutions helped the people with relief, consolation and moral support. The missionary and other priests served the people like the priests in beleaguered Malta during the siege of 1940–3. Obviously they could not have done otherwise. It was natural for the missionaries to sympathise with their parishioners; they had seen the mutilated and shocked survivors of the pogroms coming in, and now they saw people suffering from shortages, including growing food deficiency, and also from the regular Nigerian air raids, often reported in *West Africa*, which caused havoc, as they normally hit civilian targets only.

The food shortages, though not the air raids, affected civilians on the other side of the front also. From an early date there was acute suffering among people in federal-occupied areas also, as the CCN reported early on; there was particular distress, for several months, in South-Eastern State after the federal occupation. Although food could be brought freely into such areas, not everyone could buy enough and relief efforts were needed. Catholic Church agencies and others provided relief there too. Catholic humanitarian efforts on the Biafran side received most publicity from mid-1968 onwards, but those on the other side continued quietly throughout.

Bishops and clergy, both Catholic and Protestant, working on the Biafran side might or might not think that secession had been a wise choice, and all would probably have welcomed a peace settlement on any terms, but while the Biafran people around them were suffering they had to help and call on others to help. The churches with their parishes and hospitals had a built-in organisation on which relief distribution networks could be based; in the World Council of Churches–Christian Council of Biafra operation, for example, supplies were sent first to Queen Elizabeth Hospital in Umuahia and then distributed to other hospitals.[8] And the churches' overseas links provided one early channel for appeals for relief supplies for Biafra in Western countries. Missionaries' appeals were a normal feature of Catholic life in all those countries, but now they were not for restoring a church's roof but for urgently needed food and medicine; and because of the Holy Ghost Fathers and Kiltegan Fathers link there were appeals, publicity and generous response from an early date in Ireland. A good deal of the information about hunger and deprivation in Biafra which contributed to our news reports in *West Africa* came, at this stage, from the Irish Republic press. In Dublin on 12 December 1967, a press conference called by John Kennedy, whose brother Father Raymond Kennedy had just come from Biafra with a request for medical supplies, was followed by an appeal for help, and in March, Jerome Udoji and Mark Olisa, coming from Biafra, addressed a new meeting in Dublin to talk about the refugee camps; money and suitable food like dried milk were then collected by a new body called Africa Concern, whose activity expanded from then on.[9] Founded by John Kennedy and his wife, Kay O'Loughlin Kennedy, Africa Concern later developed into Concern Worldwide, which is still active in humanitarian work today.

Appeals for help for Biafran civilians also started at an early date in Scandinavia, where the Lutheran churches were to play a major part; there was a church appeal on 21 November 1967, and the Norwegian and Danish church relief organisations began to send relief materials including stockfish in the first part of 1968. This was said to have been dispatched to Fernando Po,[10] presumably to be included in the Red Cross cargoes. But the Catholic humanitarian effort seems to have been from the start separate from the ICRC operation. An airlift to Biafra was arranged by Caritas Internationalis, which is basically just a loose grouping of Catholic charitable and humanitarian bodies around the world but in this case became an organiser of relief delivery.

Father Anthony Byrne, a Holy Ghost Fathers missionary in Onitsha diocese, was in charge of this operation, which was recorded in his reminiscences published thirty years later; they are readable and generally credible, but not 100 per cent reliable, being annoyingly vague about dates.[11] There is a definite date given, late December 1967, for a journey he made from Port Harcourt via Lisbon to Rome, where he was first asked by the Vatican to help arrange for the papal delegates who had already been to Lagos to plead for peace, to go to Biafra to do the same; he arranged this in Lisbon, apparently with Wharton (the "Butch Dutting" in Byrne's story is clearly Wharton, though it appears strange to have to disguise his identity after so long). He was told in Rome, so he recalls, "Check the plane, *personally*, to make sure there are no military supplies on it. Explain to the Biafrans that the Vatican will not communicate directly with them because we do not recognise their state."[12] The delegates travelled as arranged, with a cargo of medicine, and saw Colonel Ojukwu. They returned to tell the Pope of widespread severe hardship in Biafran territory, and then Father Byrne, back in Rome, was told to organise Caritas relief supplies to Biafra, while other Catholic relief work was organised for the Nigerian side of the war front.

Byrne arranged the Biafra deliveries with Wharton (or Dutting). Caritas paid for some short-haul flights for relief supplies from São Tomé to Port Harcourt; but other relief supplies were shipped on the long-haul flights by Super Constellation that Wharton ran from Lisbon to Port Harcourt via Bissau, capital of Portuguese Guinea. These mostly carried arms, while journalists going to Biafra also travelled on them. On 10 February 1968 *West Africa* had an article

"Inside Biafra—by a Correspondent" describing this journey. I never found out who wrote this article; it was certainly not one of the editorial staff of the magazine. He or she travelled with a party of journalists on one of the Constellations on the Lisbon run (there were six planes, Super Constellations and DC-7s, flying several times a week): "Passengers sleep on mattresses between carefully weighed shipments of arms, ammunition and medical supplies." The plane landed at Port Harcourt airport with all lights switched off until the last moment. The journalists were taken to Onitsha, seeing the "flattened market", as well as Dawes Island, downstream from Port Harcourt and still in Biafran hands, though the federal forces had not been dislodged from Bonny.

The flights from Portugal and São Tomé were of course in breach of Nigerian law. This did not bother the mercenary pilots, who earned good money for precisely that reason. As for the churchmen involved, they reckoned that breaking Nigerian law was justified for the good purpose of saving innocent lives. Besides Caritas, other humanitarians seem to have used the mercenary arms flights, including Protestant and secular organisations. Moral criticism of the churches for sending food and medicine in planes mainly used for arms would be absurd rigorism; there was then no other way to get the food and medicine needed in Biafran territory except for the ICRC flights (probably very inadequate when they were operating at all), and anyone who dispatches any goods by air, sea or rail freight has no control over the other goods stowed next to his own, and is not responsible for them.

However, the mercenary pilots gave priority to cargoes of arms, as their Biafran paymasters ordered. Humanitarian bodies could not see the arrangement with Wharton as anywhere near what was needed, as shortages and malnutrition grew in Biafran territory. The churches probably thought also that it was better to avoid publicity about mixed cargoes when they decided to buy their own aircraft. When they did so, the whole Biafra relief airlift was expanded and transformed between May and July 1968 (as will be described later) and passed into history and legend. There were then persistent false Nigerian accusations throughout the war that planes operated by the churches carried arms as well as vital supplies to save lives. These accusations could well have been due partly to earlier reports of arms and food being unloaded from the same aircraft; if so, the accusers ignored the vital difference between planes operated by mercenaries on behalf of the Biafrans, which could carry some humanitarian cargo, and planes wholly operated by church organisations. The latter never carried any weapons.

In working closely with the Salazar regime in Portugal, which was fighting three wars to maintain its colonial empire in Africa, the Biafrans shocked and angered many Africans. In Guinea-Bissau, the African guerrilla fighters were winning, as was described in *West Africa* by Basil Davidson, our correspondent covering those wars; in Angola, the Portuguese had largely won for the moment, while in Mozambique they were being driven back. In all those countries, Africans were suffering acutely, hundreds of thousands becoming refugees—while the Portuguese were helping deliver relief for Biafrans suffering similarly. Salazar's aim was very obvious and non-humanitarian: Portugal could help weaken the most populous country in Africa, which supported the Organisation of African Unity (OAU) resolutions about the Portuguese territories, Rhodesia and South Africa, and could do so more actively if it won its war (which in fact happened). The help for the Biafrans cost Portugal nothing—it was not very generous, and the flights to Biafra had to pay landing fees. But the Biafrans travelling via Lisbon, Bissau and São Tomé with the aid of oppressors of fellow Africans cannot have felt comfortable. They agreed to it for a simple reason, the same reason for which Churchill embraced the Soviet Union as an ally in 1941. In an interview, Chinua Achebe said, in words resembling Churchill's, "If the devil himself had offered his air facilities we would have taken it, and I would have supported it."[13] I did not see that interview then, but it was clear that this was the Biafrans' thinking.

Biafra's links with Portugal seemed to be organised by Christopher C. Mojekwu, one of the top Biafran leaders, said to be a close relative, possibly an uncle, of Odumegwu Ojukwu. Although he was Biafra's commissioner for internal affairs, he spent much of the war in Lisbon or travelling to other countries. He was an object of suspicion, no doubt because of his power, which was certainly great. He was one of the "Nnewi clique" from Ojukwu's home town, said to surround and influence the Biafran leader. Rivalries and feuds at the top are common in any country, while it can be difficult to find the truth about them in secretive dictatorships, which the Biafran and Nigerian regimes both were. Certainly the Biafran regime remained united until the end, despite hopes entertained on the Nigerian side, for example by a *Daily Times* journalist who assured me that "the Igbos are clannish", and other sections of Igbos would not tolerate taking orders from a Nnewi man for long. True, relations between the Nnewi man and other senior people of the regime were not always smooth. Raph Uwechue, in his account written after he broke with the Biafrans in late 1968, speaks of this, mentioning for example the arrest of Brigadier Hilary Njoku in October 1967, after clashes with Ojukwu over control of the army.[14] N.U. Akpan, in his reminiscences published soon after the war, says Ojukwu "was never really sure of the army".[15] Ojukwu comes over in several accounts as superior and authoritarian; in one interview he poured scorn on General Gowon for his relative lack of education, as if that mattered in the war. Yet his great ability also comes over; he ran a team that kept Biafra going for 30 months.

S.O. Mezu's semi-fictional story, *Behind the Rising Sun*, passes through Lisbon; he describes the pilot, "Boris Henk", obviously Hank Wharton, and a Biafran representative, "Everly Nwomah", no doubt based on Mojekwu or one of the other Biafrans who represented Ojukwu in Portugal. According to the novel, the Biafran office in Lisbon "was well furnished, in exquisite taste, with chandeliers floating down from the ceilings and Persian rugs decorating the floors".[16] This fits in with Mezu's other startling tales of extravagant big spending by Biafran representatives in Europe, including a hair-raising account of gigantic shopping expeditions in Paris. Lamentably this is probably a true picture, and while Nigerians of the ultra-privileged set probably spent just as lavishly in Europe during the war (as they notoriously did in later years), it did less harm to their side than to the Biafran, which needed all the foreign exchange it could get for more serious purposes. However, the Biafrans could reasonably defend spending on travel by their representatives seeking to explain their cause to the world, and on some overseas offices (not necessarily with chandeliers). They were claiming to have created an independent state, even if nobody had recognised it in the first ten months, and needed offices to make contact with Western governments and the Western media. To make the desired impression, they needed to pay high rents for offices in districts like those where embassies were located. The Biafra office in London was in South Kensington, at 3 Collingham Gardens.

The war, the civilians and the world

Federal forces of the Second Division crossed the Niger and joined the forces of the First Division coming from the east to capture Onitsha on 21 March 1968.[17] There was heavy fighting before the Biafrans withdrew, and there was another federal war crime during this operation, the murder of about 300 people in a church[18]—not reported in *West Africa*. In this defeat the Biafrans lost one of the major cities of the former Eastern Region, a centre of both commerce and education for a century, in fact a more important historic city than Enugu, which the British had established as a new administrative centre near to the coalfields. In a military sense, however, they did not lose much then. The Third Division did not advance south of Onitsha into the Igbo heartland. And on 25 March the federal forces suffered a serious setback when a column with, according to one report, 102 lorries, 6,000 men and 350 tons of equipment, proceeding towards Onitsha from the east, was ambushed by Biafrans at Abagana. A tanker was set alight and much of the convoy was destroyed, with huge numbers killed. The Biafran officer who commanded this action was Colonel Joe (or Hannibal) Achuzia, who was to become famous within Biafra and beyond. On the federal side, Colonel Murtala Muhammed was relieved of his command of the Third Division in April, and replaced by Colonel Ibrahim Haruna.

The setback at Abagana was not admitted on the Nigerian side, and *West Africa*'s war reporting slipped up on this occasion. We never had any correspondents reporting from the Biafran side except the one reporting in the 10 February 1968 issue mentioned above; there were now Western correspondents of British daily and Sunday papers in Biafra, and *West Africa* quoted a report on Abagana from a *Daily Express* correspondent, but only a month after the event.[19] Later, the Biafrans took journalists to see the ruins of the federal convoy at Abagana; they were able to do so because they still controlled much of the country around and even further north—there was an attempt to retake Nsukka in February.

It was later said that the decisive hit at Abagana was possibly made by a mortar shell, or by a home-made explosive device called by the Igbo name *ogbunigwe*, which was often used during the war and with deadly effect. It was one of the achievements of Biafra's Scientific Group, whose skill at improvisation was widely admired; the Biafrans used home-made mortars at Onitsha.

The Nigerian forces, while they triumphantly proclaimed the capture of cities (which mattered for the Biafrans too), tended to stick to the main roads and towns and often left nearby villages effectively in Biafran hands for some time. In his January 1968 address to the Consultative Assembly, Ojukwu said the federal forces attacked with a "wall of lead", before which the Biafrans withdrew, but when the Nigerians' ammunition and supplies ran out, the Biafrans pushed them back or harried their supply lines.[20] The Nigerian forces' habitual gigantic waste of ammunition affected the course of the war greatly; it may have been a major cause of the war's long duration.

In the battles for Onitsha, the federal army lost a considerable number of men, perhaps more than in most actions. Overall, the Biafrans had probably lost more men in battle even at that early stage, but I recall no figures except the very vaguest given for either side's casualties; on the federal side, and most probably on the Biafran also, there were no next-of-kin telegrams, and I for one did not think of looking at the small ads in Nigerian dailies for notices of war dead. While the Biafrans introduced conscription quite early in the conflict, those who fought and died on the Nigerian side were volunteers; references to Nigerian conscription that I have seen in post-war writing probably allude to occasional local press-ganging, as there was no organised official conscription.[21]

Throughout, most deaths were among civilians, and most of the civilian deaths were on the Biafran side. Many of these were due to the indiscriminate air raids, but acute food shortages were widespread by early 1968, as already noted. These, however, were found on the federal side of the war front also, especially in South-Eastern State.

And in the Mid-West, violence from federal forces had not stopped with Asaba. We heard very few details of the Biafran guerrilla forces among the Mid-West Igbos, but enough to know that they were active and came to be grouped into the Biafran Organisation of Freedom Fighters (BOFF). Early in 1968 there was little news of them, but *West Africa*'s Matchet's Diary, reporting from Warri, recalled the "ferocious killings after the Biafrans left" and said, not explicitly mentioning the massacre, "Asaba itself is still a ghost town, heavily scarred by the fighting ... It is in Asaba that the tragedy of the Western Ibos is most evident."[22]

I need to record that the *West Africa* editorial office had a tendency to caution, to say the least, in the reporting of wartime atrocities. I remember being made to understand this, though I do not recall specific discussion about coverage or non-coverage of any particular incident. This is a matter on which journalists face problems when writing, in a country without press restrictions, about an overseas war (those writing about their own countries' wars face other problems). Obviously every care must be taken to be sure of the facts about a war crime, and this can be difficult when news is suppressed and rumours are rampant (as they certainly were in the Nigerian war). But too much caution can lead to the disregarding of good evidence and effective covering up of serious crimes. It is best to strive to tell the truth, ignoring warring parties' view that reporting one side's war crimes is not telling the truth but taking sides. I regret that with one exception—the Nigerian air raids—*West Africa* spoke out very little about either the federal forces' war crimes or those of the Biafrans.

The Biafrans committed many, some in the Mid-West, many in the minority areas of Biafran territory. In Biafra there was intense surveillance of the whole country, with constant encouragement of suspicion and spying on one's neighbour. Checkpoints along the roads reinforced the surveillance; *West Africa*'s correspondent reported in the 10 February 1968 issue that "roadblocks tend to be placed every 2–3 miles" and soldiers and militia were "ubiquitous." (The militia, formed from better educated people and at first separate from the army, took part in the fighting, and some joined the BOFF.)[23] Even Igbos had to submit to this, despite the popularity of the war (at least initially) among them. But Ijaws, Ibibios and other minority people were the main target of harassment in which the Civil Defence organisation was active. Later accounts said more about this civilian quasi-police corps, including many teenage girls, which had sweeping power to bully and threaten travellers. But there was an early indication in a broadcast by Akanu Ibiam, reported in *West Africa* of 29 July 1967: the adviser to the governor deplored ill-treatment by Civil Defence members of people who did not speak a particular language but were Biafrans—meaning, of course, non-Igbo Biafrans.

After the war N.U. Akpan recorded instances of ill-treatment—sometimes the killing of people of the non-Igbo minorities.[24] This was encouraged by the obsessive official concern with "sabotage". Ojukwu himself set the example of blaming every Biafran defeat on treachery and sabotage, and there was constant fear of being suspected as a "sabo". Such suspicions were directed especially at minority people because many of them were, and others were suspected of being, in sympathy with the federal side. *The Times*'s correspondent in Biafra, William Norris, reported the killing of 200 Ibibio people outside the Progress Hotel in Umuahia on 2 April; the principal of Trinity College in that city questioned the report.[25] Detailed and hideous allegations of killings by the Biafrans in South-Eastern State were given by a retired senior medical officer, Dr B.J. Imkeme, at the Kampala talks in May,[26] and by some Catholic priests in a long letter to the Pope on 16 August 1968.[27] There may have been some anti-Biafran guerrilla activity in the area assigned to Rivers State; the Rivers militant Isaac Boro, freed from gaol, was reported to be leading resistance, according to *West Africa* of 7 October 1967. This could only have worsened the Biafrans' paranoid oppression. Elechi Amadi described later the state of fear in the Rivers area, with harassment, arrests and killing. Worst of all, he saw at least 200 bodies of people killed on suspicion of aiding the federal enemy;[28] it is not clear when this happened: it may have been when the federal forces got near—their offensive in that direction began in April 1968.

During the months before then, a group of Eastern minority people—maybe visitors from Lagos, maybe students in Britain—called on the editor of *West Africa* and explained how Biafra, which the outside world admired as the plucky underdog, was for their people a police state (Ogundipe liked to compare it to Orwell's *1984*). The office also received a Rivers propaganda publication that I read, filled with horrific allegations, some stretching credulity. The magazine did not quote those allegations. Beyond doubt, non-Igbo people under Biafran rule suffered a great deal of violence—but not only from the Biafrans. Some of the Nigerian air raids hit minority areas, striking for example the Mary Slessor Hospital in the Ibibio town of Itu. While some Rivers people complained that Biafra was getting too much sympathy, one Rivers man, Ignatius Kogbara, helped to arouse such sympathy as the Biafran representative in London from 1968. He was of the Ogoni people, a small group little known at that time but later made famous by another of its sons, the writer and activist Ken Saro-Wiwa—who in the civil war supported Nigeria, becoming administrator of Bonny in November 1967.

Rivers people's view that the outside world was too favourable to Biafra was already held then by other Nigerians too, and by British supporters of Nigeria. I think it was during that time, the first months of 1968, that I took a call in the office from Cecil King, who said the Biafrans were getting too much sympathy in the British press and wanted to know more (I asked Kaye Whiteman to reply). But I also recall that at that time, before June 1968, Biafrans thought the world was against them. Certainly it was not so supportive as it later became. Efforts by the Biafrans to win support around the world had, however, been continuous since before secession, especially in Britain and the US. An *African Weekly Review* supporting Biafra was published in Britain early in the war.[29] From January 1968 Biafra employed a public relations firm based in Geneva, Markpress, whose chief executive officer was H. William Bernhardt, an American.

More will be said later about Markpress,[30] which acquired a grossly inflated reputation. It was a competent PR outfit, but it was subject to the direction of the Biafran regime; its presentation of the Biafran case was thus subordinate to the regime's own efforts, which also included regular trips abroad by leading dignitaries. And that regime was not so media savvy as some professed to believe. An example of what its publicity efforts were really like came in January 1968, when it made a wild allegation that a thousand British troops were sailing from Liverpool to reinforce the federal army; this was apparently based on a trip by sea to West Africa arranged by the Commonwealth Institute for 715 British teenage schoolchildren, sailing from Southampton. The Biafrans made strong protests and the offices of the United Africa Company and Elder Dempster in Port Harcourt were burned down.[31] The following May a similar daft allegation was made by the Biafrans: that the Hibernian Football Club then touring Nigeria were in fact British paratroopers.[32]

More rationally, in seeking worldwide support Biafrans recalled the dreadful events of 1966, especially the pogroms, and argued that they had in effect been driven out of Nigeria—so why should Nigeria force them to come back? It was quite a strong case, and many individuals in many countries responded by thinking that the Nigerian war to end secession was unjustified. Biafrans, however, sought more than that. From the beginning, Ojukwu's regime used the word "genocide" to describe the federal war effort. This was emphasised partly to ensure continued support from its own people who had their traumatic memories of the pogroms, but it also sought to persuade the rest of the world that Nigeria aimed at the total extermination of the Biafrans.

The accusation of genocide—the worst crime a government can ever commit, after all—did not gain credence quickly in the West, though it did convince some, as will be described in the coming chapters. Many Biafrans believed in it, saying that after the pogroms, "the Hausas" were invading the surviving victims' homeland to kill the rest. War crimes committed or tolerated by the federal forces strengthened this belief, and so, especially, did the bombing. There was, for example, a raid on Awgu, with hundreds reported killed or injured, on 17 February 1968; the new ICRC representative in Lagos, Jean-René Pierroz, protested against the bombing raids on civilians.[33] There were raids on Owerri on 21 April (people being strafed as they left a church) and on Aba on 22 April.[34] The Federal Government often claimed that the buildings they targeted were being used for military purposes; school buildings might have been so used sometimes, as all schooling had stopped in Biafra, but there surely wasn't really up-to-date intelligence of it before the raids; and hospitals were most certainly serving their normal function, while an open-air market or people emerging from a church could not possibly be called military targets. In fact, there seemed to be no effective concentration on military targets, and many reports suggested that the Egyptian pilots flew far too high to aim properly.

Akpan wrote after the war that "Nothing had contributed more to the prolongation of the war than the indiscriminate activities of the Federal air force for the greater part of the civil war". [35] And of course that was very obvious at the time; the pro-Nigerian David Williams said in the office, "I wish they'd stop these bloody air raids," and before long he was to condemn them in the magazine. However, many war crimes do not equal genocide, which is action aimed at the deliberate killing of an entire people. Biafrans' use of that word, recalling the Genocide Convention of 1948, did not arise from pure calculation of possible advantage for their cause, but they surely did calculate that genocide, if proved, must be a matter of proper international concern; it would sweep aside Nigerians' protestations that the war was a purely internal affair—if proved. Yet it was perfectly possible for people in many countries to oppose Nigeria's war effort, and especially to oppose helping it with arms supplies, without accepting that there was a danger of genocide.

In Britain, some opponents of the war and sympathisers with Biafra's case formed the Britain–Biafra Association (BBA), whose first public meeting I attended to report for *West Africa* in mid-March 1968, at the Holborn Assembly Hall. My report appeared in Matchet's Diary of 23 March; as that diary was known to be almost wholly written by the editor, David Williams, it referred to me as "my correspondent". It noted that the British speakers, though strongly in favour of Biafra (especially two missionaries), stuck to observed and known facts and were restrained in language, and that the final resolution simply called on Britain to stop arms supplies to Nigeria and support efforts towards a ceasefire and negotiations. Michael Barnes, a Labour MP who had just joined 41 other MPs of his party in a Commons motion calling for a halt to the arms supplies, was among the speakers.

Raymond Njoku, a leading Igbo politician who had been Nigeria's federal minister of transport, gave a vigorous speech in defence of the Biafran struggle. I thought his speech would give a bad impression and said so in my report; he alternated mockery of the Nigerian army with descriptions of its crimes, and expressed utter contempt for

Northerners and shock that Britain should have forced Easterners to live with "these people". I fear that this report revealed my inexperience. I failed to understand that the purpose of war propaganda is usually to rally support at home first, and only secondarily to convince other countries; Njoku must have been addressing, above all, his fellow Biafrans who were present. It was true, however, that Biafrans themselves often expressed the sort of tribalistic hate that had been so much directed against them—though one could not expect them not to hate Northerners after the pogroms of 1966.

Several speakers at that meeting, including Njoku, spoke strongly and with detail about the indiscriminate air raids, and it was clear, my report said, that "these air raids on civilian areas are going on continually, and that minority people are among the many civilians who suffer". The air raids, indeed, did more to arouse sympathy for Biafra than any propaganda efforts. It was probably because of them, mostly, that Biafrans commonly called their adversaries "the Vandals".

R.O. Davies, chairman of the association, wrote a letter published in *West Africa* of 13 April, calling my report "excellent" but correcting my estimate that the attendance was mainly African (he said about half were African), and saying that 90 per cent of the 200 BBA members were British, most having recently worked in Nigeria. The BBA published a weekly *Biafra News*.

I seem to recall attending one other meeting of the BBA after the first. At one meeting the Biafran national anthem was sung; I believe that its lyrics had only recently started to be heard on Biafra Radio,[36] but the tune may well have been played on the radio earlier. This was the famous tune from Sibelius' *Finlandia*, which had long been the tune of songs including "On great lone hills" and the hymn "Be still, my soul". It was widely known at the time, or supposed, that the lyrics were written by Nnamdi Azikiwe (he later tried to disown them). Anyway I learned the first two verses:

> Land of the rising sun, we love and cherish,
> Beloved homeland of our brave heroes;
> We must defend our lives or we shall perish,
> We shall protect our lives from all our foes;
> But if the price is death for all we hold dear,
> Then let us die without a shred of fear.

Hail to Biafra, consecrated nation,
O fatherland, this be our solemn pledge:
Defending thee shall be a dedication,
Spilling our blood we'll count a privilege;
The waving standard which emboldens the free
Shall always be our flag of liberty.[37]

Whoever wrote those lyrics, they were not well chosen for a national anthem. They are, frankly, morbid, without the confident, triumphal tone of other national anthems. There are indeed other lines which say, "We shall emerge triumphant from this ordeal" and "Then shall our trumpets peal the glorious song / Of victory we scored o'er might and wrong"—but only in the third verse. The lyrics generally express a mood of half-expecting defeat and death.

Defeat was coming steadily. The Biafran success at Abagana was an isolated one. Nigerian forces were soon advancing not in the Onitsha sector, but across South-Eastern State and from there into Igbo country. The Federal Government announced the capture of Oron on 21 March, Itu, Mbak and Ikot Effiong on 24 March, Eket on 25 March, Uyo on 29 March, and Ikot Ekpene on 31 March.[38] With the coastal town of Opobo captured also, the Third Division was now able to advance into the area of Rivers State. Further north, the federal forces captured the Igbo town of Abakaliki on 5 April. A huge store of three million yams was captured there, a big further blow to the Biafrans' food supply.[39]

General Gowon apparently said words suggesting the war would be decided by 31 March (maybe he was misinterpreted); that did not happen, but his forces were making plenty of progress then.[40] What did happen on 1 April 1968 was the formal establishment of the new Nigerian states' governments, apart from Rivers and East Central (Governor Udo Esuene of South-Eastern State had now moved to Calabar). For months, *West Africa* had been reporting details of the devolution of power from the Interim Common Services Agency (ICSA) covering the former Northern Region to the six Northern states.[41] Now the Northern states started functioning with their own administrations and budgets. Colonel Hassan Katsina, who had been chairman of the Interim Administrative Council for those states, returned to normal army duties, now as brigadier; he became army chief of staff a few weeks later. It was certain now that, as defenders of the Federal Government said, the former Northern Region had gone for ever; the new states in the North created vested interests that would oppose any improbable plans to revive the old region. Biafrans had been mistaken in suggesting that the division of the North was a pretence. However, it could not be enough to persuade them that no trace remained of Northern domination, still less that what had happened to their people under Northern domination should now be forgotten.

Despite the military setbacks and the prospect of more coming soon, the Biafrans were as determined as ever to fight for independence. Neither they nor the Federal Military Government would now consider a confederation as a compromise solution; Hassan Katsina said, "Aburi will never be repeated."[42] In February 1968, when Arnold Smith visited Lagos, there was a flurry of hope and speculation in London about peace talks involving the Commonwealth, but nothing came of it then, the FMG declaring that the Commonwealth peacekeeping force suggested by some could only come at its invitation.[43] Biafra continued to send high-level emissaries to defend its case, such as Nnamdi Azikiwe, who travelled to several African countries in March. While Ojukwu said he was ready for talks "without conditions", a *West Africa* editorial (rather rashly headed "An end in sight?") commented on 6 April that this must mean the FMG giving up its conditions for talks. Earlier, Edwin Ogbu, permanent secretary of the federal Ministry of External Affairs, had said the government now put "less emphasis" on one of those conditions, that there could be no talks with Ojukwu himself.[44] Nigeria now accepted in principle that talks could be with him, but still insisted on the two main conditions: the Biafrans must give up secession and accept the 12-state structure. Nigeria was to stick to these demands rigidly, and they in fact meant Biafra must surrender before any talks, which could therefore be only about the detailed arrangements for capitulation. Thus, as that editorial in the magazine said, the possibility of talks seemed remote. However, it went on to warn of the dangers to the Igbo population from a further federal advance: "more and more Ibos will be concentrated in an ever-diminishing area, with frightening risks to health and social discipline". This was already happening and was soon to get worse.

Recognition of Biafra by four African countries

On 13 April 1968 President Nyerere of Tanzania announced that his country was recognising Biafra as an independent state. In a lengthy statement in Dar es Salaam he accepted the Biafran case that "people from the Eastern Region can no longer feel safe in other parts of the Federation", and said:

> Fears such as now exist among the Ibo peoples do not disappear because someone says they are unjustified, or says that the rest of Nigeria does not want to exterminate the Ibos. Such words have even less effect when the speakers have made no attempt to bring the perpetrators of crimes to justice and when troops under the control of the Federal Nigerian Authorities continue to ill-treat any Ibos who come within their power …

> Africa fought for freedom on the grounds of individual liberty and equality, and on the grounds that every people must have the right to determine for themselves the conditions under which they would be governed …

> Surely when a whole people is rejected by the majority of the state in which they live, they must have the right to life under a different kind of arrangement that does secure their existence.

> States are made to serve people … when the machinery of the State, and the powers of the Government, are turned against a whole group of the society on the grounds of racial, tribal, or religious prejudice, then the victims have the right to take back the powers they have surrendered, and to defend themselves …

Nyerere argued that other federations had broken up (the Federation of Rhodesia and Nyasaland and the Mali Federation), as had the short-lived United Arab Republic of Egypt and Syria, and the resulting separate states had been recognised. "We recognise Mali, Egypt, Syria, Malawi, Zambia, Pakistan and India. What right have we to refuse, in the name of unity, to recognise the fact of Biafra?"[45] That point was also made by Ojukwu, but it was a weak point. The other federations had joined together, fairly briefly, political units that had been separate and working effectively for a long time before, which was not the case with Nigeria; and Nyerere might have considered that mention of Pakistan and India could recall the hideous mass killings of the 1947 Partition—not a happy precedent to cite in arguing for partition of another country. But his point was clear, though he did not need to back it with those comparisons: political arrangements are not sacrosanct, they can be altered, and they should be when there are strong reasons for not continuing them.

Nyerere, unlike most African leaders, had the reputation of a thinker; in his general arguments about the role of the state, he followed centuries of both Christian and Enlightenment thinking. On the specific case of Nigeria, he made valid points, such as the importance of Nigeria's failure to have the authors of the pogroms punished. What he said about the Igbos genuinely fearing extermination, whether the fear was justified or not, was certainly true, as *West Africa* noted. But he went too far in speaking of Nigerian troops continuing to "ill-treat any Ibos who come within their power". He seems to have been thinking of the frequent foul behaviour of soldiers at roadblocks in the Lagos area, but the words could suggest that the federal military operations were generally of that character (however, he did not use the word "genocide").

Tanzania's action was a shock to the Federal Government and its supporters. Nyerere had a high reputation in Africa, as a strong defender of African interests and needs, especially against South Africa, Rhodesia and Portugal; Tanzania was the vital rear base for the Frelimo fighters in Mozambique and sheltered large numbers of Mozambican refugees. To have such a man against them was not easy for Nigerians. Their media attacked Nyerere forcefully, and could find some things to hold against him, as his government was a dictatorship and his people suffered many impositions in the name of egalitarian socialism. But he was known everywhere as a man of principle and nobody could plausibly suggest any base reason for him to recognise Biafra; it could only be an honest decision for the reasons he gave.

Nyerere's recognition gave a great boost to the Biafrans' morale but could not give them any real help. It coincided closely with the start of a new offensive by the Third Division towards Port Harcourt. While Biafrans talked of renaming the big city "Port Julius Nyerere", the federal forces marched inexorably towards it. They also marched into the eastern Igbo country, the capture of Afikpo being announced on 22 April, and this was rich agricultural country whose loss made the food crisis in Biafran territory worse. While the Nigerians' cap-

ture of towns commonly left nearby villages unoccupied and in practice free to trade with the Biafran side, for the refugees and many
others on that side food prices had already become prohibitive. It
made little difference that the Biafrans were able to launch a raid into
the Mid-West, entering Asaba for a time on 18 April, and defeat one
federal attempt to cross the Cross River south of Arochukwu.[46]

Evidence of that minor Biafran victory was seen by British journalists reporting on the Biafran side, William Norris of *The Times* and
Norman Kirkham of the *Daily Telegraph*. More and more Western
journalists were going to Biafra now, and one was living there full-
time: Frederick Forsyth, who resigned from the BBC early in 1968
and went to Biafra, where, so he recalled long afterwards,

> Ojukwu offered me half a tin-roofed Nissen hut, food from State
> House kitchens, a Volkswagen Beetle and a petrol allowance. Plus
> access to the communications company he had engaged to get news
> despatches from Biafra to Geneva and thence to the world. After that
> I could go anywhere, see anything and report anything.
>
> I made plain that I would not report what his own propaganda bureau
> wanted, but only what I saw with my own eyes or learned from reli-
> able sources. But what I wrote would be fair.

"That's all I want," he said. "Fair. After that the story will tell itself."[47]

Forsyth helped to tell the story very sympathetically, writing for
many British papers, but what Ojukwu foresaw happened: the story
told itself. It was not Ojukwu, not Forsyth, not Markpress (whose
bulletins Forsyth thought were useless)[48] that won the world's sympathy for the Biafrans; it was the facts of what happened, especially
the facts of starvation. The Biafran government sought expert reports
on the food crisis and took what action it could take itself, but was
not concerned to publicise the crisis to the outside world at that
time. It was mainly relief agencies and churchmen who reported it
in the West then, as already mentioned, and *West Africa*, quoting
them, said a little.

In Lagos, in April 1968, the Nigerian Red Cross launched an
appeal for relief services and assistance, saying more than 2 million
children and 1.6 million nursing mothers would be in danger of malnutrition as a result of the war; 25,000 people or more would need

Red Cross aid every week, as well as 500,000 displaced people now in Red Cross refugee camps and villages in federally occupied areas; the secretary of the Nigerian Red Cross, Timothy Udondek, estimated that over 200,000 were still in hiding in those areas, and conditions were bad in East Central, Rivers and South-Eastern States. As for the people in areas not yet occupied, their situation would become "serious and dangerous" as the federal forces advanced. Sir Adetokunbo Ademola, the Nigerian Chief Justice and president of the Nigerian Red Cross, who launched the appeal, said talks were continuing on the airlifting of aid to secessionist territory.[49] The appeal showed that people in areas "liberated" by federal forces were in dire need, which indicated, even if the Chief Justice could not say so publicly, extreme negligence on the part of the military and civilian authorities. The 200,000 people hiding in the bush were afraid of the Nigerian forces, and they must have had cause, even if in some areas those forces were helping displaced people in cooperation with relief agencies. Many of those people in hiding were probably in the Mid-West, where vicious behaviour by the federal forces remained common. There was a detailed report of murder and torture by them in the Mid-West village of Ishiagu in April; Gowon ordered an inquiry.[50] On 27 June two officers were shot in Benin for the murder of four civilians at Ogwashi Uku.[51]

The likely consequences of further federal advances into Igbo country, as well as the ongoing advance on Port Harcourt, gave added urgency to efforts to arrange peace talks. Out of the limelight there were some contacts between the two sides, presumably through some intermediary or another; we heard about them but of course kept the secret. Frequent visits to London and other world capitals by senior federal and Biafran representatives were probably connected with those contacts. There was one puzzling question (never examined by our magazine, I think) about the travelling Biafrans: what passports did they use? In August 1967 Chief Enahoro complained that Biafran agents were "very active" in the US even though the FMG had cancelled their passports.[52] In fact, the Federal Government could have cancelled all the Nigerian passports of people travelling to defend the Biafran cause; if it did, what travel documents did they have? Anyway they went on travelling. On the federal side, three permanent secretaries—Allison Ayida (economic affairs), Philip Asiodu (industries) and Ahmed Joda (information)—often came to London, where David Williams and Bridget Bloom knew them well.

A strange fact that I never learned at the time was that Asiodu, a prominent defender of the Nigerian case around the world, was an Igbo—not only that, an Igbo from Asaba who lost a brother murdered by federal troops there. Decades later he said that he had concluded that his brother must be dead only on visiting Asaba near the end of the war, but in the weeks after the massacre, as informal reports spread, he had sent a memorandum to Gowon saying, "We can't allow this to continue, because it'll destroy the whole hope of trying to keep one country."[53] The British government officials hearing Asiodu defending the cause of "trying to keep one country" probably had no idea about this—though the Commonwealth Relations Office did know about Nigerian atrocities.

In late April, through the efforts of the Commonwealth Secretariat under Arnold Smith, what *West Africa* called "talks about talks about talks" were held in London. Arikpo travelled there and met Smith, Harold Wilson (who had written to Gowon earlier), and the Commonwealth Affairs secretary George Thomson. Then, early in May, what the magazine called "Peace Talks Preliminaries" were held, organised by the Commonwealth Secretariat, to pave the way for more substantive peace talks. Enahoro and Ayida were among the federal delegates; Mbanefo and the new Biafran representative in Britain, Ignatius Kogbara, among the other side's. There were long discussions about the venue for the real talks, until agreement was reached on Kampala, the capital of Uganda.[54] Fierce arguments about the agenda for Kampala led to a compromise with two broad items: conditions for the ending of hostilities and arrangements for a permanent settlement.[55] The hopes placed in the Kampala talks were slender, for Arikpo had said that while preliminary talks could be held without preconditions—as happened—for true peace talks or a ceasefire the Federal Government's two conditions remained: the Biafrans must renounce secession and accept the 12 states.[56]

While in London during those days, Sir Louis Mbanefo visited David Williams at the *West Africa* office. This was of course kept secret, though the two knew each other well. Mbanefo talked about the Nigerian air raids; Williams, who was already against those air raids, was convinced completely by the testimony of that thoroughly good man. On 11 May a *West Africa* editorial declared: "the bombing of Biafran towns … should at once be discontinued. Independent visitors to Biafra all agree that the bombing affects civilians indiscriminately … Even if the London talks do not, through further peace talks, lead to cessation of hostilities, the indiscriminate bombing should still be stopped." I was not always proud of what the magazine said editorially, but I was then. I cannot say whether it was because of that editorial that Edward Enahoro, deputy permanent secretary at the Nigerian Ministry of External Affairs (brother of the other Enahoros), said soon afterwards, "All bombing of non-military targets has been stopped." When reminded by a questioner that the FMG had never admitted such raids, he said there had been "fresh instructions".[57]

As preparations for Kampala went ahead, on 8 May Gabon announced its recognition of Biafra. A government statement accused Nigeria of a "veritable genocide with the aim of wiping out the State of Biafra and the Ibo people".[58] Gabon was a minor African state and its president, Albert Bongo, only in power for a few months, did not have the stature of Nyerere. But he could have been influenced by a much more prominent African head of state, Félix Houphouët-Boigny of Ivory Coast, who had already indicated on 22 April that recognition of Biafra was being considered. On 9 May, at a packed press conference in Paris, Houphouët-Boigny spoke of the "inexplicable and culpable indifference of the whole world about the massacres which have been taking place in Biafra for more than ten months". He added that 60,000 people had been killed in this conflict, more, he said, than in Vietnam; Matchet's Diary in *West Africa* questioned this, having obtained official figures of the Vietnam war dead from the US embassy in London: 425,325 since 1957, including 118,769 in 1967 alone.[59] After a big meeting of the single party in Ivory Coast, recognition of Biafra was announced on 14 May. It was considered possible that Houphouët-Boigny and Bongo imagined the Nigerian situation to be like that in the French African territories at the time of decolonisation, when those territories were formed into two federations— French West Africa (AOF) and French Equatorial Africa (AEF)—

which soon broke up, being opposed by the leaders of Ivory Coast in one case and Gabon in the other, fearing that their wealthier countries would have to subsidise the others. Arsène Usher, the Ivory Coast foreign minister, said federations had a habit of coming unstuck.[60]

The recognitions by Ivory Coast and Gabon were attributed by the angry Nigerian media to pressure by France. Those countries were both very close to France, but so were a dozen other ex-French states in Africa, and these did not recognise Biafra; that interpretation of the actions by Houphouët-Boigny and Gabon turned out to be mistaken. But Nigerians were not mistaken in noticing a pro-Biafran trend in Paris. *West Africa* followed the reactions to the Nigerian war in France. On the one hand, there was business as usual: normal diplomatic relations between Paris and Lagos (though these had been severed for years and only resumed in 1966), and flourishing economic relations—France was the biggest customer for Nigerian groundnut exports, the French firm Safrap was one of the three oil-producing firms in Nigeria, and the giant French construction firm Dumez built the Niger Bridge opened in 1965. Nigeria had its embassy in Paris, headed by Alhaji Abdulmaliki, previously high commissioner in London; the Biafrans had their office there, with no diplomatic status, headed by Raph Uwechue. While the French government banned arms sales to both sides, the French press was taking a close interest in the war, like the press of many other countries. *Le Canard Enchaîné*, the crude satirical weekly (to which the *West Africa* office subscribed), suggested that France might be playing "a double game".[61] It was, but the covert French assistance to Biafra was still limited in early 1968. In May, soon after Houphouët-Boigny's visit, President de Gaulle and his government were distracted by the great French student revolt and strikes; they overcame the threat well, and their double game regarding Nigeria could resume, if it had ever stopped.

The federal Third Division moved steadily through Rivers State territory in April and May 1968, against fierce Biafran resistance. They took Okrika, Elelenwa, Aletu and Obigbo, and the battle for the big city itself began on 16 May, with Colonel Achuzia commanding the defence. The next day, Biafra's vital airport was captured. In that area of rivers, estuaries and swamps, Port Harcourt lies on a peninsula, but the federal forces—deliberately, it was reported—did not at first cut it off, which left an exit route for hundreds of thousands of civilians. On 18 May federal forces entered Port Harcourt.[62] Most of the population escaped towards Biafran territory. The city's population had for long been mainly Igbo, and almost all the Igbos now left, fearing the federal army but still more the civilian Rivers people who could take revenge for Biafran oppression. Numerous Rivers people, however, retreated with the Biafrans, including, probably, people who had collaborated closely with them. But others stayed put and went over to the winning side. Nabo Graham-Douglas, who had resigned as attorney general of the Eastern Region in September 1966 and had been detained by the Biafran authorities, escaped when his guards at Port Harcourt fled; the popular bandleader Cardinal Rex Jim Lawson, a Rivers man who as the "high-life king of Biafra" had been performing in Port Harcourt shortly before it fell, slipped over to the Nigerian side.

In the fighting in Rivers State, Isaac Boro was killed in action, and other Rivers people also helped the federal forces. Many welcomed those forces, though some regretted doing so as their widespread brutality did not spare Rivers people, according to a later account by Frederick Forsyth.[63] General Gowon, in a press conference on 21 May, admitted there had been atrocities, but said those committed by the Biafrans were not reported.[64] The war crimes record of both sides was indeed worsening; a *New York Times* report spoke of some committed by Biafrans before and by Nigerians after the fall of Port Harcourt,[65] and Akpan later wrote of seeing at Igrita mass graves of people murdered as suspected saboteurs by civilians.[66]

As a result of the obsession on each side with the other side's real or supposed mercenaries, two British businessmen who were present on the federal side soon after the fall of Port Harcourt were beaten up by troops, until Colonel Adekunle intervened, and were described by the Nigerian press as mercenaries. That obsession was to continue; the Nigerian newspapers, which absurdly used to quote prisoners and deserters as if their words were reliable, cited such reports as speaking of hordes of mercenaries, including Tanzanians, on the Biafran side. But, as pilots, mercenaries were really important for both the Biafrans (who during 1968 had no working aircraft left) and the Nigerians.

In a broadcast on 19 May, Ojukwu said Biafra would welcome a referendum in "disputed areas", meaning the Eastern minorities, after a cessation of hostilities.[67] This offer came late in the day, after Biafra had lost almost all the territories concerned, and it depended on Nigeria accepting a ceasefire as a first step, which it seemed, as the talks in Uganda approached, to be certain to go on rejecting. In that broadcast Ojukwu appeared to suggest that "the second phase of our struggle" would be guerrilla war; some who followed the conflict thought this might be possible, but in the end it was not to happen, except (during the war) for the Biafran Organisation of Freedom Fighters in the Mid-West.

Fighting continued in Rivers State after the fall of Port Harcourt; some weeks passed before Abonnema, Degema, Bakana, Nembe and Yenagoa fell to the Nigerians.[68] Although they also lost Awgu in the north on 18 June, obviously the Biafrans were very far from beaten. They had proved to be good fighters, and their enemies must have regretted the jibes made at the beginning of the war about Igbos at war, such as them being an "army of pen-pushers". That foolish jibe referred to Igbos' success with clerical jobs all over Nigeria; now, in the war, the high level of education among the Igbos was put to good use, especially in devising home-made weapons such as mortars and the *ogbunigwe*. With the loss of the Alesa-Eleme refinery Biafra's scientists were to start successful small-scale refineries using petroleum deposits that were still accessible. To a remarkable degree the Biafrans kept ordinary life going despite hardship. Government departments and courts continued functioning, the Catering Rest Houses (all now renamed Progress Hotels) continued to serve customers, and some newspapers were produced—an Agence France-Presse (AFP) journalist came back from Biafra with copies of the *Daily Flash*, the *Star*, the *International Daily News* and the *Daily Standard*[69]—though they came to be printed on crude material like school exercise book paper. This could have been widely available because education was one part of normal life that had not resumed; another missing part of normal life, for many people, was having enough to eat.

The loss of Port Harcourt, a major defeat for the Biafrans, may have deterred some countries thinking of recognising Biafra (the Federal Government claimed this), but President Kaunda of Zambia declared recognition on 20 May. A statement said that "the indiscriminate mas-sacre of innocent people has filled us with horror".[70] Kenneth Kaunda was respected all over Africa in the same way as his close ally Nyerere and, like him, he had been convinced of the Biafrans' case; Tanzania, Zambia and some other African states had recently been visited by Nnamdi Azikiwe. As a staunch anti-colonial campaigner now confront-ing the Smith regime on Zambia's doorstep, Kaunda gave a diplomatic and publicity boost to the Biafrans. But a military boost would have helped them more when their delegates left a country reeling from a major defeat to attend the peace talks at Kampala. The recognitions of Biafra could not alter the Federal Nigerian attitude, which military success reinforced. Before the talks, I recall, Bridget Bloom said to a visitor to the office who followed the situation, "Well, will Ojukwu surrender?" That was about the size of it. *West Africa* said in an editorial, "A Year of Secession", on 25 May that while the federal advances had cemented support for Biafra, whose leaders still wanted a ceasefire before any talks on a settlement, "unless the Biafrans are prepared, under whatever formula, to renounce secession and accept the states, no peace settlement will be possible".

Such editorials aroused mixed reactions among readers. Williams's custom was to analyse the situation and set out what he thought likely to happen (not necessarily what was desirable). This is a normal enough editorial approach, and is what many readers expect. Thus he consistently described the Nigerian position in the war as a given, as something that had to be faced. But to Biafrans and others who thought the Nigerian side could and should give way, the editor of *West Africa* seemed to be advocating what he in fact simply thought to be inevitable; some said the magazine was simply the tool of British commercial and political interests backing Nigeria. Williams told us once that he was annoyed by people saying to him such words as "Of course, you've got to write those things, haven't you?" when he in fact wrote what he believed. I do not believe that his editorial policy was dictated by Cecil King; more probably Williams and Babatunde Jose encouraged King, if that were necessary, to support Nigeria. There were no changes to Overseas Newspapers, *West Africa* or the Daily Times group resulting from Cecil King's dismissal as chairman of the International Publishing Corporation on 30 May 1968, except that he resigned as chairman of the Daily Times of Nigeria Ltd, to be succeeded by Jose.[71]

The Kampala talks started on 23 May with Enahoro heading the federal negotiators, also including Asika, and Mbanefo the Biafran ones, who also included Achebe. The Biafrans continued to demand an early ceasefire before talks on a permanent settlement; Mbanefo also called for an end to the blockade and said Biafra would agree to the policing of a ceasefire by an international force and to supervision of points of entry into both sides' territories to enforce a general arms embargo. To make the Biafran demands even more impossible for the FMG to accept, he called for the withdrawal of each side's troops to the pre-war borders. This was an extraordinary proposal after the Biafrans had lost almost all the territory of South-Eastern and Rivers States. The proposal on an arms embargo was also far-fetched; it would have been easy to have international observers checking the Biafran airfields, but who could imagine the federal side agreeing to the examination of all ships entering Lagos harbour, not to speak of Nigeria's land borders? However, it made little difference that the Biafrans demanded so much after all their defeats, because the other side rejected any ceasefire before Biafra agreed to renounce independence and accept the 12 states of the Federation. All the efforts of Arnold Smith and President Obote of Uganda failed to bridge the gap between the two sides. After several days, talks were held on 29 and 30 May on proposals that were not revealed to the representatives of the world's media who had flocked to Uganda for the talks; there was talk of some concessions by both sides, but the impasse was not broken (possibly, it was suggested, because of a broadcast by Ojukwu on the anniversary of secession). Enahoro stuck to his insistence that there was "no solution outside one Nigeria … That means the other side giving in. But we are trying to ease the process …" But Mbanefo, at a plenary session requested by him, said on 31 May that Nigeria had proposed "a programme of insulting arrangements for a Biafran surrender", and Biafra saw no point in continuing the talks.[72]

Defeat and desolation

The fall of Port Harcourt was a major blow to the Biafrans, but they were prepared for the loss of its airport. Back in November 1967 *West*

Africa had carried reports of the Biafrans building an airstrip, and by the time Port Harcourt fell, the Uli airstrip, which was to serve the Biafrans well and become world famous, was ready. Also called the Uli-Ihiala airstrip or airport, or by its code name Annabelle, it was a widened stretch of road, 2,000 yards long, equipped with many of the features of an ordinary airport, including customs and immigration desks. It was designed for night flights, because of the danger of federal air raids; it had anti-aircraft defences, but by now Biafra had no more working military aircraft. The control tower was mobile and there was good camouflage to conceal the airstrip at dawn every day. Uli was a triumph for Biafran resourcefulness; we heard it was partly the work of an Igbo engineer who had worked on airports in Nigeria.

Two or three other airstrips were also built. There were reports of airstrips at Obilago, Uga and Uturu, but much less was reported about them than about Uli. On 1 June *West Africa* quoted a report of four airstrips, codenamed Annabel (*sic*), Beatrice, Dominique and Caroline; soon afterwards the *Nigerian Observer* of Benin said the location of four Biafran airstrips was known.[73] Obviously it must have been known to the Nigerian side quickly.

Very soon the gun-running planes from Lisbon were landing at Uli; the *Daily Express* correspondent Walter Partington reported having flown on a Constellation from Lisbon to an airstrip "somewhere in Biafra" about mid-May.[74] They carried some food and medicines for civilians, but the World Council of Churches (WCC) and the Catholic agency Caritas had begun chartering a few flights from either Lisbon or Portuguese São Tomé, a short distance off the Nigerian coast; this was to become the main base for relief flights to Biafra, but in May and June 1968 there were hardly any of these, though a WCC charter flight landed at Uli on 21 May. Now church aid agencies were actively discussing the purchase or chartering of their own aircraft.

In late May the ICRC appealed for more aid and decided to send three medical social teams to Biafra, mentioning that famine was now spreading in the bush.[75] It continued its flights to Biafran territory from Fernando Po, now landing at Uli; the Federal Government reaffirmed that it was allowing those flights, but the ICRC said it could only airlift about 25 tons of relief in one flight, and it had about 3,000 tons ready to be delivered. Dr Georg Hoffman of the ICRC travelled to Lagos to discuss the growing crisis.[76] It was clear that much more food and medicines were needed as the plight of civilians on the Biafran side was worse than ever.

The mass exodus from Port Harcourt was probably the most massive and pitiful of all the displacements of people in the war so far. Our news pages briefly summarised reports (there was never enough room for details, though readers probably wanted many more), saying, "reports from inside Biafra speak of great distress among the refugees from Port Harcourt, with many dying on the way".[77] Most of the fleeing men, women and children walked long distances, carrying household goods or pushing some in handcarts, until a good many of them were able to reach the home villages of their families; people who had lived all their lives in the great port city might never have been to those villages, but they were of course welcomed there. But some Igbos may well have been from villages now under Nigerian occupation, and the Rivers people among the refugees were simply stranded. Many people staggered into the refugee camps, often sick and starving.

It was not only refugees in the camps that were facing starvation. In the villages there were local crops which could be and were cultivated more, and wild fruit and vegetables and game, but there were also swollen populations of extended family members coming from other areas. By mid-June, surveys in some villages showed widespread malnutrition; some feeding centres were set up in some refugee camps.[78] Not many accounts of village life in Biafra reached the West during the war. An Englishwoman married to an Igbo since before the war and resident in Biafra throughout the conflict has now written about her experiences.[79] After leaving Enugu, where she had been a teacher, Rosina Umelo lived in her husband's home village, where she gave birth to the fifth of their six children. Her account mentions that as everything became scarcer, especially protein food, people in rural areas began to suffer from *kwashiorkor* by the middle of 1968.[80]

The food shortages and multiple health crises in the Biafran enclave had been serious before, but the Port Harcourt exodus clearly tipped them over the edge. More aid was urgently needed, and the church agencies set about responding. At first their plans were not widely known. It was two or three months before the churches' mercy air-lift, which was to become justly famous, got properly started, as will be discussed briefly in the next chapter.

West Africa asked in an editorial on 8 June whether it was really impossible for the Federal Government to accept a ceasefire without the Biafrans first abandoning secession. That government pointed out that it had been common for talks to go on while a war was still in progress. This was correct historically, but there were many calls for a ceasefire before talks in the Nigerian case; it could help ease the crisis facing the crowded, dense, displaced population in Biafra, which went on swelling with each new federal advance. Lagos did not listen to such calls. After so many victories, the Federal Government wanted to press on to victory and thought a ceasefire would help the Biafrans, who were beaten already, to hold on. In fact, both sides could have used a ceasefire for rest and recuperation for the troops, but for the Biafrans that was more urgent. The Nigerian troops were ready to press on, and Gowon said on 5 June that they would do so, entering the Igbo heartland, unless Biafra responded to appeals to abandon the struggle. *West Africa*, in that editorial of 8 June, urged the Biafrans to reflect on their situation and consider seeking security through negotiations.

This implied that they had lost the war—and in reality they had. They had lost virtually all of South-Eastern and Rivers States, and considerable Igbo areas also. They claimed to be a united nation of Igbos and non-Igbos, but now it was more true than ever that the Biafrans were the Igbos, as many had been saying anyway—not only pro-federal Nigerians but also others such as President Nyerere had called the Biafrans simply "the Igbos". They had lost valuable sources of food, and also the vital oil industry. Shell-BP started work rapidly to get the oil flowing again; while oil exports had been halted; Nigeria had still been able to pay for the war, though the cost was high—an article on "The War Budget" in *West Africa* noted that Nigeria was borrowing more and investment in industry had fallen drastically in 1967[81]—and now the Federal Nigerian economy could soon recover.

But I do not recall, in discussions of the war in London at that time—May and June 1968—predictions that the Biafrans would be completely defeated or would agree to surrender in a short time.

They were not finished. Although several people from the minorities were still prominent among them, now there was a struggle of the Igbos to defend their hearths and homes. They would certainly do so fiercely, and they had one military advantage: a small compact territory where it was fairly easy to move forces from one sector to another. They were able to strike into Rivers, South-Eastern and Mid-West territory, and were to go on doing so constantly.

Obviously the Biafrans were inspired to keep going by the recognition granted by four African states. They hoped for more, and there was in fact considerable sympathy for Biafra in Africa. In Ghana, where the military regime had wide powers over the press, on 29 May the two main morning newspapers, the *Daily Graphic* and the *Ghanaian Times*, carried *in memoriam* notices commemorating the Easterners murdered in Northern Nigeria, paid for by the Biafra Union of Ghana. In the next few weeks, the minister of information of the Congo Republic (Congo-Brazzaville) expressed hope that the Nigerian government "may soon realise that there is nothing to gain in continuing a civil war which is the shame of our continent";[82] and, more strikingly, President Bourguiba of Tunisia declared, "under the pretext of unity everything was being done to destroy an ethnic group of 10 million Ibos ... one cannot stand idly by before such a massacre".[83] His attitude was a breach in the generally solid support for Nigeria among Arab and Muslim countries (not entirely surprising, as Islam did not have a prominent position under Bourguiba's highly secular regime). And it supported the Biafrans' accusation that Nigeria was aiming at genocide.

It emerged later that in that same month Bourguiba received a Biafran delegation including Nwokedi, Dike and Uwechue, and suggested they consider a loose federal arrangement; but Nwokedi rejected the idea at once, saying Biafra would not go back to Aburi after so much sacrifice.[84] This showed that the Biafrans, who were losing, were as intransigent as the Nigerians, who were winning. The latter also rejected a return to Aburi, but maybe the Biafrans could have offered to accept it and asked African states like Tunisia to persuade Lagos. In fact, Bourguiba did not go further after going very far by expressing belief in the genocide accusation.

The Biafrans were now getting more sympathy for that accusation, especially in the West, where it could potentially make the most difference. In Britain, *The Spectator*, edited by the future Conservative minister Nigel Lawson, had an editorial on 31 May 1968 calling for recognition of Biafra and saying Britain had become "an accomplice in genocide". This conviction was not generally shared—among others, Colin Legum in *The Observer* rejected it, speaking of people increasingly willing to return to their villages in federally occupied areas.[85] But with or without belief in genocide in Nigeria, opposition in Britain and other countries to all military assistance to the federal side was growing. Seventy backbench Labour MPs called for a halt to that assistance, as did the General Assembly of the Church of Scotland.[86] Czechoslovakia, during the period of relaxed Communist rule and reduced Soviet dominance in the "Prague Spring" of early 1968, halted all arms sales to Nigeria; the Netherlands did the same in June.

The Nigerian government protested that the Dutch action would give false hope to "the rebel leaders and their friends".[87] It surely did give them some hope, and Biafrans hoped, and the Federal Government feared, that in Britain the mounting pressure would also force Wilson's government to halt the arms supplies. The Biafran leaders were now regularly condemning the British government, and within Britain there were increasing protests. The protestors did not usually support Biafran independence as the only solution, few called for recognition of Biafra, and not all believed the genocide allegation, but there was a growing call for an end to the arms sales. And it was already growing when the starvation in Biafra, though very serious, was not yet known to the general public in the West.

6

FAMINE AND RELIEF IN THE HEADLINES
(JUNE–DECEMBER 1968)

The Biafran Baby in the British papers

On 12 June 1968, *The Sun*, which had been started by the International Publishing Corporation in 1964 to replace the *Daily Herald* and which was not yet part of the Murdoch empire, published a highly disturbing front-page story on Biafra, "The Land of No Hope", by its diplomatic correspondent, Michael Leapman, with photos by Ronald Burton. They had travelled to Biafra on the Lisbon run, with Markpress arranging and paying for the journey. They witnessed fearful starvation among refugees; Leapman wrote:

> Hundreds of thousands of Biafrans will starve to death this summer as they are hemmed into an ever-shrinking area in the middle of their country.

> By the end of the rainy season in August, more than a million of the country's 14½ people may have died.

Some people, he said, got help from extended families, but others went to "hundreds of refugee camps established by the Government in temporarily closed schools". People fled before the Nigerian forces because "Biafra's Ibo people fear that, if they stayed in occupied territory, they would be massacred by the invaders. Several thousand

Ibos in Nigeria were killed in 1966 and 1967." Some of the most fertile areas of Biafra had been occupied, the blockade prevented supplies getting in, and of the roughly four flights each week from Lisbon only two at the most carried food and medicine. Dr Clyne Shepherd, at Queen Elizabeth Hospital in Umuahia, said there were about 2,500 cases of malnutrition each week, and the number was going up, with adults affected as well as children; about 200 tons of protein were needed each day, and nothing approaching that was available. The front-page story concluded, "Only if the war ends and the Nigerian blockade is lifted can there be any serious international rescue operation to relieve the disaster."

Before the *Sun* story appeared, a House of Commons emergency debate on British policy on Nigeria had been scheduled for the same day, 12 June, a culmination of months of concern and protest by politicians, churchmen and others about British arms sales. The *Sun* report mentioned British arms supplies as important for Nigeria, and from then on the reports of starvation in Biafra gave more urgency to the calls for a halt to British arms sales. There had also been the calls for efforts to end the war, and these continued after the failure at Kampala. In the emergency debate, the foreign secretary, Michael Stewart, said Britain would try to persuade Nigeria to accept an international peace force, and both sides would be urged to accept no more arms supplies. Stewart and the prime minister, Harold Wilson, then mentioned this proposal to Chief Enahoro, who was in London. It got nowhere, and calls for Britain to halt its own arms sales continued and grew. A *Sun* editorial on 13 June said Britain should make a "much more vigorous effort" to bring about peace, through the Commonwealth and the United Nations, and urge a general embargo on arms supplies to both sides, adding, "There is a moral case against continuing to supply arms to Nigeria, whether other countries do or not", noting that Britain had rightly halted arms supplies to South Africa unilaterally. Many others were to say the same in the coming months.

There were many other reports from Biafra quickly following Michael Leapman's in the British press and that of many other Western countries. They included shocking photos of starving children in particular, suffering from *kwashiorkor*, the protein deficiency disease which produces a distended stomach and skin hanging loosely over bones. These reports put Biafra on the map, but they associated its name for ever with a sick and starving small child, a "Biafran baby". Naturally the reports led to instant action in many countries to try to relieve the starvation. Oxfam began efforts immediately, and started concerted action with other bodies belonging to Britain's Disasters Emergency Committee. For the next months there were appeals for help, which aroused an enormous response.

That response was one of genuine compassion based on facts accurately reported. That may seem obvious, but to some it was not. Some supporters of Nigeria in Britain at once suggested that the journalists' and others' reports were part of a campaign of deception to arouse support for Biafra. It was suggested that inexperienced reporters were simply seeing hunger that was common in Africa. However, Dr Shepherd said there had been very little malnutrition of that sort in the area of the Biafran enclave in peacetime.[1] Doctors, aid workers and others had been observing a drastic decline in ordinary people's nutrition due to the war, massive displacement and the blockade. Now it was worse than ever, and the reporters observing it included experienced Africa hands like Lloyd Garrison of the *New York Times* (well known to the *West Africa* staff). Any reporters who were new to the country could learn plenty from Biafrans and from expatriate doctors and clergy.

The fact was simply that people who had always been living near the edge, in an area of unusually dense rural population, were tipped over the edge by the war and the almost total halt to food imports from within Nigeria and from overseas, especially of protein food. The Biafran government had been organising relief for months. A study published long afterwards by Arua Oko Omaka recorded that on 15 June 1968 Biafra had 688 refugee camps with 482,923 displaced people in them (*West Africa* at the time reported 628 camps).[2] There was a Biafran Rehabilitation Commission headed by S.E. Imoke.[3] At the same time, the situation was dire in parts of the now federally occupied South-Eastern State. Before long, foreign reporters saw that situation too, and it was known in other parts of Nigeria, but in the West the fearful crisis in the Biafran enclave was most publicised.

For a while I heard people in London suggesting that the Biafrans were manipulating and deceiving the world through the reports of starvation. "I don't want to see any more Biafran propaganda," said one journalist after reading one of the reports in a newspaper. "It's all geared, isn't it?" said another. They were wrong; it was not Biafran propaganda, it was not geared. Such ideas expressed a confusion, still sometimes heard even today, between the Biafran leaders' propaganda efforts, employing Markpress as a major channel, and the reports of independent journalists. The impression was given—highly offensive to those journalists—that they were agents, pawns or dupes of an efficient propaganda machine. What many individual reporters, aid workers, doctors, nurses and clergy saw with their own eyes was depicted as a piece of propaganda by Markpress, which soon gained legendary proportions in the eyes of some.

In the debate in parliament on 12 June, John Cordle, a Conservative MP who had business links with Nigeria and supported its government's cause, spoke of the Biafrans' PR activity. Leapman replied in *The Sun* of the next day, saying that there was nothing wrong with Markpress helping reporters travel to Biafra, not in great comfort in his case, and adding,

> There was no attempt to show us things in which we were not interested, and we were not pumped full of propaganda. Neither were we wined and dined in traditional public relations style.

> My reports, like those of other Pressmen who have been to Biafra, were based on what we had seen for ourselves.

What Leapman did not say explicitly in his 12 June 1968 story, but did say later,[4] was that the Biafrans had not wanted the famine conditions reported in the world's press. Indeed, they had wanted to show that they were coping. The fact that the journalists taken to Biafra by another PR firm in late January did not startle the world with stories of food shortages, which were already there, confirms this. Things had become much worse when Leapman was there, and impossible to conceal—how could starving people filling up a major hospital in the temporary capital be hidden? But the Biafran authorities did not pester that journalist or others into telling the world of mass starvation.

But many journalists did their professional duty by reporting it. In June, July and August there were repeated horrific reports, especially about starving children kept alive by a few cups of milk, or not kept alive at all. Doctors, nurses and priests, both local and foreign, told of what they saw daily and would go on seeing when the reporters had gone home to report; they had been treating starving and sick people for months, before the tabloid headlines began, and now saw the crisis getting worse. For such witnesses, even those able to give some help, it was a highly exceptional and heart-rending experience. Reports spoke of one journalist with plenty of African experience crying in his bed during his Biafra assignment, and one priest engaged in relief work muttering, "I don't know how the Lord can permit this."

Or was all this a massive, elaborate operation to deceive the world? Anyone who believed that could believe anything. In fact I recall that suggestions of a fake famine invented by Markpress quite soon ceased to be heard at the time, except occasionally; white supporters of the federal side were angered by the famine story with the pictures of starving babies; they felt it was hitting below the belt, but the facts could not be doubted for long. Much later, when the evidence of the true situation was no longer available to most people, some writers seemed to revive those suggestions of a propaganda deception. Of course, such ideas must be consigned to the dustbin of fake history.

While few could continue to suggest that the reports of starvation were baseless, the idea of a cunning and effective Biafran PR campaign deceiving the world was to spread, and is still found in some of the literature today. Indeed, Biafra did have its Propaganda Directorate, and Markpress did a lot of work, for example sending its bulletins about the war to all British MPs and many others it sought to influence. But a good deal of Markpress material consisted of Ojukwu's speeches and reports of real or invented Biafran military victories. I only saw a few Markpress bulletins once, and they were not such as to arouse passionate reactions. But Markpress has been depicted as the origin of all the world publicity about Biafra, especially about famine there. That legend has served to discourage belief in truthful reports about the plight of the Biafrans, though Arua Omaka, who certainly has no such agenda, also exaggerates the influence of

Markpress.[5] Some writers on the war seem to prefer the legend to the simple fact that ordinary people in a dozen or more countries, and many eminent church people, politicians and others, reacted with horror and compassion to accurate reports of a real man-made disaster. Instead they insult the honest and independent witnesses who made those reports by lumping them together with Biafran official propagandists as one imagined hostile force of fiendish efficiency.

For example, Harold Wilson, in his book published the year after the war ended, says on Biafra that "the purveyors of Biafran propaganda flooded the Western press and Western legislatures with literature, and secured a degree of moral control over Western broadcasting systems, with a success unparalleled in the history of communications in modern democratic societies".[6] Did Wilson mean that the newspaper and television journalists who in fact reported on what happened in Biafra did nothing, or that they were all "purveyors of Biafran propaganda"? The recent historical work by Michael Gould says Markpress "not only created awareness throughout the international community of the plight of Biafra's population, but gave it access to aid on an unprecedented scale, both armaments and humanitarian support";[7] but it was journalists, aid workers and clergy who created the awareness and the humanitarian support, while the Biafran regime's emissaries obtained the arms. Graham Harrison, in a study of British campaigns on behalf of Africans, including the slave trade abolition and Biafra campaigns, says, "the disaster journalism that emerged from Biafra in 1968 and 1969 was pivotally a result of the Biafran government organising a public relations operation through a (what is now called) public relations company called Mark Press" [sic]; but he admits that the journalists who in fact reported on the situation from Biafra did not do quite what the Biafran government wanted—naturally not, as they were independent operators, not mere agents.[8] Maggie Black, dealing with Oxfam's role in relief for the Biafrans in her history of the organisation, says that "The version of the Biafran situation which burst so spectacularly upon the world in mid-1968 was put out by a European public relations firm hired by Ojukwu to present the Biafran case in its most heartrending light"; to confirm her dismissive view of the reporters and other witnesses of a truly heart-rending situation, she speaks of "journalists and missionaries passionately persuaded in their cause".[9]

Such dismissal of the evidence of people on the spot is unwarranted. Certainly many journalists who went to Biafra either had already, or acquired when there, a strong sympathy for the Biafran side, and missionaries already had that. But a number of journalists reporting on the Nigerian side, and probably the majority of expatriates working on that side, sympathised with the Federal Government. This was not new or strange—how many of the reporters covering the Spanish Civil War were without sympathies for one side or the other? This does not usually mean that any such reporters, or other witnesses to human disasters, tell lies to back their cause. They may make honest mistakes (journalists are not infallible). They may go wrong when they get away from reporting facts to make estimates or forecasts (some of the estimates of Biafran famine deaths may have been ill-founded). They may report one incident truthfully but assume too rashly that there are others. They may, when reporting the opinions and policies of certain people, believe too readily those on one side—I saw that happen. But they rarely if ever invent stories out of nothing—when a reporter in Biafra, sympathetic to the Biafrans, said he saw children starving, he saw children starving. In assessing reports of mass suffering and disaster, to dismiss everything said either by victims or by eyewitnesses sympathetic to the victims is absurd and offensive, and in practice likely to be propagandist. Such people have ensured that unpleasant facts are known to the world, as in the Biafran war.

It was not a PR operation, it was the *facts* that horrified the world. The response was of two kinds. First, there were the appeals for funds and donations to help the suffering people in Biafran territory. But, secondly, at the same time, there were increased protests at British arms supplies to Nigeria. Those protests had begun months before, but now Britain was seen to be supplying the weapons for a war leading to massive displacement of people and starvation. The passionate controversy over the arms supplies in the next 18 months made Biafra a major public issue in many countries. It was extensively reported at the time, and has been covered by many accounts written during and since the war.[10]

The appeals for help and the political campaign against British arms continued at the same time, but often separately. The overseas aid charities like Oxfam and Christian Aid concentrated on appealing for aid, as they had done for other overseas emergencies; others did the same. But journalists, editors, church leaders and politicians, while supporting the appeals for help, also called on the government to stop the arms sales to Nigeria. It was inevitable that people shocked by the consequences of the war waged by Nigeria should widely take such a stance, and it did not show that the famine reports were part of a conspiracy to help Biafra. The starvation was a fact; that it was due to the war and blockade imposed by Nigeria was a fact. And that British arms supplies were very important for Nigeria's war effort was also a fact. It would have been absurd to expect British people learning these facts not to query, at least, the supply of arms to Nigeria.

Protests and polemics

Of course most of the ordinary citizens of many countries who reacted to the Biafra famine in that way knew very little about the war and its causes. But what they said was not very different from what many well-informed people were saying. I heard it said that those who knew the full facts were on the side of Nigeria; many of them were, but not all. British people with experience of work in Nigeria and knowledge of its recent history were found on both sides of the argument about the right policy for Britain to follow.

Some of those opposed to the arms sales were pro-Biafran in the fullest sense, but not all. Some wanted a complete international embargo on arms supplies to both sides, and wanted Britain to take the initiative for this and start by halting its own sales. Many thought it wrong in principle for Britain to fuel war in another country. Such people might well have been glad to see any peaceful solution, with or without Biafran independence; they could, like President Nyerere, favour Nigerian unity but not Nigerian unity imposed by force. But all that said, opposition to British arms supplies was seen by some as aimed in effect, if not in intention, at a military advantage for Biafra. The British government tried to avoid admitting that the Nigerian army depended heavily on British weaponry—by repeated lies, which were eventually exposed.[11] The exact proportion that the UK supplied does not matter; certainly a halt to British arms supplies would have caused serious problems for the federal war effort. Hence the Biafran regime, which had not planned the publicity about starving children and may have been surprised by its impact, quickly saw that it could help the Biafran cause and encouraged foreign journalists—and ordered Markpress, of course—to continue it.

While the public Western response to the reports of starvation arose from genuine compassion and desire to help the needy, a question remains: why did this particular disaster arouse such a response? Of course there had been such generous responses before. Britain has a long tradition of large-scale public donations to help relieve suffering in other countries; just before the Nigerian war, for example, there was a big response in Britain to fundraising for relief in the Bihar famine in India. But not all disasters have aroused the same response. The response to Biafra appeals in Britain, the US and many other countries was exceptional; however, it was to be repeated in response to the Ethiopian famines in 1973 and 1984. Examination of these public outpourings of pity[12] makes it clear that there is an accidental, unpredictable element to them, not easy to explain. Certainly political manipulation is not the explanation in any of these cases, nor in another case of extraordinary public giving, the response to the plight of the Kurds in northern Iraq in late 1991.

In 1960–1 there was an appeal by the Oxford Committee for Famine Relief (to become Oxfam in 1965) for relief for the Kasai region of the Congo, where mass starvation had set in during the descent to anarchy and mayhem; terrible photos of skeletal children were shown then, as in the reports from Biafra a few years later, and these shocked people particularly.[13] In the case of Biafra, the situation in which people were starving could also appeal to the outside world. The image of a "beleaguered" country or people can arouse an elemental urge to send help. Biafra was in a real sense under siege, even though it was larger than the cities besieged throughout history and was not totally invested. And a siege has often proved able to arouse feelings in many countries, as people wait for news of relief or surrender—Vienna in 1683, Londonderry in 1689, Khartoum in 1884–5, Madrid in 1936. As on those earlier occasions when there was no

Markpress, where Biafra was concerned it was the situation, as correctly reported, that aroused feelings.

What aroused them more was that there was a possibility of helping. After reading the shocking press reports of children slowly wasting away from starvation, and thinking "Something's got to be done", people in the West soon realised that something *could* be done. The *Daily Sketch*, headlining the crisis on 17 June 1967, sent half a ton of full-cream dried milk and appealed to readers for more. Such gestures were just the beginning. Money donated to the main charities was commonly used to buy food and medicines transported by sea to Fernando Po or São Tomé and then by air into Biafra. The knowledge that starving people could be helped made all the difference; and, indeed, they were helped.

The humanitarian desire to send help was obvious and inevitable. The other response—to call for an end to British arms for Nigeria—was not so inevitable; it was not the only possible response. Nigerians commonly admitted the great suffering in the Biafran enclave—if my memory is right, the idea of a fake disaster invented by Markpress was uttered more by white supporters of Nigeria than by Nigerians—and blamed it on Ojukwu, saying the solution was for Ojukwu to surrender. However, to concerned non-Nigerians, except for those committed to supporting Lagos, it seemed obvious that the British arms were being used in a war effort that had led to mass starvation, and should stop. This eventually became the majority view of the British press, and not only the tabloids like the *Daily Sketch*, which said on 17 June, "Scandal of Biafra: the *Sketch* says the children need milk—Britain sends bullets."

Nigerians supporting the Federal Military Government admitted that that government had started the military action, and admitted that it was causing great suffering, but thought the rest of the world should accept the action as justified. In the *West Africa* readers' letters page and in conversation, we heard many arguments they used. The editor of the magazine supported some arguments but not all, though he was overall on the FMG's side. However, as Williams often said and some Nigerians admitted, the government was hopelessly incapable of making a credible defence of its war to end secession. Some statements by Gowon and others might give a good impression, but statements and actions by Nigerian officials in the country and abroad often had the opposite effect, and ordinary Nigerians in writing and conversation often ended up increasing sympathy for the Biafrans.

For example, it was common to defend the war by placing all the blame on "the Igbos" and especially on "January the 15th". One *Daily Times* journalist said to me, "When the Igbo man is happy, Nigeria remains united; when the Igbo man is not happy, Nigeria must break up." That was in private conversation, but in July 1968 the Mid-Western State government published a seven-page advertisement in *The Economist* and, on 20 July 1968, in *West Africa* (it was clearly headed "Advertiser's Announcement", but should not have been published at all), which said in the course of a long historical account, "Since 1947, certain Ibo leaders have embarked on a plan of unparalleled audacity to dominate Nigeria", and devoted twelve paragraphs to the "Ibo urge for domination".

This advertisement expressed common Nigerian attitudes, but in a major official document intended to make the world more favourable to Nigeria. It did briefly condemn the pogroms, whereas Nigerians defending their cause commonly did not like anyone to mention that crime and, when it was mentioned, went on about "January the 15th … the Igbos … January the 15th … the Igbos … the Igbos …", suggesting that the killing of a dozen people on that day was somehow a good reason for the murder of thousands a few months later and the expulsion of Easterners from most of the Federation—"a thousand eyes for an eye", presumably. To foreigners such propaganda suggested that, in the eyes of Nigerians, the Igbos, numbering several millions, were all criminals and deserved all they got.

The Federal Government at the top level made more reasoned defences of its position. In his speech at Kampala, Chief Enahoro, describing the lead-up to secession, admitted the pogroms; but, like many others, he relativised those "tragic and regrettable killings"; he said they could not be justified, but "all this is in the past", and emphasised that many people in the North had saved Easterners' lives.[14] While it was right to give all honour to those people, it did not efface the dreadful memory of the thousands killed: do African Americans forget the generations-long horror of lynching in the South when told of the brave white police officers who died trying to save people from lynch mobs?

Enahoro and others also spoke often of the 30,000 Igbos still living in Lagos. This was of course to answer the allegation of genocide; if it were not for that consideration, the FMG would have done better to keep quiet about those Igbos in Lagos. To anybody who knew that hundreds of thousands had lived in the federal capital before, and especially to anybody who had witnessed what happened to them in 1966–7 (some British people who had been in Lagos recalled this with horror), 30,000 still living there was not much to boast of. They were alive, but they were obliged to carry special passes ("Like South Africa," I said in an office conversation; "No!" colleagues protested). And they were the special target of the menacing roadblocks mounted by soldiers and police in the region of Lagos throughout the crisis years, following the descent into arbitrary violence by troops in mid-1966. Foreigners were not usually affected personally by the brutality at the roadblocks (I was not, on a short visit to Lagos and the Western State in early March 1968), but it did no good to Nigeria's reputation abroad. Because the roadblocks were directed against Igbos, one of the few prominent Igbos who supported the Federal Government, the trade unionist Armstrong Ogbonna, was harshly treated by them. He wrote about it in a Nigerian newspaper sometime in 1969; I wanted to write an opinion piece in *West Africa* quoting this, but it was suppressed because Ogbonna had once led a demonstration against Cecil King. I was annoyed, not because I had any special regard for Ogbonna, but because I had wanted to work in some words about the vile roadblocks. They were to continue for years, involving many crimes.

General Gowon promised that if the Biafrans accepted the unity and 12 states of Nigeria there would be a general amnesty and they would have full equality with other Nigerians. Meanwhile, the FMG banned overtly tribalistic language in the newspapers—an Igbo had to be described as a "Nigerian of East-Central State origin". However, the newspapers were still filled with extreme vindictive language about the "rebels" and their backers. In one office conversation, Kaye Whiteman said, "Reading the Nigerian papers makes one feel completely and utterly Biafran", and Williams and I agreed. The radio was worse, especially Kaduna Radio; I often read its fierce language in the *Summary of World Broadcasts*. It was just as well for the Federal Government's publicity efforts that few people in the West read the *Summary of World Broadcasts*, fewer still the Nigerian dailies (though foreign diplomats in Lagos saw them). True, nothing put out by either side could equal the excesses of Biafra Radio, but most British people never heard them. Instead they saw and read reports of the suffering in Biafra and knew it was a man-made disaster due to war and blockade; federal publicity efforts were up against that.

Those publicity efforts may have had a hopeless task anyway, but they were also deplorably organised. Staff at the Nigeria High Commission in London, in Northumberland Avenue, were disagreeable in manner and the atmosphere at that High Commission unfriendly. The high commissioner, Brigadier Ogundipe, had a hot temper and a thundering voice, shouting at journalists as if they were insubordinate soldiers at the regular press conferences he held during the war. Officials dealing with the press in Nigeria itself were as inconsiderate and unhelpful as those in London. Nigerian official representatives had a reputation as abrasive, arrogant and intolerant of any views contrary to theirs. For example, they sometimes objected to people even using the word "Biafra". This showed lack of understanding in what was, admittedly, a rather exceptional situation: nowhere in the world, in recent decades, had a region of a country broken away, established itself for a time with a working government, and adopted a new name. In the Katanga secession, the name had not been contested; nor in the Algerian war of independence (which the French called secession) or the movement for independence (secession to the Chinese regime) in Tibet. The question of what to call the secessionist former Eastern Region of Nigeria had no recent precedent. In fact there was no question, except from Nigerian government officials, who could only look ridiculous in apparently wanting the whole world to speak of "the rebel enclave" or some other such phrase. When a country called Biafra by its initially effective government established itself on the ground, the outside world began to use that name automatically, without thinking it was granting a sort of diplomatic recognition. *West Africa* spoke of Biafra by that name throughout, and I did not hear of any arguments about it.

The FMG at that time had power, official recognition, flourishing trade relations, easy access to all the money it needed, and all the arms it required—but not much sympathy and affection around the world, which went rather to the Biafrans. Journalists who travelled to Biafra more than ever after the famine story broke recounted that they were treated in a more courteous and friendly way there than in Nigeria; they were escorted, but not restricted. There were ugly sides to the Biafran situation—Nigeria's glaring inequalities continued there, Biafra had nasty roadblocks too, and, above all, there was the loathsome treatment of people of the minorities; yet many foreigners seemed ready to ignore or forgive such things on the Biafran side.

The minorities were in truth the weakest link in the Biafrans' case, as the pogroms were in the federal case. It was not enough for the Biafrans to say that many minority people were with them, as it was well known that a large number were against them. Federal propaganda, including Enahoro's lengthy speeches during the peace talks, naturally devoted plenty of attention to the Rivers and South-Eastern peoples—that was its strongest card. In answer to Biafran claims to the right of self-determination, their adversaries asked why Biafra denied that right to the minority peoples. By mid-1968 the future of Rivers and South-Eastern States had been resolved on the ground, as they were almost totally under federal military control, but the Biafrans did not see it as settled; instead they called for a referendum in those states. As Raph Uwechue said after he resigned as Biafra's Paris representative later in 1968, this proposal came too late.[15]

But after all that could be said about the Eastern Nigeria minorities, the facts about what had been done in 1966–7 to Easterners, including minority people, remained. Because of them the Biafrans were seen by countless people outside Nigeria as a persecuted people—"overwhelmingly the wronged party", as Margery Perham said—and their sufferings in the war confirmed the picture. Nigerians ought to have known that this would be a widespread reaction.

In Britain, France, the US and many other Western democracies there was a long tradition of public concern and protest about oppression, persecution and exploitation in other parts of the world; also about foreign wars and, more recently, about preparations for nuclear war. Marches, demonstrations, meetings, letters to the press, lobbying of politicians, on many such topics—all this was an important part of recent history in the West, even though the active participants were always in the minority. To recall only the few years before 1967, there were the Campaign for Nuclear Disarmament (CND) and the Anti-Apartheid Movement in Britain, the Civil Rights movement in the US, and, to crown them all, the worldwide protest movement against the Vietnam War, with strong support in Britain and France but backed by great numbers of Americans opposing their own country's war. The Nigerian war came at a time when the Vietnam protests were at a peak, with the major demonstrations outside the US embassy in London on 17 March and 27 October 1968. The thousands of Nigerians living in Britain and the US witnessed all this, and some may well have joined in student "demos". When their own civil war came, did Nigerians backing the Federal Government really expect there to be no protests?

Many of the same public figures involved in other protest campaigns protested also against the Nigerian war and British support for it, which was often seen as implicitly backing the Biafrans, or else supported Biafra more completely. There was, for example, the Rev. Donald Soper, Lord Soper, a famous Methodist minister, pacifist, and campaigner on all sorts of causes, including South African apartheid and racism in Britain. There was Fenner Brockway, Lord Brockway, the veteran campaigner against colonialism, who founded the Movement for Colonial Freedom (MCF) in 1954 and was its chairman for some time; he opposed the arms sales to Nigeria from an early date, asking many questions in the House of Lords. There was Stan Newens, a left-wing Labour MP who served as chairman of the MCF and opposed the arms sales in the Commons. There was James Griffiths, a veteran Labour MP who had been colonial secretary in the Attlee government; he condemned arms sales to Nigeria but still hoped that some sort of Nigerian unity would continue. Similarly, Brockway headed a British Committee for Peace in Nigeria, which as its name shows was not committed to Biafran independence (it was backed initially by Sir James Robertson, former governor general of Nigeria) but wanted peace. I do not recall from the time what William Ajibola's study later recorded that many of the early backers of the committee, including Robertson, withdrew support when it called for a unilateral British arms ban.[16] Brockway and others saw no inconsistency in making that call while seeking peace; for them, the two had to go together.

Many campaigners against the arms sales to Nigeria were on the political left, as one would expect from the history of left-wing anti-militarism. But in contrast to the Vietnam protests, those directed against the Nigerian war involved people of all political parties and allegiances. In fact there was considerable support for the Biafrans among Conservative politicians and newspapers, though the Conservative leadership backed the Labour government on Nigeria. Hugh Fraser was the most prominent; among the others were two journalists and future Tory politicians: Nigel Lawson, who as editor of *The Spectator* supported the allegation of genocide and called for recognition of Biafra, and Jonathan Aitken, who was to become a well-known supporter of the Biafran cause.

Some other Conservatives commenting on the Nigerian war were unfortunately imbued with colonialist and racist feeling, which was widely aroused at that very time by British supporters of Ian Smith: besides venting prejudices against Africans, Tories of that sort could pursue their opposition to Harold Wilson's Labour government by contrasting the sanctions against Rhodesia with the arming of Nigeria. I recall a cartoon by Cummings in the *Daily Express* showing stereotyped Africans—Nigerians and Biafrans—fighting and Wilson passing by proclaiming his crusade against Smith. Peregrine Worsthorne, a diehard Tory journalist who defended Smith's UDI, wrote in the *Sunday Telegraph* of 4 August 1968 about "primitive savagery" and asked, "How much longer can the civilised world be expected to treat men like General Gowon as ordinary heads of state? If they behave like savage chieftains, that is how they may come to be treated." Such comments combined imperialist prejudice with extremely short memory: the mass savagery committed in the Second World War far exceeded anything ever seen in Africa. People too blinded to reality to see this may have considered themselves to be friends of Biafra, but if so, they were undesirable friends. In fact, attitudes of white superiority were found among supporters of Nigeria. A pro-Nigerian French journalist who reported from the front, Jean Wolf, wrote in a book published during the war, "It is true that they [the federal forces] wage total war, African-style war, brutally, without mercy."[17] Was it Africans who had carried out massive war crimes in France just a quarter of a century before?

Each side in the Nigerian war sometimes compared the other side to the Nazis, and certain European supporters of Biafra, commenting on the starvation, made comparisons with Belsen. Such propagandist language was quite wrong. But it was also wrong for supporters of the Nigerian government to dismiss all Western criticism of its conduct of the war because of the monumental war crimes record of Western countries. Individual Europeans and Americans who had nothing to do with their countries' historical crimes were, if they rejected any attitude of white people's superiority, as many did, quite entitled to criticise Nigeria, whose war crimes were truly criminal regardless of what Westerners had done before.

My own impression at the time was that racist twisting of the criticism of Nigeria's war effort was untypical of the protest movement, and that, while prominent individuals opposing the war could be of many political persuasions, the active campaigners were mainly on the left, with the major exception of *The Spectator*. Prominent people who opposed apartheid and the Rhodesian regime, supported the American Civil Rights cause, and opposed racism in Britain (voiced loudly at that very time by Enoch Powell) were also opposed to Nigeria's war to end secession. For example, *Peace News*, the militant weekly supporting the CND, was a determined opponent of the war, sympathetic to the Biafrans though not uncritical of them. This was not a mainstream paper, but *The Guardian* was, and it was opposed to the war for most of its duration. Walter Schwarz (formerly on the staff of *West Africa*), who had been the *Guardian*'s correspondent in Lagos until the crisis, was one of the strongest opponents. He was one of the prominent Africa specialists working for British newspapers. Of the others—most or all of them well known to the *West Africa* staff—one, Colin Legum, Commonwealth correspondent of *The Observer*, supported the FMG, even though he had angered it greatly by his honest reporting of the pogroms. His view was that of David Williams also: that while the Biafrans' feelings in response to the mass crime in the North were justified, secession was not the answer. Legum, a South African anti-apartheid exile, and Basil Davidson, the eminent Africanist who wrote often for *West Africa*, were left-wingers who backed Nigeria; but many more, probably the majority, were on the other side.

It must be noted again that calling that other side simply "pro-Biafran" is an over-simplification. Many prominent speakers against the British arms supplies wanted a total embargo on arms, a ceasefire and peace talks, not necessarily acceptance of Biafran independence. But to Nigerians such distinctions did not matter much; such protestors were viewed as wanting in practice to see Nigeria deprived of necessary military supplies and Biafra, at the very least, better able to fight on. Such an attitude, like that of Americans who said the anti-Vietnam War protestors were working for the Communists, was to be expected in wartime, but in retrospect the many differing sincere views that were expressed need to be recalled accurately.

When the British press, after the famine story hit the headlines, adopted a general editorial attitude that was pro-Biafran or seemed so to Nigerians, many of the latter reacted with apparently total incomprehension. Unable to understand how the world seemed to be against their country, they thought of many explanations. One was that the press was quite simply bribed, and, of course, there was the myth of the mighty Markpress mentally enslaving the world's journalists. And there were paranoid ideas of a vast conspiracy by hidden forces in the West determined to destroy Nigeria and using the press to that end.

Obviously none of these fantasies is found in a serious study of the British press's coverage of the Biafran war by the Nigerian scholar A. Bolaji Akinyemi, who later became Nigeria's minister of external affairs.[18] However, this thorough study is imbued with the author's pro-federal attitude. He says for example, "The *Guardian* completely lost its head in its opposition to the war."[19] He gives interesting details of how major British daily and Sunday papers dealt with the war itself, the famine and relief, and other aspects. He notes that there was apparently some disagreement within editorial offices; that was certainly true of *The Times*, whose feature writer Roy Lewis was pro-federal[20] while his editor, William Rees-Mogg, came out as a strong sympathiser with the Biafrans. But in noting some inconsistencies over time in newspapers' policies, he seems not to consider that editors might simply have changed their views by learning more about the situation, or in the face of new facts—as when *The Times*, the day after the *Sun's* report on 12 June 1968, called for an end to the arms supplies. Anyway there may not have been so many inconsistencies as suggested, for writers did not have to be always totally on one side or the other—those opposing arms sales did not believe the Biafrans incapable of doing wrong. There was nothing strange about the *Daily Mirror* generally supporting a united Nigeria but employing "shock tactics treatment of the victims of starvation" and carrying articles by both the pro-federal Labour MP Woodrow Wyatt and the anti-federal journalist George Gale:[21] why not let readers see arguments on both sides? Akinyemi, who exaggerates in saying the *Financial Times* was fully pro-Biafran,[22] is overall highly critical of the British press. In truth, the FMG was lucky to have the limited support it had in the British media despite the obstacles, largely self-inflicted, to an understanding of its point of view.

A more fair-minded and objective study of the British press, and public opinion and the pressure groups, was published in Nigeria by William A. Ajibola in 1978.[23] While it has many inaccuracies, it analyses the media coverage fairly thoroughly except, strangely, the *Financial Times* (in fact broadly sympathetic to Biafra). Examining the editorial attitudes to the key issue of British arms supplies, it notes how *The Times*, *The Guardian*, *The Sun*, the *Sunday Telegraph* and the *Daily Express* came out against them, while *The Observer*, *Sunday Times*, *Daily Telegraph* and *Daily Mirror* were in favour.[24] Examining radio and television coverage also, Ajibola confirms what was obvious at the time: that the British media were mainly sympathetic to Biafra rather than Nigeria.

That attitude stung and hurt Nigerians—in the 1970s I was struck to hear people in Nigeria who supported the federal war effort remembering Britain in retrospect not as an ally in the war, but as an enemy, because of the press and public hostility. The FMG could constantly fall back on a legalistic defence—it was the legal ruler of the whole country, it had a right to suppress a rebellion by force—but it decided belatedly that it ought to try to get more genuine support in the world, in fact to be better liked. The government engaged a public relations firm in London, Galitzine, Grant and Russell, in mid-

1968. It put out a well-produced magazine, *United Nigeria*; I cannot remember what was in it.

That PR effort showed recognition that critics of Nigeria had a case that needed to be answered. But the understanding of the critics' reasons was still defective. Nigerians, for example, stuck to the idea that Catholic opponents of their cause were agreeing with the Biafrans' constant claim that the war against them was a religious war of Muslims against Christians. Nigerians seem to have worried about that propaganda too much. Of course it was quite false. The federal military action was not the same as the civilian gangsterism of the Northern pogroms—even though soldiers had joined in that—and the Northern mass violence had been political and criminal violence, not jihadist violence; it was totally contrary to Islamic law. And as Nigerians often repeated, most of the senior leaders of the government were Christians, a large proportion of the troops were Christian, and great numbers of Nigerian Christians lived and worshipped freely around the country, with missionary and local clergy.

Did the missionaries on the Biafran side support the official Biafran view that this was a war of Muslims against Christians? It is not necessary to suppose so. If they sympathised strongly with the Biafran cause, as many certainly did, it was not necessarily for that reason. When the Irish missionaries worked hard to help people suffering around them and sought more help from the West, as was their duty, countless Catholics responded in Ireland, Britain and especially the US, and among them some may have believed that there was a religious war against Christian Biafrans.[25] Seeing all this activity, and the Biafran claims, supporters of the federal side seem to have put two and two together and concluded that the whole Catholic Church saw the war as a religious war. But I did not see any proof at the time that the Pope ever said this.[26] The Vatican, well informed about the Church in all countries, knew very well that the Catholics on the Nigerian side were in no danger or trouble and were helping relief in the war zone on the federal side, with steady contributions from Caritas.

Yet the Pope did criticise the Nigerian war, and so did the priests working on the Biafran side. What some Nigerians seemed unable to understand was that Catholics, like others, could oppose the war without believing it to be a religious war. Yet that should have been easy to understand for anyone who knew about trends in the Catholic Church in the previous two decades. A number of priests and lay activists had been proclaiming the need for Catholics to stand up in the public domain for peace and justice in the world. This included campaigning against flagrant social inequalities and injustices in the world economic system and within many countries, especially in Catholic Latin America. Campaigning against war included the creation of the Pax Christi organisation in 1945, the opposition to France's Algerian war by the Catholic weekly *Témoignage Chrétien* and the famous Abbé Pierre, and the protests against America's Vietnam War by the brothers Berrigan, both priests. A prominent cleric who followed this trend in Britain was Monsignor Bruce Kent, then chaplain to the University of London, who later became general secretary of the CND, and during the Biafran war was a forceful protestor against British policy. Such people did not call for narrow sectarian solidarity with fellow Catholics; they followed orthodox Catholic teaching, which went back centuries, about the "just war", ready to condemn unjust wars against Muslims or Communists.

Those activists went further than the Vatican recommended, but they helped remind Catholics of the mainstream Church teaching on war. That teaching was developed with wars between states in mind, but there was now a wider Catholic opposition to war. Catholics could oppose the Biafran war on the grounds that it was an unjustified war, not because they believed it to be a Muslim jihad. Some might believe that it was not a jihad, but genocide (to kill Igbos, not Catholics); in May, *L'Osservatore Romano*, the daily newspaper of Vatican State, said the war was a "war of extermination" and Biafra's secession was "a step forward for the new nations of Africa towards total independence and self-determination".[27] Contrary to common opinion, *L'Osservatore* is not an official organ of the Holy See and does not necessarily reflect the Pope's thinking. But certainly there was opposition to the Nigerian war among many Catholics, including Pope Paul.

On 2 June 1968, Whit Sunday, the Catholic archbishop of Westminster, Cardinal Heenan, gave a sermon at Westminster Abbey, which no head of the Catholic Church in England had done for four centuries, and said some words about Biafra. This was in the

159

context of a criticism of "selective indignation" about public affairs; he spoke of the countless marches and demonstrations against the Americans in Vietnam, and added, "But how many marches and demonstrations have there been against the massacre in Biafra?" He referred to Houphouët-Boigny's words about the death toll and said, "It is we, the British, who have supplied many of the instruments of death";[28] hence the British were not in a position to cast the first stone at the Americans. His remarks on Biafra angered Nigerians greatly. They were in fact not well phrased; in Nigeria there was a war in which massacres occurred, not one big massacre. But anyway, FMG supporters were angered by his mention of Biafra by that name and his accusations against the Nigerian and British governments. If they looked at the prelate's words, they would have seen he said nothing about a war of Muslims against Christians.

In August, the federal commissioner Joseph Tarka, in Rome, said angrily, "I was brought up a Catholic. Now you had better just call me a Christian."[29] What had been said to him to arouse such indignation? Perhaps he had been told the real reason for Catholics' criticism of the war, as opposed to the reason imagined by federal representatives like Edwin Ogbu, now Nigerian ambassador to the UN, who said the Pope believed the war was a religious war.[30] Nigerians were also angry with Rome for the Caritas flights to Biafra. In August, Chief Justice Ademola led a protest delegation in Lagos; the papal delegate to Central and West Africa, Monsignor Luigi Bellotti, told them that the Pope had been "moved by the human suffering".[31] Later in 1968, Archbishop Aggey of Lagos, returning from Rome, told a conference of Catholic bishops that the Pope was distressed at media representation of his "constant concern and practical efforts for the charitable relief of suffering".[32]

The simple fact was that Catholics reacted to the Nigerian war, for or against, for the same reasons as other people did. People of common sense of all religions or none agree that war is a very serious step which should be undertaken only for very good reasons. Many Nigerian Christians thought their government had such very good reasons and was waging a just war, but other Christians and others around the world were not convinced.

Because of this, Catholics especially were subjected to paranoid suspicions. Soon after the end of the war, Woodrow Wyatt MP complained in the Commons, "It is remarkable and disturbing how the Press and television have fallen for little pressure groups and propaganda put out by them—by Markpress and other organisations all this time", and then proceeded to a truly 17th-century description of popish activity in the cause of Biafra:

> I fear that some of the organs of information have been in the hands of Roman Catholics. It is a serious matter. It does not seem to me to be any coincidence that the Director-General of the B.B.C. [Charles Curran] is a Roman Catholic. And it does not seem to me to be a coincidence that the Editor of The Times [William Rees-Mogg] is a Roman Catholic.[33]

In the same vein, Akinyemi later wrote that "it was a Catholic group which was responsible for the conversion of the editor [of *The Times*] to the Biafran cause".[34] Why not consider that Rees-Mogg might have thought for himself about the Nigerian war? Of course, that is what people of all religions did, reaching their own varying conclusions. Among Catholic politicians, the Conservative MP Hugh Fraser was strongly pro-Biafran, but Maurice Foley was for years the junior Foreign and Commonwealth Office (FCO) minister responsible for Africa in the Wilson government, constantly travelling to Nigeria and defending its case in the Commons. Among journalists, Auberon Waugh, a passionate supporter of Biafra, was a Catholic, but also a provocatively independent character like his father Evelyn; and Tom Burns, editor of the respected Catholic weekly *The Tablet*, was strongly pro-Nigerian. In Ireland, many Catholics championed Biafra, but so, prominently, did Conor Cruise O'Brien, who was not a devout Catholic and was strongly opposed to the Catholic Church's power in the Irish Republic.

A worldwide plan by the scheming Church of Rome to support Biafra was one more mental construct to explain away worldwide opposition to Nigeria's war against secession. The simple fact was that ordinary people around the world learned about the facts, or some of the facts, and decided what to think.

The disputes over famine relief

Various agencies were already distributing food and medicines and providing other aid for war victims before the starvation became worse and hit world headlines. On the Nigerian side of the front, for example, there were the Nigerian Red Cross, the Catholic Relief Services and the Christian Council of Nigeria's Relief Committee, with the International Committee of the Red Cross (ICRC) in overall charge. Supplies from money raised overseas were sent to these agencies on both sides; Caritas and Oxfam, at least, took care to send them to agencies working on both sides impartially. Local agencies and the relevant governments were responsible for distribution on the spot. On the Biafran side, the government was ultimately in charge—it had to grant landing rights and visas for aid workers—but properly left the aid agencies to do their job. Reports from mid-1968 showed that they did the job as well as they could, but there was a desperate shortage of food and other aid.

On the Nigerian side of the front, the government and the army gave some help to the local aid agencies, but in South-Eastern State there was suffering comparable to that on the other side. A team of 30 young Nigerians, mostly students, volunteered to help the Nigerian Red Cross and the Christian Council of Nigeria and went to Calabar, Uyo and other places in August and September 1968. Four of them wrote a report in the *Nigerian Christian*, with grim details. At a refugee camp run by the army in Calabar, people "suffered from acute starvation and had little or no hair on their heads, scaly bodies and swollen feet that burst and dripped water". At the Government Teacher Training College at Uyo, "The compound was full of people reduced to mere shadows by starvation. A nasty smell lingered all over the place from the bodies buried in shallow graves all over the compound ... Heavy rains were falling and this quickened the deaths of many people." It was reported that no less than 25 people were dying each day in that college alone. The volunteers, who went close to the front line where fighting was going on, gave out gari (cassava flour), rice, wheat, salt, tinned meat and other food. Their report said:

> We regard it as a failure on the part of the Nigerian Press for keeping quiet about the thousands of people on the Federal side who die of starvation. The world press has whipped up sympathy for Biafra by pictures and news but no one hears of starvation on the Nigerian side, though many perish daily. It is not altogether the fault of our people

in other parts of the country to have what we regard as criminal indifference to the sufferings of others.[35]

This testimony, which we at *West Africa* did not see at the time, is quoted here to show how starvation caused by the war was very real on both sides of the front line; details here are similar to those reported by journalists on the Biafran side, and where was Markpress? In fact the shocking situation in South-Eastern State was also seen by two British MPs who went there in August, James Johnson (Labour) and Nigel Fisher (Conservative), and by some foreign journalists, and was reported in *West Africa*.[36] On the federal side there were some genuine problems of delivery of bulk supplies, but there was no blockade, money was available, and the utter failure to provide adequate relief was due solely to "criminal indifference". On the Biafran side, the aid distribution system was efficient, but there was simply nothing near enough to be distributed.

For several months relief supplies for the Biafra side were mostly transported on the Lisbon gun-running flights. Oxfam made a first grant, of £10,000, for goods to be carried on those flights in March 1968. Then there were a few flights from Lisbon chartered by the churches. Far more help was needed, and efforts to provide it went ahead between May and July 1968. In later years, several accounts of this were published. In the present work, the contemporary coverage by the magazine is supplemented by some reference to two of those later accounts, in a limited way—there cannot be a full account of the Biafra relief airlift here, though such a full account is still needed, as the published accounts leave gaps to fill. One of these is the short but detailed account published in Nigeria in 1978 by Emmanuel Urhobo, a Mid-Westerner who headed the Christian Council of Nigeria's National Rehabilitation Commission;[37] as noted earlier, in a good sign of the post-war reconciliation, his account is very objective and does full justice to the relief work on the Biafran side. The major work published is a much later and longer academic work by Arua Oko Omaka.[38] Father Tony Byrne's reminiscences, lively reading but too imprecise about dates in particular, add some details; Frederick Forsyth, in his book published during the war, adds some more from the Biafran side.[39]

The government of West Germany donated DM 4 million to Deutscher Caritasverband and DM 4 million to the corresponding Protestant relief agency, Das Diakonische Werk. Byrne did much to secure this and then arrange for use of the funds to buy or charter aircraft, eventually four DC-7s. These were to make possible a much enlarged humanitarian airlift, but it took time to organise (the plans were probably unknown, except to a few, when the *Sun* report appeared, mentioning only the Lisbon run). Storage and distribution within Biafra were well organised; Caritas set up its central store about a kilometre from Uli airstrip, and the Christian Council of Biafra–World Council of Churches central relief distribution store, previously at Queen Elizabeth Hospital in Umuahia, was moved to Awo-Omamma, about 126 km south of Uli. Urhobo notes that there was cooperation between the church agencies and the ICRC at Uli and in the distribution operations;[40] this was necessary, but the ICRC's flights were still approved by the federal side and the churches' were not.

Regrettably, *West Africa*'s news pages at the time, and the sources mentioned, do not make up a full picture of how the churches' relief airlift was pieced together in the early months. Various agencies were involved, including of course the Biafran government, and apparently Hank Wharton was involved in the planning, though the churches' operation was separate from his and carried no cargo except the necessities of relief operations; however, at this time there were disputes between Wharton and the Biafrans. Several aircraft were involved, and two islands, Fernando Po and São Tomé. There were problems, hitches, and delays while people starved and food and medicines donated by governments and the generous public in many countries were steadily unloaded from ships on the two islands and piled up in warehouses there.[41]

But gradually more relief flights were organised through the efforts of church agencies, especially in Scandinavia (whence stockfish, once supplied to the former Eastern Nigeria commercially, was now sent as aid for Biafran war victims). In August 1968, Protestant church relief organisations of Denmark, Norway, Sweden and Finland agreed to form Nordchurchaid, which in cooperation with German churches began regular relief flights from São Tomé into Biafra. With Caritas taking part also, the airlift fully commenced in September, with priority given to the delivery of protein food, medicines and clothes.[42] For about a month the Nordchurchaid airlift was commanded by the famous Swedish pilot Count Carl Gustaf von Rosen, who had gone to the help of Ethiopia against the Italians thirty years before; but he was away for some days in September, revisiting Ethiopia, and he resigned on 26 September. Plenty more was to be heard from von Rosen later.

The much-enlarged airlift to Biafra was a long way from starting when, following the worldwide publicity about starvation, several governments and humanitarian bodies engaged in urgent new discussions of how to deliver aid. The Federal Government had already said it would allow Red Cross supplies to be delivered by road to the front line and across it into Biafran territory.[43] It continued to propose this, while another proposal was for delivery by river boats from the Niger Delta to Oguta in Biafran territory. But after the Biafran government appealed to the world for aid on 13 June, Biafra Radio on 17 June broadcast a declaration that no food could be sent through Nigeria, because it could be poisoned.[44] The Biafrans did not win much outside support for this outlandish claim; in fact there was unease among Biafra's sympathisers. The Biafran government also made another objection, that arrangements for overland delivery of relief supplies from Nigerian into Biafran territory would require the dismantling of Biafran defences along the route chosen, and the Nigerian army could exploit this to send in troops behind the Red Cross lorries. This objection had a bit more support, but still not enough to prevent a distinct cooling of sympathy for the Biafrans; *The Times* on 26 June accused Ojukwu of "using the misery of his own people to extract diplomatic and other advantages to counterbalance defeats in battle". Amid the arguments on this subject, many failed to examine whether the overland supply route was practicable at all. An article in *West Africa*, noting that "This situation has long been predictable" though it had turned out to be worse than predicted, pointed out that the route from Lagos to the front line would be a very long one via Makurdi, and Nigeria had very few lorries to spare.[45] The article suggested an alternative route northwards from Port Harcourt.

However, the overland route from the north might have been feasible; the FMG proposed flying supplies initially into Enugu, not far from the front, and announced on 8 July a detailed proposal for transport to Awgu and then southwards to the front line. A "no man's land" would have had to be established along the road with Red Cross representatives at each end, checking the lorries through and keeping an eye on the troops stationed behind—successful cheating would not have been easy—and this would have required a local truce; but obviously the FMG was ready to accept that, despite its rejection of any general ceasefire without a prior Biafran surrender. The food delivered would probably have included African vegetables besides dried milk and other industrial high-protein foods, and if yams and cassava were bought in the area to the north of the enclave—a major food-producing area—or other parts of Nigeria, that would encourage the Biafrans' genuine or contrived fears of contamination. It might have been necessary to airlift those food items too, from outside Nigeria to the collection point, at high cost. The big problem, as pointed out in the magazine, would have been finding enough lorries, with all the demands of the military and ordinary civilian needs like produce transport. In retrospect, another problem can be seen, which I do not remember anyone discussing at the time—there was bound to be opposition within Nigeria to so much effort to "feed the rebels", and how long could that operation have been continued? There was also the inefficiency, obstruction and negligence shown in Nigeria even in delivery of relief for people on the federal side, as in South-Eastern State. Even so, the overland route was feasible, given enough vehicles. But one fact evident at the time was that Biafrans—that is, Biafrans who were not starving themselves—saw it as a humiliation to be fed by their enemies.

With the agonising delays in relief for the starving, protests in Britain mounted. At the end of June, Leslie Kirkley, general secretary of Oxfam, visited Biafra; on his return he said, "Unless we pull out all the stops … we will have a terrifying disaster on our hands. By then two million may have died." Wilson's government had to do something, and during 5–20 July it sent Lord Hunt—formerly Sir John Hunt, organiser of the successful expedition to reach the summit of Mount Everest in 1953—at the head of a mission to Nigeria to assess relief needs, for which the government committed £250,000. These efforts were for the benefit of people on the Nigerian side only.

On that side, Oxfam sent its own team to South-Eastern State (only the second time Oxfam, which normally sends help to others working on the ground, had worked in an actual scene of famine); the team found the appalling situation already noted, but worked to provide aid at Itu, distributing ICRC and UNICEF rations of milk, stockfish, garri, rice, beans and corn soya milk, until conditions improved in late December.[46] While Oxfam, Caritas and others continued to send help to the Nigerian side, the situation of the beleaguered, starving enclave had its special appeal for the public; it was for "Biafra" that people wanted to give. And this caused problems with the FMG.

West Africa on 6 July 1968 said that while Ojukwu was accused of playing politics with hunger, in the hope of getting British arms sales to Nigeria stopped, "If the Federal Government makes every effort to relieve that hunger it will save Ibo lives and fulfil its responsibilities towards all Nigerians." Yes, all Nigerians—in the Federal Government's view, Biafra had no legal existence and thus the people in areas under the secessionists' control were Nigerians, so that the humanitarian agencies in those areas were saving the lives of *Nigerians*. But that consideration did not stop constant attacks on the humanitarians in the Nigerian media, which cast doubts on their sincerity. On 19 July, Gowon summoned the relief agencies' representatives in Lagos and warned Caritas and Oxfam in particular against political involvement. Kirkley reassured Nigeria that "An appeal on purely humanitarian grounds … does not involve us in political judgements on the rights and wrongs of this tragic situation".[47] Nigerian suspicions were increased by a suggestion that RAF planes could drop supplies onto Biafran territory; it was apparently this (accounts vary) that led to a warning by the FMG that unauthorised flights over Nigerian air space would be shot down (in fact an RAF Hercules took 18 tons of relief supplies to the Nigerian side in July).

What riled Nigerians greatly was the use of the name of Biafra in charitable organisations' fundraising in the West. Appeals for funds for Biafra were in fact calls for help for starving people in the area that was called Biafra at that moment, and probably most of the fund-donating public understood them that way, but Nigerians could see them as expressing political support for Biafran self-determination; Ogundipe said this in a protest letter to Kirkley on 28 June 1968.

Nigerians who had not lived in the West, or (like Ogundipe, perhaps) did not know that very genuine humanitarian sentiment can be aroused there among people who know nothing whatever about the people they pity and want to help, could easily see such sentiment as concealing a hidden agenda. Gowon did accept that the humanitarian sentiments were genuine, and in practice his government merely grumbled when the Western charities continued to use the name of Biafra in appeals. After all, what were the alternatives? To appeal for funds to help the starving in "the Nigeria–Biafra war", or "Nigeria and Biafra", would have seemed no better in Lagos. And whatever wording was used in appeals, Caritas, Oxfam and other agencies saved lives on the Nigerian side of the front also, making up to some extent for the very inadequate official relief efforts. These were eventually improved under the direction of a National Rehabilitation Commission, set up in July 1968 under Timothy Omo-Bare, who had headed a National Rehabilitation Unit in the Cabinet Office established earlier, and allocated £1 million.[48]

Talks at Niamey and Addis Ababa

Following the failure of the talks arranged by the Commonwealth Secretariat at Kampala, it was the Organisation of African Unity (OAU) Consultative Committee on Nigeria—which had achieved nothing thus far except a trip to Lagos to declare support for Gowon—that got the two sides to agree to meet for more talks. These were at Niamey, capital of the Niger Republic; the populated southern part of that country is almost an extension of Northern Nigeria, and its president, Hamani Diori, was strongly pro-Nigerian, but in a non-geographical sense Niger was close to France, and both sides accepted the venue.

The Niamey talks, held from 15 to 26 July, were different from the Kampala talks in that both General Gowon and Colonel Ojukwu attended, though not for long periods and not at the same time. Awolowo headed the federal delegation at the start, while other delegates included Femi Okunnu, commissioner for works, and Allison Ayida; many of the top Biafrans attended, including Nnamdi Azikiwe, Michael Okpara, Louis Mbanefo, Eni Njoku and N.U. Akpan. Gowon flew in on the 16th and then the 17th, Ojukwu (boarding Houphouët-Boigny's personal Mystère 20 at Libreville) on the 19th. Five of the six heads of state of the OAU Consultative Committee were there, the Congo sending a deputy foreign minister, and the OAU secretary general Diallo Telli played an active part. These talks were intended to prepare the way for full-scale peace talks, and it was agreed to hold these the following month at Addis Ababa. In Niamey, unlike Kampala, the question of relief for victims of the war was actively discussed, and agreement was nearly reached on an overland "mercy corridor" from federal-held to Biafran-held territory; but Njoku for Biafra demanded an armed international force to police the "corridor", while the FMG agreed to policing by civilians from relief organisations or the OAU.[49]

Before the talks at Addis Ababa began, there were some further discussions about relief. As an alternative to the overland route it recommended, the FMG came round to accepting in principle an enlarged relief airlift; this had the advantage of simplicity, and although it would be expensive, the money would have been found. The FMG insisted on the right to inspect the cargoes, but this was not new; the Nigerian consul in Santa Isabel on Fernando Po had been inspecting ICRC cargoes flown to Biafra for months, and the Biafrans had accepted the arrangement; since April, the Red Cross had been flying in regularly.[50] Nigeria insisted that if it authorised an enlarged airlift to Uli, this must take place by day, which would be better anyway to deliver the vast amounts needed, and the Biafrans did not oppose this. But arguments continued while people continued to die in vast numbers, with Hank Wharton (whose role in this situation seems unclear, and who gave priority to arms anyway) and the church relief organisations unable to make much difference at that stage. Meanwhile, Nigeria's Third Division advanced steadily northwards into Igbo country on the way to Aba, where many of Biafra's government functions had their centre.

The talks at Addis Ababa were opened on 5 August by Emperor Haile Selassie, who played an active part as they went on. Ojukwu attended on the first day and gave a two-hour speech, a long historical account to justify Biafra's stance.[51] Enahoro gave another long speech in rebuttal, as head of the federal delegation, and then another speech even longer than Ojukwu's;[52] Gowon had declined the emperor's invitation. After Ojukwu and others left, Eni Njoku headed the Biafrans, who also included Christopher Mojekwu, Matthew Mbu and Pius Okigbo; Allison Ayida, Femi Okunnu and Anthony Asika were among the Nigerian delegates, for some of the time at least. These talks were meant to get on to the heart of the matter, the war and how to end it; hence, presumably, the long, grand-standing speeches. The prospects for bridging the gap between the two sides' positions were very poor from the start. Enahoro repeated that secession must be renounced, while also repeating the FMG's agreement to an external force to be present at the ceasefire and surrender, and saying the areas now held by the secessionists could be policed by Igbo police. But Njoku's proposals on 9 August included, first on the list, acceptance of Biafra's sovereignty. David Williams, editor of *West Africa*, was at Addis Ababa and spoke to Njoku, who emphasised that for Biafrans their people's security was most important; Biafran spokesmen had said this before, and it had led some to hope they might accept an alternative to full independence, but now Njoku said security meant control of their own army, which is a prerogative of a sovereign state.[53] The gap had not been bridged at all, but the talks went on for a time, and turned their attention to relief.

The FMG was informed, apparently at Addis Ababa, that an agreement had been signed in Biafra between the Ojukwu government and the ICRC for use of an airstrip for daylight relief flights. On 10 August the ICRC's DC-6 was fired on, and it suspended its aid flights, but on the 14th August, Lindt, the ICRC's commissioner for Nigeria, said daylight flights to Biafra were expected to start soon, to an airstrip offered by the Biafrans, and he seemed optimistic about federal approval.[54] Lindt, however, said the airstrip was not yet ready. According to an account published the following year by Frederick Forsyth, who was in Biafra, the Red Cross installed electrical equipment and a fully fitted control tower at Obilago airstrip, and on 13 August signed an agreement with Ojukwu on the use of that airstrip for daylight relief flights; troops were moved away from the airstrip, and big Red Cross signs were painted on the ground, but then the Nigerian Air Force attacked Obilago on 20, 24 and 31 August.[55] *West Africa* quoted a Reuters report of one raid on the airstrip in the 24 August issue.

Gowon said, in an interview with the editor reported in that same issue, that the airstrip offered for the aid flights did not exist, and the Federal Government was supposed to agree to equipment being flown in for it. He presumably meant that the airstrip, being basically a stretch of road, was not then able to function as an airport. Anyway the FMG said it was unacceptable that "any portion of Nigeria should be internationalised and handed over to a foreign agency".[56] But an ICRC statement said that, in view of the increasing urgency, "the ICRC, in close cooperation with National Red Cross Societies and other relief organisations, will nevertheless assume responsibility for taking every possible step to deliver the most urgently required relief supplies to the famished population".[57] This was ambiguous; it could be taken to mean that the ICRC, which had always adhered to the strictest legality so far, was ready to go ahead without clearance from Lagos. This episode remains obscure; maybe the ICRC somehow obtained equipment to get the airstrip in working order, or maybe the Biafrans did so through some other channel, as they had possibly done for Uli earlier. But it is certain that Lagos rejected use of Obilago, and Gowon told the editor of the magazine that it was because Obilago was on the main road from Afikpo to Okigwi, and as a demilitarised zone it would block the way for Nigerian forces to advance along that road. In arguing thus, the FMG would of course consider Obilago airstrip, not accepted by it for relief flights, as a military target. Very blatantly, the Federal Government blocked a proposal for relief delivery to Biafra for its own military reasons; its forces were making progress then.

Maybe the Biafrans, on their side, had proposed Obilago for their own military reasons. The FMG said daylight relief flights could go to Uli, and Gowon asked in the interview why the Biafrans did not agree to that. Two weeks later, Gowon said the government would agree to "a neutralised airstrip in the Uli-Ihiala area under strict conditions of control which will ensure that it is needed only for handling relief supplies". But in an apparently separate statement, the FMG said it would approve Red Cross daylight flights to Uli for ten days from 5 September, apparently not insisting on neutralisation (which would have meant, if enforced somehow, that the Biafrans would have to stop the arms flights landing there).[58] The Biafrans did not agree to any federal proposals for Uli. In fact they suspected that their enemies were secretly planning to send a bomber in among the relief planes to cause major damage to Uli airstrip, enough to deny it to the night-time arms flights. For a time, both arms flights and relief flights used both Uli and Obilago (the ICRC had resumed its flights); then the Nigerian forces captured Obilago on 23 September.[59] That settled the question of Obilago, but the Biafrans still rejected the federal proposal on Uli.

On that the Biafrans certainly let their suspicions run away with them; the chances of a Nigerian bomber slipping in among the Red Cross planes unnoticed were very small—the Red Cross pilots would have seen and reported it—and the world's eyes would have been on the relief operation; a raid on Uli during that operation would have shocked even backers of Nigeria and put Gowon flagrantly in the wrong and in international trouble. No agreement was ever reached on daylight airlifts, or on the river or land routes which the ICRC said were the only ones able to deliver sufficient quantities.[60] Meanwhile, the Nordchurchaid flights came in regularly at night without bothering to ask for Nigerian permission, but could not yet stop the starvation.

France declares support for Biafra

On 31 July 1968 a statement in Paris after a meeting of the cabinet under the new prime minister, Maurice Couve de Murville, said the Nigerian conflict should be resolved "on the basis of the right of people to self-determination"; it said "the blood spilt and the suffering borne for more than a year by the population of Biafra show their will to assert themselves as a people".[61] This confirmed what had been steadily becoming clearer in recent months. While the French Foreign Ministry on the Quai d'Orsay strove to maintain correct relations with Lagos, another agency of the French government aided the Biafrans. That was the office of the secretary general for African affairs at the Presidency, Jacques Foccart. One of the most prominent Gaullists for two decades, he was responsible for one side of the close relations established under de Gaulle with the governments of ex-French African states.

Foccart had for long been involved in the seamy secret or semi-secret side of Gaullist politics. He was a leader of the Service d'Action Civique (SAC), a corps of strong-arm men supporting de Gaulle, and was linked with the violent counter-terrorist group called unofficially the Barbouzes, which fought, by its own methods, against the French-Algerian terrorist force trying in 1961–2 to halt Algerian independence and assassinate de Gaulle, the Organisation Armée Secrète (OAS). As de Gaulle's right-hand man for Africa, Foccart was involved again in intelligence and security activity. He did not head the official secret service, the Service de Documentation Extérieure et de Contre-Espionnage (SDECE); his reputation as a spook, an *homme de l'ombre*, arose in part from the intelligence and security links run by him between France and the mostly dictatorial governments in the French sphere in Africa. Foccart's *réseau* (network) helped keep those governments in power, foiling actions and plans by their opponents. And from 1967 it extended its operations to help the Biafrans.

Foccart's network had close links with President Houphouët-Boigny of Ivory Coast and with Gabon, where after the death of President Mba in November 1967 Albert Bongo became president. French aid to Biafra was organised by Foccart, Bongo and Houphouët-Boigny, with two leading Foccart lieutenants: Jean Mauricheau-Beaupré, in Ivory Coast, and Maurice Delauney, France's ambassador to Gabon (his position shows that the separation between official French foreign policy and Foccart's parallel activity was not total). At the head of it all was General de Gaulle, to whom Foccart answered directly.

Much of this activity was already known when Jacques Foccart himself confirmed it decades later, in reminiscences published in the form of an extended interview in two volumes.[62] He confirmed suspicions that his network had arranged for mercenaries to go to Biafra, saying Delauney and Mauricheau-Beaupré handled this.[63] As French mercenaries had gone there in late 1967, the Foccart network was already working for the Biafrans then. He recalled that three weeks after the start of the war de Gaulle said, "We should not intervene, or give the impression of having chosen sides. But all things considered, the breaking up of Nigeria is desirable, and if Biafra succeeds, it will not be a bad thing."[64] Behind his words lay the general's lasting resentment against Britain and America ("*les Anglo-Saxons*") going back to the Second World War. There was also the considerably older French resentment against Britain over the colonial partition of Africa in which Britain was thought to have secured the best bits; that colonial view survived African independence.

In addition, Nigeria had angered de Gaulle by breaking off relations with France over its nuclear tests in the Algerian Sahara in 1961. The five-year diplomatic breach (ended only in 1966) had not affected economic relations, and there was nothing economic in de Gaulle's opposition to Nigeria. It was generally supposed to be due in part to a fear that Nigeria, as a large and apparently promising country, would become a leader in Africa and lead smaller and less well-endowed francophone states astray from their allegiance to France. In fact Nigeria under Tafawa Balewa had not sought to be a leader among African states as Nkrumah's Ghana had sought to be, and certainly had not threatened any other African state. The only neighbour state with which it had had any problem was Cameroon, whose president, Ahmadou Ahidjo, resented the decision of British Northern Cameroons to join Nigeria rather than Cameroon in the 1961 referendum, and that problem did not affect generally good relations; Ahidjo supported Nigeria throughout the war.

Nigerians were clearly right to be suspicious of France's role from an early date, though nothing eventually came of the proposed Rothschild Bank deal. But Nigerian commentators were mistaken in thinking that the recognition of Biafra by Ivory Coast and Gabon was simply due to French pressure on African lackeys. It was common then and later to assume that in relations between African states and major powers the former were simply serfs or puppets; although it could be a Western colonialist reflex, this assumption was made by Africans also. Houphouët-Boigny, often seen in Africa as a faithful servant of France, was in fact a forceful character, and it was he who urged de Gaulle to support the Biafrans. Foccart said Houphouët-Boigny had "constantly put pressure on France", and without his persistence France's help for the Biafrans would have been "more moderate"; de Gaulle was "very reluctant" but agreed to some help if it was kept secret.[65]

A glance at the rest of francophone Africa shows that most of the states there did not recognise Biafra. No African leader loved France more than President Senghor of Senegal, but although he showed some sympathy for the Biafrans, he accepted the FMG as legal ruler of all Nigeria. So did President Eyadéma of Togo and President Keïta of Mali. And so did President Tombalbaye of Chad, who called in French troops, to add to a permanent French garrison, to deal with a serious rebellion, or serious unrest at least, in August 1968 (the Nigerian press naturally noted how France was supporting rebellion in one African country and suppressing it in another). Clearly de Gaulle did not really press his African allies into supporting Biafra; they showed independence in foreign policy in other ways also.[66]

While some help was given to the Biafrans from an early date, large-scale arms supplies seem to have started in mid-1968. On 3 August a *West Africa* editorial said Biafra "will clearly hope to get arms from France"; it surely did, and was not disappointed. On 24 August the magazine quoted Lloyd Garrison, one of the most respected journalists covering the Biafran war, reporting from Paris in the *New York Times* that an Air Gabon DC-3 was flying to Biafra from Libreville every night, carrying arms, ammunition and food for the Biafran army; a DC-4 would soon be added to this airlift. Air Gabon was the national airline of Gabon, which recognised Biafra as a sovereign state entitled to acquire arms. But the Libreville–Uli arms airlift, soon confirmed by many reports, was taken to be a French operation to arm the Biafrans, and it clearly was.[67] In Paris the official line was that the embargo on arms sales to both sides remained in force. It was soon reported that, to maintain this pretence, Ivory Coast shipped arms to the Biafrans and France sent arms to replace them. Foccart recalled that de Gaulle agreed to this subterfuge.[68] But he said the arms being sent from Ivory Coast were old captured Second World War weapons; were they the only ones passed to the Biafrans? Possibly other French weapons were sent to Biafra, maybe with a stopover in Abidjan, with creative paperwork saying they came from Ivory Coast. Foccart did not mention any similar subterfuge in the case of Gabon, but said the arms supplies were organised mainly by Delauney and Mauricheau-Beaupré.[69] Foccart evidently ran the show.

The French press took a keen interest in the war, and was generally very pro-Biafran, but possibly no more so than the British and

American press; when Foccart was asked much later who had organised the press campaign in support of Biafra, he said, "I think it was spontaneous," while adding that "we" helped to take reporters and television teams to Libreville and "from there, via the networks serving Biafra".[70] There is no reason to doubt this. In the *West Africa* office we saw a number of the French press reports, usually very favourable to Biafra; an article in the left-wing magazine *L'Evènement* said the Biafrans must be sent arms, not food[71] (presumably the author was ignorant of, or not satisfied with, the French arms that were in fact being sent). The pro-Biafrans were not unchallenged in Paris; two French reporters who went to the front, Jean Wolf and Claude Brovelli, wrote a pro-federal book afterwards.[72] *Le Canard Enchaîné* had some sympathy for the Biafrans, but not for the de Gaulle–Foccart policy; when the war ended, it had a heading, "Biafra: Les crocodiles sont en larmes." The Paris weekly *Jeune Afrique*, which we read regularly in the *West Africa* office, was largely on the Nigerian side. It had been started in 1960 by the Tunisian Béchir Ben Yahmed as *Afrique-Action*, published in Tunis and backing the Algerian National Liberation Front. It was moved to Paris and given its new name later, retaining its links with the French left; it also continued its North African orientation, but it covered sub-Saharan Africa as well, not only the French-speaking countries, and was the leading magazine for francophone Africa. Another defender of the Federal Nigerian case in Paris was the Nigerian film-maker and writer Ola Balogun, who studied film-making in Paris from 1966 to 1968 and then, after working in the film unit of the federal Ministry of Information in Lagos, returned to Paris as press attaché in the Nigerian embassy in 1969.

On 9 September President de Gaulle himself defended France's support for Biafra at a press conference. By that time the Nigerian forces had taken Aba—of this more shortly—but de Gaulle could have seen this as a reason not to assume that the Biafrans were rapidly losing the war, but to offer them more help to stop that happening and spite the "Anglo-Saxons": the British parliament had just debated the arms sales to Nigeria and failed to stop them, while the US government, which had never supplied any arms in this war, in late July urged the Biafrans to admit defeat.[73] In addition, the Addis Ababa talks, which had dragged on without reaching any agreement on relief or anything else, broke up early in September; the emperor, who had met the Nigerian and Biafran delegations jointly or separately over 35 times, said he hoped the "few remaining details" on relief for Biafra could be worked out by the Consultative Committee at Algiers,[74] where the OAU's annual gathering was to take place straight afterwards (the Council of Ministers on 4–11 September, the summit on 13–16 September).

President de Gaulle said, "I am not sure that the system of federation which replaces in certain places the concept of colonisation is always a very good one, or very practical … Why should the Ibos, who are mostly Christian, who inhabit Southern areas, who have their own language, be subordinate to another ethnic group in the federation?" He claimed that the Federation, to reduce the rebellion, employed "war, blockade, extermination, famine". However, France was not now giving Biafra recognition, as that was a matter for Africans, but it "cannot be excluded in the future". He suggested that the Nigerian Federation might transform into "some sort of union or confederation which could reconcile the right of Biafra to dispose of itself and the links which would remain between it and the whole of Nigeria".[75]

The arms and genocide issues

In Britain, the summer of 1968 was the summer of Biafra. Nobody over 60 who was in Britain then can forget how the reports of the Biafran famine and the terrible photos filled the newspapers, with many television and cinema newsreel reports added. It was the number-one public issue. There were appeals and collections for Biafran relief all over the country. *West Africa* recorded a very small part of all this activity, for example schoolchildren organising a "mile of pennies" in Nottingham to aid the Biafrans,[76] and a collection in Luton which raised funds for the airlifting of over 80,000 tons of baby food.[77] Some people wanted to do more than contribute money. I went to a press conference in the *Daily Mirror* building where two men, one or both ex-RAF, talked of plans to fly food into Biafra aboard a light aircraft, an ill-thought-out scheme that predictably failed; it may have been devised when the churches' flights into Uli were still being organised and were far from sufficient, and the discussions of other ways to deliver relief were getting nowhere.

That deadlock over relief added to public anguish, which turned to anger directed above all against the Wilson government. There were marches and lobbies of MPs, all directed at one aim: to end the government's support for the Nigerian government, especially its arms supplies. That demand brought together people of all political parties and all trends of opinion. There were the relatively small groups of activists, the Britain–Biafra Association and the separate Save Biafra Committee (later renamed the Save Biafra Campaign), but there were far greater numbers of churchmen, politicians, journalists and ordinary citizens supporting the cause.

Those demanding an end to arms for Nigeria did not always, or even usually, believe that Nigeria was committing or planning genocide. But following the *Spectator*'s editorial of 31 May, Auberon Waugh, its political correspondent, visited Biafra in July; he was to be one of the Biafrans' strongest supporters, convinced that they were facing genocide. Another prominent supporter of the genocide accusation in Britain was Mrs Suzanne Cronje, a South African anti-apartheid émigré freelance journalist. Other writers alleging genocide, mainly in the US, are quoted by Chinua Achebe, in his lament for Biafra published the year before his death in 2013.[78]

The word "genocide", coined to describe the systematic murder of the Jews of Europe by Nazi Germany, was adopted officially in the 1948 Genocide Convention. Its use was bound to arouse memories of the Nazis' greatest crime; the only comparable crime on such a scale in history until then, the extermination of the Armenians in Turkey in 1915–16, was little remembered around the world. Nobody knowing about the fate of the Jews and the Armenians could have believed that anything similar was going on in Nigeria. The Committee of Union and Progress regime in Turkey and later the Nazi regime in Germany ordered the mass rounding up of the victims for deportation over short or long distances, to be methodically murdered without the outside world seeing; and despite attempts at secrecy by efficient police states, the facts were known to the world within weeks. In Nigeria such a systematic operation could not have been organised and could not have remained secret for even half a day. And nobody could have imagined anything in Nigeria like what was to happen when an African state did carry out genocide later, in Rwanda in 1994, a planned genocide in which there were no preliminary deportations, and no attempt at secrecy. In the Nigerian conflict there was never any reason to believe that genocide was going on; in fact it was never even contemplated.

Why were allegations of genocide believed? Partly because of a failure to distinguish war crimes from genocide. War crimes, including mass killing of civilians and POWs, have regularly occurred throughout history; they were never defensible but were not the same as the planned, thorough, deliberate mass murder of a particular people, the complete or at least overwhelming destruction of that people. Genocide is a quite exceptional crime which, on the largest scale, may have occurred only three times, all in the 20th century. In all three cases the genocides, while they took place during wars, were quite distinct from military operations.[79] Thus they were different from military actions which may kill great numbers but whose aim is military victory, not extermination; in the case of German South-West Africa (Namibia) in 1904–7, those responsible for the operations had a clear intention to kill all the Herero and Nama peoples, which justifies the description as a genocide, but in many other cases, probably the majority, the victors may have cared nothing about how many died but still did not aim to kill everyone.

Many massacres do not make one genocide. Britain enforced a rigid "hunger blockade" against Germany in the First World War, and carried out massive indiscriminate air raids on German cities in the Second; these were major war crimes, each killed hundreds of thousands, but they were not genocide—the Allies did not make a decision to kill every single German. In the Nigerian war, the federal forces carried out highly criminal air raids on civilian areas, and killed civilians on the ground on several occasions, as at Asaba; these were war crimes, but were not genocide.

Of course the main reason for the Biafrans' fear of genocide, which was certainly genuine for very many of them, was the memory of the Northern Nigeria pogroms. It was natural for survivors and witnesses of an air raid by a MiG on a crowded market to think that "the Hausas" were coming to finish the job of murder. Supporters of the federal side should always have admitted this before protesting against the allegations of genocide. However, those making the allegations needed to go beyond the traumatic memory of the pogroms and show that systematic murder of Igbos was being organised regularly, as state policy, during the military operations. Air raids and crimes like Asaba did not show this.

Some concerned people expressed fears not of genocide, but of massive punitive violence after a Nigerian victory. Conor Cruise O'Brien, after his visit to Biafra, urged the United Nations to arrange an immediate truce to prevent "mass murder on a scale unparalleled as yet in Africa".[80] The editor of *The Sun* said on 13 June 1968, "If the war does not end, there could well be massacre as well as famine." Probably many people had such fears. While real genocides have been few, brutal indiscriminate reprisals after a victory have quite often occurred. Examples in recent history before the Biafra conflict included Spain after Franco's victory in 1939 and Algeria after the end of the war of independence in 1962, with great slaughter of people accused of siding with the French. In sub-Saharan Africa, insurgency had recently met brutal response from the Portuguese in Angola, Mozambique and Guinea-Bissau and from African governments in Cameroon and the Congo. In the case of Nigeria, the unpunished pogroms, the lawless violence of soldiers in Lagos after the July 1966 coup, and the virulent tone of the Nigerian media did not encourage confidence in General Gowon's words about amnesty, reconciliation and welcoming back the Eastern "brothers". But although fears of mass punitive action were less extreme than fears of genocide, they were mistaken even so. Gowon's words were categorical and often repeated before a watchful world community, which, after all that had taken place, could justifiably keep a close eye on what happened with a federal victory—whether the victorious troops would be under proper discipline, and whether relief efforts would be better than they were in federally occupied areas during the war.[81]

Fears about that were not entirely without cause. Killings of civilians following Nigerian victories occurred often enough to justify concern about officers as well as common soldiers in an army which during the war expanded at an incredible rate, from 8,000 to 200,000 according to one estimate (others were considerably lower: 120,000–

130,000), making proper control of its conduct very difficult, if it was even adequately attempted. Frederick Forsyth and other reporters saw clear proof of repeated massacres by Nigerian troops of the Second and Third Divisions.[82] It can seem indecent quibbling about definitions when the subject is mass murder, to argue whether these killings amounted to genocide or at least, as Forsyth argued in 1969, justified preliminary UN investigation into possible genocide.[83] But the difference between sporadic killings in the course of military operations, on the one hand, and planned extermination, on the other, is important. The former, however criminal, can at least sometimes be expected to stop when those committing them achieve victory. Pitiless brutality in the pursuit of victory can be followed by proper treatment of the defeated afterwards, as in Japan in 1945.

The accusation of genocide came to be based, after the onset of mass starvation became known around the world, on that consequence of the war and the blockade. Military operations, even if directed against hostile armed forces only, can lead to mass flight of whole populations and immense suffering with many deaths; this happened, for example, in the flight of the Serbs before the Austrian forces in the winter of 1915–16, and something similar happened in Biafra. But in the Biafran case there was also the blockade halting food supplies. In truth, the Federal Government could not deny responsibility for the onset of starvation: anyone deciding to wage war and impose a blockade is primarily responsible for the consequences, whatever the other side does or does not do.

The Federal Government in fact placed the secessionist territory under siege. There have been sieges throughout history, and every time the aim has been to starve the defenders until they surrender. Only in the 1949 Geneva Convention did the nations of the world take the first steps (very limited) towards outlawing the use of starvation as a weapon in war in that time-honoured way. I do not recall any of us on *West Africa* taking the trouble to look up the relevant parts of what was usually called the Geneva Convention, in the singular, but what in fact consisted then of four Geneva Conventions signed on 12 August 1949. The fourth Convention, "Relative to the Protection of Civilian Persons in Times of War", declared in article 59, "If the whole or part of the population of an occupied territory is inadequately supplied, the Occupying Power shall agree to relief schemes on behalf of the said population, and shall facilitate them by all the means at its disposal." However, this seemed to outlaw only the starving of civilians after their territory is occupied, not the use of starvation as a weapon to make them submit. And it was not clear whether that article applied to occupation which is being resisted—whether the occupying power must facilitate civilian relief in an area of resistance. But in any case, those provisions only applied to international wars, not civil wars.

However, all the four Conventions had a common article 3 on "Conflicts Not of an International Character", which declared, "Persons taking no active part in the hostilities, including members of armed forces who have laid down their arms and those placed *hors de combat* by sickness, wounds, detention, or any other cause, shall in all circumstances be treated humanely, without any adverse distinction founded on race, colour, religion or faith, sex, birth or wealth, or any other similar criteria."

"Treated humanely": that was vague, but sufficient. That article seemed to cover—at least it did not exclude—treatment of people outside the control of a state's forces. Blockading a rebel area and preventing any food from reaching civilians known to be starving in large numbers there cannot be called humane treatment. Can it be called genocide? Several Western commentators said so about Nigeria from the middle of 1968. The starvation and the blockade became the main counts in the accusation of genocide. That article of the Convention could also apply to the Biafrans: blocking food supplies for their own people was certainly not humane treatment. However, it must be recalled that the FMG originally ordered the blockade.

The siege of the Biafran enclave was not total; people could and did cross the lines frequently. The FMG did want to stop all cross-border trade, but it did not stop people coming over from Biafran-held to federal-held areas; on the contrary, it welcomed this and accused the Biafran regime of preventing it, which probably did happen on some occasions at least. Lamentably, those who crossed over in that way did not find adequate help, but they were still encouraged to cross over, and a number did. So the Nigerian authorities did not want everyone in the Biafran enclave to starve. But inviting individuals to cross the lines while not helping those staying (willingly or under compulsion) on the Biafran side would still be using starvation as a weapon—unless the FMG agreed to the delivery of relief supplies through the blockade. And that it did.

General Gowon's offer to allow food and medical supplies for civilians to pass across the lines into Biafran territory was praised by many as a wonderful magnanimous gesture. But it should rather be seen as an obligation. If the Federal Government had flatly refused to allow any relief to reach civilians on the other side, after enforcing its own blockade for a whole year with very obvious consequences, that would have been a serious war crime—though probably not genocide. The FMG proved by its actions that it was following the Geneva Conventions and natural justice in this case—unless it imposed conditions that were totally unreasonable.

Thus the question of relief supply routes into Biafra, already mentioned, was vital. It came to a head in the middle of 1968, and then again in the middle of 1969, without being forgotten in the meantime. It aroused strong passions among the belligerents and among the millions in other countries following the terrible story of starvation. Each side was highly suspicious of the other's proposals. The outside world, anguished to read of starvation continuing unabated, would have welcomed any agreement on any means to deliver the relief needed. Who, in mid-1968, was to blame for the lack of agreement? Fifty years later, I would say both sides, but the Nigerian side more, as its objection to the use of Obilago airstrip for relief flights was, quite openly, that this would block a planned advance by the federal army; yet the FMG had said it was ready to close the road south from Awgu to military operations, and only one part of the many-pronged federal advance would have been blocked at Obilago. However, the Biafrans could have overcome their suspicions and agreed to daylight relief flights to Uli; they had no good reason to oppose that proposal.

The Biafrans, contrary to the myth of their superhuman propaganda skills, did not convince all sympathetic people on this matter. In addition, the fact that a rich few among them were far from starving must have become known, for at one point in 1968 I recall a cartoon in *Peace News*—a vehement campaigner against arms sales to

Nigeria—showing a skeletal child and nearby a fat man munching roast chicken and saying, "We Biafrans would rather starve than surrender!" I do not recall whether any Biafran leader ever said those exact words, but the mass starvation did not bring the Biafran regime anywhere near giving up the struggle. That regime and Gowon's both put military and political considerations above all others.

The accusation of genocide was reasonably doubted even by those very critical of the FMG, but they could still oppose the arms sales. With many more reporters now going to Biafra, where they were shown captured British weaponry, it was obvious that the Nigerian army depended on British small arms and armoured cars (Ferret, Saladin, Saracen) and some other equipment. Besides licensing exports by private firms, the government provided arms from its own stocks—20 Saracens in July 1968, for example.[84] It was slow to admit this, and even slower to admit how heavily the Nigerians depended on Britain for arms. The extent of the dependence was concealed, no doubt to avoid admitting that the Nigerian war effort, whose effects were so shocking, would not have been possible without British arms. The protests continued even as the federal forces pushed the Biafrans further back. Besides Britain, there were constant protests in France, the Netherlands, West Germany and other Western countries.

I believe not all opponents and supporters of the British arms sales fully examined the worldwide questions that the debate raised. The heart of the matter was the unequal distribution of wealth in the world. Industrialised countries could afford armaments industries producing aircraft, warships, tanks and other military hardware in ever newer and more expensive versions. African countries could not. They sought to establish industries, but naturally wanted industries producing cotton textiles, groundnut oil, cement, beer and refined petroleum products, not weapons of war. Nobody in his senses would have advised the newly independent states, with all they had to spend on the urgent needs of their people, to establish the sort of "defence industries" developed in the West; they might at the most set up small arms factories like Nigeria's at Kaduna. And yet those states all had armed forces which needed adequate equipment. There was no choice but for them to buy this from Western Europe, the Soviet bloc, the US, Israel and a few other suppliers. Of course these expensive purchases have themselves been a drain on the struggling economies of African states; this has troubled some Africans, but it will not stop until perhaps, in the distant future, African states agree to scrap national armed forces. Meanwhile, those national armed forces depend on arms supplies from the industrialised world.

And the se supplies are subject to special arms export licensing in the supplier countries; where it is decided that licences to private exporters should be granted, there is no obvious reason why supplies from government stocks should not be added. Commonly, licences in Britain and other countries are granted without difficulty, and decisions on licensing are of course usually based on either commercial or strategic and foreign policy considerations. But there is always the possibility of arms exports coming under scrutiny at the top political level, which in turn gives democratic parliaments influence over them. Thus arms exports to a particular country can be examined from a plainly moral point of view: does it deserve to have British arms, especially if it is using them to wage war? African customers for British arms do not like to be subjected to such moral scrutiny. They perceive a sort of discrimination: Britain, France and America can wage any wars they like because they manufacture their own weapons, but African states which cannot do that must be judged to see whether they deserve to buy necessary weapons for war. Judging whether an African government deserves to have arms to suppress a rebellion can seem like arrogant assertion of the wealthier countries' power, a sort of neo-colonialism. In the case of the Nigerian war, resentment about British arms came first from the federal side: how could the British dare even to hesitate before supplying arms to a friendly Commonwealth country facing a rebellion? This argument seems to have put the British government under moral or emotional pressure; its own statements suggest that the decision to arm Nigeria was due mainly to this. But of course there is the other side to the question.

Moral protest at the international arms trade has been voiced strongly in Western countries since the 1930s campaign against "merchants of death", if not earlier. Even governments of arms-producing countries have come to accept, at least sometimes, the moral argument that arms exports fuel conflicts overseas and may need to be curbed to help restore peace. Shortly before the Nigerian war, Britain halted arms supplies to India and Pakistan when they went to war in 1965. Such actions will always anger one or the other belligerent, but that should not be an overriding consideration. Arms exports to countries at war encourage continuation of war and reduce any incentive to make peace. Halting them may be seen as rich countries manipulating less rich ones through their economic power; but if that is done for the sake of peace, so be it, say Western campaigners on the arms exports question. Such campaigners are people of serious Christian or secular humanitarian principles, who are sure to be well aware that the West has no claim to higher morality than African countries. Indeed it has none, but it does have greater economic power, and the question is how to use that power: to fuel conflict in Africa or help bring about peace there?

There is no way around this issue. African countries buying armaments have to submit to possible scrutiny of their fitness to receive those armaments; it is useless to complain. Moral scrutiny of arms exports by Western countries with a hideous record of destructive wars, some of them actively preparing for destruction of the whole world by nuclear weapons, can seem most objectionable. In fact it is commonly demanded by pressure groups that are also opposed to the West's military record and activity; this was shown in the campaign against arms sales to Nigeria. In any case, single-issue protests always attract a variety of support with varied motives, and common sense requires judging them by what they say, not who joins in saying it.

The present work will not deal with the role of the British government at length, especially since I cannot add much to what was written at the time and later; I myself had no contact with any minister or official of that government at the time, though my colleagues had a good deal. The editor of the magazine was constantly in touch with the senior civil servants in the Commonwealth Relations Office (CRO) and then the FCO, which came into being during 1968 to merge the CRO and the Foreign Office; particularly, I seem to recall, with Donald Tebbit, assistant undersecretary. Those mandarins' advice favoured continuing normal relations with the government of a major country with close ties to Britain for many decades, a government effectively ruling most of the country. Following their advice, itself influenced by Sir David Hunt's advice from Lagos, the British government spoke in defence of the FMG, agreeing with its view that Biafran secession would lead to the break-up of other African states. It also stressed that the FMG was the recognised legal government, which was true—but there was no legal obligation for Britain to supply arms to the recognised legal government of any country. However, the British government constantly suggested that there was a sort of moral obligation, that refusing to do so would mean backing a rebellion. That was the core of its defence of an unpopular decision. Lord Shepherd, minister of state (who travelled to Nigeria in June and again in July 1968), said back in January 1968, "There is a legal government in Nigeria and we are bound to support it."[85] There was also the argument that Britain, by supplying arms to Nigeria, had some influence over the government there and could use it to good purpose. This probably had some justification, though its implications did not please Nigerians; it suggested that they needed to be kept on a leash, and it rubbed in their dependence on Britain for arms to win the war.

The opponents of arms sales to Nigeria believed that they fuelled and prolonged the conflict; and, once the extent of famine was known, that British arms were being used in a campaign that caused enormous suffering in the war zone. Some pro-Biafran activists like the Britain–Biafra Association also opposed the Federal Government's military action because of the Biafrans' grievances leading to secession. Besides these core objections, some of the opponents of British government policy went further, saying for example that Britain had been wrong to try to keep the Federation together in the lead-up to the war—a mistaken view, I believe, for at that time a break-up seemed likely to produce immediate worse bloodshed.

Opponents of arms sales often suggested that Britain decided on them in order to preserve a colonial creation, or to follow the supposed dictates of British business in Nigeria, especially Shell-BP. There were also regular accusations that the British government had been misled into thinking the war would be won by Nigeria in a short time. In particular, Sir David Hunt was accused of making this rash prediction. We learned very reliably at the time that this charge was not true, and in his memoirs Hunt indignantly rejected it, saying that as late as October 1967 he reminded London of the uncertainty of the war.[86] However, those memoirs reveal, with startling clarity, that what was said during the war about Hunt's pro-federal bias was well founded. While he says the pogroms were "a shocking crime" (incidentally casting doubt, with reason, on the Radio Cotonou story), he devotes inordinate attention to showing that Ojukwu exaggerated the death toll.[87] But there is worse. Discussing the July 1966 coup, he says, "The Ibos, who had never had it so good, discovered that they had pushed their luck too hard. In a violent reaction they turned to an alternative course: if they could not rule the whole of Nigeria they would make the existing Eastern Region into a state of their own."[88] "The Ibos ..."! All seven million of them? Just piqued by losing their supposed power over the country? These words from an experienced diplomat echo the common paranoid myth among pro-federal Nigerians at its crudest, and are grossly insensitive towards people who suffered a real "violent reaction" in July 1966 and later. It scarcely matters if he did not predict an early federal victory if that was his attitude to the conflict generally.

By August 1968 the opposition to the arms sales was stronger than ever. Harold Wilson, in his book published after the war, recalled "bitter and indescribably unhappy sessions at question-time and in debates":

> As we travelled through the country, demonstrations were increasingly hard to bear, as more and more Vietnam gave place to Biafra for their inspiration. But added to those who had urged the case on Vietnam were many, many more, most of them politically uncommitted, who regarded Biafra's sufferings as an outrage. Many of them were young, idealistic students, devout Churchgoers, United Nations Association liberals, socialists, pacifists, idealists of every kind. They demonstrated in the streets, often silently—with dignity and sorrow—many for the first time in their lives. In the churches, the Roman Catholics with their strong missionary connection with largely-Christian Biafra denounced us from pulpit after pulpit ... The nonconformists all, bar a few, condemned us ... in the life of a Prime Minister, these are things that hurt.[89]

An article in *West Africa* made the indisputable comment that "today, a veil of almost total incomprehension seems to separate Nigerians and British".[90] As the article said, the reaction of British public opinion was truly humanitarian; it needed to remind Nigerians of this, as many saw blatant bias and suspected a hidden agenda, while to many in Britain Nigerians, in talking about the war, seemed callous and unfeeling. Nigerian attitudes often showed sheer bewilderment—why were people so against them?—but sometimes showed total contempt for world opinion. On their side, some British commentators remarked on the fact that Nigeria, like other African states, owed its existence as a separate state only to arbitrary colonial partition, which was of course true, but sometimes went further and suggested that only Britain, as the creator of Nigeria, was interested in a wholly artificial Nigerian unity. I recall the famous historian Denis Brogan writing in the press in this vein and referring to "Nigeria" always in quotation marks, to suggest that it was not a real country. Conor Cruise O'Brien contrasted the genuine national feeling of the Biafrans with the artificial "facades" which he saw in established African states.

The truth, as we saw it from the *West Africa* vantage point—I myself from the readers' letters in particular—was that apart from Igbos and some other Easterners, Nigerians at that time very commonly felt that Nigeria was a real country to which they belonged, a real country which the secessionists were trying to destroy. Only two or three generations had passed since Britain created a united Nigeria, but that had been enough for great numbers of people to have contact with each other as work colleagues, friends, even sometimes spouses, for example through education—especially the University of Ibadan, whose multi-ethnic alumni were prominent in many fields—and through many sorts of employment such as teaching and work for the Nigerian Railway, and, until the horrors of 1966, service in the army. Much more united great numbers of people than colonial-drawn borders.[91]

This feeling of unity was especially strong among Southern and Christian Nigerians, and the gap between them and the North—that is, the heartland of the Northern emirates, not the former Northern Region as a whole—was very obvious. Those who saw Nigeria as an artificial British imposition were thinking of that gap, and many saw a similar or greater gap between Northern and Southern Sudan: the British, it was said, had in two major African countries forced different peoples of greatly differing cultures to stay together at independence, the result being war in both. The British might indeed have followed another policy, though it was rather late to say so in the late 1960s. But whatever might have been done differently in one or two countries, almost all African states were bound to comprise many differing peoples, and it was simply necessary for those peoples to work together; if a country was divided, the same would still be necessary. It was pointed out, rightly, that Eastern Nigeria was also a colonial creation (in 1939).

African states' borders had indeed been drawn up by top-hatted Europeans in treaties among themselves in the 1880s and 1890s; but going further back, one sees European states' borders created by the wars and marriages of various kings. Until 1918, Europe had had one multi-ethnic state, Austria-Hungary, which had in many ways been a successful state. Since then, Europeans had been used to the idea of a state having one dominant people with a prevailing national language. But this did not need to be followed by Africans, and in fact could not be. Multi-ethnic states were and remain the only possible sequel to colonial rule in Africa.

Those who condemned a war to maintain unity, which was originally a colonial creation, and those who defended a war to prevent other Africans challenging the colonial frontiers, both missed the essential point. What matters is not how a country's borders were drawn, or when, or by whom, but how the people living within those borders are treated. As Julius Nyerere said about Biafra's secession, the state exists to serve the people, not the other way round. Regardless of how its borders are fixed, a state is a political arrangement that can be changed and historically often has been. A particular state arrangement should not be maintained always and at any human cost; there may come a point when, owing perhaps to its own actions and failings, maintaining it is not worth the cost. Biafrans said that point came in Nigeria in 1967. There is nothing wrong with a multi-ethnic state, but there is plenty wrong with a state where one numerous and important ethnic group is violently attacked and driven out of the greater part of the country.

The Nigerian war and its implications were obviously examined in the academic arena among others. In July 1968 there was a teach-in at the School of Oriental and African Studies (SOAS) in London, where Dr U.U. Uche, a Biafran lecturer in law at the SOAS, and G.I. Jones, who after working as a colonial official in Eastern Nigeria had turned to academia and became a prominent social anthropologist at Cambridge, were among the speakers. Among them also were Obi Egbuna, a well-known Igbo writer and radical campaigner then in London, where he was often seen at Speakers' Corner and at the Africa Centre; and Samuel Grace Ikoku, an Igbo left-wing politician who had been general secretary of the Action Group and then, in Ghana, editor of the radical newspaper *The Spark* and one of the pan-African left-wing group assembled under Nkrumah. Extradited to Nigeria after the fall of Nkrumah, Ikoku had now joined the small band of prominent Igbos supporting the federal side, declaring his stand in a *Daily Times* article in March 1968; later he wrote an article in *West Africa* on "Nigeria Tomorrow", airy ideological dreaming about a coming conflict between "neo-colonialism and the new nationalism".[92] Egbuna told the SOAS teach-in that in Nigeria the real enemy was "white oppression", with Africans being used by whites; he developed this idea in a short pamphlet he produced about that time, *The Murder of Nigeria*. This illustrated the variety of left-wing views about the Biafran war, which was, whatever Egbuna said, very plainly a war fought by Africans for their own reasons. There was another teach-in at the London School of Economics (LSE) where speakers were Jones, Uche, Professor Keith Panter-Brick of the LSE—who was to publish in 1970 an important study, *Nigerian Politics and Military Rule: Prelude to the Civil War*—and C.C. Wrigley, a prominent Africanist at the University of Sussex and a strong opponent of the war.[93]

Besides the debates, meetings and protests in the country as a whole, there were regular questions in parliament about the arms sales, for example by Hugh Fraser and the Liberal leader, Jeremy Thorpe, in late July.[94] Parliament went for its usual summer recess, but it was recalled because of the Soviet Union's invasion of Czechoslovakia on 21 August. Among the worldwide chorus of condemnation of this action was criticism by the Communist *Morning Star*, which also criticised the Soviet military aid to Nigeria (proving that the British Communists were part of an old British left-wing tradition, not just agents of Moscow). When parliament reassembled to debate Czechoslovakia, it met again for a second day, 27 August 1968, to debate Nigeria. About that time *The Times*, *The Guardian* and the *Financial Times* all called for an end to British arms supplies.

West Africa reported some of the contributions to the parliamentary debate in the issue of 31 August. I was on holiday then and did not study the full debate. Examining the House of Commons debate fifty years later,[95] I see that the government line was based essentially on the sense of obligation to Nigeria already noted: the secretary for Commonwealth affairs, George Thomson, said that when the war began,

> Neutrality was not a possible option for Her Majesty's Government at that time. We might have been able to declare ourselves neutral if one independent country was fighting another, but this was not a possible attitude when a Commonwealth country, with which we had long and close ties, was faced with an internal revolt. What would other Commonwealth countries have thought?

He also said, "it must be for the Nigerians themselves to decide upon what form their State should take," but added, "Whatever the hopes and fears of the Ibos, we cannot believe that they would not now do better to see what conditions they could negotiate for themselves within the framework of a united Nigeria, however this was expressed." There were, he said, "many degrees of federation or confederation"; on that the British government seemed to suggest the FMG might consider a looser sort of grouping, but this was now rejected on the Nigerian side. Apart from that, and its call for the earliest possible ceasefire, the government supported the Nigerian views, and said the arms supplies would continue—while denying reports, quite often made, that these included bombs for air attack. But it stuck to claims that were to be proved false or misleading, for example that "Our supplies have amounted to about 15 per cent by value of Nigeria's total arms purchases". There was also a debate the same day in the House of Lords, with Lord Shepherd defending the government policy.

The government was clearly trying to make excuses for its policy. Labour ministers defending the policy showed little confidence in their rightness; they were wriggling. Much was said in the debate about the present and likely future conduct of the federal army; some MPs expressed confidence in the troops' discipline and proper treatment of civilians, while others doubted whether the army was fully under General Gowon's control; Gowon himself was praised by many speakers. Plenty of attention was paid to the current federal advance towards Aba, which was taking the war right into the Igbo heartland; the government was embarrassed because it had expressed a belief that there would be no offensive of that sort. Relief operations were obviously discussed, and since at that very time there were active talks involving Dr Lindt, Haile Selassie, the United Nations and others, which seemed to be making progress, there was optimism expressed—prematurely. But there were many references to the shocking failure of the Federal Government to relieve starvation in areas under its control, especially in South-Eastern State; this had been exposed in the report by Lord Hunt and his team, which proposed ways to start faster relief transport.[96] Nigel Fisher and James Johnson had seen this negligence themselves on a recent tour organised by those responsible for it, and spoke severely about it. John Mackintosh, a Labour MP who had previously been a professor of politics at Ibadan and was sympathetic to the federal cause, said the British government should "say to the Lagos Government that if we are to continue as the arms supplier for part of the arms needs of Nigeria the Federal Government must do a much better job of organising food distribution and relief supplies in the area now under its control as well as help to get relief into areas held by Colonel Ojukwu".

Here Mackintosh was expressing what was the main theme of most of the speakers in this debate: that Britain had a duty to persuade the Nigerians to do the right thing. It was with that in mind that the Wilson government continued to supply arms. It had said in June that it would "more than reconsider" its policy if the FMG was aiming "not merely to preserve the unity of Nigeria but to proceed without mercy either with the slaughter or the starvation of the Ibo people". In truth the British parliament was putting Nigeria on trial, or on probation: if you are a good boy, you can have guns. This obviously did not please either side. On one side, Nigerians resented British attitudes to the war; Mackintosh said in the debate, "We have a bad Press in

Nigeria; we are not universally regarded as the greatest friends of the Federal Government in Lagos. We are often attacked, and we do not get all that much credit."

On the other side, some believed that the war effort using British arms was leading to genocide or the imminent threat of it. The prominent left-wing Labour MP Frank Allaun said in the most extreme wording in the debate,

> It is possible that in the next few days the world may witness the greatest human tragedy since 1945: the slaughter and starvation of millions of men, women and children. We may see an attempt at what Hitler called the final solution of the Jewish question, and this may be the attempted final solution of the Biafran question. Even if every human being is not shot, as many Biafrans fear, I believe that they are right in thinking that every person capable of giving leadership locally will be killed.

Hugh Fraser said, referring to the reported federal advance into Igbo country, "If this invasion takes place and if resistance continues, there is the gravest possible danger of genocide." However, the word "genocide" and its equivalents were used very rarely by opponents of the arms sales in this debate, while other MPs condemned use of the word as unfounded. James Griffiths, strongly opposed to the arms supplies, did not use that word; while expressing hope for the Addis Ababa talks, then still going on, he said, "If there is now no chance of negotiations and peace, if all that is to take place is the final assault, I implore my right hon. Friends to stop supplying arms now." He also said, "I hope that there will be a united Nigeria, but this is not the way to unite the country."

Fraser and others were wrong to talk of genocide, but there were verbal excesses among pro-Nigerians also. Nigel Fisher spoke on an earlier occasion of a "quick kill" as the best solution, a most unpleasant and stupid phrase; berated for it in the 27 August debate, he said lamely that he had meant a quick federal victory. And William Whitlock, undersecretary of state for Commonwealth relations, who wound up the debate—and angered many by talking beyond the agreed deadline and preventing a vote—repeated the myth of the power of Markpress. While recognising the truth of reports of starvation and suffering, he said, "In the propaganda field the Ibos have often seemed to be winning the war of words while losing the battle of arms. Behind this success is a highly professional operation conducted by an advertising agency in Geneva. The Ibo official line is regularly telexed to Geneva and distributed wholesale and undiluted by the agency to world-wide outlets." Absurdly, he went on to mention the ridiculous Biafran stories like the one about British soldiers disguised as footballers; those stories, which nobody except perhaps a few Biafrans had believed, showed precisely how incompetent Biafran propaganda was in the "war of words".

That was further shown by a striking fact about that debate: the opponents of British arms supplies said nothing to support Biafra's case for independence; they did not go into the reasons for secession, except for one phrase by Fraser: "The Ibo people have shown their right to self-determination more clearly, perhaps, than any other people in the world." The contrast with the long-winded historical surveys by Biafrans—and their adversaries—at peace talks was striking. True, the attacks on the FMG and the calls for an end to the arms supplies served to support the Biafran struggle for independence. But whereas many MPs showed understanding of the Federal Nigerian case for war, while also recognising the Biafrans' real fears, MPs opposed to the war showed compassion and concern for the Biafrans' present suffering and possible worse suffering in the future, rather than sympathy for the Biafran case—which was that the people of the former Eastern Nigeria had been driven out of the Federation, no longer belonged to Nigeria, and must have their own independent state.

That debate made no difference to the war or to people's attitudes. But it probably strengthened the anti-British feeling among the Nigerian media and public. The opponents of British arms sales to Nigeria and supporters of Biafra may have been amazed to hear about the suspicion of Britain in Lagos, but it was real. In July there was a demonstration against the "double-faced" role of the British government, including the prominent far-left trade unionist Wahab Goodluck (another example of the varied left-wing responses to the war) and a prominent member of the Federal Executive Council, Alhaji Aminu Kano, commissioner for communications.[97] He was to remain a "hawk" over the war and a critic of Britain and, implicitly, of Gowon. He and others of similar views saw the Soviet Union, rather than Britain, as the right ally for Nigeria—while Wilson saw British arms sales to Nigeria as necessary to stop Moscow getting more influence there. After the Commons debate, *West Africa*'s editorial of 31 August, commenting on the British government's argument about opposing Soviet plans and acting as a restraining influence on Lagos, said, "In Nigeria this argument has distasteful implications."

These Nigerian reactions were to be expected but deserved no sympathy. They showed once again a general failure of understanding and sympathy not only for the other side in the war, but for the feelings naturally expressed in the outside world. It seemed many Nigerians simply expected the world to help their government defeat a rebellion and not ask any questions. In an already globalised world such people showed extreme insularity. They were fortunate in getting the support they did have, with the British government accepting that it had a moral obligation to supply arms. In that editorial, David Williams adopted that Federal Nigerian view completely: "It would be an extremely hostile act, amounting to gross interference in domestic affairs, if the British suddenly decided that they no longer agreed with the role which the British themselves originally planned for the Nigerian forces."

At some point during the war, I cannot recall when, my editor asked me to say straight out what I thought of British arms sales to Nigeria. I said I thought Britain should halt arms sales to countries involved in both international wars and civil wars. I said this on the spur of the moment and would, on reflection, not be so categorical; there have been clear cases where help to a government to suppress some sorts of rebellion was justified. But I did not think then and still do not think that the Biafra war was such a case. Refusing to arm a government fighting a rebellion is indeed interference, as my editor said. But is deciding to arm it not interference also, as the Biafrans said? Everybody discussing the moral implications of arms to Nigeria—and the whole debate was always highly moral in tone— should in my view always have accepted that the Biafran case was unusual. It was not a case of criminals breaking up a country out of bloody-mindedness. What happened to the Eastern Nigerians in 1966–7 was highly unusual in the world. Normal principles about governments and rebels must have exceptions; the events that drove the Biafrans to secede provided one exception.

Lamentably, the campaign against arms sales came a year too late. The Conservative MP John Tilney (sympathetic to the federal side) said in the debate,

> I do not agree that the British Government could not have taken some action a year or more ago. At that time I said I thought that an embargo should have been put on all arms to both contestants. I am not convinced by the argument of the Secretary of State [George Thomson] that that was impossible at that time. I think we should have tried for at least a month or two to get the countries of the world to dampen down a war which it was obvious to so many of us would be a terrible civil war. Had we done so, a number of lives could have been saved, and also much destruction of property and much bitterness.
>
> At that time Biafra, or so-called Biafra, was viable. It had its oil and its routes to the Cameroons. It also had no really embittered minorities. How different it is today!

Indeed, in August 1968 Nigerian forces controlled all the minority areas and a considerable Igbo-peopled area also. By then, one argument made by the FMG and its supporters, that halting British arms would make no difference to the war, had something in it. I for one would have supported a halt to the arms sales then even so, and some good might have come from it—it could, at least if France took similar action, have encouraged more serious peace efforts; but the prospects would have been poor. A year earlier, however, Britain could have refused to supply arms and intervened to secure some sort of settlement; if only that had been done, or at least attempted.

New federal advances and the military observers

Further advances by the Nigerian Third Division, which had in fact been in action for months, began in July 1968, and on 24 August they turned into a new full offensive, the objective being to capture Owerri, Aba and Umuahia, the main cities still in Biafran hands. These were Igbo cities, and if there had been any intention to avoid attacking the Igbo heartland, it was dropped. In fact, Gowon had made it clear that sooner or later his forces would move in there, unless the Biafrans accepted federal peace terms. Enahoro said in late July that the troops had paused outside Igbo country "on advice from all quarters—from our friends".[98] But an article in *West Africa* of 31 August, "Is It the War's End?", said,

> Now, however, whether the relative federal inactivity has been due to a desire not to upset the Addis Ababa talks, whether it was due to the abnormally heavy rains, or whether to the need to strengthen, reorganise and regroup units and replenish supplies, the three Federal divisions surrounding Iboland are preparing for what is likely to be the final attack.

Against fierce resistance, the Nigerian forces crossed the Imo River, losing many casualties, and launched an attack along the main road to Aba on 24 August. The population of Aba had begun to leave a week earlier, adding to the crowded refugee population in Biafran territory, and the city fell on 4 September.[99] Further west, men of the Third Division crossed the Oguta Lake and took Oguta town on 11 September, but the Biafrans retook it after two days, fortunately for them as it was close to Uli airstrip; however, the federal forces continued to advance in other directions.

Many foreign journalists accompanied this Nigerian offensive. Their reports spoke of the battles but also of the personality of the division's commander, Colonel Benjamin Adekunle, a violent, hot-tempered, loud-mouthed exhibitionist. He was thoroughly hostile to journalists (he ordered the shaving of one reporter's head) and relief workers. He got constant media attention around the world for months and must have relished it. Within Nigeria he may have embarrassed Gowon, but he got popular attention for winning victories. A ferocious disciplinarian towards his own men, he may have restrained their conduct towards civilians and POWs usually, but there were war crimes under his command. Of course not all reports and allegations of war crimes were true; David Williams, reporting with the federal forces, wrote from Asa, ten miles south of Aba, that he had checked a village where a massacre had been reported and did not believe it had happened. In a separate piece, he wrote that "the army leaders have restored a degree of discipline which would have seemed impossible in 1966. A strong corps of Military Police is also now functioning; its absence in 1966 was one reason why the troops got out of hand."[100]

During the Aba offensive a federal officer killed a Biafran soldier who had surrendered, in front of foreign journalists. When pictures of this were broadcast in Britain, a furious Adekunle ordered a court martial at which he himself presided, and the culprit was executed. This too was televised, and in a horrible twist, the TV crew asked the firing squad to wait until they were ready.[101] This episode became notorious and has been mentioned in later books on the war. This was a blot on the record of the foreign reporters in the war, who generally did not deserve the attacks often made on their work.

The concerns about the troops' conduct were all the more urgent because it was widely expected that this offensive would defeat Biafra finally. It was probably for the same reason that the Nigerian and British governments now went ahead with a plan, agreed in principle in June, for a small force of observers to accompany the federal forces and report on how they were conducting the war. General Henry Alexander, former chief of staff of the Ghanaian army, was the main British representative on the group of military observers, who assembled in Lagos on 19 September. Others were from Canada, Poland, Sweden and the OAU, and there was a civilian United Nations observer, Nils Gussing, who had come earlier to deal with relief measures. Individual members of the observer team were changed several times, Alexander leaving after two months.

It seems that the observers were explicitly told to find out whether genocide was planned or in progress; at least, their public statements responded to that allegation.[102] In fact they were to go further, looking at real or reported breaches of the Geneva Convention. Of course they did not have full freedom to investigate; the many critics of the observer team noted that their movements were controlled by the Nigerian army. It was also apparent that as military officers they obviously understood war well, but at the same time were bound to feel some affinity with the Nigerian officers whose messes were probably familiar to them. In fact, one of the British observers—Major Ian Walsworth-Bell—also gathered intelligence and gave advice to the Nigerian army, before being dismissed in September 1969.[103] Despite that improper unneutral behaviour, some criticisms of the observers were unjustified. It was suggested that they would not understand the meaning of genocide, but that word recalled Nazism, and Alexander and other members of the team had served in the Second World War; one of the others was a Pole. And they obviously knew the difference between killing civilians and not killing them, and between sporadic and systematic killings.

The word "genocide" was now widely used about Nigeria, as *West Africa* noted in an editorial on 14 September, which rejected the charge but noted that federal supporters encouraged it by loose talk about the Igbos and the relief agencies. On 9 September, the same day that de Gaulle spoke of "extermination", Richard Nixon, the Republican candidate for the coming US presidential election, spoke about the "terrible tragedy of the people of Biafra", with an estimated 6,000 dying daily of starvation. He said, "Until now efforts to relieve the Biafran people have been thwarted by the desire of the central government of Nigeria to pursue total and unconditional victory and by the fear of the Ibo people that surrender means wholesale atrocities and genocide." (This was presumably a muddled reference to the impasse over delivery of relief to Biafra.) Then he declared, "But genocide is what is taking place right now—and starvation is the grim reaper."

If one assumes that Nixon and his advisers were thinking first and foremost of votes in the election, it is significant that they thought such words on Biafra could win votes. From before secession the Biafrans had been working hard to win support in the US. The Federal Government had done the same—comparing the Nigerian war to the US's own civil war, with Gowon as Lincoln—and the US government, while selling no arms to either side, supported the Nigerian side diplomatically: President Johnson said the US was "today sincerely sympathetic to the desire of the Federal Military Government to preserve Nigerian unity", while it had "ardently hoped for the earliest possible peaceful resolution".[104] But despite Americans' preoccupation with Vietnam and domestic problems, concern about the Nigerian war grew—Martin Luther King was planning to visit Nigeria and Biafra when he was murdered on 4 April 1968—and then the starvation in Biafra led to the same shock and desire to help in the US as in other Western countries, and to considerable political support for Biafra as well as humanitarian concern. An American Committee to Keep Biafra Alive campaigned actively. Support for Biafra spread among Irish Americans and Catholics—even if the Catholic Church did not officially endorse the claim of a Muslim versus Christian war, many ordinary churchgoers probably believed it, and Biafran emissaries emphasised it—and among the Jewish community. These communities commonly voted Democrat, and Nixon must have hoped to win some of them over by talking of genocide in Biafra.

Even before the prospect appeared of the world's most powerful country coming under the rule of someone who believed Nigeria was committing genocide, that belief was spreading and Nigerians had to reckon seriously with world opinion; that was no doubt why Gowon accepted the British proposal for the military observers, which many in Nigeria opposed. In the same spirit of conciliating world opinion, which those other Nigerians wanted to disregard, Gowon invited Dame Margery Perham, who had for months been expressing concern about the war, for a ten-day visit to Nigeria. He gave her a three-hour audience and lent her his personal aircraft to travel around. The veteran scholar was convinced of the Federal Government's good intentions for the Igbos, and gave a broadcast message in Nigeria, addressed to Ojukwu personally and to "the Ibo people with you", to say this and urge the Biafrans to abandon a hopeless struggle. She referred to the outpouring of sympathy around the world for the Biafran people, and said, "The world which is watching would condemn you if they now believed that you [Ojukwu] were using your leadership to prolong a hopeless struggle at their expense." From what she had seen and heard in Nigeria, "I do not believe that your people would be in danger of massacre or revenge."[105]

Dame Margery did not repudiate her earlier statements sympathetic to the Biafrans—it was she who had brought the Asaba massacre to world attention, though without giving the town's name. But she was strongly criticised for the stance she now took, for example in a letter from Chinua Achebe to *The Times*. Her basic point, that whatever had happened before, the Biafrans now had nothing to gain by fighting on, was valid and reasonable; and there were certainly leading Biafrans who thought that way by now. The federal offensive going on as she spoke did not in fact end the war then, but it drove the Biafrans further into a small enclave more crowded and distressed than ever. In the Rivers and South-Eastern States, normal conditions were far from resuming, but on 6 September *West Africa*'s Griot columnist saw the first oil flow from the Shell-BP terminal at Bonny since the start of the war.[106] This did not benefit the people starving not far away in South-Eastern State, and there were still many repairs needed for the oil installations, but Nigeria was on the way to having enough oil revenue to pay for the war. The chances of the Biafrans getting control of those oil installations again were more remote than ever.

Many Rivers and South-Eastern people would have supported the federal forces in resisting any Biafran attempt to reoccupy their areas. Biafran oppression there was outlined in a pamphlet published by Nabo Graham-Douglas,[107] *Ojukwu's Rebellion and World Opinion*, giving the pro-federal Rivers point of view; it was brandished by the Nigerian delegation at Addis Ababa and mentioned (with a word of caution about all the propagandist works being put out) by John Tilney in the Commons debate. Although not all the people of those states agreed with Graham-Douglas, one cannot doubt that a Biafran reoccupation there would have been an operation of massive vengeance. In fact the war now had only three likely outcomes: a prolonged war of attrition, a federal victory with subjugation of Igbos, and a Biafran victory with subjugation of Ibibios, Efiks, Ijaws, Ekois, Ogonis and other minorities. The last would only happen with a spectacular reversal of military fortunes. If it somehow happened, the referendum that the Biafrans proposed would produce a big majority for Biafra; otherwise, with federal forces in occupation, there would be a big majority for Nigeria. The idea of Biafra being independent but confined to Igbo territory, briefly floated by *West Africa* a year earlier, was now discussed again, using the term "Ibostan" by analogy with the South African Bantustans; Gowon told *West Africa* that Nigeria would not consider this,[108] and Ojukwu and his colleagues would most probably not have been satisfied with it either, though they implicitly accepted the possibility by their offer (never likely to be even considered) of a minorities' referendum.

The OAU meetings in Algiers, where the FMG delegation was headed by Awolowo, included a whole day's discussion of Nigeria.

Of the heads of the Biafra-recognising states, only one, Kenneth Kaunda, attended. The representatives of Sierra Leone and Tunisia made speeches which Awolowo thought non-committal, but they voted for the resolution, which called on the Biafrans to cooperate with the federal authorities to restore "peace and unity in Nigeria"; it also called for an end to hostilities and a general amnesty, but on the whole it was unambiguously on the side of Nigeria.[109]

In the next two or three weeks, some Biafran representatives in Europe decided to see if a compromise peace might be possible, and made some approaches to the federal side. Almost nothing was reported in *West Africa* about these moves, which were largely semi-secret. According to de St Jorre's post-war account, Michael Okpara (Ojukwu's special political adviser), Nnamdi Azikiwe, Kenneth Dike and Francis Nwokedi met senior officials of Jacques Foccart's department in a Paris hotel on 7 September and were told that France's aid would remain limited (as de Gaulle confirmed two days later), and then decided, with the exception of Nwokedi, to urge Ojukwu to accept a united Nigeria on conditions. This, it seems, infuriated Ojukwu,[110] but it was not the only move of this sort by Biafrans seeking not to defy Ojukwu, but to persuade him. Raph Uwechue, the Biafran representative in Paris, considered that the Biafran leaders were "bent on formal sovereignty much more than I considered reasonable" and should rather be considering a confederation as a solution; in September he expressed his views in an official communication to the permanent secretary of Biafra's Ministry of External Affairs.[111] Early in September the British government heard that some Biafran leaders might be ready to agree to talks on the basis of a united Nigeria. According to Suzanne Cronje's post-war account, Ignatius Kogbara, Biafra's representative in Britain, approached Arnold Smith and then had a meeting with Lord Shepherd, but advised that any initiative should wait for Ojukwu's statement to the Biafran Consultative Assembly.[112] Lord Shepherd, however, travelled to Lagos in late September, and mentioned the approach made by some Biafrans.

The Biafran Consultative Assembly and Council of Chiefs met, in the wake of weeks of steady defeats, and heard a defiant speech from Ojukwu; Biafra would fight on, he said in a broadcast on

26 September, and "we are stronger today than we were two weeks ago".[113] How were they stronger? They had beaten off the attack close to Uli, but Ojukwu may well have been referring to the new arms supplies, now regularly reported. Despite these, there may have been doubts among leading Biafrans in Umuahia, not only abroad. After the war, Akpan recalled that at one point, apparently in September 1968, delegates left to tell the recognising countries that Biafra was ready to accept it had lost the war, but the delegates "came back with assurances of an immediate supply of arms and ammunition". Akpan commented, "As far as I know, it was from this time on that Biafra started receiving military aid from outside countries."[114] This account is vague and apparently not first-hand (Akpan, though head of the civil service, was clearly excluded from many decisions). It may be that Ojukwu did not really want to say he was ready to abandon the struggle, but to suggest that possibility in order to get more arms from Ivory Coast and Gabon; yet he must have been in constant touch with those countries, so why a special delegation? Anyway, more arms flowed in and Ojukwu could ignore the senior Biafrans who urged him to consider a peace settlement on the basis of a confederation (which, incidentally, de Gaulle supported). However, the Nigerians were not ready even to consider this, and must have told Lord Shepherd so.

The important Igbo city of Owerri was captured by federal forces on 16 September. Three days later the military observers assembled in Lagos, whence they soon travelled to the war zone. The First Division advanced slowly, because of problems of supply lines, as John de St Jorre, the *Observer*'s special correspondent, reported from Awgu on 21 September for *West Africa*; he said the Biafrans were still running a rudimentary administration in areas north of Onitsha, but Abakaliki now had 80 per cent of its pre-war population, though Enugu was still almost empty.[115] After occupying the section of road intended for the Obilago airstrip, the First Division captured Okigwi on 30 September. There, an elderly missionary couple, Albert and Marjorie Savory, who worked at the Oji River Leprosy Settlement, were killed by a drunk Nigerian soldier, together with a Swede and a Yugoslav working for the ICRC; all were wearing Red Cross badges. The observers condemned the killing as "unprovoked and inexcusable".[116] Their first and second general reports, in October, said they had seen no evidence of genocide, though they mentioned rough treatment by both sides and made some criticism of POWs' conditions; soon afterwards they criticised the treatment of POWs at Kiri-Kiri and Ikoyi prisons in Lagos.[117] After the capture of Okigwi, the federal offensive ground to a halt. Probably one cause was the usual gigantic waste of ammunition by the Nigerian army, but the arrival of French arms for the Biafrans was another cause.

Ojukwu declared at this time that Biafra's strategy was to "delay the enemy until the world's conscience can be effectively roused against genocide".[118] The French arms supplies helped Biafra to hold out with that aim; an editorial in *West Africa* of 5 October said, "There can be no doubt that as a result of greatly increased supplies from Gabon, whether these have official French approval or not, the Biafran army now has a more regular supply of ammunition, and probably of other things than it has had for a long time." By "official French approval" the editor no doubt meant approval by France's established institutions like the Foreign Ministry; Foccart's parallel network was really very official in a sense, but the French embassy in Lagos was of course totally against the de Gaulle–Foccart operation. Such differences among the French obviously did not deter Nigerian protests; there was an eight-mile anti-French march in Lagos in September.[119]

Although there was a relative lull in the fighting for some months from the end of September 1968, there were many other developments relating to the war, and the *West Africa* staff were as busy as ever in recording them. We who wrote the news pages felt rewarded for hard work every week by knowing that readers appreciated our information on a war arousing more interest than ever before at this eventful time—not only West African readers, but they very much: many of them were to be seen queuing up at lunchtime on Fridays to buy each new issue in Orbit House, where there was a little alcove in which they sat to read it. From September 1968, for several months, there were only three of us to produce the magazine, for Bridget Bloom then left *West Africa* (where she had been a strong supporter of the federal cause in the war) to work for several years for the *Financial Times*. She said in the issue of 14 September that there had been "never a dull moment" in work on the magazine. Very true, and much else besides the war was interesting. In fact it was pleasant to get away from the war and write about the almost totally peaceful affairs of other West African countries—such as Ghana, where a programme of returning to civilian rule, routinely promised by military regimes, was genuinely going ahead—and, indeed, about peaceful developments in Nigeria, such as the closing of the intake gates of the new Kainji Dam on the river Niger in August 1968.[120]

Mercy flights and arms flights

From persistent reports it was clear by October 1968 that French arms were being flown into Uli at a rapid rate; some flights landed at Uga also, but much less was written about that airstrip. The mainstream Western media were picking up the story and *West Africa* quoted their reports (I recall no attempt to send its own reporter to Gabon or Ivory Coast at that time). A *Daily Telegraph* report from Accra said French arms were being shipped to Ivory Coast in an unmarked Boeing and transferred to Super Constellations for the flight to Uli.[121] *Newsweek* reported from Libreville on the arms flights from Gabon to Biafra.[122] Both Ivory Coast and Gabon denied the stories; the Ivorian foreign minister, Arsène Usher, went to London in November for a Central Office of Information tour planned well before, but the Biafra arms reports added public interest to the visit, during which he had lengthy talks at the Foreign Office; however, nothing was clarified or resolved.[123] The *Financial Times* reported eight aircraft, presumably delivering arms, flying from Gabon, with 18 Rhodesian and South African pilots.[124] Estimates of the amounts delivered varied; the *Sunday Telegraph* spoke of 80 boxes of arms and ammunition each night.[125] *West Africa* quoted Professor Dike as saying Biafra was receiving 100 tons of arms each week.[126] Most or all of them were probably coming from France via Gabon and Ivory Coast, for at this time the uneasy relations between the Biafrans and Hank Wharton ended in a complete breach. The dispute was of course about money, while the Biafrans, typically, accused the American of sabotage.[127] This was apparently not the end of arms flights from Portugal; it was reported that a Cuban firm (presumably Cuban-American) had taken over from Wharton.[128] But it was the French arms flights that helped make Uli airport one of the busiest in Africa for some time. One report spoke of 28 aircraft landing each night, 14 with arms, 14 with relief supplies.[129]

In September 1968 the churches' airlift from São Tomé to Uli was operating well, with five to eight aircraft initially, and, together with the ICRC flights from Fernando Po and French Red Cross flights from Gabon, delivered large amounts of food and medical supplies. It was to go on operating for the rest of the war, and in the end saved countless lives. At a meeting in Rome on 9–10 November 1968, called by Monsignor Bayer of Caritas Internationalis, a new coordinating body, Joint Church Aid (JCA), was set up, grouping all the agencies involved in the airlift, which henceforth used that name.[130] JCA had no offices or staff of its own, and it operated through the member agencies. The main aircraft used in the elaborate operation was the DC-6B, carrying about ten tons; Super Constellations and Boeing C-97 Stratofreighters were also used.

In September, Caritas made 180 flights to Uli in ten days,[131] and Nordchurchaid delivered 700 tons in a week.[132] In the first two weeks of October, 94 ICRC flights brought in 990 tons of relief supplies.[133] All these deliveries, plus an effective distribution system on the ground,[134] had their effect. The Red Cross said in late October that the food situation was better on both sides of the war front, and suggested that an estimate of 2.5 million children being fed by relief organisations was too high.[135] The number of children and adults still starving and in danger of death was still dreadfully high; Oxfam reckoned that 200,000 died in October and 300,000 in November,[136] and estimates of the total number who had died of food deficiency diseases and other illnesses due to destitution now ranged up to a million. On the Nigerian side of the front, the serious food shortages, for which the authorities had no excuse whatever, continued and half a million displaced people were thought to be suffering in the Uyo area of South-Eastern State in September;[137] in the same area, a senior Christian Council of Nigeria team headed by the Anglican bishop of Lagos, Seth Kale, to deliver relief materials found a situation better than before, but still bad with widespread *kwashiorkor*.[138] One problem in those "liberated" areas was that many people hid at first in the bush, although the army fed some who came out and others were later helped by the relief efforts coordinated by the ICRC. The military observers said civilians were more afraid to come out of hiding in the Third Division's zone than in the First's[139]—even though those in the latter were Igbos. Colonel Adekunle could well have been a cause of this; he was openly hostile to both the observers and relief agencies, though he had to cooperate with both—an agreement with the Red Cross on relief in the Port Harcourt sector was reported in *West Africa* of 12 October.

The observers' reports and those of others all showed that the Federal Government and its forces were not committing or planning genocide, but were guilty of some sporadic war crimes, widespread negligence and indifference towards civilians, and a lack of urgency about helping relief efforts. All this was deplorable enough, and it was not really a great compliment to the Nigerian forces to say that they were not committing the extreme crime of genocide. Still, they were not committing it; but as *West Africa*'s editorial of 2 November said, belief in genocide "is as important to continued resistance as the supplies now flowing into Biafra". However many or few people in the West shared that belief, huge numbers supported and aided the remarkable relief airlift.

The airlift put the Portuguese "cocoa islands" of São Tomé and Príncipe (or, in fact, the main island of São Tomé) into the world's news pages again. They had been there sixty years before, when their cocoa plantations employing Africans as virtual slaves had become an international scandal. Later, as Portugal's oppressive colonial rule continued, São Tomé was the scene of an infamous massacre of protesting workers in 1953. Later still, when Africans fought to end Portuguese rule in bigger territories, on São Tomé they could not organise armed resistance—not easy on small islands—but they had their nationalist movement in exile in Gabon. São Tomé was an important staging post for the Portuguese, and now for the Biafrans also, whatever they—and the left-wing Westerners who travelled through São Tomé on the way to and from Biafra—thought about Portuguese colonialism.

The Biafra airlift transformed São Tomé, at first stretching its hotel space, its supplies of aviation fuel (provided by a subsidiary of Shell), and its capacity for handling goods arriving by sea. These problems were overcome by the efforts of JCA and the Portuguese authorities.[140]

1. Nigerian Head of State Yakubu Gowon © Keystone Press / Alamy Stock Photo

2. Lt. Col. Odumegwu Ojukwu © Keystone Pictures USA/ZUMAPRESS.
com/Alamy Live News

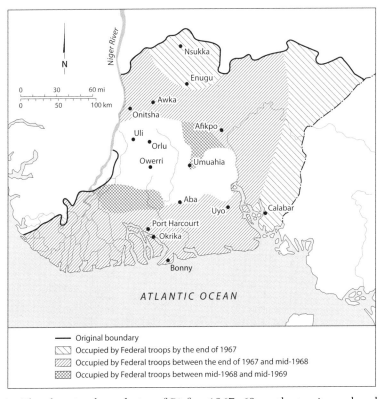

3. The changing boundaries of Biafra, 1967–69, as the territory shrank from the entire former Eastern Region into a small enclave in the Igbo heartland. Cartography by Bill Nelson..

4. Biafran soldiers carrying a wounded comrade. Credit: Al J. Venter.

5. Biafran recruits under training towards the end of the war. Credit: Al J. Venter.

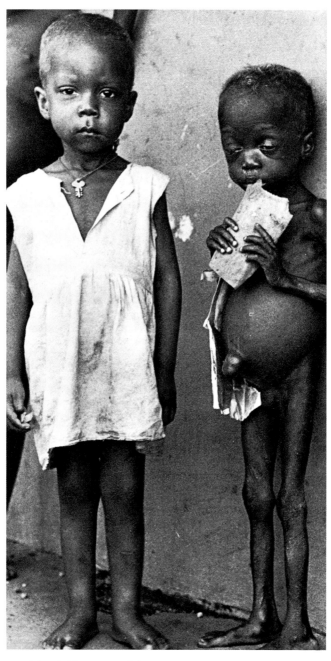

6. Two of the child victims of the conflict, near Uli. Credit: Al J. Venter.

7. A Biafran propaganda poster. Credit: Al J. Venter.

8. A rural scene in Biafran territory in the war. Credit: Al J. Venter.

The island became a hive of activity as up to 30 or more flights left for Uli each night, except when the weather or technical problems interfered, and ships regularly docked with food donated in Europe and America for the Biafran war victims. Such an operation as that airlift has rarely been seen. The perilous night-time landings at Uli must have reminded some British and French people of the RAF Lysanders landing at night to help the French Resistance in the Second World War. But those had been less frequent and had not carried food, and comparisons have rather been made with the Berlin Airlift of 1948–9.

The Portuguese aid to Biafra was not affected when the dictator António Salazar had a severe stroke and was replaced as prime minister on 27 September 1968 by Marcelo Caetano. He continued with the wars to suppress the African insurgents in three countries, and with the aid to the Biafrans. Ojukwu sent a message of sympathy to the sick Salazar; *West Africa*'s Matchet's Diary, mentioning this, added, "But before supporters of the Federal government raise their hands in horror they should reflect that in the first six months of this year, Portugal was still Nigeria's fourth most important customer for groundnuts (60,000 tons), way ahead of the United Kingdom; and the first customer was France."[141] That little-known fact was no secret; I had found it out for our commercial news pages from one of the useful publications of the Commonwealth Secretariat that we received.

In contrast to its neighbour, General Franco's regime in Spain cooperated with the ICRC aid flights (subject to Federal Nigerian approval) from Spanish Guinea, and decided to give independence to that colony. After free elections (not allowed in Spain itself), Equatorial Guinea became independent on 12 October 1968, under President Francisco Macías Nguema, whose base of support was in Rio Muni, the mainland part of the country. From the other part, the island of Fernando Po, the ICRC flights to Biafra continued for the moment.

The Red Cross refused to let journalists travel on its relief flights, but JCA readily carried them. The world's media now carried many stories of the hazardous flights to Uli, the mercy airlift that inspired the world. Many journalists, and other travellers who sometimes went to Biafra in that way, gave hair-raising descriptions of how the plane descended in total darkness until, just before touchdown, the pilot called out "Lights!" and the runway lights were switched on, just for long enough to let the plane land, and then switched off before any Nigerian bomber above could take aim. It was a terrifying and exciting experience (a *Daily Mirror* reporter told me it was "f—ing awful"). The reporters told how the stockfish, dried milk and other life-saving goods were quickly loaded onto lorries for distribution. The scene was hectic all through the night, but everything generally worked well. Very few of the aircraft and crews were lost, but the pilots were a brave mixed bunch (it is said that some airline pilots took holiday jobs to fly the Biafra airlift). Equally or more heroic were the doctors, priests, nurses and nuns who distributed the food and cared for the sick and starving, a grim task when only a limited number could be saved; the foreigners who did this work were widely praised, and deserved it, but there were of course many Biafran doctors, nurses, drivers and others who did equally vital work. For example, Biafrans paid by the government ran the refugee camps and drove the 300 lorries used by JCA for distribution.[142]

Journalists on the JCA flights sat on boxes of stockfish, not ammunition. There were strict orders against carrying anything of a military nature, and they were obeyed. I never doubted this at the time, and Dr Clyne Shepherd, who was regularly on hand at Uli to watch over the unloading, confirmed it to me in 2017. From an early date the Nigerian press published allegations that the churches' relief planes carried arms; Caritas was accused in particular. The Social Welfare Department of the Nigerian Catholic Secretariat made a public declaration saying, *inter alia*,

(1) Caritas is supplying food and medicines to those Nigerians caught behind the rebel lines. It flies these supplies in specially chartered planes. These planes are open to inspection before take-off.

(2) Caritas is not supplying and has never supplied arms to the rebels.

(3) Caritas has never at any time recruited or transported mercenaries to the rebel-held areas. Caritas does not fly her planes from Gabon.[143]

In his book published in Nigeria after the war, Emmanuel Urhobo did not support the allegations against the churches' relief airlift, simply mentioning briefly that they were made and rejected.[144] At the time obsessively suspicious Nigerians would of course dismiss any denials. But no evidence of the allegations was produced. The Federal Government itself sometimes supported the allegations, but still with no proof. I am sure that one reason for the common belief in the story was confusion with the Wharton airlift from Lisbon, which did carry both arms and relief materials. If Nigerians read reports of both sorts of cargo being unloaded from the same plane at Uli, and did not check whether that plane was operated by JCA or not, they could easily jump to conclusions.

Michael Gould, in his 2012 book, revived this false accusation, not with proof but by ambiguous wording. In the introduction he writes, "Unfortunately, some aid agencies were not averse to supplying arms as part of their aid programme to Biafra."[145] No details, no source for this wild accusation. It may have been a distortion of what he says later in a paragraph, itself very inaccurate, about the disputes over delivery of relief to Biafran territory: that the FMG was against airborne delivery because "it left them with no control over the contents of the air supplies. The inference was that arms would be flown in with humanitarian aid, which to a greater or lesser extent was exactly what happened."[146] Very inaccurate sentences leading to a highly misleading conclusion. The last phrase could be taken as supporting the allegation of JCA planes carrying arms, but Gould's source, the former squadron leader Alfred Anowai of the Biafran Air Force, could simply have meant that both arms flights and relief flights landed at Uli, which nobody ever denied. Further on, Gould says that "as the war progressed the Federal Authorities became increasingly obsessed with the idea that much military aid was being airlifted into Biafra with the humanitarian aid. Their obsession was justified, and evidence comes from pilots' reports confirming that often the only way humanitarian aid could reach Biafra was in aircraft chartered to carry arms."[147] This point was always well known, but it related only to the period before the churches' and the ICRC's airlifts combined, never carrying arms, were fully operational. Anowai, quoted here again, may simply have meant again that both relief flights and arms flights used the same airstrip, without suggesting that their cargoes were mixed.

As relief flights and arms flights both used the same airstrip, bomber crews could not distinguish the two at night, but it would be quite wrong to suppose that the Nigerian Air Force (NAF) refrained from attacking Uli for that reason.[148] Even the ICRC, whose flights were approved by Lagos, was told that its crews flew at their own risk. In fact the Air Force, which still made regular raids on civilian targets (on which *West Africa* again declared that they "cannot be justified either militarily or morally"),[149] was simply incapable of causing severe damage to the airstrip. There were some raids on it, but they did not succeed in causing serious damage even in daytime; however effective the Biafrans' camouflage during daylight hours was, since the coordinates of the airstrip were obviously known exactly, that failure must have been due to the Egyptian pilots' inclination to fly high to avoid Biafran anti-aircraft fire. Ojukwu said those Egyptians were "the most yellow-bellied pilots in the world".[150] Until November 1968 the NAF caused little trouble for night flights to Uli; but then things changed. *West Africa* of 9 November reported a Lagos press conference by Yusufu Gobir, permanent secretary of the Ministry of Defence, who said the NAF was now better able to intercept night flights but added, "there are safeguards which will prevent any incidents to relief planes operating through the International Red Cross Committee". This was taken to mean that the ICRC was giving the Nigerians details of the flights and coded signals to identify an ICRC flight to an air force interceptor. I have not seen any reference to this arrangement working successfully. Most of the relief flights, ICRC and other, and most of the arms flights still got through, and it could have been simply because the NAF planes missed them. But in November, *West Africa* carried a report of a rocket attack on two aircraft at Uli, with a Caritas plane said to have been destroyed.[151]

At this time when the Biafra relief operations were making a real difference to a terrible situation, allegations began about their possible side effects helping the Biafran war effort. These were to continue and spread, and will be examined in the next chapter. *West Africa* of 19 October 1968 published an article by Kennedy Lindsay, "Financing Biafra's War", which set out with some detail how missionary and humanitarian work in Biafran territory involved considerable payments in foreign exchange to the Biafran authorities, which they could use for arms purchases or any other purpose. According to Lindsay, missionaries in Biafra, for example, were paid in Biafran pounds, but their employers overseas paid corresponding sums into a Biafran account at the African Continental Bank, in hard currency.

This article raised many questions, including some about the running of Biafra's economy. There was a working administration using the Biafran currency, and banks were still working at least part of the time, but what revenue did the government receive? How, for example, did it, or the Bank of Biafra, provide local currency to a missionary body corresponding to an overseas in-payment of hard currency—by printing money? Lindsay was not wholly convincing. A businessman wrote a letter questioning him; as he wanted to remain anonymous, I published his letter under the Latin alias "Mercator". He rightly asked how Lindsay had got such apparently detailed information. We also published a letter from a missionary's wife casting doubt on what Lindsay said about missionaries' salaries.[152] But Lindsay's main point was surely correct; Biafra was paid in hard currency for the legitimate costs of necessary humanitarian work, and could use that hard currency as it liked. Lindsay persisted for years, with strangely concentrated zeal, in writing in many places about this. Naturally the Nigerian press seized on his *West Africa* article. But the generous public around the world knew nothing of it and properly went on giving for relief of victims of the war. Exposure of possible side effects benefiting one party in the war was never a good reason for not sending badly needed humanitarian aid.

7

BIAFRA ON LIFE SUPPORT
(DECEMBER 1968–NOVEMBER 1969)

Defiance and deadlock

West Africa of 7 December 1968 appealed to the Biafrans to abandon a hopeless struggle: "The world respects and admires the courage and resourcefulness your people have shown; you have made your case thus far. There is no danger of genocide. Politically the 'northern domination' you feared is dead."

Others were certainly appealing to the Biafran leaders in the same sense by then, including some leading Biafrans. Raph Uwechue resigned from his key position as Biafra's representative in Paris in December 1968, and worked on a book in which he said he had explained in his letter of resignation that "the only serious point at issue was the government's attitude towards a negotiated settlement". He believed the Biafrans should give up sovereignty in return for "an arrangement which like the Aburi accord guarantees for Biafra adequate control of her security".[1] He set out detailed proposals for this in the book, which was completed in March 1969, with forewords by Nnamdi Azikiwe and President Senghor of Senegal, and published about three months later. Earlier, though this may not have been publicly known, Azikiwe had written to Colonel Ojukwu on 25 September urging negotiations.[2] Azikiwe had then moved to

215

London, where I saw him at a party to celebrate the 80th birthday of Fenner Brockway, at which Stan Newens presided and Sybil Thorndike spoke;[3] Zik also spoke there, not mentioning the war.

The British Committee for Peace in Nigeria, of which Lord Brockway was chairman, looked tirelessly for some way to bring about peace. In December 1968, as the committee's representatives, Fenner Brockway and James Griffiths MP, travelled to Biafra and had talks with Ojukwu. After visiting Nigeria also, on their return they reported to the British government, which did not listen to the committee's suggestions on arms and peace initiatives. When they addressed a meeting in London I heard them report, among other things, that Ojukwu had said something about death being preferable to surrender, and they had replied, "You have a right to say for yourself that you prefer death to surrender; you have no right to say on behalf of all your people that death is preferable to surrender"; Ojukwu said nothing to this. Probably he had meant that to die fighting was better than surrendering to face slaughter, the usual Biafran argument; but of course the response of those veteran socialist men of peace was the right one. It should be recalled again that they both denounced British arms supplies to Nigeria consistently; Williams of *West Africa* admitted that Jim Griffiths was one critic who had some effect on him.

I recall that at that meeting or another that I attended, Griffiths expressed his hope that some sort of Nigerian unity could continue, but Biafrans in the hall protested loudly, "No!" "Impossible!" In fact some Biafrans may privately have agreed with those calling for a compromise peace involving some sort of Nigerian unity, but those people, such as Uwechue, faced a major difficulty: the federal side was no longer willing to consider anything like the Aburi agreement, and it would not change its mind unless it faced a major military setback. That was highly improbable; the Biafrans now controlled only about one tenth of their original area, and, though well supplied with French weaponry, they did not recover much lost ground. However, in December (when both sides declared truces at Christmas time) the federal First and Second Divisions had still not linked up along the Onitsha–Enugu road, the Biafrans still held the east bank of the Niger for some distance south of Onitsha, and they were attacking in the

Aba and Owerri sectors.[4] In February and March 1969 the First and Second Divisions did link up, but the Biafrans surrounded Owerri.[5] The fighting in these months was on a relatively small scale, but it showed Biafra was still not beaten. At a meeting of the Biafran Consultative Assembly and Council of Chiefs and Elders on 10 February 1969, Ojukwu said, "We cannot give up."[6] About that time the Biafran regime, perhaps as a sign of confidence, perhaps in response to complaints at the strange closure decision, ordered the reopening of primary schools.[7]

Some Biafrans may have hoped that unrest in the Western State starting in November 1968 might help them. If so, they were disappointed, but this unrest, directed above all against taxation, was serious for some weeks. The palace of the Oba of Ishara was burned down, and troops fired on rioters outside offices in Ibadan, killing 11, in late November; after more disturbances a curfew was declared just before Christmas in Ibadan itself and in Ishara, Ede and Oyo.[8] The basic grievance in the West was direct taxation, which had been an oppressive feature of colonial rule over most of Africa and had been continued after independence in Nigeria and other countries. The cost of the war may have increased taxpayers' resentment, but an article in *West Africa* of 22 February 1969 by "a Nigerian correspondent" said this was increased more by the blatant self-enrichment of several army officers: "Nigerian newspapers, like *The Tribune* at Ibadan, had earlier confirmed speculation that many of the magnificent buildings springing up in parts of Lagos, Ikeja, Illupeju [*sic*] and Ibadan are in fact owned by army men and those close to them." Ostentatious money-grubbing by "big men" using all sorts of means, begun by politicians, was quickly taken over by military men. The press was able to speak out against such abuse of power; in January 1969 the *Daily Times* ran a campaign with the slogan "Keep Nigeria one—but clean", and forced the business tycoon S.L. Edu to resign as a commissioner in Lagos State. But illicit self-enrichment was to continue and multiply for decades to come. Criticism of it during the war did not diminish support for the war effort; the Yoruba unrest was not motivated by any political project like that of the gaoled Wole Soyinka, and Biafrans' dreams of Yorubas rising up to help them remained dreams.

Support for the federal war effort remained solid throughout, apart from the Biafrans themselves. Obviously there were great numbers of Nigerians interested only in getting on with their own lives in the villages and towns, and not very interested in the war or any political outcome of it. But there were many others to whom winning the war mattered. A propagandist play, *Keep Nigeria One*, was produced by Hubert Ogunde (who toured Britain in 1968 and again in 1969 with his troupe, performing the usual non-political Yoruba-language repertoire). There was a song in praise of Gowon which was always being played at Nigerians' social occasions in London.

This was a genuine civil war, in which one's neighbour, workmate, classmate, friend or lover of today became the enemy of tomorrow. Civil wars produce exceptional bitterness and hatred, and this one was no exception. The venom expressed on each side about the other was extreme, and on the Nigerian side it did much to support outsiders' suspicions; *West Africa* noted this, and Colin Legum, while rejecting the allegation of genocide, also noted how pro-federal Nigerians indulged in genocidal talk. One journalist of the *Daily Times* told me, "If either side had nuclear weapons they would use them." It was natural to wonder if Nigerians and Biafrans could ever live together again in one country. Yet survivors of other civil wars had done just that, many times—but with lasting ill feeling going on for generations, as in the US, Spain, and the Irish Republic.

With the relative lull in the fighting in the latter months of 1968, fewer refugees arrived in Biafran territory for a time, but the situation of both displaced people and ordinary village dwellers there was still critical after the increase in protein food supplies through the airlift. Reports emphasised that this improvement in the situation was only relative, and precarious. In November 1968, UNICEF and Joint Church Aid (JCA) said the famine in the war zone could get worse than ever in December and January, after the new yam harvest had been eaten.[9] The food shortages did not affect protein intake only. The basic carbohydrate root and tuber crops, quite sufficient in peacetime, were now too scarce or prohibitively expensive; a single yam was reported to have cost £2 in Owerri just before its fall;[10] displaced people had abandoned crops in the fields. The Biafran leaders did not depend totally on the food airlift; they saw that more production was urgently needed.

Biafran's Directorate of Food Production organised a "land army" of young people between 12 and 17 with the slogan "Dig for victory", and encouraged production of protein-rich food crops like beans and groundnuts, among other crops. In late January, Ojukwu declared that these efforts would "mount the assault against the challenge of starvation regarded by our enemy as a legitimate tool of war".[11] Protestant church organisations started an agricultural programme to supplement the official one, increasing local production of crops, including rice.[12] The funds raised from the Western public were used partly for this effort and local purchases of crops, but a good deal was devoted to the airlifts by JCA and the Red Cross; in November the Red Cross in Geneva appealed for another £10 million.[13] In the new year,, Anthony Asika warned of a starvation threat on the federal side of the front;[14] in late February *West Africa* reported from Calabar that in South-Eastern State, "compared with last autumn, with its high death rate from malnutrition, food supplies are now more or less adequate", but still there were about half a million people on the "feeding list".[15]

Public concern over the starvation, and readiness to contribute, remained high at the end of 1968, and later, in the US, Canada, Britain, and Continental Europe. I do not know if the term "compassion fatigue", to describe some responses among the Western public to disasters and emergency appeals, had been coined at the time of the Biafran disaster; if so, it could not have been applied to responses to that disaster. There was no compassion fatigue through 1968 and 1969. Biafra might not always be in the headlines, but it was an ongoing story which the press, radio and television of a dozen countries pursued constantly. While the media also recorded the political and military situation, what affected the public most was the continued truthful reporting of starvation, especially among children. What Harold Wilson later recalled as "the steady drip, drip of pro-Biafran propaganda on the television screens"[16] was in fact, usually, reporting of starvation and relief. The BBC launched a special Biafra appeal at Christmas 1968 in the children's programme *Blue Peter*; there was a big response to the appeal for wool and cotton to raise funds for three hospital trucks, six emergency doctor's cars and various other equipment and drugs to aid children. The presenter, Valerie Singleton, said, "We're not going to say who is right or wrong. All we can say is that war is always wrong."

There were, of course, other prominent overseas news stories, such as Rhodesia, which was in the headlines for a time when Wilson and Ian Smith met for talks aboard HMS *Fearless* in October 1968, but Smith stuck to UDI even though he was offered many concessions for a negotiated settlement. It was obvious that the Commonwealth Heads of Government Meeting in London in January 1969 would have Rhodesia high on the agenda. But it was obvious too that the Nigerian war could not be completely avoided there, however much the Federal Military Government might protest that it was a purely internal affair. In December 1968, 140 MPs signed a motion calling for an immediate ceasefire and a halt to arms sales, but the FMG protested at continued discussion of these matters in the British parliament, saying they were likely to give the Biafrans false hopes and MPs should rather concentrate on Rhodesia.[17]

In the US there was no arms supply issue, but the public anguish over Biafra led to strong pressure for more help for humanitarian efforts, backed by the Democrat senators Hubert Humphrey, Eugene McCarthy and Ted Kennedy among many other prominent Americans. As an example of the US public response, in January 1969 dock workers suspended a strike to load a ship with food to be taken to the Gulf of Guinea for the Biafra airlift. Lyndon Johnson, however, had always accepted the FMG as the legal government of all Nigeria, and had even gone further in verbal support for it; while after Nixon was elected the new president in November, it was soon apparent that in briefing the incoming administration, the civil servants of the State Department, whose view on Nigeria was like that of their counterparts in Britain's new Foreign and Commonwealth Office (FCO), would quietly prevent any following up of Nixon's words on "genocide"—no doubt explained away as campaign rhetoric. But when Johnson announced in December that the US government would make eight C-97 Stratofreighter aircraft available at a bargain price ($4,000 each) for relief flights, four for the ICRC and four for JCA, the FMG protested, saying this would allow Caritas "and other rebel supporters" to use their present aircraft for arms only.[18]

The general state of public opinion in Britain about Nigeria was shown, to name two of many illustrations, by a new editorial in *The*

Spectator on 27 December 1968, headed "Lord Lugard Is Dead" and saying the frontiers established under his governorship of Nigeria "can no longer claim any special justification"; and by a cartoon during the Commonwealth meeting in one of the London evening papers, showing a big heap of corpses in the background and in the foreground a man at a desk marked "Nigeria" saying, "Mind your own business, let's talk about Rhodesia" (another example of the way some British Tories used the terrible ordeal of Biafra in support of Ian Smith). At the end of 1968 the Britain–Biafra Association published a booklet, *Aspects of the Biafran Affair*, by George Knapp, who was, with Greville Jones, a partner in External Development Services, a firm advising several African and Middle Eastern governments on political and economic matters; they were retained as advisers by Eastern Nigeria in 1959, and later by Biafra. It gives a brief description of the war situation, the problem of relief delivery, the propaganda by FMG supporters, the position of the minorities, and notably British policy. Answering the question people were asking, Why don't the Biafrans give up?, Knapp concluded that what Biafrans had faced and were to face was possibly genocide, or at any rate mass killing regardless of the definition, and they could at best hope for subjugation, which they would see as slavery.

At the Commonwealth summit in London in early January 1969, Chief Awolowo headed a large delegation including Anthony Enahoro, Brigadier Hassan Katsina, Aminu Kano and the regular travelling permanent secretary trio of Allison Ayida, Philip Asiodu and Ahmed Joda; he was met at London airport by 15 coachloads of Nigerian students (while 1,500 Biafrans took part in a torchlight march). Awolowo opposed putting the Nigerian war on the agenda, which Wilson ruled out anyway in his opening address. Awolowo had long informal meetings with Presidents Nyerere, Kaunda and Obote; Wilson, after discussion with Awolowo, invited delegates, outside the conference proper, for a "discussion over gin-and-tonic". The Nigerian delegates did not meet Kenneth Dike, Francis Nwokedi and other senior Biafrans who were in London. The excited speculation about some move towards peace had never had any basis and led to nothing. Enahoro said, "There is no way of dealing with armed rebellion in any country other than with force of arms."[19] The unpopularity—outside Nigeria—of his government's stand was shown again when the BBC television programme *24 Hours* devoted most of one hour to Biafra, emphasising the suffering there, and allowed Enahoro just six minutes to reply, after which some dockers at Tees Dock near Middlesbrough, who saw the programme, refused to load arms for Nigeria aboard the Nigerian National Shipping Line vessel *Oba Ovonramwen*.[20] Another shift loaded those arms, and some measures taken against the BBC in Nigeria by an angry FMG after the pro-gramme—cancelling some facilities given it in Lagos, and recalling people from training with the BBC in London[21]—were soon rescinded. The FMG and its supporters had to endure the hostility of unofficial Britain while getting support from official Britain.

World opinion generally, in attitudes to Nigeria, was divided into an official world and an unofficial world. For the official world it was business as usual with Nigeria; Awolowo, speaking at the Commonwealth summit, said Nigeria's current balance of payments problem was "temporary",[22] and this reassurance could be believed because Shell-BP's oil production was already up to 200,000 barrels per day by November–December 1968,[23] and it was expected to reach the pre-war level of 500,000 barrels per day by end of 1969.[24] The official world witnessed or joined in the ceremonial opening of the Kainji Dam—the major project of Nigeria's Six-Year Develop-ment Plan, costing £100 million—by General Gowon on 15 February 1969. The unofficial world neither knew nor cared about this but was concerned with what was happening a few hundred miles away in the war zone, where great numbers of civilians and numerous soldiers were dying each day. In Western Europe, the US and Canada, the official world had to take some notice of the unofficial world's unabat-ing concern over just two big topics relating to Nigeria: the starvation in the war zone, and British arms sales.

Hence there was no let-up in the Western scrutiny of the Nigerian conduct of the war, however much that angered Nigerians. That con-duct was far from satisfactory, in the treatment of POWs for exam-ple; while there were reports suggesting that prisoners were not always being taken in this war, in fact many were taken, but their treatment was very poor. The international military observers made strong new criticisms of their treatment at Kiri-Kiri prison in Lagos—

whose superintendent said his staff did not know the Geneva Convention—and recommended that they should be moved to a separate camp run by the army.[25] Even so, it was right for the observers and others to repeat that genocide was not being pursued or planned, as *West Africa* did on 15 February 1969 in an editorial "The Word and the War". It said, "Anybody who has seen Nigerian soldiers looking after Ibo refugee camps will angrily reject the comparison with Hitler's treatment of the Jews which the Federation's critics imply." In fact, people coming under the control of federal forces had not been adequately assisted, but negligence, however inexcusable, is not genocide. The editorial noted that "the word"—"genocide"—was based on the accusation that the Biafrans were being deliberately starved into submission; it asked, was there evidence that Gowon and his colleagues, "who thought this would be a short war", intended to use starvation as a weapon? Earlier, Auberon Waugh had suggested that the federal forces' advance was deliberately slow, so as to starve the Biafrans rather than defeat them in battle;[26] this was absurd, and all that we heard suggested that the Nigerian leaders badly wanted to defeat the Biafrans as quickly as possible.

West Africa's editorial on 8 March 1969 was headed "Secession or Security?"; this was the question some senior Biafrans had been posing as defeat followed defeat. The magazine's editorial pointed out that secession had not provided Biafrans with security. It also said some of the major arguments against secession—that it would encourage secessions in other parts of Africa, and within Nigeria—were debatable: other secessionist movements in Africa would need to have local sources of support (indeed, the Eritrean secessionists in Ethiopia, and the Southern Sudanese, were determined to fight anyway without consideration of Biafra). But then it said the federal case for war was right because a successful secession by a Biafra confined to East Central State alone would not be good even for the Igbos, and would not make for lasting peace.

Earlier, Nnamdi Azikiwe, in a speech at Oxford on 16 February, seemed to accept the possibility of agreeing to the 12-state structure of Nigeria; however, he called for United Nations intervention, an international peace force established by the Security Council, a total arms embargo declared by that council, and a referendum in the war zones, with an independent Biafra one of the choices. All this was rejected by Lagos. The FMG stood firmly against any peace proposals, including Uwechue's published later, that involved a confederation or something similar; by creating the 12 states it had ruled out that sort of compromise. In fact there were no serious peace moves for months in 1969. So the war went on, and so did the hunger and disease. Biafra had a measles outbreak but it was contained with vaccines flown in by the airlift; the relief agencies' efforts were very effective in medical care as well as food distribution, so far as resources allowed—besides working in several hospitals, they had mobile medical teams for outpatient treatment.[27]

While JCA, which about the new year announced its thousandth relief flight[28] and held a meeting in Copenhagen in late January 1969, went ahead with its São Tomé airlift, ignoring the Federal Government's views, the Red Cross airlift ran into difficulties with newly independent Equatorial Guinea from December 1968. It suspended the ICRC flights briefly in December, and for a longer period in January. There was a dispute over the carrying of fuel aboard the ICRC planes (it was needed for relief distribution by motor vehicles within Biafra and for hospital generators there, but there were reports of its being used for generators at Uli airstrip, which the Red Cross denied); and there was speculation about pressure from Nigeria, whose external affairs commissioner, Okoi Arikpo, visited Santa Isabel in December. In fact the FMG continued to approve the ICRC airlift, but the Nigerian press and public hostility to relief agencies extended to the Red Cross flights. The Equatorial Guinea government held talks with the ICRC (whose Biafra operation brought in money to Fernando Po). But during January, President Macías, addressing a meeting of Nigerians on Fernando Po—a large community resident there for many years, now including many who considered themselves Biafrans—accused the Biafrans of making contact with separatists on the island and joining in a plot.[29]

As permission to resume the flights from Fernando Po was delayed, the ICRC sought another base for the Biafra airlift, and Dahomey soon agreed.[30] It had not been involved before, but President Émile Zinsou, since he took office a few months before, had shown a humane and fair-minded attitude to the war in its giant neighbour, saying he was against secession but against waging a war to end it,[31] and later declaring, "Dahomey is neither for Nigeria nor Biafra in the conflict."[32] So it was not surprising that he agreed to help the airlift to Biafra. His general attitude cannot have pleased the FMG, and when the new airlift started early in February 1969, Enahoro said the Dahomey government had not given any advance notice; it was the ICRC that had informed Lagos.[33] But the airlift went ahead, and on 12 February the flights from Equatorial Guinea resumed, though under some restrictions imposed by the Macías regime. Soon afterwards, that regime was involved in a crisis involving accusations against Spanish timber companies, armed Spanish intervention to save Europeans, and a reported coup attempt on 5 March and the killing of the foreign minister, Atanasio Ndongo.[34] This began a downhill slide into dictatorship, which became a nightmare regime of sadistic terror equalled only by Idi Amin in Uganda. That lay some way ahead, and in 1969 both Equatorial Guinea and Dahomey, a very different country (not quite a democracy, but one of the freest countries in Africa), continued for a while to help save lives with the Red Cross airlift to Biafra.

The ICRC, JCA and French Red Cross relief airlifts could amount to 30 landings per night at Uli, but it was sometimes less, as the precarious operation on the ground did not always work well, and there were threats from anti-aircraft fire on the planes' route to Uli and from Nigerian bombers hovering over the airstrip during the night, though not always all night. For that, the Nigerian Air Force (NAF) had some expert mercenary pilots. During the war something became known about them, and later published works said more. Recently, more has been described in the book published in 2015 by Al J. Venter,[35] a veteran South African journalist who has written two dozen books on various countries, including several on African conflicts. He visited Biafra towards the end of the war, reporting for the *Daily Express*. About aircraft and pilots his book is a good read with many details and good illustrations, several in colour.

There were many reports during the war of a Nigerian Air Force pilot who attacked planes landing at Uli frequently and, with the usual gallows humour of war pilots, sent radio calls saying, "This Is Genocide." Venter records that the pilot flew a Dakota C-47 adapted to carry canisters of explosives, and had a South African accent.[36] There were reports of an NAF pilot called "the Intruder", who may have been a Belgian flying a DC-3, different from the "Genocide" pilot.[37] If the latter was a South African, he was not the only one flying for the Nigerians. Venter's book has many details about Ares Klootwyk, a South African who flew a Soviet MiG-17.[38] South African, British and Australian pilots with the NAF gave more effective service than the Egyptians, while Nigerians were trained at Kano to operate the Russian aircraft. Venter's account confirms what was clear at the time, that the Nigerian air attacks on Uli were not wholly ineffective—they could cause damage to the runway, taking some time to repair, and destroyed a few incoming or landed planes—but were unable to put the airstrip out of service; very few planes and crews were lost. Rather improbable stories were told in some books on the war (not Venter's), and possibly at the time also, of mercenary pilots serving both sides meeting secretly and the Nigerians' pilots agreeing to avoid shooting the others down.[39] If this ever happened, the agreements only lasted a short time.

Bombs, Churchill and Wilson

West Africa regularly criticised the indiscriminate Nigerian air raids, saying on 8 February 1969 that they did more harm than good to the federal side. That obvious fact was not well understood in Lagos. In mid-February there was a report of an air raid on the village of Umuohiagu, with over 400 people killed. The head of the Red Cross in Biafra, H.K. Jaggi, spoke at that time of five hospitals hit by air raids. There was an air raid then on the most densely populated part of Umuahia.[40] The correspondent of *The Times*, Winston Churchill, confirmed that the market at Umuohiagu had been raided and, in *The Times* of 27 February, reported a raid on a market crowded with hundreds of people at the village of Ozu Abam, destroying a maternity clinic and a post office, devastating an area of 10,000 square yards, and killing over 120 people; he was on the scene four hours later. He returned to Britain then, but the press reported other raids later, including one hitting the outpatients department of Queen Elizabeth Hospital in Umuahia, reported (from UPI and AFP) in *The Times* of 3 March.

These air raids caused renewed shock and anger in Britain. The foreign secretary, Michael Stewart, expressed the government's anxiety to Nigeria's high commissioner, Brigadier Ogundipe, but the British government was now under attack. It had been widely denounced for months, not only in Britain but in Continental Europe, where there was great sympathy for Biafra and opposition to Britain's arming of Nigeria—in Sweden, for example, whose prime minister took the matter up with Wilson, and in West Germany, where in February 1969, Wilson, on a visit, was pelted with what looked like a sack of blood by angry demonstrators. Now over 150 backbench MPs supported a motion for a halt to British arms supplies; although the air raids did not use British bombs or planes, Britain was seen as an accomplice in the waging of total war.

In response to all the condemnation, the Federal Government said again that there were strict orders against the bombing of civilian targets. As it was very obvious that those orders were being ignored, military observers in Lagos and the UN representative called on Colonel Shittu Alao, head of the NAF; there was "some tough talking", it was reported, but Alao repeated the FMG denial.[41] In the columns of *The Times*, filled with letters about the air raids, Ogundipe said reports of non-military targets being attacked would be investigated. On 8 March the high commissioner gave a press conference, where he said there had been accidental bombing of civilian targets, but action would be taken against pilots who deliberately bombed them. But he also launched a fierce tirade against Winston Churchill. Although many air raids were reported by a particularly experienced and respected American reporter on the war, Lloyd Garrison, as well as Churchill, supporters of the FMG singled out Churchill for extraordinary abuse. His editor was also attacked, for using the famous name the reporter shared with his late grandfather to win support for the Biafrans.

The vehemence of the attacks on Churchill was startling. I think nobody dared actually to say he had lied, but those attacks implied it. He had not: reports of indiscriminate air raids came from many witnesses. When Umuahia fell to the federal forces in April, a *Daily Express* reporter went there and sent a report headed "Where did those bombs go?", saying, "There was little evidence of the bombing damage so frequently proclaimed by Colonel Ojukwu", with hardly any damage seen to Queen Elizabeth Hospital and the market square.[42] However, there had been more than a month to repair damage (not reported by Churchill but by news agencies) to the hospital, which had to be in constant use, and all the markets attacked from the air could have been back to normal within a day, with stalls easily replaced. Later, A.B. Akinyemi charged that *The Times* "ignored the report of the team of International Observers which contradicted Churchill's reports on the deliberate bombing of Biafran markets, churches and hospitals".[43] But the observers were never able to enter Biafran territory, and on 10 March 1969 said, obviously, that they could not rule on the accuracy of the air raid reports.[44] There should be no doubt about the indiscriminate bombing reported by Churchill, Garrison and many others.

At *West Africa* we had no doubt at the time. Matchet (the editor) wrote on 8 March that the indiscriminate air raids probably strengthened Biafran resistance; the Egyptian pilots might be incompetent or their planes unsuitable, or they might just not care, and perhaps the FMG should send them home. It declared that the raids "serve no military purpose", which was true according to legitimate military considerations. The raids did cause enormous disruption inside Biafra, with a great deal of activity having to stop during daylight hours— troop movements, but also plenty of ordinary civilian activity— because of the fear of enemy aircraft. This constant disruption no doubt affected Biafran military operations, but that could not possibly justify the air raids except according to the principles of total war. Britain had followed those principles in the area bombing of Germany in the Second World War, but there was by the 1960s increasing recognition that this had been unjustified, and anyway Nigerians could not properly talk of Hamburg and Dresden to defend what they were doing now. Ogundipe on 8 March said the Umuohiagu market was close to an important crossroads, which seemed to imply the total war logic which his government claimed not to follow. However, a group of pro-federal MPs wrote to Ogundipe restating their support for Nigeria but calling for an end to air raids on civilians, saying the Second World War had shown such raids were "barbarous" and likely to fortify the spirit of those attacked.[45]

While controversy raged in the British media, with Hugh Fraser and Woodrow Wyatt clashing on BBC television, the House of Commons debated the whole Nigeria arms supply issue again on 13 March. Maurice Foley, undersecretary for foreign and Commonwealth affairs, called the air raids "cruel and militarily useless", but defended the government's policy, saying, "We could not avoid involvement; we had no other honourable option." Frank Allaun, just back from Biafra, was one of the Labour MPs who spoke on the other side. In the end, only 62 MPs voted against the government. *West Africa*'s reporter (I cannot recall who it was) noted that no speakers made accusations of genocide.[46] Churchill did not allege this either in an article he wrote in *The Times*, where he said Nigerian unity made sense and there was no reason to dispute borders simply because of their colonial origin. He claimed that the British arms sales were due mainly to fear of increased Soviet influence in Nigeria, but said that influence was in fact rising anyway.[47] It was quite true that the Cold War-oriented Wilson government feared that the USSR could acquire a powerful position in Lagos; Wilson said this plainly in his later book—the Russians "were tightening their grip on Nigeria's life".[48] Those fears were fairly ridiculous. *West Africa* said in an editorial that there was no evidence of Moscow having or going to have "real political influence in Nigeria's government".[49] As for any idea that Nigerians would ever adopt anything resembling Communism, that was laughable.

Churchill, who had been to Lagos as well as Biafra, also noted that what was said about the war in the Nigerian capital, by British officials among others, was far from what was known to be happening on the Biafran side—that is, far in facts, not opinion. This had been noted by journalists since the beginning of the war. British officials, anxious to try to curb the media criticism of their government's policy, found that dismissing reports from Biafra as "propaganda" could achieve the opposite effect to that intended. On *West Africa* we strove to stick to the principle "Facts are sacred, comment is free". The editor's comments were pro-federal—he defended British arms supplies again during the air raids controversy, while suggesting the use of aircraft might be inappropriate except "in close support of ground troops"[50]— but our news pages sought and, I believe, obtained full objectivity. At

this time there were only three or sometimes only two of us producing each issue; then, in April 1969 I believe, the editorial staff was
joined by Danny Nelson, who had been editor of *The People* in Uganda.
The offices of Overseas Newspapers had earlier been moved a short
distance to Cromwell House, Fulwood Place, with effect, for *West
Africa*, from the issue of 8 February 1969.

At the end of the Commons debate on 13 March, it was announced
that Harold Wilson would travel to Nigeria. The idea had been discussed earlier, but now it was apparently thought important for
British domestic politics that Wilson, who had often sent ministers to
Lagos at times of pressure at home over the arms, should go there
himself. He went to Lagos on 27 March. He visited Enugu, Port
Harcourt and Calabar, and went also to Kano, where one demonstra-
tor had a placard saying "Wilson, your press is bought". This was one
expression of the Nigerian public's very critical attitude to Britain—
though Biafra Radio, in a raving comment, said the demonstrations
showed that "even aggressor Nigeria" was rebelling against "Britain's
insistence on total genocide". Wilson expressed support for Nigeria
clearly, as in Enugu, where he said he now knew Igbos could live at
peace under the FMG.[51] But in his talks with General Gowon he
spoke strongly about the air raids, and while Gowon continued to
protest that the air force was ordered to attack only military targets,
he must have got the message that such orders were well known to
be constantly flouted and this would affect Britain's attitude. In his
memoirs, Wilson wrote later that "one of the concrete results of my
visit was an end of those bombing raids".[52] In fact, the heavy indiscriminate air raids almost ceased for several months.

Before and during the visit there was frenzied speculation about a
possible meeting between Wilson and Ojukwu, even perhaps in Biafra
(where his name was execrated), perhaps at another venue; there was
then a flurry of argument about who said what to whom, but it seems
clear that a meeting was considered, and there was at one point agreement to meet in Abidjan. Then, however, Ojukwu said he could not
leave Biafra at that time, as a federal offensive was in progress.[53]

What the Biafrans called the "Wilson offensive" began on 26 March.
Troops of the First Division reached Uzuakoli, a few miles north of
Umuahia, and evacuation of the Biafran capital began on 4 April; on

15 April Bende was taken. It was reported in the French newspaper *Le Figaro* that there had been a halt in French arms supplies, angering the Biafrans, but that arms deliveries to Uli had since increased.[54] Later, *West Africa*'s Griot columnist heard that de Gaulle had ordered a halt to the arms supplies for three weeks but had been persuaded by Foccart and Houphouët-Boigny to restart them.[55] The increased arms supplies could not save Umuahia, which was captured on 22 April. Biafra Radio went off the air for four days, presumably because of a forced move. The telex link between Umuahia and Lisbon ceased to function, at least for a time;[56] it had been an important link between Biafra and the outside world.

While the Biafrans showed great skill in adapting to the vagaries of war to keep things running, the loss of Umuahia clearly caused serious disruption. But Nigerian celebrations of the capture of what had been Biafra's capital since the fall of Enugu did not last long. Biafran troops withdrew from Umuahia to join others who had been besieging Owerri for four months, and quickly took the city; the FMG admitted it had withdrawn from there on 28 April. This was the first time in this war, where the taking or defence of cities was considered vital, that the federal forces had lost an important city after capturing it. The Biafrans established some government offices at Owerri, though it had been severely damaged, and continued to advance southwards. Their Consultative Assembly met on 1 May and voted to offer Ojukwu the rank of general; he had refused this before, but now accepted it.

The recent federal advance had ended with the Biafrans on the offensive. They had remained active in the Mid-West, which the Biafran Organisation of Freedom Fighters (BOFF) and other Biafran forces were easily able to enter; they had retained control along both banks of the Niger. The rivers, forests and swamps of the delta area, ideal country for guerrillas and infiltrators, included areas of onshore oil exploration and production by Agip and Shell-BP, and on 9 May Biafrans attacked an oil camp near Kwale, killing 11 foreigners working for Agip and capturing 18 others, including 14 Italians. This led to an international incident much headlined at the time. At the end of May the captives were tried and sentenced to death for helping the Nigerian enemy, but there were appeals by the Pope and the UN secretary general, and the Italian deputy foreign minister, Mario Pedini, went to Biafra (the only member of a Western government ever to do so); on 4 June the Portuguese government announced that the 18 would be freed, and they shortly were.[57] Ojukwu said the world had shown more concern about the fate of a handful of white men than about great numbers of Africans; this had been true of attitudes to the Congo wars, but it was not true about Biafra, for there had been great anguish in the West for the past year about starving Africans there. Ojukwu would, however, have lost support in the West if the captives had been executed. In the event he may not have lost any, and that attack in the Mid-West was the beginning of many Biafran attacks on the oil industry, further proving that Biafra was far from finished.

There were reports of more fighting and new displacements of people in the Mid-West in May and June 1969. The Second Division there had proved as ineffective—against military adversaries—under Haruna as under Murtala Muhammed. Haruna lost that command when, following the federal setbacks—but not because of them, it was officially stated—all the three divisional GOCs were replaced in mid-May. Haruna was replaced by Lt Colonel Gibson Jalo, Colonel I.D. Bisalla became GOC of the First Division in place of Colonel Shuwa (who did not in fact hand over for another four months), and for the Third Division Colonel Olusegun Obasanjo, commander of the Ibadan Garrison Organisation, took over from the notorious Colonel Adekunle.[58] The Biafrans were now making some advances against the Third Division, and a *West Africa* editorial on "Two Years of Biafra", on 7 June 1969, said, "there can be no certainty of a quick or easy Federal military victory".

Frustrated at their army's lack of progress, many Nigerians were ready to blame the outside world: the British press, the world attention concentrated on the Biafrans and the constant repetition of the name of Biafra, the relief agencies, and even the British government, forced by British public opinion to place conditions on its support for Nigeria and keep it under constant scrutiny. Such feelings were widespread in the North, where there was also vicious hatred of the Igbos. I read the venom of Kaduna Radio in the *Summary of World Broadcasts*, but did not hear at the time about a vile chant in Hausa broadcast regularly on that station, summoning people to murder and rape to complete the killings of 1966.[59] On one occasion, I think in the summer of 1969, I attended a meeting of the Britain–Nigeria Association—a group of former governors and colonial officials, business executives and others linked with Nigeria—where David Williams spoke about the war. When a questioner asked if Williams saw any signs of regret among Northerners for the pogroms or among Igbos for "January the 15th", he said he saw some among the latter, but not among the former, who said the pogroms "should be forgotten".

This disgraceful attitude to the great crime which had caused the war was not confined to the North. The annual report of the Nigerian Railway Corporation for 1966–7, the year including the pogroms, stated that 6,000 workers "absconded" (these were Eastern Nigerians fleeing for their lives). At one of Ogundipe's press conferences I asked him if the Federal Government was planning to bring the authors of the pogroms to justice. He shouted back, "Do you think two wrongs make a right?" I replied, "Certainly not, sir", and he said, "That answers your question." It did not, of course. But it may be that any effort by Gowon to bring those major criminals to justice—apart from some soldiers who, it was reported, were charged—would have led to his fall. For the North, imbued with a fierce chauvinistic attitude, was still very powerful. The FMG's assurances that the old Northern domination had ended were true in the sense that the outsize Northern Region dominating the whole Federation was gone, as had much of the old emirate local government system,[60] but a major part of that former region—the Hausa–Fulani emirates and the similar Borno and Bida (Nupe) emirates—still had great power as a populous and economically important area. Northerners could often disregard the FMG's words about the war being only against the rebel leaders and not against the Igbo people, about the need to allow relief for civilians on the secessionist side on agreed conditions, about a general amnesty after the war, and other such things, and accuse Gowon of being under the influence of fellow Christians and the Western world. And yet, the careful protection of Eastern Nigerians' "abandoned property", with rents collected for handing to the owners in due course, was enforced in the North. This was one aspect of federal policy that rightly impressed the world.

It was clear to observers of the conflict who were won over by Gowon's friendly and conciliatory manner that many Nigerians did not share his humane and decent views expressed in his Code of Conduct and his concern to have it followed, and his willingness to agree to overland daylight delivery of relief to Biafran territory. He was rightly admired for sticking to those views, but his foreign admirers did not always understand him right. He was very firm and uncompromising about winning the war, and demanded that it must be ended by the Biafrans accepting the 12 states of Nigeria. The virulent propaganda in the media, backed by at least one senior member of the Federal Executive Council (Aminu Kano), implicitly criticised Gowon for being too soft, but did not attack him openly, so far as I recall. The public knew he was not soft at all about carrying on until victory; he seemed in fact to be popular. On 19 April 1969 the country celebrated the wedding of Yakubu Gowon with Victoria Zakari (a girl-next-door, from the Wusasa Anglican Christian community where he had grown up).

Africa and Biafra

In France, a Biafra Week was held in March 1969, sponsored by the government with, it was stated officially, a humanitarian focus. But there were calls for French recognition of Biafra; celebrities including François Mauriac and the famous Resistance leader and journalist Emmanuel d'Astier de La Vigerie signed an appeal for recognition in January 1969.[61] Much of the French reporting on the war was pro-Biafran, and so were several books now beginning to appear, such as *Biafra an II* (reviewed in *West Africa* of 25 January 1969) by François Debré, son of the prominent Gaullist politician who was at that time foreign minister, Michel Debré. But formally and officially the French government continued normal relations with Nigeria, and French business there was unaffected; the elder Debré wrote to Lagos saying France would continue to recognise only the FMG, and four French deputies visited Nigeria. Two Gaullist deputies visited Biafra about the same time and, on their return, called for recognition of Biafra's independence.[62] France had a Comité d'Action pour le Biafra (headed by Raymond Offroy, former French ambassador to Nigeria), an

Association France–Biafra, and a Comité International de Lutte contre le Génocide au Biafra.[63]

The arms supplies, officially denied in Libreville and Paris, went on apart from the three-week halt already mentioned. But the man behind them, President de Gaulle, put his job on the line by calling a referendum on his proposals for reform of the French Senate and a new sort of "partnership" in industry; and when voters rejected these proposals on 27 April 1969, he resigned as promised. The interim president, Alain Poher, promptly sacked Foccart. Foccart recalled later that in May 1969 Nigeria's foreign minister visited Paris and held talks with Debré, in which he gave details of deliveries from Abidjan and Libreville, all exactly correct;[64] this must have been the visit by Arikpo to Debré on 2 May, the day Foccart was sacked. But in June, Georges Pompidou, who had been prime minister under de Gaulle for six years, was elected president; de Gaulle was gone, but Gaullism reigned again, and Foccart was recalled to his position (with a slight variation in the description of it). The aid to Biafra continued; but without de Gaulle, who had said it was possible, French recognition of Biafra was no longer to be expected.

Biafra did receive one more recognition to add to the four African ones in 1968: in March 1969 Haiti declared recognition, which was announced in Umuahia at a reception for a visiting Zambian delegation.[65] Haiti is one of the most African parts of the African diaspora, and in the past was highly regarded in Africa because of its struggle for independence; but in 1969 it was ruled by the vicious dictatorship of François "Papa Doc" Duvalier, not a reputable friend for the Biafrans (though they could not pick and choose).

Elsewhere in the African diaspora there was plenty of humanitarian sympathy for Biafra, and Nyerere was much respected, but many people were probably impressed by Nigeria's potential to be a strong African state. A US State Department official, asked by *West Africa*'s Matchet who were the supporters of Biafra in the US, answered, "Well there's the Catholics, then there's the Protestants, then there's the Jews, then there's the atheists; and I suppose the Buddhists and anybody else ..."[66] But, the editor added, "the Negro establishment leaders appear to have no doubt about the disastrous consequences to Africa of Biafran secession", an example being the African American congressman Charles Diggs, who had led an official mission to Nigeria and Biafra soon after Nixon took office. In May 1969 Williams, visiting Washington for a conference organised by the Georgetown University Center for Strategic and International Studies, wrote again of an "almost total lack of support for Biafra from the Negro-Americans", illustrated by an address to that conference, very critical of the idea of US intervention, by Theodore Brown, director of the American Negro Conference on Africa.[67] However, some supporters of Martin Luther King and civil rights were sympathetic to Biafra. On 29 August 1968 Joan Baez, the great Hispanic songstress of the Civil Rights Movement, and Jimi Hendrix, a supporter (though not very prominent) of that movement, performed at a Biafran Relief Benefit Show in Manhattan.

The general African official support for Nigerian unity was made clear once again when the OAU Consultative Committee met in Monrovia from 18–20 April 1969. All the committee's six heads of state were there except for General Akwasi Afrifa, who had just taken over as head of Ghana's National Liberation Council (NLC) after the resignation of General Ankrah (for accepting a large bribe from an Igbo businessman). The concluding statement urged both sides to accept "a united Nigeria which ensures all forms of security and guarantees of equality of rights and privileges to all its citizens".[68] This reasserted strong support for Nigeria, thanks—it was reported—to insistence by Diallo Telli and President Ahidjo of Cameroon. But there had been an apparent readiness to discuss a compromise solution of a looser political union in Nigeria which Biafra could join, renouncing independence. There was probably a good deal of support for such ideas in Africa. Many African governments may have supported Nigeria out of a sense of obligation, without much sympathy, longing for some flexibility from Lagos. President Senghor wrote a foreword to Raph Uwechue's book, whose proposals were far from FMG policy, though his support for those proposals was partial and cautious. Several African governments showed a reserved or ambiguous attitude, such as Sierra Leone, Tunisia and Congo-Brazzaville. It was reported in Uganda that President Obote had been close to recognition of Biafra but had held back when there was a chance of him helping to make peace as host to the Kampala talks. President Zinsou of Dahomey said, "In Africa, when two brothers are quarrelling, we don't say that it is an internal affair, neither do we say that one or the other is guilty."[69] The FMG did not like such talk, but its reaction was restrained—so long as a country did not actually declare recognition of Biafra, lukewarm or ambiguous support for Nigeria was tolerated.

Ordinary African citizens around the continent did not all support the OAU collective viewpoint on Nigeria; far from it. There was considerable sympathy for the Biafrans in many African countries.[70] In Sierra Leone it grew steadily during 1969, when Francis Nwokedi stayed there for some time as Biafran representative. David Williams, who liked visiting Sierra Leone, now found himself constantly challenged when in Freetown about his support for Nigeria. Eventually, Sierra Leone's House of Representatives unanimously passed a motion calling on Prime Minister Siaka Stevens's government to "use its good offices" to resolve the conflict, and eight members asked it to recognise Biafra.[71] There was plenty of sympathy for Biafra in Ghana also, doubtless encouraged by the many Biafrans living there; supporters of Nigeria were annoyed by the Ghanaian media's coverage of the war.

During the war there was some speculation that ex-president Kwame Nkrumah, now in exile in Guinea, sympathised with Biafra. He was not known to have made any statements on the war, and that could have been difficult because the president of Guinea, Ahmed Sékou Touré, was a strong supporter of Nigeria. Nkrumah apparently did take a quite contrary stand; when in power, he had been very hostile politically to Northern Nigeria, and, most significant, during the civil war the magazine *Africa and the World*, founded by the Nkrumah government in 1960, backed Biafra strongly. Published in London, it was financed by that government until its fall, and after that Nkrumah provided funds to help it continue publication.[72] Each monthly issue was received in the *West Africa* office, presumably by subscription or exchange, and there were full-page advertisements of issues of *Africa and the World* in *West Africa*, although it totally opposed Williams's support for the Ghana NLC, continuing to champion Nkrumah. *Africa and the World*, a radical pan-African magazine, supported Biafra so firmly and so consistently that Nkrumah must have been at least inclined towards sympathy for that side. But that did not mean giving it full support. Nkrumah became more radically left-wing in exile, and left-wingers who had sympathy for Biafra were aware that it was not socialist or egalitarian at all. Nkrumah wrote in 1968, in a letter published much later, "Neither Ojukwu or Gowon are socialist", and said the solution was for Nigeria to be "divided into four independent separate states, all pursuing a socialist pattern of society within the framework of an All-African Union Government". He approved of Obi Egbuna's *The Murder of Nigeria*,[73] which was published by Panaf, the London publishers of books by Nkrumah, operating then from the offices of *Africa and the World*.

In Cameroon there was widespread sympathy for Biafra, especially in West Cameroon, the former British Southern Cameroons, which had been closely linked with Eastern Nigeria. Since its voters in the 1961 referendum chose union with former French Cameroun rather than with Nigeria, and since that was seen as an anti-Igbo vote—there was resentment against Igbo traders living in Cameroons as well as against the Eastern Region government dominated by Igbos—it might have been thought that in the Biafran war West Cameroonians would sympathise with the South-Eastern and Rivers opposition to Igbo Biafran rule. The contrary happened. Soon after secession, *West Africa*'s correspondent found West Cameroonians backing Biafra, and suggested they identified with it because they themselves were already resenting the hegemony of the much-larger francophone part of the country and its dictatorial leader, President Ahmadou Ahidjo.[74] I encountered pro-Biafran sentiment among Cameroonians on a visit to the country in 1968, for the tenth anniversary of Ahidjo's coming to power, and later in London, where I quite often met Cameroonian students. Both anglophone and francophone Cameroonians were often pro-Biafran, in contrast to President Ahidjo. The president was still sore about the former British Northern Cameroons—at those tenth anniversary celebrations he spoke of "our brothers separated from the motherland"—but supported Nigeria strongly in the war; he restated this support emphatically at a congress of his single party (the Union Nationale Camerounaise) at Garoua in March 1969. But in the first months of the war two Cameroonian newspapers, the Protestant *La Semaine Camerounaise* and the Catholic *L'Effort Camerounais*, expressed support for Biafra.[75] West Cameroonian students I met in London commonly spoke just like Biafrans about the war.

In contrast, some African governments went beyond words and actively helped Nigeria. There were the notorious Egyptian pilots; Algeria sent a military medical team for the Third Division (badly needed as the Nigerian army's medical service was very deficient); and that division, it seems, also employed some Chadian soldiers. There were reports during the war and later[76] of Chadian mercenaries called "Gwado-Gwado" (with some variation in spelling), but with few details; I have never found out the full story of them. The name seems to be Hausa, but that language is widely spoken in Chad. Were they individuals leaving a bankrupt country to earn money with the Nigerian army, or were these troops—said to be two battalions—recruited through the Chadian government? How did Colonel Adekunle find them useful? Did President Tombalbaye not need troops at home where there was serious unrest, or did he want to get some troops out of the way and earn money in the process? This is one of the more obscure episodes in the war.

Biafran resilience and the Ahiara Declaration

By 1969 Western journalists were travelling frequently to Biafra; many took the route via Paris and Libreville, which was shorter than the one via Lisbon, though that was still being flown. The Western public was seeing regular reports from inside the besieged enclave, with photos; although television crews at that time had problems with bulky equipment, many brought back film of life in Biafra, and photojournalists like Don McCullin used ordinary cameras to great effect. Besides newspaper, magazine, radio and television reports, by mid-1969 books about the war were coming off the presses.

Raph Uwechue's book *Reflections on the Nigerian Civil War* was reviewed, soon after publication, in an article in *West Africa* of 14 June 1969. After examining the crisis and civil war, Uwechue concluded that the Biafran leaders had wrongly continued to insist on full sovereignty when their people's legitimate demand was rather for security. He suggested immediate steps starting with simultaneous renunciation of the Biafran secession and the Nigerian decree creating the 12 states, and a ceasefire supervised by a mixed OAU and Common-wealth force, with UN observers, to be followed by moves towards civilian rule and a census. He further suggested that for a "transition period" the country should be divided into six states—three in the North and three in the South—and that these states should have more powers than the existing 12 states; Nigeria must be "a *loose federation—a United States of Nigeria* based with suitable modifications ... *on the Aburi accord*."[77] These proposals could have been a good basis for an end to the war and a better and more secure future, but they would have required years of dedicated effort based on sustained all-round goodwill. In fact, neither the FMG nor the Biafrans considered them for a moment.

The same article in *West Africa* also reviewed another new book, *The Making of a Nation: Biafra*, by two recently graduated Biafrans, Arthur Nwankwo and Samuel Ifejika.[78] A strongly committed defence of the Biafran case, speaking of Gowon's "genocidal war" and saying "Biafra, as a political reality, has come to stay", it is, however, not written as a polemic to arouse popular backing for the cause; it seems to be meant for scholars, consisting largely of a detailed history of the background to the war, with documents reproduced at length. But a postscript by Nwankwo, on the situation in Biafra up to October 1968, is more like reporting for the general public, with horrific descriptions of the starvation and the rise in food prices to impossible levels. Genocide is asserted as a certain fact—except for a small minority of dissenters ready to change sides, says Nwankwo, 95 per cent of Biafrans "are today faced with total extermination".[79] There is also an insight into internal problems within Biafra: "While some children pine away in the houses of death, others still have monthly gifts of expensive toys to play with while their well-fed par-ents indulgently watch them in air-conditioned rooms, sipping beer and smoking cigarettes."[80] And there were the tensions between civil-ians and soldiers and between civil servants and the civilian director-ates involved in some war work; this problem was also mentioned by N.U. Akpan in his book after the war.[81]

The extreme wealth flaunted by some Biafrans amid the torment of so many others was obviously noted by writers and journalists besides Nwankwo. A correspondent of the French daily *Combat* wrote of a former politician with immense power over the region of Orlu, with a villa and a private beach, charging the Red Cross rent for the Awo-Omamma hospital.[82] Such people must be clearly distinguished from other Biafrans who avoided the extremes of destitution but were not among the super-rich. There were many such people—civil servants, professional people, clergy—who managed to keep going with difficulty, with a big fall in their living conditions. It is such people who are portrayed in Chimamanda Ngozi Adichie's *Half of a Yellow Sun*. Though they did not starve, they were short of almost everything, struggling to get some scarce goods such as batteries for radios, much sought after. I recall hearing of one family asking a Biafran traveller from Britain to Biafra to bring teabags.

Biafrans in Britain and other Western countries mostly did what they could to help their people at home. I did not hear many details of how they did so, but they raised considerable sums of money. Some may have been donated to the relief agencies; I do not know if ways were found to send money to individuals, but they probably were—ordinary money transfers were impossible, but it must have been possible to give foreign currency to travellers who would pay the Biafran currency equivalent to people in Biafra. I did not hear of food parcels being sent regularly to people there. But while delivery of food to the starving refugees must have been left to the Red Cross and JCA and their local distribution networks, for individuals— mostly, no doubt, in the category of the hard-hit but not totally destitute—occasional gifts could be sent with the help of travellers. Biafran travellers must usually have been people on government business, but there were no doubt others, a fortunate few; I remember a good article in *The Guardian* by a 15-year-old Biafran girl on her return from a trip to the home country. Western travellers carrying presents for Biafrans could be journalists and aid workers, but especially missionaries, who were vital as carriers of letters. It was vitally important for Biafrans abroad to get news from home, and for their people at home to hear from them. In fact, many spent long periods without news of their own people but with dismal general news constantly reported in the media. Not surprisingly, we heard of Biafrans in Britain having mental breakdowns. For the particular problems of students, stranded with no family or scholarship money coming in, an Africa Educational Trust was founded in London; it had its offices in the same building as the Africa Centre.

In Biafra, a more or less normal money economy still operated after two years of secession and blockade, despite the extreme inflation; new shilling and threepence coins were issued then, with a palm tree, a rising sun and the words "Peace, unity and freedom" on one side and an eagle on the other.[83] Markets were open regularly as many people could still buy and sell. But there was the utter destitution and starvation which horrified the world. The help sent by the world made a difference, but not enough. August Lindt, the ICRC commissioner, said in late April 1969 that the famine in Biafra was under control, but he meant only that it was not spreading out of control as in the year before; he added that protein deficiency was widespread still, and tuberculosis also.[84] And amid the suffering there were a few flaunting great wealth, and the contrast disturbed many Biafrans.

Ojukwu came out to condemn the gross inequality and call for higher ideals in a long speech on 1 June 1969 in which he set out an ideology or philosophy that Biafra should follow, going beyond the winning of the war, which of course he spoke of as well. It was given at the village of Ahiara, where Ojukwu had his headquarters at that time in "a camouflaged colonial building", so Chinua Achebe recalled much later. Achebe was a member of a National Guidance Committee under the Ministry of Information, set up to study what sort of country Biafra should be, what principles it should follow.[85] The document it produced was called the Ahiara Declaration, a name recalling the Arusha Declaration of 1967 issued by Biafra's ally President Nyerere; it was delivered in an address by Ojukwu to the Consultative Assembly.

The very long declaration[86] spoke of the ideals of freedom and excellence and condemned the Nigerians, mentioning the blockade and the air raids, but also faults within Biafra, where, Ojukwu said, people had not thrown off Nigerian habits. He said,

> We accuse the Nigerians of inordinate love of money, ostentatious living and irresponsibility; but here, even while we are engaged in a war of national survival, even while the very life of our country hangs in the balance, we see some public servants who throw huge parties to entertain their friends; who kill cows to christen their babies.

He called for an end to "rigid class distinctions" in the army, perhaps thinking of the reform of the Tanzanian army by Nyerere. He denounced the international foes of Biafra, including the Arabs, aiming to control all of Africa, and the Soviet Union, which he called "Bolshevik Russia".

In his book published after the war, N.U. Akpan, head of the Biafran civil service, said the declaration was influenced by "intellectuals and professionals" contemptuous of the civil service and institutions;[87] his tidy administrative mind was put off by such people. But others approved of the declaration, which was followed by action against corruption and other misconduct,[88] and the establishment of an orientation college for training in Ahiara principles.[89] It did not talk of socialism but it said, "every individual must consider all he has, whether in talent or material wealth, as belonging to the community", while adding that this did not mean "the abolition of personal property". Akpan later said some people were worried about what this might mean. But Ojukwu's commitment to greater equality may have been popular at a time when almost everyone was suffering in Biafran territory, and it may have won some approval in the West. The printed version of the declaration was issued with a photograph of the bearded Ojukwu looking like Fidel Castro or Che Guevara, heroes of young and less young left-wing Third-Worldists in the West; that must have been intentional, though such people's backing, if it came, could not help Biafra much.

In the Ahiara Declaration, Ojukwu mentioned Biafran troops' successes in the war, saying they were holding positions in Elele and on the outskirts of Igrita, well south of Owerri on the way to Port Harcourt, while federal forces on the Onitsha–Enugu road, he said, dared not leave that road. Some Biafran gains could be followed by retreat, but the overall picture for some months after April 1969 was of Biafrans advancing. And by the time of the declaration, Biafra had a new and more effective air arm, as will be described shortly.

Mercenaries and spies

Frederick Forsyth's book *The Biafra Story* was published as a Penguin Special on 29 June 1969, its 30,000 print run being sold out in four weeks; it was reviewed in *West Africa* of 30 August 1969. It concisely describes the prelude to the war, the actual fighting of which Forsyth witnessed a good deal; the British government's role which he condemns absolutely; and the crisis of starvation and quarrels over relief. The author showed the same skill in writing for the intelligent average reader that he was to show in his novels in later years, but this time in writing fact. Fact written from a viewpoint highly sympathetic to Biafra, but still fact: what he and others wrote was dismissed by others because of their pro-Biafran sympathies, but that prejudice was unwarranted—obviously, mass disasters have usually been reported by those sympathetic to the victims. But his interpretations can be questioned. He suggests that Britain culpably acted to support the unity of Nigeria even before the war, whereas then the break-up of the country did not seem to be a way to peace, but to further bloodshed; diplomatic efforts to avoid a break-up were justified for that reason, as they were not the same as help to reimpose unity by force later. And, as noted earlier, Forsyth is too ready to see the hideous massacres that he records as evidence of planned genocide; troops in war can behave unpredictably towards civilians, sometimes murderous, sometimes decent—the Vietnamese villagers of My Lai saw American soldiers coming one day to give out chocolate, another day to kill everyone, and similar things happened in Biafra.

Forsyth was fascinated by mercenaries and inclined to romanticise them, as was shown a few years later in his novel *The Dogs of War*, about an African state under a murderous despot—a very thin disguise for Equatorial Guinea under Francisco Macías Nguema—and an attack by mercenaries (aided by ex-Biafrans recruited through a barely disguised Ojukwu) to overthrow him.[90] But in *The Biafra Story* he deflated the reputation of mercenaries, saying, "the contribution of the white man to the war on the Biafran side must be reckoned as well under one per cent."[91] However, he describes in some detail the real contribution made by Rolf Steiner and Taffy Williams and the Biafran Fourth Commando Brigade they put together, especially in resisting the federal advance on Aba.[92] Steiner, who was mad and admitted it, was eventually forced onto a plane out of Biafra. This presumably lay behind a statement by Ojukwu, reported in *West Africa* of 25 November 1968, that eight Europeans fighting for Biafra (unnamed) had been expelled for "indiscipline and brigandage".

There is some information on the Biafrans' mercenary pilots, and those who supplied Biafra on the Wharton Lisbon run, in the recent book by Venter, who shows admiration for these mercenaries and sympathy for the cause of the white Rhodesians, among whom some of the pilots were recruited. Besides Jack Malloch, a Rhodesian who also took part in Ian Smith's sanctions-busting, the Biafrans' foreign war pilots included Freddy Herz, a German, and Jan Zumbach (alias John Brown), a Pole. There were also the numerous pilots who flew the relief supply planes; not much has been published about them. Although the relief deliveries and arms deliveries were quite separate after the end of the Wharton operation, and both were obviously different from bombing operations for Biafra, probably some of the mercy flight pilots also flew arms planes or bombers on other occasions, or at any rate were mercenaries like the others—those relief pilots may not have been saints, even though they saved countless lives.

There was never any doubt about foreigners in the Nigerian Air Force, which depended heavily on them, and there were known to be some in the Nigerian Navy. Reports of British military personnel assisting the Federal Nigerian army are not supported in Venter's book. They were made by Forsyth frequently—after the war, an SAS veteran told him he had once had him in his gun sight in Nigeria[93]— but by others also, including Jean Wolf and Claude Brovelli.[94] At *West Africa* we brushed aside too hastily reports of mercenaries with the army, perhaps because we were tired of the wild stories of mercenaries in the Nigerian and Biafran media. Quite early in the war there was a British TV programme apparently showing mercenaries on the Nigerian side (I did not see the programme and do not know exactly what it showed), and Nigerians wrote angry protests that we published in the magazine. Later, Ogundipe told David Williams that he had rejected one individual's offer of military service; mentioning this in the office, Williams said, "So he admits he sees such people." That man may simply have demanded too much money, and others may have been recruited.

In the House of Commons debate on 27 August 1968, James Davidson (Labour) mentioned information he had received, originating from a federal officer POW, about British officers with the federal army, possibly mercenaries. Such reports need to be taken with caution but, added to other indications, make it safe to assume that there were most probably British officers with the Nigerian army—maybe true mercenaries, maybe not. On the Biafran side, mercenaries were recruited through the Foccart network, as was well known and as Foccart later admitted; it is quite possible that there was some secret British operation involving mercenaries on the other side—the British secret state is more truly secret than the French and American ones, as was shown when the SAS's advisory role in the Indian military assault on the Golden Temple in Amritsar in 1984 was kept secret for thirty years.

Mercenaries fought in other African wars in later years, in Angola for example, and fascinated the Western public; they were portrayed in the film *The Wild Geese* in 1978, a horrible film but no worse than the reality of mercenaries like Peters in the Congo and Callan in Angola. There should be no surprise that African belligerents, like others, have been ready to employ the most disreputable people to help them to victory. What is surprising is the amazing faith placed in such people, only some of whom earned their lavish pay, and the utter obsession of both Nigerians and Biafrans with each other's mercenaries, imagined to be far more numerous than they were.

During the war, a report reached London that Frederick Forsyth, who accompanied Biafran troops in the field, was actually fighting with the Biafrans as a mercenary. We heard the report but did not take it seriously. Decades later he explained in his memoirs how a mistaken report of him taking part in the fighting had arisen.[95]

Forsyth also revealed in those memoirs that while in Biafra he had been an agent of the British Secret Intelligence Service, the SIS (or MI6). Although the SIS comes under the FCO, whose policy Forsyth condemned, its main purpose is getting information, and he readily agreed to provide good information from inside Biafra.[96]

We heard little and reported less about intelligence activities in the war. Nigeria had its Military Intelligence and its police CID and Special Branch; Biafra must obviously have had its counterparts to those. Biafran intelligence work included getting plenty of information from the federal side of the front, perhaps even from Lagos, where many Igbos who had stayed behind were loyal to Biafra and willing to help it; there was a report of Biafran agents in Lagos using a secret transmitter,[97] but I never learned any more details of this. There were some Nigerian intelligence operations in the West, against arms suppliers to the Biafrans. David Williams mentioned (off the record) meeting one agent in London and hearing about his tracking down an arms sale. That may have been a planned sale of aircraft; we heard of the Biafrans trying to buy at least one Gloster Meteor located at Blackbushe airport (near Camberley), and the defence secretary, Denis Healey, said in December 1968 that the export of six planes had been stopped.[98] One can assume that the British secret services helped the Nigerians, and the French secret services helped the Biafrans, in intelligence work. The SIS had its man at the British High Commission in Lagos during the war, following a normal pattern.[99] Elsewhere the SIS probably helped thwart Biafran arms deals, not necessarily by sabotage, though that was (inevitably) alleged by the Biafrans and cannot be ruled out.

Auberon Waugh, in a report from Lisbon in July 1968, said that British diplomatic efforts to stop the Wharton gun-running operation had failed, but some "scruffily dressed foot-tapping 'spooks'", alleged to be from the Commonwealth Relations Office (CRO), seemed to be offering $200,000 to deliver Wharton to Lagos, $100,000 for destruction of one of his Constellations, and $200,000 for delivery of one of the planes with its cargo to Lagos, payment to be made in Frankfurt; and when one plane was blown up in Bissau, the South African pilot, who had had nothing to do with the explosion, went to Frankfurt and tried in vain to get the money.[100] It is an entertaining account, as one would expect from a Waugh, but requires grains of salt. Did the CRO have its own dirty tricks department? A Constellation was in fact destroyed at Bissau on 7 June 1968; *West Africa* quoted a report suggesting that there was an explosion of nitric acid being shipped to Biafra for the Scientific Group.[101] This does not exclude sabotage, and Venter quoted much later an account by the pilot of that plane, a Rhodesian, who said an American pilot of another Constellation "had been nobbled by a Nigerian agent and 'persuaded' to stop our flight, 'at whatever cost'".[102] This second- or third-hand account coming from the shadowy world of international skulduggery cannot be relied on, but the story is possible.

The relief crisis of mid-1969

From February to June 1969 the airlift of food and medical supplies to Biafra proceeded at an impressive rate, with the ICRC, JCA and the French Red Cross helping to make a difference for thousands of displaced people and ordinary villagers. The ICRC, for example, made 65 flights in the week from 26 February to 5 March 1969. Food brought in by the airlift included corn soya milk, milk, fish meal, ground stockfish, baby food and salt. But the situation in the crowded enclave was still grim. Food distribution was well organised, but Churchill reported that the rations were very small and large amounts of starch food staples were needed.[103] In late February a yam was reported to cost £4.[104] Despite this high cost, relief agencies bought up local food for the destitute people (presumably adding to the inflation in the process). Some food was obtained from the other side of the front, in the "attack" trade; Ojukwu said in an interview with *Newsweek* that these purchases were important, and declared confidently that Biafra could survive for four months if there was no serious interruption in relief supplies, and then "we have made it".[105] What did he mean—surely not that no more relief aid would be needed then? But the steady inflow of relief may have encouraged the Biafran leaders to hope that the airlift would be enough, if added to the "dig for victory" efforts by villagers on which they placed hopes also.

There was no such optimism about the airlift among those helping the relief effort. Western governments had for some time been contributing to Biafra relief, as well as the Western general public, which was still giving generously. By January 1969 the US had provided $22 million for relief on both sides. The new Nixon administration promised more, while continuing the previous administration's political support for Nigeria (it merely expressed "deep concern" over the air raids). Senator Charles E. Goodell visited both sides and promised more help; he also called for an immediate ceasefire,[106] which even countries sympathetic to Nigeria commonly proposed. Nixon sent Professor Clarence Clyde Ferguson to look for ways to get more food to the victims. After visiting Biafra, Ferguson said the airlift could not possibly meet the needs.[107] This seemed to cast doubt on Ojukwu's optimism in his (ambiguous) *Newsweek* interview, which could have suggested that he did not see it as very urgent to reconsider proposals for bigger supplies under some agreement with Lagos. But the Biafrans did express readiness to do so in principle, Ojukwu mentioning again the idea of a land and water route to take supplies to Oguta. On its side, the FMG, rather oddly, now suggested that supplies could be flown to Obilago airstrip, the object of controversy when it was in Biafran hands, but which was now in federal hands.[108]

It was announced in April 1969 that the ICRC was feeding about 960,000 people in Biafran and 989,000 in federal territory. On the Nigerian side, it had 22 distribution centres and used two ships, plying from Lagos to Port Harcourt and Calabar, and one aircraft, a DC-4; on the Biafran side, where it had eleven distribution centres, it used 46 lorries, four DC-7s flying from Santa Isabel and three DC-6Bs, two Stratofreighters and a Transall from Cotonou; two more Stratofreighters were waiting in Switzerland.[109] This impressive effort was matched by that of the churches, which had 470 relief centres in Biafran territory by early May.[110] All this saved countless lives but was not enough for the mass of people in need; the airlift was bringing in 200 to 240 tons per night in April, but experts said a minimum of 460 tons per night was needed.[111] That would only be possible under an agreed plan for massive daylight deliveries.

In the absence of such a plan, the FMG continued to maintain the blockade and order air attacks on the Uli airstrip. It was wrong for Wilson to claim in the House of Commons, on 2 April 1969, that Gowon had allowed food supplies through to the secessionist side "even knowing, in so doing, that he was letting arms supplies through". Gowon never agreed to this; he simply approved a potential agreement under which relief supplies, and no others, could be flown in, carefully checked, during daylight hours; whether the Biafrans could have arranged for arms supply planes to slip in among Red Cross planes one cannot tell, as no agreement on daylight flights was ever made. Pending such an agreement, the FMG agreed to the night flights by the ICRC but did not stop attacks on Uli's night-time traffic for them or for anyone; the NAF did in fact hit several planes approaching Uli or on the ground there. Yet some Nigerians, too, thought that Gowon's conciliatory approach to relief supplies meant not attacking flights to Uli for fear of hitting humanitarian flights.[112] This view was certainly mistaken. In working on the magazine's news pages I devoted particular attention to the relief question, and I never heard of any decision to refrain from attacks on Uli so as to avoid hitting relief supply aircraft. Nigerians who wrongly believed that Gowon had made such a decision would have contributed to the ugly chauvinistic mood already mentioned.

Where the churches were concerned, the fact that their humanitarian organisations sent help to suffering people on both sides—in wholly separate operations—caused problems on the Nigerian side, where both Caritas and the World Council of Churches were accused of supporting Biafra, and the accusation that their relief flights to Biafra carried arms was widely believed. But although there were Nigerian protests and demonstrations on the subject, the churches themselves suffered no harassment or ill-treatment, or any restrictions on their work, including extensive relief work in the war zone. On 15 February 1969 *West Africa* reported a meeting of the Catholic bishops of Nigeria and Biafra in Rome. More remarkably, on 22 March 1969 *West Africa* reported that Monsignor Jean Rodhain, president of Caritas Internationalis, had visited Nigeria and called on Gowon. In front of the Nigerian press, Gowon accused Caritas of ignoring Nigerian sovereignty over air space and mentioned the accusation of its planes carrying arms; Rodhain denied this, but that is not what is significant about this episode. It seems to show clearly that Gowon did not himself believe that Caritas was carrying weapons. If he had, how could he have allowed the head of an organisation of gun-runners to enter Nigeria (Rodhain could easily have been denied a visa) and then gone much further, to invite him to his office in front of the press? He must have repeated the gun-running allegation because the Nigerian public was convinced of it, and given Rodhain the opportunity to deny it for publication.

Besides flying relief to Biafra, as already noted the ICRC was also in overall charge of relief work on the Nigerian side from early in the war, with local bodies like the Christian Council of Nigeria (CCN) doing much of the work under its direction. The CCN established a Commission on Relief and Rehabilitation, headed from 1 March 1969 by Emmanuel Urhobo, a lawyer and industrial consultant. They all achieved a good deal, but the ICRC aroused a good deal of criticism for its running of the aid operation. Some years later, Urhobo accused the ICRC (called International but in fact a Swiss body) of not recognising the work of other agencies under it, and of laying down its own rigid rules about priorities for aid, neglecting the Mid-West.[113] There was another problem, too: some Westerners in Africa offend Africans by insensitive and thoughtless behaviour, and I heard of Swiss ICRC staff in Nigeria being accused of this. An article in the London *Sunday Mirror* spoke of bureaucracy in the ICRC and the expensive lifestyle of its staff.[114] Such things did not help when its position in Nigeria was uneasy. But it was because of their work on the Biafran side, above all, that many Nigerians, either ignoring or not caring about the countless innocent lives saved in that work, were persistently hostile to the "wicked humanitarians", as a writer in one newspaper actually called them.

Despite all the worldwide scrutiny of Nigeria's conduct of the war, and continued allegations that it amounted to genocide, one serious investigation into the genocide charge in 1968–9 attracted very little attention and has remained little known until today. An International Committee for the Investigation of Crimes of Genocide considered a Biafran complaint of Nigerian genocide and its representative travelled to Biafra and Nigeria to get evidence, after which the committee met in Paris and a report was published in Britain on 31 May 1969. This was made known in a book published soon after that called *Biafra: Britain's Shame*,[115] by two particularly active campaigning journalists already mentioned, Suzanne Cronje and Auberon Waugh, who in their strong condemnation of British policy believed that Britain and the FMG were prepared to condone genocide. A chapter by Waugh states:

> The enquiry, conducted in Biafra and Nigeria from December 1968, took evidence from six hundred and fifty people in Biafra and four hundred and ninety in Nigeria, of which three hundred and forty-two were combatants. The officer responsible for conducting the enquiry, Dr Mensah, from Ghana, interviewed members of the International Observer Team and people serving in the administration on both sides. He records that no impediments were put in the way of his enquiry by either government. His conclusion, which was accepted

by the International Committee, was that prima facie evidence of genocide and also of genocidal intention existed.[116]

This investigation is also mentioned in Cronje's post-war book, which adds some details.[117] But her information and Waugh's do not explain exactly what this "Paris-based unofficial organization of lawyers" (Cronje's words) was, what status it had, and on whose initiative it had been founded. *West Africa* recorded nothing about it in 1969. Perhaps journalists reporting on the Biafran war did not know what to make of this reported investigation, for the whole thing is odd. "Dr Mensah" is referred to just like that, with no forename; Mensah is a very common Ghanaian name. Who exactly was he? And who helped him carry out so many interviews? In Biafra he would of course have been given every assistance, including secretarial help, and the number of interviewees there seems possible. But did he really do all that he was said to have done on the Nigerian side? The FMG was not obliged to cooperate with such an investigation. Did it really allow Mensah to proceed? This episode is full of puzzles. Since the war, very little has been said about that committee and its report. None of the contributors to the recent volume *Post-colonial Conflict and the Question of Genocide: The Nigeria–Biafra War, 1967–1970*[118] has given any fuller explanation of the report and its origin, though some mention it briefly and one notes that it received "very little attention outside of Biafra".[119]

However, Waugh saw the report, and so did others. W.A. Ajibola's study of British public opinion, examining parliamentarians among others, mentions that all MPs were sent copies of this 102-page document by the Britain–Biafra Association, but it did not convince most of those he interviewed, who said it was very long and had strong elements of propaganda.[120] While information unfavourable to Nigeria was too readily dismissed as "propaganda", there was some cause to be sceptical about that document. However, there clearly was a group of concerned and legally qualified people who wanted to examine whether there was genocide in Biafra, and sent a representative to Biafra who heard evidence of mass killings. Waugh quoted a little from what Mensah had heard, probably from survivors of massacres interviewed in Biafra. There are utterly horrific details of mass killings by the foulest means at ten places, mostly in the Mid-West.

And such killings certainly happened many times. In the Mid-West the federal forces were fighting the BOFF guerrillas, and the usual brutality of counter-insurgency operations occurred. There seem to have been special efforts to conceal what was happening in the Mid-West, but reports came out. In that state, too, in 1967 many Igbos were killed in mob violence, and Mensah probably heard about that as well as later killings by troops. Certainly there was, as Mensah said, hatred of the Igbo people behind such killings—when gangs of lay-abouts in Benin went out to "get Igbos", they were thinking of geno-cide in a sense, but on a local scale and for a moment; that was not true state-organised genocide, even when soldiers were involved in a sporadic way. However, in view of what is now known about Asaba, the full truth about war crimes in the Mid-West, if it was fully docu-mented as it still could be, would most probably be a dreadful indict-ment of the federal forces.

While Mensah said he found "prima facie evidence", it would have been necessary to prove—if the matter ever came before any court, which was impossible at that time anyway[121]—that orders for a gen-eral killing of all Igbos came from a senior authority. As that did not happen, if the word "genocide" and the puzzles over that International Committee[122] are set aside, the real and provable fact should be accepted: that the Nigerian forces committed numerous serious war crimes and tolerated others by civilians, most often, quite probably, in the Mid-West. These crimes occurred in the course of military operations whose aim was to defeat the Biafran forces, not to slaugh-ter all Igbos after victory. That does not make the war crimes excus-able, nor does the certain fact that the Biafrans committed war crimes of their own.

In the Mid-West fighting near the river, the Biafrans captured Aboh, or parts of it, at the end of April. The federal forces in the Delta area were reinforced, but the Biafrans went on to attack the oil installations near Kwale, as already recorded, and posed a threat to oil production, a threat increased soon afterwards from the air. After more than a year with no air power at all, they acquired some Swedish aircraft with the help of Count Carl Gustaf von Rosen, who also piloted them for Biafra. These Minicon planes were light aircraft said to have been originally manufactured for training or sport, but in this case adapted at a base in France to carry rocket launchers.[123] Small and manoeuvrable, flying low and escaping radar detection, the Minicons were successfully used for low-level precision air attack. Eventually eight or nine second-hand Minicon MFI-9Bs were provided for Biafra; the Swedish nobleman, a quixotic adventurer, was said to have paid for the planes out of his own pocket to help the Biafrans. Besides von Rosen himself, some other foreign pilots and at least one Biafran flew the Minicons.

The Minicons raided Port Harcourt airport on 22 May and Benin airport on 24 May, then Enugu airport on 26 May. The aim was to hit Nigerian military aircraft, and von Rosen, travelling back to Sweden soon afterwards, said twelve had been hit and two destroyed. Soon afterwards there was a raid on the Ughelli power station in the Mid-West on 29 May, causing some damage.[124] The Minicon raids caused shock on the Nigerian side; all flights by light aircraft were prohibited, and there was a prolonged federal air attack on Uli on 23 May. Sweden was now denounced like France in Nigeria, but von Rosen said the Minicons had been exported legally as aircraft for non-military use, before being adapted in France (that is, he had tricked his government); the Swedish government later declared this aircraft to be war material, so that its export would be subject to special licensing.[125] However, five more Minicons, beating the new regulations, were exported from Sweden, adapted for rocket attack, and delivered to Biafra, von Rosen coming back with them.

On 5 June 1969 an ICRC aircraft carrying baby food, a DC-7B flying from Fernando Po, was shot down by a Nigerian Air Force MiG-17; its crew, including the American captain David Brown, were killed. Various accounts of this incident were published at the time and later. They tend to show that the plane was flying before sunset and the pilot did not obey the NAF crew's order to land, but also that the air force pilot (most probably a mercenary) had time to radio for instructions before firing. But there are puzzles. Was the Red Cross plane not supposed to be inspected at Santa Isabel and allowed to proceed? And the ICRC said (angering the Biafrans) that it had given details of its flights to the federal authorities—had it done so this time? At any rate, this incident either arose from or coincided with a hardened state of feeling in Nigeria following the Minicon raids. Von Rosen had flown relief planes before returning—in a quite separate venture, months later—to start a new Biafran air force; it could all be seen as a grand plot involving various planes, foreign pilots and "wicked humanitarians". There were now almost daily attacks on the ICRC in the Nigerian press.

The federal Ministry of Information at first described the shooting down of the ICRC plane as a "disaster" and the ICRC briefly resumed its flights. But very soon they were suspended again and the ICRC asked for guarantees for the safety of the mercy flights. JCA also suspended its flights, except for a few; there was a report, carried in *West Africa*, that it too had asked for guarantees, which was strange if correct, because it had never had FMG permission for its airlift anyway. The ICRC had had such permission, so its request for guarantees was reasonable in principle. But it was made against the background of fierce Nigerian hostility, directed equally against the Red Cross, which respected Nigerian laws and wishes, and JCA, which did not. Lindt was declared persona non grata and later resigned, and Okoi Arikpo made various accusations, denied by the ICRC.[126]

In this situation it would not have been easy for Gowon to agree publicly to guarantees for resumed ICRC night flights to Uli. What sort of guarantees could there be which would not arouse public suspicion in Nigeria? So it was back to the search for an arrangement accepted by both sides for daylight relief deliveries. Both sides had remained committed to the idea in principle, but now the issue came to a head in mid-1969, as it had in mid-1968. But while those controversies revived, the Nigerian government turned on the ICRC operations on the federal side. At a meeting with relief agencies called by the government in Lagos on 30 June 1969, it was announced that the ICRC's coordinating role on that side would end and would be handed over to the Rehabilitation Commission.[127] It was agreed to make the handover gradual, and other agencies like the CCN would continue to do most of the actual work; they held a meeting in Lagos with the Rehabilitation Commission soon afterwards—the Nigerian Red Cross Society, the CCN, Catholic Relief Services, UNICEF, Oxfam, CARE, and the Muslim International Relief Organisation.[128] But the ICRC, despite some controversies, had used its plentiful experience to do great work, and was being booted out for no other

255

reason than Nigerian public prejudice. And yet Lagos agreed that the ICRC flights to Biafra, the reason for that prejudice, could resume, though in a different way.

Enahoro explained on 30 June that daylight flights to Biafra must be cleared at a federally held airport; later it was specified that this must be Lagos. He went on to make a string of accusations against relief agencies. He quoted the military observers as saying that some of the relief food was being consumed by the Biafran forces, though in fact the observers were only quoting POWs and a defector. He said relief flights must no longer be used to help "communications" between Biafra and the rest of the world (so relief workers and pilots could not carry people's letters?).[129] And he repeated the fable about relief aircraft carrying weapons—which Arikpo repeated soon afterwards to the Pope himself, accusing Caritas and the Canadian organisation Canairrelief, which was prominent in the JCA airlift.[130] If there had been any proof to back this accusation, the Nigeria High Commission in London would not have failed to send it to the *West Africa* office; and the magazine only mentioned the accusation as a news item, never backing it.[131]

As discussions on relief arrangements for Biafra continued, JCA started sending more planes again, as feeding stations were closing and food was getting very short in Biafra for those needing aid. JCA did not get involved in discussions on a new agreed daylight airlift. The British government was involved in those discussions, and on 5–6 July talks were held in London between Britain, Nigeria and the ICRC, whose new president, Marcel Naville, then travelled to Lagos.[132] Naville had recently denounced forcefully the suppliers of arms for the war, and his words were widely assumed to have Britain in mind, but he did not name any country. The British foreign secretary spoke on 3 July of a new British initiative for a land "corridor" for relief. Since mid-June there had been plans for delivery of food up the Cross River from Calabar to the area controlled by Biafra on that river's bank, aboard ships called *Donna Mercedes* and *Donna Maria*; the Biafrans agreed to this in principle, the FMG did the same after talks with Professor Ferguson, and the vessels were sailed to Lagos. But the South-Eastern State governor, Colonel Esuene, publicly opposed the plan.[133] This river-borne food delivery never sailed; it was also put in doubt by fighting near the river, but the governor was probably voicing common Nigerian hostility to plans which would be described as "feeding the rebels".

Worse soon followed. In late June, Chief Awolowo, the senior civilian member of the FMG, declared, "All is fair in war, and starvation is one of the weapons of war." Brigadier Hassan Katsina similarly said that he "personally would not support anybody we are fighting".[134] These remarks echoed around the world. They contradicted Gowon's repeated words about readiness to help fellow Nigerians on the other side of the fighting front. Awolowo, a lawyer, seemed unaware that the Geneva Conventions to which Nigeria had adhered in 1961 rejected the idea that "all is fair in war" and obliged its government to ensure "humane treatment" for civilians in the civil war. He and Hassan Katsina were following, from positions of higher rank, the widely reported words of Adekunle in August 1968, where he said "I want to stop even a single Ibo being fed as long as these people refuse to capitulate."[135]

Those remarks were unoriginal: combatants had been saying such things for centuries. Relief of suffering among civilians in wartime is not a straightforward business. There will always be the belief that it helps the military operations of one side or another. There can be, in fact usually are, careful safeguards to ensure that food and medicines go only to civilians and not the troops; in Biafra these were usually stringent and well enforced until near the end, when soldiers were hardly able to eat themselves and sometimes seized food meant for refugees. But some can always argue that if outside agencies care for civilians, that relieves the military of their duty to do so and, if food is brought in from outside, leaves local food supplies available for the troops. It can also be good for the troops' morale if they know their families are being cared for by the Red Cross or other agencies. So *any* aid for civilians in a war zone can help the military indirectly, on one side or the other or both. So what is the answer—to let them starve? Nigerians recalled that Britain had declared a total blockade of Germany in the Second World War; *West Africa*'s editorial on 21 June 1969, however, said "there should be no analogy" with a civil war in which the people needing aid were people of the same country, and the aim was to treat them as such after the war.

Gowon showed his rejection of Awolowo's ideas but without blatantly opposing his number two in the Federal Executive Council, by continuing talks on daytime flights. Talks between the FMG and Marcel Naville on 12 July, however, failed. Naville said later in July that the food situation in Biafra was not catastrophic but could deteriorate badly in weeks.[136] While the ICRC would not resume flights without a formal deal agreed by the FMG, JCA and the French Red Cross resumed their airlifts as before, but these were very inadequate without the ICRC contribution; soon JCA was reporting that deaths among children, having declined, were now over 1,000 per day again.[137] Under a one-off arrangement, two ICRC planes went to Uli with doctors and 30 tons of medical supplies,[138] but talks on a lasting arrangement dragged on while people starved.

The Biafrans apparently accepted the plan agreed with the ICRC but said Uli airstrip must be kept open for other purposes.[139] This was (if correctly reported) an odd suggestion, but it related to a real problem—although some arms flights and others used the Uga airstrip, most flights of all sorts apparently went to Uli, and it was absurd to think either that the Biafrans would stop using Uli at night, or that the Nigerians would stop interfering with night flights there. Maybe this problem was evaded in the draft agreement, which included a federal concession called for by *West Africa* on 12 July: it agreed that inspection of cargoes could be done at Cotonou by observers including Nigerians. The FMG insisted that it had a right to call down an ICRC flight on its way from Cotonou, after inspection, to Biafra, which seemed quite unnecessary[140]—it would be very easy to ensure that a plane, after inspection, was not secretly loaded with arms by Biafran agents before take-off. Even so, there was, after an inordinate delay, a workable arrangement, concluded between the ICRC and the FMG on 13 September 1969. But the next day Biafra's relief coordinator, Dr S.J.S. Cookey (a Rivers man), rejected the agreement; Ojukwu repeated the earlier suspicion that the Nigerians would take advantage of the mercy airlift to send in military planes.[141]

On this occasion, in 1969 I believe, the Biafrans were plainly in the wrong about daylight relief flight plans. There was no danger that Gowon would risk the shocked reaction around the world that would come if an NAF bomber slipped in among the Red Cross aircraft. The truth must be that the Biafrans were concerned above all with *control*: under the ICRC–Nigerian deal the airlift and the lives of very many people would depend wholly on others, but the night flights were entirely under Biafran control—the relief agencies were completely subject to Biafran orders. Control mattered more than saving lives.

So the ICRC emergency airlift to Biafra ended. The ICRC continued its more traditional activity on both sides in this war for prisoners of war, and said later that it would now concentrate mainly on that work—which, however, was insufficient and probably obstructed on the federal side. Some POWs at Kiri-Kiri prison in Lagos told the military observers in January 1969 that they had not sent or received mail for 18 months, and their conditions were heavily criticised then by the observers, whose recommendation for a separate camp run by the army was, however, carried out later, as they reported after their visit to the war zone in May and June 1969.[142] We heard very little about the POWs in Biafran hands; they were estimated to number 6,000 in September 1969.[143]

The Red Cross's relief operations had been on an exceptional scale, and involved tricky relations with the two belligerents, not only the Nigerians. But a great job of saving lives was done and the Red Cross deserved to retain its high reputation. Its strict adherence to neutrality and avoidance of partisan political comment were criticised, notably by a group of French doctors who worked for it in Biafra and later formed a new organisation, the now celebrated Médecins sans Frontières. Their view that those relieving suffering should on occasion speak publicly about the man-made causes of suffering has some merit; so also has the Red Cross view (bind the bandages and accuse nobody)—neither is wholly right. What is lamentably certain is that the Red Cross's neutral stance did not save it from quite unmerited hostility in Nigeria. It continued its attempts to get agreement on daylight flights, as JCA also did, but the Biafrans maintained their objection ostensibly based on an absurd fear.

The Times, which on 28 June had said starvation was now the deliberate federal policy and this had "the effect of a policy of genocide", three months later accused Ojukwu of intransigence over both relief delivery and negotiations.[144] But Nigeria came out badly in the eyes of the world from the mid-1969 relief crisis, because of Awolowo's vile comment. In London, 80 MPs signed a motion calling for the government to work for agreement on relief for both sides, and for a general arms embargo; a debate was held in the Commons on 10 July, with only 44 MPs voting against Wilson's policy, though the Conservative opposition, normally on the side of the government over Nigeria, abstained this time. The British government—represented in Lagos from June 1969 by Sir Leslie Glass, in succession to Hunt   was far from changing its policy. Efforts in London to present the FMG's case included a symposium at the House of Commons in late April 1969, arranged by James Johnson MP, and accompanied by an exhibition of painting and sculpture by Ben Enwonwu,[145] who deplored the war, having earlier appealed to the Biafran leaders to end the fighting and expressed hope for "a new Ibo leadership" and "a worthier future in a nobler Nigeria".[146] But in the latter months of 1969, new FMG immigration regulations made it very difficult to obtain entry permits for Nigeria, and this affected journalists among others, which showed how the FMG continued to undermine its own attempts to get the world's understanding.

There was vague talk of peace moves in July and August, some of it linked to the Pope's visit to Uganda (31 July to 2 August), where he talked about Nigeria with President Obote; nothing came of it, but there was a widespread feeling, in Africa and elsewhere, that the FMG should soften its stance and accept a compromise like a confederation. The FMG sent special envoys to African states in August, knowing that there was unease.[147] The wavering in support for Nigeria was due very much to the military stalemate. Biafra now covered an area of only about 10,000 square miles, about 150 miles WNE–ESE wide and 20–100 miles deep, stretching from the Niger to the Cross; yet it was holding out, and overall it had lost hardly any territory for a year. After confident forecasts of victory, Nigerian representatives felt humiliated.

It had always seemed that federal supporters, unable to understand worldwide opposition, thought it might be due to a belief that the federal side could not win. I noticed that Brigadier Ogundipe, the Nigerian high commissioner, often held his press conferences just after Nigerian victories, as if to say to the world, "So there!" There were commentators talking of an "unwinnable" war, probably because most recent wars had been guerrilla wars like the one still going on in Vietnam; but in fact the Nigerian conflict was a conventional war of armies and fronts, except for the BOFF in the Mid-West, and in the end the defeat of the Biafran army was not to be followed by guerrilla operations, as some had predicted.

From June to September 1969 there was considerable fighting both in the south, where the Biafrans had advanced, claiming in June to have taken the Owaza oil and gas field about 15 miles north of Port Harcourt; and in the north, where the road from Onitsha to Enugu seemed still not secured by the federal army, which meant that the Biafrans could at least sometimes get food through from the important agricultural area north of the road. While the Owaza defeat was denied by Lagos, the Biafrans were said to have reoccupied oil-producing areas where they set up makeshift refineries; among other reports, *The Times* of 5 March 1969 reported the success of those refineries, from which rationed amounts of fuel were allocated to the army and relief distribution. The Nigerians, however, claimed to have captured one of them at Ebocha in August. In the Mid-West, where fighting went on, *West Africa* of 16 August reported over 6,000 people being evacuated along the Niger during operations; this sounded like classic regrouping of civilians for counter-guerrilla action. The Second Division now dealt with the Mid-West alone, Onitsha being handed to the First Division. All this fighting was indecisive for months; but for long the Nigerians had been expected to achieve something decisive.

They did score a political success in August 1969, when Nnamdi Azikiwe arrived at Lagos airport and was driven from there to Dodan Barracks for talks with Gowon on 17 August. It was said that he had been at Ikeja airport for a stopover, but in fact his re-entry into Nigeria had probably been arranged. Huge crowds welcomed Zik, who did not stay long but went to Liberia, as planned, and joined President William Tubman and Gowon for talks.[148] Not long afterwards he spoke in London at the Nigeria High Commission, declaring that he believed in "one Nigeria, which is indivisible, indestructible and perpetual" provided that there was "adequate security" for all citizens, and said it was not true that Igbos were destined to be exterminated. Although his proposals for a settlement were different from the

FMG's, he had abandoned Biafra for Nigeria. Ignatius Kogbara, Biafra's representative in London, said, "Biafra is a purer and better place without him."[149] In the following weeks *West Africa* published several letters praising or condemning Zik's defection (he wrote to protest at the hostile letters being published). In mid-September Zik began a tour of Nigeria, starting with East Central State. Later I heard him give a speech in London to the Britain–Nigeria Association, where he set out with his well-known eloquence how the older generation of African politicians, including himself, had let Africa down.[150]

In that speech, Azikiwe quoted an estimate that 1.5 million people had died in the war. Such estimates were quoted by many people, Nigerians included, and from all the reports published in *West Africa* it can be safely said that the number killed, mostly by starvation and disease, was at the least many hundreds of thousands. As many may have been saved, but by September 1969 the airlift was even more inadequate for staving off hunger and disease than before, with the ICRC gone. JCA said then that 15,000 tons of food per month were needed but less than a third of that was coming.

The suffering can be better understood if the appalling statistics are supplemented by first-hand descriptions of individuals' lives and deaths. There is a very good inside account in Rosina Umelo's reminiscences (cited earlier), but these were written in 1972, two years after the end of the war, from notes taken during the conflict, and published in 2018;[151] they describe in detail how people helped themselves or were helped by the relief operation in villages, and Umelo makes clear that very many were helped to survive, though she also mentions the fairly inevitable trafficking in relief food and accusations against those handling distribution.[152] At the time, few accounts of the Biafran civilians' plight by individuals affected appeared in Britain. In *West Africa* we were able to publish one, in the issue of 16 August 1969: a heart-rending letter from an Igbo man in Lagos describing how his family had suffered. J.M. Igwebuike wrote:

> In the heat of the confusion of 1967 I sent my wife and all my three children home to the East, while I stayed at my work, hoping things might settle down after a time. But later the war broke out and I lost contact with my family. Not very long ago I received a letter from my wife through the help of a Federal soldier. She is now receiving treatment in a clinic; here is her story:

When they could not get my monthly allowances any more and there were not much foodstuffs available to buy in Biafra, she made a little farm around the house, with the help of my two sons and daughter, to help them eat fairly well. It was from this farm that my sons Joe, 16, and Peter, 14, were taken away and conscripted into the Biafran army last September.

About a month later she had to flee our home with my daughter Josephine, 10, at the approach of the Federal troops, and stayed in a refugee camp in another town. It was in this camp that a soldier who was in the same platoon as my two sons told her of their death in one of the war sectors, exactly two months after they were conscripted. The older boy was first hit by a bullet, and when the junior boy saw his brother writhing in agony he knew no better than to go and help him, when he too was hit, and the two of them lay in the bush for the vultures.

Back in the refugee camp they were having one meal a day, not even what you could call one square meal, and they began to suffer from kwashiorkor, and my daughter became very sick and died. That was when my wife made up her mind to work (sic) back to our village to face one of two alternatives—to get shot by the Federal soldiers, for that was what they strongly believed in, or feed on the farm. She said that she was no longer afraid of death since her only three children were gone, and she believed that all the Ibos in Lagos and elsewhere in Nigeria had been killed. She was told by the Biafran soldiers that they had cleared the Federal troops in our village, though she no longer took such stories seriously.

So she decided to walk on to face anything. When she finally staggered, sickly, into the village one evening, after two days following the bush path, she received her greatest surprise. Her surprise was not that she met such a number of Federal soldiers in the village but that the soldiers took great pity on her, rushing about, giving her this and that just to see that she did not die. After she was given some treatment by the soldiers she was taken in the army vehicle to one of the clinics run by the ICRC in the federally controlled area, where she is now receiving treatment. It was there that she was told that Ibos are still living in Lagos, and so she decided to write and tell me everything in case I did not meet her alive when the war ends. I have already applied to get her out to Lagos but the doctor in charge of the clinic wrote encouragingly to me, advising me to hold on for a while, that she would be all right in a few weeks' time.

But the most unfortunate thing in the whole episode is that I happen to be the only surviving child of my parents who died a long time ago. I am 53 and my wife, now sickly, is 36. It is clear that our chances of ever having a child again are very remote, and that means my family name disappears forever with my death. The lesson I have bitterly learned now at 53 is that one's security is not found only in one's home town or soil. Perhaps my children might have been alive and happy today had I not rushed into sending them back to my region; that has been the most costly mistake of my life. Events in this war have shown clearly that the further away you are from home, the better for you.

We normally had a rule that a letter would not be published in the readers' letters page unless the author gave an address, though that did not need to be published; but although Mr Igwebuike gave no address except simply "Lagos", I waived that requirement, with colleagues' agreement, to publish an eloquent account of one man's suffering from the war, certainly typical of very many people's experiences, though I do not recall seeing any other such letters.

The Lagos *Sunday Times*, using a long-standing arrangement with *West Africa*, took this letter and made it into a front-page story, headed "The Lost Family". It said the story would "touch every human heartstring", and I think it reproduced the letter in full; but it spoke in the subhead of "the horror of the rebellion visited on an innocent father" and added a read-out saying, "I sent my two sons home but they became food for vultures—thanks to Ojukwu". Maybe the editor of the *Sunday Times* wanted to satisfy the authorities by these insertions. I thought the distortion wrong: the original letter should have stood exactly as it was written and reproduced in *West Africa*.

Paris and Pretoria

France's military aid to Biafra was beyond doubt; in July 1969 there were reported to be two arms flights per night from Gabon every night.[153] But there were reports of some other countries' governments supplying arms to Biafra, in addition to the black market sales which some governments failed to stop or perhaps winked at.

The Federal Government claimed that South Africa was aiding the Biafrans. Reports of such aid appeared in the British press now and then, but they did not seem very convincing, and *West Africa* did not take them up. Some reports of such arms supplies published in August 1969 were unreliable, as Cronje argued in her later book.[154] But there really was South African military aid to Biafra, arranged in collaboration with Foccart's organisation in France, and it was not confined to arms supplies. The details of this were kept secret for nearly fifty years. Venter has now given a full and convincing account of a group of South African officers headed by Major Jan Breytenbach training Biafrans for a new Special Forces unit and accompanying them in action. Helped by the Foccart network in Paris and Libreville, the South African team operated in Biafra for a considerable time (the dates are not clear in Venter's account). Its members were made French subjects and given documents as such, which helps explain why their presence remained a secret long after the war—if ex-Biafrans talked about it they would presumably have said those white soldiers were Frenchmen, and the presence of French mercenaries was well known.[155] Towards the end of the war the *Sunday Telegraph* seems to have got near the secret, reporting French–South African collusion involving Foccart's lieutenant Mauricheau-Beaupré; but it mentioned only military supplies.[156] Venter notes that one man involved in the top secret activities of the apartheid regime, Paul Els, published a book in South Africa in 2000, mentioning the mission; then Venter published his own account in London in 2015. If this secret had got out during the war, the Biafran leaders would have faced real trouble among Africans, even sympathetic ones who understood the need for Portuguese help.

There were various reports during the war of Israeli aid to the Biafrans, though with few details apart from humanitarian aid, which was admitted; probably some other aid was sent, and Biafrans struck a chord with many Israelis and other Jewish people by comparing their fate in Nigeria with that of the Jews in Europe (there are indeed parallels). Another country said to have assisted the Biafrans was China, but the Nigerian allegations of Chinese military aid were not easily credible, and Mao's regime may have offered no more than verbal encouragement motivated, one may assume, by its Soviet enemy's aid to Nigeria.

An article in *West Africa* of 15 November 1969 said France's policy on Biafra was being reconsidered and there was division in the government; the minister of posts, Jacques Marette, was a member of the Comité d'Action pour le Biafra. In late December, Nigerian representatives arranged for some French journalists to go to London to hear an address by Nnamdi Azikiwe, who urged France to reconsider its policy.[157]

A *West Africa* editorial on 7 December 1968 said, "Biafra's friends not only appear to supply the arms either free or on credit, but to deliver them." This impression presumably came from sources in Paris, and was probably correct. Very likely the Biafrans never paid for the French arms supplied from mid-1968. Nearly thirty years later, Philippe Gaillard, in his extended interview with Jacques Foccart, raised the question: "Arms, ammunition, chartered aircraft, pilots, mercenaries are expensive. How was all that paid for?" Foccart replied, "Il est certain que nous y avons aidé." Pressed for more detail by Gaillard, he said, "Essentially, anyway, it came from state funds. Several ministries were told to contribute." Several ministries—not just Foccart's department and its own funds. That would presumably have required a direct order from President de Gaulle. But how much was contributed? On that, Foccart gave no hint.[158]

There has been plenty of highly critical writing in France about the semi-secret world of "la Françafrique": the intertwined political, security service, and financial links between France and several African regimes, a peculiar Afro-French world of slush funds, spooks, mercenaries and shady deals. There have, for example, been exposés of this world in books by Pierre Péan[159] and François Verschave.[160] But although they say a good deal about Foccart and the French aid to Biafra, they say nothing about the financing of Foccart's operation. A similar muckraking work by an Ivorian dissident about Houphouët-Boigny[161] says nothing about this either. Some facts may well have been unearthed by others. N.U. Akpan, who fled with Ojukwu to Ivory Coast in January 1970, recalling the Ivorian president's welcome for them states that Houphouët-Boigny spent much of his own income helping the Biafrans and "must have personally guaranteed a number of loans contracted by Biafra to buy arms".[162] After the war, Suzanne Cronje suggested that the French military aid involved the sale of arms, which the Biafrans paid for with loans signed and guaranteed by the Ivory Coast and Gabon governments, and quoted a figure, given by Ignatius Kogbara, of no more than $5 million for that aid.[163]

Foccart's statement that French government funds were used to help Biafra would suggest that the aid was a gift, not a loan. But perhaps arms were sold on credit? Even if the Biafrans had to borrow to pay for some of their arms, did they service the loan or loans at all, before they lost the war and (presumably) could not be made to pay anything back (but perhaps the president of Ivory Coast could)? It is all very obscure, but it seems highly likely that the Biafrans never paid anything for those French arms.

Protests and lobbying

From 1968 there was a noticeable "Biafra lobby" in Britain, an informal group separate from the more organised Britain–Biafra Association and Save Biafra Committee. They included British people with African experience who knew about the situation and opposed government policy, notably Peter (or E.V.) Gatacre, who had worked for the United Africa Company (UAC) in Lagos and became an active campaigner against British government policy on Nigeria in 1967–8. His role is largely forgotten but was a very active one according to Jonathan Aitken, then a journalist and a prospective Conservative candidate for parliament, who travelled to Biafra and then to Lagos for the *Evening Standard* in September–October 1969, and on his return began writing strongly against the arms sales and joined the "Biafra lobby".[164] He and others of the lobby repeated the common criticism of British officials' refusal to accept some known facts about Biafra. *The Observer* spoke of "a small tireless lobby which had been meeting and scheming in the drawing room of Hugh Fraser's Georgian house on Campden Hill [in Kensington]". Their circle included editors like Nigel Ryan of ITN and Rees-Mogg; they made many contacts with politicians and others, and they helped organise meetings and marches. The influence of this lobby must not be exaggerated—its members, and others, had been supporting Biafra individually for a long time, and, as Aitken says, "no small group could possibly have been responsible for the tremendous welling up of nation-wide concern about Biafra".[165]

In September 1969 a group of journalists started producing a regular Biafra supplement to *Peace News*, which had been campaigning against the war and the British arms supplies from an early date; the Britain–Biafra Association was using the paper's office as its own address by late 1969. Suzanne Cronje was a prominent member of this group; she was a tireless campaigner for Biafra, often seen at press conferences and other occasions, where even those who did not agree with her stance must have admired her courage—she had a disability (extreme obesity) which would have made less determined people go out as little as possible. Others of the group included Richard West and Francis Wyndham. They attacked not only the Wilson government, whose concealment of the truth about the arms sales they gradually brought to light, but also journalists who supported Nigeria and Britain, possibly under pressure—the FCO regularly leaned on journalists sympathetic to Biafra. The left-wing *Peace News* group overlapped with the other, for the cause of opposing British arms supplies to Nigeria united people of all political sympathies. It brought together, for example, Peter Cadogan of the Save Biafra Campaign, a militant opponent of nuclear weapons who had joined the Committee of 100 advocating Gandhian tactics against those weapons, and Hugh Fraser, a former secretary of state for air. There was increasing opposition among Conservatives to their front bench's support for Wilson on Nigeria, and many Labour MPs had for long opposed the government policy. What united these campaigners was not insistence on Biafra's right to independence—only some were committed to that—but support for a ceasefire and peace talks to achieve some sort of settlement and, as a perceived priority, an end to British arms for Nigeria.

In 1968–9, opponents of the Nigerian war, especially in Britain, regularly condemned Shell-BP as an ally of the Nigerian and British governments, even suggesting that the war with all its huge death toll was being fought for the oil company. Car windows had stickers saying "Boycott murder—boycott Shell-BP" or "Put a dead Biafran in your tank" (alluding to the company's advertising slogan "Put a tiger in your tank"). The group of campaigners writing in *Peace News* claimed that the commercial interests not only of Shell-BP but also of the big West Coast trading and industrial firms such as the UAC were the real reason for Britain's military and other backing of Nigeria.

For the belligerents themselves, from the beginning of the war or earlier, the oil industry was vitally important. The Biafrans did not emphasise their hopes for oil income to make a success of independence, but they obviously had such hopes. On the Nigerian side, suspicions were quickly aroused when Shell-BP seemed ready to pay taxes to the Biafrans. The size and power of multinationals make them always liable to invite suspicion. In Africa, there were recent memories of the immense power of the Union Minière, which lay behind the Katanga secession of 1960–3. Sir David Hunt wrote later, "I could foresee Shell-BP cast in the role of Union Minière, and Britain in the role of Belgium."[166] But although a conglomerate like Shell-BP had enough money on paper to buy and sell many African states, in reality its power was distinctly limited, as the FMG proved very quickly by extending its blockade to oil and capturing Bonny, thus preventing the Biafrans from exporting any crude oil. This amply proved that Shell-BP was not running the show.

Nigerians were quite right to suspect that Shell-BP, and other big firms too, were not at heart committed to Nigerian unity or the cause of the Gowon regime. Their primary concern, naturally, was to go on trading and, if possible, recover from the setbacks they had endured from the crisis. They would have been quite willing and able to adapt to a successful Biafran breakaway; there would soon have been a Shell-BP (Biafra) Ltd and a UAC (Biafra) Ltd. When the war began, foreign companies would have welcomed a return to peace and normal trading conditions, even if this meant Biafra being established as an independent state following either a military victory or a negotiated settlement; they doubtless appreciated Nigeria's big domestic market but could have managed without it—the UAC had done business in tiny The Gambia for decades. But when it was clear that the only likely outcome of the war was a federal victory, the companies waited for that, and hoped that it would come quickly.

In Nigeria, British firms outside the East were obviously hit by the crisis of 1966—the tin mines lost their usual rail link to the sea and many Eastern workers, for example—but some trading could continue then and after the war began. Their managements may have commonly wanted a quick Nigerian victory to restore peace, but basically they just kept on running their businesses, helping the war effort involuntarily—through taxes, including Shell-BP's big payments, and occasional requisitioning: the *Enugu Palm* of UAC's Palm Line was requisitioned in January 1969 for a journey from Lagos to Port Harcourt.[167] But firms working in Biafran territory soon had to close up for the duration. It may have been known to some in London, though not to us in *West Africa* as I recall, that a few days after secession the deputy chairman of UAC, Frederick Pedler, wrote to Margaret M. Green—a prominent anthropologist, expert on the Igbo language and culture, and active supporter of relief efforts in the war—saying the company had urged Easterners not to secede and now was "very actively doing all it can to maintain economic relations with Biafra … We have already found one rather ingenious route to establish a trickle of goods."[168] Such efforts did not succeed; industries like the UAC's Onitsha textile mill and the Nkalagu cement factory closed down; and produce exports stopped except for small amounts of cocoa and rubber flown out aboard returning planes in the airlift.

As the war went on, Biafrans vented their general anger against Britain by attacking the idle offices of British firms, and a decree of 31 May 1968 empowered the government to take over the businesses and assets of foreign companies that had suspended work in Biafra.[169] But the Biafran regime was not at all left-wing even after the Ahiara Declaration, and if it had won it would probably have welcomed all the British business firms back. And if that had happened, Biafra would have readily sold oil to Nigeria, Britain and everywhere else. It was Nigeria that most wanted to prevent such a scenario. Britain could have done without the oil in the former Eastern Nigeria—it did in fact do without it, for a whole year. Shell-BP managed well without that oil too—being a multinational means that loss of production and revenue in one country can be compensated for from other countries. It was for the Federal Government of Nigeria that recovering access to that oil was vital. Its determination to do so was not dictated by Shell-BP or Harold Wilson. But these also wanted the oil to flow again, and only a Nigerian victory seemed likely to achieve that if there was not a peace settlement.

Similarly, although Nigeria's palm products trade had been badly disrupted,[170] the UAC could manage well without the palm oil and palm kernels in Biafra's temporary territory. Its own plantations had always provided only a small amount of the supply, and its share of the smallholder production marketed (no longer by UAC since the early 1960s) for export could be replaced from UAC's other sources. There was a world surplus of vegetable oils and fats at the time; the 1968 annual report of Unilever said profits in tropical Africa as a whole rose in the year, enough to make up for the loss of business in Nigeria.[171] The UAC did not need to promote a war to get enough palm oil and kernel supplies. However, D.K. Fieldhouse records that "UAC's position was that its first priority must be to maintain good relations with the Lagos government, since most of its business was in federal territory".[172] Margaret Green apparently thought the UAC had considerable power to influence events, as she suggested it might persuade the British government to recognise Biafra. It did not have that sort of power. Pedler and Lord Cole, the chairman of Unilever, and other British businessmen went to see Nigeria's high commissioner, Ogundipe, to urge a more conciliatory Nigerian policy in the war, but they were not heeded.[173]

That initiative was right and proper, but another initiative by Pedler was not: he joined with other businesspeople in Britain to urge the government not to stop arms supplies to Nigeria.[174] British businesses operating in an overseas country engaged in war can properly support reasonable efforts to restore peace, but to call for arms supplies is quite improper. If this had become known to the public at the time, it would have been seen as full confirmation that the war was being fought for West Coast big business. Gordon Wilson, chairman of UAC (Nigeria) Ltd, told Pedler that if arms supplies stopped, "Government and public reactions in Federal Nigeria will deteriorate to anti-British with adverse effects on trade and security."[175] That, as well as a desire to see a quick end to the war, was a reason why firms working in Nigeria backed British policy on arms. Their fears for themselves may have been exaggerated or not real at all; no harm came to French people in Nigeria, and French business interests there[176] were not affected. British firms would probably have suffered no more than demonstrations and a few broken windows—one cannot imagine the FMG taking drastic action against numerous major firms in the middle of a war. However, the Nigerian public distrust of Britain was real.

Powerful firms operating in colonial and Third World countries have been properly criticised; some in West Africa had disreputable pasts in the colonial era, such as forced labour on the Nigerian tin mines and near-monopolistic practices by UAC, which Africans condemned and attacked from the 1930s onwards. They still had great power in the 1960s, but it need not be exaggerated. In the Nigerian war, they supported the federal side as their bread was buttered on that side, but they did not have the power to give orders for it. In the latter part of 1969 I heard Richard West tell a meeting that "Nigeria is a neo-colony" (he added that Gabon was another); addressing some pro-federal Nigerians in the hall, he said he was sorry for their people, who were being used by Britain (they seemed baffled). That was not the real situation, but the oil companies and the established West Coast firms did support the FMG's war effort, as that alone seemed likely to restore normal trading conditions. And the British government certainly wanted oil production to resume as soon as possible and, having done nothing to secure a peaceful solution which would have had that effect, hoped that arming Nigeria would achieve it; that is obvious even though ministers did not state it as a reason for the arms sales.

Thus the attacks on big business by critics of Nigeria and Britain had basis in fact. The corresponding attacks by pro-federal Nigerians, suggesting that some Western financial power was promoting the press coverage of the war so as to cause Nigeria's destruction, had none. A number of Nigerians had such a notion then and later, such as Ola Balogun, who wrote after the war,

> Western interest … thus lay in encouraging the disintegration of Nigeria, not in ensuring the preservation of Nigeria's unity, the more so as the gigantic oil reserves located in the breakaway Eastern Region were an irresistible magnet for Western imperialist greed.

> Once Western financial circles (which own 95% of the mass media in Western Europe and America) had decided to support Biafra, the mass media threw in their full weight behind the Biafran cause with devastating effect.[177]

No names or other details, of course, in this fantasy. The real Western financial and business circles had always been fond of Nigeria, where Western business did well and oil (which greedy imperialist firms did not need to aim for, as they were already pumping it) promised much more; Nigeria's large internal market, unrivalled in independent Africa, was an asset for Western business. The real attitude of Western big business to Nigeria was shown in February 1969 when Lonrho made a successful £3 million bid for John Holt, and became owner of several subsidiaries of that long-established Liverpool firm in Nigeria, including Holt's Transport, John Holt Agricultural Engineers and Holt Maritime Enterprises. As for the Western financial circles behind the press, they had nothing against Nigeria, which the press lord Cecil King admired and supported. There was no pre-existing hostility to Nigeria; it had a generally good press under the Tafawa Balewa government, which was on good terms with all Western countries except two—France and Portugal.

Only those two Western countries fitted Balogun's weird description a little. Only there was Western self-interest on the side of the Biafrans, and even there it was only political self-interest, not economic. Elsewhere in the West, power and money were on the side of Federal Nigeria. But a number of Nigerians thought that even Britain was at heart hostile to them. That view was encouraged by the Soviet Union, which in its efforts to make Nigerians see it as their true ally suggested that the British government and the British press were both manipulated by a hidden financial power, playing a double game. A correspondent of the French Communist newspaper *L'Humanité*, supporting Nigeria, said Britain had allowed arms sales to both sides.[178]

The political protests aroused by the Biafran war—as distinct from the humanitarian response of giving for relief operations—were overwhelmingly dominated, in Britain, by the opposition to arms supplies, which were denounced in other Western countries also. There was also opposition to the Nigerian government, obviously, and to big business, but attention was concentrated on the British arms sales. Largely absent was backing for the Biafrans' case for independence, which the Biafran leaders wanted to convey whenever possible, as in

Ojukwu's mammoth speech at Addis Ababa. The activists of the Britain–Biafra Association, mostly people who had worked in Eastern Nigeria and knew the background to the conflict, echoed the Biafrans' calls for acceptance of their claims, but the general public hardly did so, and even MPs, in the parliamentary debates about arms, rarely showed any positive support for Biafran independence.

Such political support must be distinguished from compassion for the suffering of the Biafrans. Some Nigerians and pro-Nigerians did not make that distinction, seeing publicity about starving children and the *Spectator*'s calls for recognition of Biafra as just two parts of the same propaganda operation, organised by Ojukwu through Markpress to win support for Biafra's independence. The genuine humanitarian feelings of the Western public were admitted, but, it was thought, those genuine feelings were manipulated by a vast deception operation. That was paranoid imagination. The common view of Markpress needs to be consigned to the realm of myth. The famine was real; it was reported by aid workers, clergy and journalists and led to a huge relief operation that no PR efforts could have invented; and the facts about the Nigerian war effort, the blockade and the arms supplies were known to the world from many sources. There was no deception by Markpress, or anyone, about these basic facts. The only important deception involving Markpress was the allegation of genocide, which a great many protestors against the war did not believe. Markpress doubtless said a lot about federal war crimes, but if one recalls that 1969 was the year when the My Lai massacre in Vietnam was headlined all over the world, one can see that Asaba would have become a household word like My Lai if Markpress had had half the domination over the world's media that it was thought to have. And with such a hold over minds, Markpress, which followed the instructions of the Biafran government, would have secured wide-ranging political support for Biafran independence.

What was in fact aroused was pity for the Biafrans as suffering victims, which was not what their leaders really wanted. Those leaders did not initially want the starvation to be shown to the world. They invited journalists, with Markpress making the arrangements, but wanted them to report on a brave, just struggle and a functioning new country, not a pitiful disaster. The famine could not be concealed, however, and it became the journalists' main story, which put Biafra on the map—but as an object of pity, a mass of unspeakable suffering calling for help with food and medicine. In her 1972 book, Cronje wrote, "On the whole, the emphasis on suffering and the relief of it damaged Biafra's chances of gaining international recognition."[179] Those chances may have been poor anyway—I recall that in Britain few people were calling for recognition before the famine story broke in June 1968. But when that happened, people appalled by the starvation typically rushed to send help for the victims, rather than take up the cause of the Republic of Biafra.

This point is made at length in a recent book by the German scholar Lasse Heerten.[180] The fullest study of worldwide media and public reactions to Biafra, it examines newspapers, television, magazines, books, charities, celebrities, politicians, campaigns and organisations in several countries. Heerten notes that there was more political support for Biafra in France; I would add that African backers of Biafra also adopted a political attitude, though that did not exclude humanitarian concern and—in France—generous contributions to relief. But in the West generally, there was more pity for Biafran victims than support for Biafran independence.

But that distinction was not total. The newspaper and television reports of starving children said something about the war causing the starvation, and most of the readers and viewers probably reacted with some sympathy for the Biafrans as the underdog fighting back, doubtless in a vague way like "Why should they be forced to stay in a country when they want to break away?" Heerten says the turnout at pro-Biafra marches in Britain was not very large, and certainly it contrasted with CND marches at that time; one reason was surely that people shocked and distressed about Biafra could help by sending cheques to Oxfam—more practical than marching. But as well as rallies and demonstrations there was the constant coverage in the press, radio, television and cinema newsreels, many letters to MPs, constant fundraising events, appeals in churches and by churchmen elsewhere, student meetings, grassroots political debates, and much else, adding to a steady undercurrent of protest; Harold Wilson's reminiscences testify to the effect all this had.

As Heerten notes,[181] the Biafrans, who had not wanted the foreign press to highlight the starvation, found that there was some advantage for them when it did. The press coverage fuelled the British campaign for an end to arms supplies to Nigeria, though that had begun earlier. Heerten, I believe, does not emphasise enough how central the arms supply issue was in Britain. Opponents of the arms sales included people who did not care particularly whether Biafra became independent or not. If the arms supplies had been halted, British recognition of Biafra would probably not have followed—France and the US did not recognise Biafra. A halt to British arms would have greatly helped Biafra, but it does not follow that MPs aimed at this as a deliberate calculation; many simply thought Britain should not be fuelling another country's civil war but should rather help make peace.

The protests and lobbying concentrated on the arms issue went on until the end of the war. Heerten's statement that "the interest of most contemporaries began to decrease quickly in late 1968, and media coverage tapered off"[182] does not correspond with what I remember. During 1969 there was the media and parliamentary outcry over the Nigerian air raids, the anguish over the halt to ICRC flights, the activities of the lobbyists; a Biafra Week in London in early November, including a Trafalgar Square rally and a teach-in at Kingsway Hall where Biafran and Nigerian representatives spoke; the interruption of the 1969 Remembrance Sunday service at the Cenotaph by Peter Cadogan and some others shouting "Remember Biafra!"; and finally a new parliamentary debate on 9 December, after 151 MPs put down a motion calling for a change to government policy, and 86—more than in any previous debate—voted against the government.

It is not surprising that protests against the arms supplies continued in Britain, for nobody knew how long the war would last. The military stalemate encouraged talk of an "unwinnable" war, and while it went on, huge numbers were starving. As time passed, the Wilson government's reasons for continuing the arms sales still failed to convince the majority of British people, to judge from opinion polls.

What were those reasons? There were four principal ones, already mentioned. Two were nonsensical, based on fears of non-existent dangers from a halt to British arms supplies—a danger of harm to British residents in Nigeria, and a danger of Soviet domination of Nigeria. A third was rather strange, as it was a flimsy reason in principle but had some basis in the real Nigerian situation: that Britain, as supplier of arms on which the FMG depended, had power to influence its conduct of the war. It did have that power, and used it, however much Nigerians resented the fact; undoubtedly, Wilson let Gowon know, in March 1969, that continued regular indiscriminate air raids would make it impossible for him (Wilson) to go on defending arms sales. But supplying arms to a country at war in the hope of manipulating that country is not really a defensible policy (it was tried again with US arms sales to Iran in 1986).

In fact, the British government emphasised most of all the fourth reason: that there was a moral obligation to help Nigeria. That was of course the Nigerian view: Nigeria is facing an armed rebellion, it needs arms, so arms must be supplied, end of story. The rest of the world could not have been expected to agree with this without question. There are rebels and rebels, not all are the same; many states of the modern world originate from rebellions, including the US; talk of sovereignty and rebellion raises fundamental questions about the state and its rights and duties, as Julius Nyerere explained. A rebellion may be in response to such extreme provocation, such extreme dereliction on the part of the state authority, that armed action to stop it loses moral justification and there is no obligation for others to help such action. That, Biafrans said, was the case with Nigeria in 1966–7: Eastern Nigerians were violently driven out of the greater part of their own country; Nigeria rejected them before they rejected Nigeria.

And they were right to say this, as I personally concluded then, watching from the fairly good vantage point of a magazine concentrating on West Africa and closely following the Nigerian crisis. While I agree that the Easterners should have accepted Decree no. 8, as some sensible people in Enugu urged, in view of all that had happened there were good enough reasons to break away from Nigeria: it was not an act of one man's "mad ambition".

When the Biafran leaders ignored good advice and declared secession, the right response from Nigerians, if they really understood what their fellow countrymen had suffered, would have been to refrain from military action and appeal to African states to help work out a temporary arrangement with Eastern Nigeria/Biafra, which could have led to some sort of union coming back in the future. Really this should have been attempted before the two decisive actions of 27 May 1967—the Eastern Nigeria Consultative Assembly's vote to authorise Ojukwu to declare independence, and Gowon's decree a few hours later creating the 12 states. Both were provocative moves, but the second rapidly became the FMG's burning of boats. Possibly, at an early date after that, the creation of states—in principle a good idea, but not the most urgent priority in the crisis—could have been put on hold; before 27 May it could certainly have been postponed until the proposed conference on a future constitution. As it was, by creating the states the Federal Government boxed itself in and made it almost impossible to turn back and agree to something like Aburi. When Biafrans considered a compromise peace as they steadily lost the war, they came up against that obstacle—though Raph Uwechue's proposals could have been a way out.

Recalling all the details of who did what when in 1966–7 may seem pointless now, but during the war it was important to both sides. Continuing the war and continuing to provide arms for it became more indefensible when it led to mass famine, but the original reasons for it remained the main issue. However, for the aroused public around the world, who may or may not have understood those reasons, the rights and wrongs of the conflict did not matter much. The Biafrans' explanation was easier to understand and agree with, but for many people what mattered most was the mass starvation that the war had caused, and while commonly condemning the British arms sales they basically wanted to see the war ended and hungry children fed, regardless of which side was right or which side won.

How could it be said that the aim of "one Nigeria" justified such a loss of innocent life? But many including myself also asked, how could the aim of Biafran independence justify such a loss of innocent life? I sometimes suggested to Biafrans in the latter part of 1969 that their leaders should consider giving in, but that simply angered them. The Biafrans' common view was that surrender meant genocide—but it did not. They should surely have abandoned the struggle in 1968; but to blame them alone for the myriad deaths is wrong. My own view, which I told to colleagues on the magazine, was that "Neither Nigerian unity nor Biafran independence is worth that amount of suffering".

Mercy and money

Apart from the nonsense about JCA as a gun-runner, there were other criticisms of the relief operations for Biafra, not all by people biased against the Biafrans. Because all sorts of contact between the Biafran enclave and the rest of the world were very restricted, almost all money transfers for expenses in Biafran territory had to go through the Biafran regime—its overseas offices and its bank, the African Continental Bank. This meant the Biafrans receiving hard currency, which it could use for all sorts of purposes, and the beneficiaries receiving allegedly equivalent sums in Biafran currency. Kennedy Lindsay, who pointed this out in his article in *West Africa* of 19 October 1968, returned to the theme in an article about sales of Biafran stamps—for collectors, as they had no validity for international postal services—in Amsterdam.[183] Others also pointed it out, for there was no doubt about the basic fact, even if there was about the amounts involved. Enahoro said in his attacks on the relief agencies on 30 June 1969 that their operations had given Biafra foreign exchange reserves of over £50 million.[184] The amount might have not have been exactly that, but it was probably considerable, from spending particularly on two items: landing fees for the relief aircraft, and purchases of local food for distribution to the most needy.

The Biafrans charged landing fees for aircraft to raise revenue and to assert their sovereignty; Nigeria must also have charged such fees for relief supplies brought in by air, as well as Dahomey, Gabon and Portugal. But the fact must be faced: the Biafran regime practised pure extortion. The Red Cross, JCA and other relief agencies had to pay; they were forced, as their overriding concern to save lives prevented them from refusing. Akpan recorded later that Dr Akanu Ibiam had written to Ojukwu strongly objecting to charging the relief agencies for landing rights; he, Akpan, had not known it was going on.[185]

The local purchases of the main items of starch food like yams were made both within Biafran-held territory and from across the lines. ICRC officials said in July that 70 to 80 per cent of food then distributed in Biafra was locally bought.[186] Of course the Biafran regime could have made its own currency available for food purchases without demanding a refund in hard currency.

This situation raised acutely the issue mentioned earlier, of the side effects of any aid sent for civilians in a war zone. Those side effects can never be avoided altogether, and the only answers are Awolowo's—to send no aid at all—or to send aid knowing that there will be indirect benefits for one or both of the belligerents. Few would question that the latter answer is the only acceptable one; but since the Biafran war there have been many studies of serious problems faced by relief operations in war-hit countries. Notable are the books by Alex de Waal,[187] Zoë Marriage,[188] and Suzanne Franks.[189] From detailed study of relief operations during later African civil wars, especially in Sudan and Ethiopia, they show how such operations can be manipulated by parties to a conflict. They make points worth considering, but they seem unfairly to blame the humanitarians who are manipulated more than the manipulating parties, as some did in the Biafran case.

Many writers on the Biafran war have expressed complete conviction that the relief agencies' payments prolonged the war by enabling the Biafrans to buy more arms. Ian Smillie, in his book *The Alms Bazaar* (1995), writes that the Biafra airlift was "An act of unfortunate and profound folly. It prolonged the war for 18 months, because the relief agencies believed, incorrectly as it turned out, that an unrestrained Nigerian Government would unleash a final genocidal bloodbath against Ibos, should Biafra collapse."[190] This is a propaganda excess; it suggests without proof that the relief agencies all believed in the danger of genocide (in fact many worked on the Nigerian side of the front also) and, worse still, that they deliberately set out to help arm the Biafrans, for only that—and not the saving of civilian lives, which was in fact the aim—might have been seen as a way to prevent a Biafran collapse. If we leave this nonsense aside, Smillie is in agreement with many other sources that the relief operations provided Biafra with plenty of foreign exchange; he says the landing fees brought in thousands of dollars per day.[191] De Waal quotes Smillie with approval in a brief, and in parts inaccurate, section on Biafra.[192] Gould says that the reports on famine in the Western press brought "great support for Biafra's survival, but its incidental and unknowing effect was to help Biafra for a further eighteen months and so prolong the agony of the war".[193]

This dogma about the Biafrans using relief agencies' payments to buy weapons to prolong the war repeats the period of 18 months, presumably calculating this as the period between the start of the main Uli relief operation and Biafra's defeat (in fact it was more like 15 months, as the airlift was not fully operational until September 1968). That was also the period of the big French arms deliveries. It would be easy to imagine a connection, except that, as already noted in this work, it is highly probable that the Biafrans paid nothing for those French arms. In addition, Count von Rosen is said to have paid for the Minicons himself. It remains true that the Biafrans received a large amount of foreign exchange from the relief agencies and could use it for many purposes—the offices in London, Lisbon and some other cities, travel by Biafran representatives, perhaps some arms sent via Portugal. But the categorical assertions about prolonging the war for 18 months must be in doubt until the full truth about payment for the French arms is established.

But even then, the basic truth will remain: innocent victims of war must be aided, full stop. To deny this means accepting the principles of total war. In the last resort, Maggie Black's history of Oxfam—despite her excessive criticisms of relief agencies for believing Biafran claims spread by the semi-legendary Markpress—was absolutely right to conclude regarding Biafra:

> The most that can be said is that the maintenance of the food airlifts was one factor among many that helped to keep the war going. In the balance of military forces, the relief of hunger in the enclave—where starvation was being used as a weapon—cannot rate higher than the arms delivered by the French; the inexperience of the Federal forces; or the bravery—spurred by the conviction that they were fighting for their very survival—of the Ibo.

> In the end, the principle that the lives of innocent civilians count for more than the political aims of belligerents must be the mast to which the agents of humanitarianism nail their colours.[194]

As JCA was running most of the airlift to Biafra from June 1969, it was the main target of criticisms about humanitarian work enriching the Biafran regime. In particular, those involved in Nigerian church humanitarian work were uneasy because they were linked by many of their countrymen with JCA and with many Westerners' support for Biafra.

Because of Nigerian Protestant churches' complaints, the matter came to a head at the top level of the World Council of Churches. Its conference in Geneva in December 1969, attended by representatives of JCA, passed a resolution which was submitted to the WCC's Division of Inter-Church Aid, Refugee and World Service (DICARWS). This in turn made recommendations restating the over-riding need for peace, and recognising "that the JCA has saved the lives of many people", but expressing "deep distress at the ambiguous position in which efforts of Christian people have political side effects, which include exposing the churches to the charges of prolonging the war and adding to the suffering of people". It raised the question "whether the churches through JCA should prolong the massive airlift in its present form".

In response, JCA, at a meeting in Sandefjord in Norway, recalled the churches' efforts to provide relief on both sides, and the overrid-ing need for peace; it recalled also that it had "supported directly and indirectly all initiatives to establish more regular and effective alterna-tives to night flights". But as these had failed, it said, it must continue the night flights: "To stop the airlift now would not only have political consequences but result in death of millions of innocent civilians. It would establish starvation as a legitimate instrument of war but also as a partisan tool in the hands of groups pursuing their own motives." It concluded, "Finally, relief is based on divine law which commands that above all we serve our neighbour and we have no alternative but to continue relief work as long as it is an effective means of alleviating the present suffering."[195]

The organisers of JCA knew of course that their critics thought the airlift was adding to suffering, not reducing it. They were right to reject that argument; the facts backed up divine law. Stopping the airlift would have halted payments for landing fees except for arms flights, but arms already ordered would still have arrived in the com-ing weeks while people starved. Did anyone seriously think that if JCA stopped its food and medicine deliveries, Ojukwu would instantly agree to the plan for daylight flights? It is most unlikely—JCA had been urging him to do so for a long time and he could con-tinue to refuse, knowing JCA would not feel able to continue refusing to help. As for Ojukwu actually surrendering to save lives if JCA

flights stopped, that is even more improbable—he would have proclaimed to the world how churchmen were cooperating to starve
Biafra into submission, and fought on with whatever arms were available (did anyone suppose a relief organisation could give orders to
Foccart?). It was unimaginable that dedicated doctors, nurses, priests
and nuns working hard to save destitute people should say to those
people, "Sorry, we're not going to help you any more, we want to
force Ojukwu to surrender. If he does you will get help." All this was
obvious even if people believed that Biafra was spending vast sums
extorted from humanitarians on the French arms, but most probably
it was not. Of course JCA was also right to say that it was a moral
duty for those able to help save innocent lives to do so. From the
beginning it had believed that this duty overrode the normal obligation (always emphasised by the churches) to obey a country's laws.
The most law-abiding people everywhere will usually admit, at least
in principle, that laws may be disobeyed for a very good cause.

Hungry but holding on

Dr Pius Okigbo said in New York in July 1969 that Biafrans had
"never been more confident" of ultimate victory.[196] Probably not all
Biafrans felt so confident, but the fighting in recent weeks had not
brought much gain to the Nigerians, and the Biafrans' air raids were
a spectacular success. The Biafrans must have wished they had
acquired the Minicons earlier: they flew so low that they could not be
detected before they attacked; none was shot down; they used Uga
airstrip but could land and take off in all sorts of places. They attacked
an oil control centre at Ughelli on 18 June, a Shell-BP flow station at
Kokori on 28 July, a Gulf Oil storage tank at Escravos on 10 August,
a power station and factory at Sapele in September, Benin airport
again in October—all in the Mid-West. Then, too, there was a very
successful raid on the Shell-BP terminal off Forcados on 30 October
1969, hitting an oil tanker. These attacks were deliberately aimed at
the oil industry, which financed the Nigerian war effort, and caused
serious damage. The Biafrans also acquired four T-6 Harvard planes
and used them for some air raids in November 1969.[197] The
Portuguese pilot of one of them, however, lost his way and crash-

283

landed in Benue Province on the Nigerian side.[198] Meanwhile, the Nigerian Air Force failed to put Uli airstrip out of action despite repeated attacks, and had now resumed quite frequent indiscriminate bombing. The head of the air force, Colonel Shittu Alao, said shortly before his death on 15 October (in a private plane crash in the Mid-West) that raids on secessionist territory had been increased from 28 to 50 per day.[199]

The lack of progress by the federal army for several months aroused some speculation that it might be deliberate. This had been suggested in earlier phases of the war, and some FMG statements seemed to support it; on 1 October, Independence Day, Gowon said the delay in ending the war was intentional, to make post-war reconciliation easier.[200] But as the FMG had many reasons for wanting to end the war as soon as possible, this may have been said to put a humanitarian gloss on what was due to other reasons. The federal army's logistical problems were considerable, much greater than the Biafrans'. The army's notorious waste of ammunition was admitted by Gowon to the editor of *West Africa*: "We have had a lot of trouble over ammunition supplies, particularly since our boys tend to blaze off with their automatics."[201] This alone could have delayed further advances against a Biafran army which had been reported in July as seriously short of ammunition itself.[202] (There may have been a problem with French supplies then; in fact there were suspicions that the French deliberately kept the supplies within limits.) In September 1969 there were massive new shipments of British arms to Nigeria; this was made known soon afterwards by the group of activists in London mentioned earlier.

Nigeria was not short of hardware for finishing the war, nor short of money, though it was feeling the financial strain. The Biafran air raids reduced oil production considerably—Shell-BP's production fell from 350,000 barrels in June to 309,398 barrels in July,[203] and later production figures were kept secret. But there was no early prospect of the war effort being seriously affected even if there were many more such air raids. There was no political danger to the Federal Government either, though there was renewed Yoruba agitation from July 1969, including violence culminating in a mass prison break at Ibadan on 16 September. Chief Awolowo and Governor

Adebayo met leaders of a militant organisation of farmers called Agbekoya, whose demands included a big increase in the cocoa price, and some concessions were made, but Adebayo spoke of a "rebellion" to be suppressed.[204] The FMG's hold on power was not threatened by this, or by a Central Bank workers' strike which led to a draconian anti-strike decree in December—though all this indicated major underlying social problems. Its secure position was shown when Gowon announced on Independence Day an amnesty for everyone detained in the civil war but no longer considered a security risk, "as soon as possible";[205] Wole Soyinka was then freed and returned to the University of Ibadan as head of the Drama Department.

The administration of relief in the war zone on the federal side—in East Central, Rivers and South-Eastern States, and in areas of Kwara State (the new name for West Central) and Benue-Plateau hit by Biafran incursions—did not go well after the end of the ICRC's coordinating role. The FMG announced in September that the Nigerian Red Cross would take over that role, not the Rehabilitation Commission as announced earlier, though the commission would have overall supervision. The Nigerian Red Cross Society duly took over on 2 October, but its chairman, Chief Justice Sir Adetokunbo Ademola, said it did not have the financial or human resources to do the work done by the ICRC, having to feed and clothe 650,000 people.[206] An article in *West Africa* of 1 November said the lack of funds for transport had led to a "drastic reduction" in food distribution. There was to be foreign aid, but the expulsion of the ICRC with all its resources and expertise was already shown to be a big mistake. *West Africa*'s Matchet said on 8 November that the Nigerian Red Cross had only £16,500 per month but needed £110,000, and food was waiting in warehouses for lack of transport, and asked why the government was not helping. But the agencies that had been doing the work on the ground continued to do so; Lutheran churches in Scandinavia paid for a "floating doctor service" in Rivers State.[207]

Things were worse on the Biafran side. A report by Eric Pace in the *New York Times* in September[208] said there were signs of demoralisation; hunger was creating division, troops were deserting, there was more call on conscripts, and soldiers were commandeering relief lorries. Hunger was undermining the resistance. There was reported

285

to be massive starvation and disease in parts of the southern area where the Biafrans had been advancing.[209] A grim detailed report by Jim Hoagland in *The Scotsman* said marasmus—total starvation following deficiency of carbohydrates—was now a worse problem for many children in Biafra than the now very familiar *kwashiorkor*; about two million displaced people received only about three relief meals per week.[210] JCA announced its 4,000th flight in November and its 5,000th at the end of December. The French Red Cross, on which little was reported in *West Africa*, said it sent 2,135 tons of relief into Biafra between 1 September 1968 and 1 November 1969—not much by comparison with JCA and, before June 1969, the ICRC.[211] There were also flights by Africa Concern, in two aircraft from Gabon. All this saved many lives, but it was not enough.

A report in July 1969 said there were more orphans than before;[212] the extended families had cared for most children who had lost their birth parents, but were now increasingly unable to cope. From September 1968 *West Africa* quoted reports of children being flown to Gabon, or sometimes Ivory Coast or São Tomé, for treatment and care, by the Swiss organisation Terre des Hommes and the Knights of Malta. Susan Garth, a wealthy British businesswoman, became a passionate but somewhat unbalanced defender of the cause of Biafra's children, launching a Biafran Babies' Appeal in 1968 and calling for general evacuation of children; this was rejected by the Biafran government.[213] But eventually about 5,000 children were evacuated by air. They may not all have been orphans—relatives caring for them may have wanted them to be taken away to safety for the time being. One may ask, in fact, how the children for evacuation were chosen. The Biafran authorities insisted that they must be returned eventually; presumably they were always given tags with their names and home areas. *West Africa* carried a report on the camp for Biafran children in Ivory Coast, noting that the Biafrans said there should be no individual adoptions and education should not be in Ivory Coast's ordinary (French-language) schools.[214] A few thousand children were saved in this way, but almost all Biafran children and adults were saved or, in many cases, not saved in Biafra.

With starvation increasing, in the latter part of 1969 many people began crossing the lines to return to their home villages or seek help from relief agencies. It had always been possible to cross the lines. Presumably many more—it is impossible to say how many—now crossed over, either not believing that they would be killed by federal troops or, like the stricken Mrs Igwebuike, no longer caring if they were. People could cross over in both directions, and word must have got back that in East Central State at least it was safe. There were in fact many signs of normal life resuming there, including the reopening of markets with plenty to sell.[215] Relief agencies, helped by the army, were at work there, with some foreign aid workers who got a mention in the British press. One, a British nurse named Sally Goatcher, accidentally drove into Biafran territory (which showed how unfortified the front line was) and was detained for three weeks;[216] I interviewed her after her release and return to England, and she spoke reassuringly about the situation where she had worked, mentioning that the military observers had consulted her about it (presumably they always sought such independent testimony when they could). Another British aid worker was quoted in a London evening newspaper as saying, "It's all malarky about genocide."

During the long period of limited military activity there could have been more fraternisation and small individual truces (for example, seeing an enemy soldier and deciding not to fire) between Nigerian and Biafran troops. Many stories of this were heard during the war. One told to us by David Williams arose from the delivery of the *Daily Times* to federal troops at Onitsha; when the newspaper's representative met the troops, one man said that "we" had not been receiving the *Daily Times*; it turned out that "we" were the Biafran troops nearby, and that man had come over for a visit. Gowon said in May 1969, "I have been most impressed by the happy, almost joking, relations which you find between the rebel boys and our own when they lie side by side in our hospitals."[217] But the "boys" on both sides were still sometimes in action, and were being prepared for more action.

There were all sorts of indications by September 1969 that the Biafrans had no hope and might as well surrender. The advance southwards had halted and there was no prospect of reoccupying Rivers State; the Minicons and T-6s could damage oil installations but not feed Biafran children or soldiers. But there were no moves by anyone to make surrender easier. In September 1969 the OAU, at its regular

summit in Addis Ababa, passed a resolution appealing "to the two parties to preserve in the overriding interest of Africa the unity of Nigeria
and to accept immediately a suspension of hostilities and the opening
of negotiations, intended to preserve the unity of Nigeria and restore
peace that will assure for the people every form of security and every
guarantee of equal rights, prerogatives and obligations".[218] President
Nyerere circulated a 12-page document defending his recognition of
Biafra. Sierra Leone abstained from the vote; and pro-Biafran feeling
in Freetown grew so much that the editor of *West Africa* devoted an
editorial on 11 October to urging Prime Minister Stevens not to recognise Biafra. But this did not much affect the overwhelming support
for Nigeria by official Africa. It should be noted that the FMG's allies,
African and British, regularly disagreed with it by calling for an immediate ceasefire. A ceasefire on its own (not accompanied by an arms
embargo, which was constantly advocated and was ideally desirable but
would be difficult to enforce) would have at least allowed a new relief
supply agreement to go ahead, and refusing it showed unjustified
intransigence. But Nigeria naturally voted for the OAU resolution even
though it called for a ceasefire, because it said this must be followed by
negotiations "intended to preserve the unity of Nigeria".

In the weeks after the summit there was some coming and going
among African leaders about the war. One, the newly elected prime
minister of Ghana, Kofi Busia, said at one point that prospects for
peace in Nigeria were better than for a long time. But Dr Busia's
government, a short while later, ordered the brutal deportation of
hundreds of thousands of African immigrants without proper immigration documents, who flocked over the borders during November
and December 1969 in a pitiful mass exodus back to their home countries including Upper Volta, Niger and Nigeria. Thousands of
Nigerians arrived back in a wretched state, and the Nigerian anger at
Busia was increased when the Biafrans in Ghana were exempted from
deportation and given refugee status (it was withdrawn after the end
of the war). Meanwhile, Sierra Leone's foreign minister said his country might recognise Biafra if peace talks were not started before the
end of the year.[219]

The conversations on Nigeria in October and November[220] did not
lead to any serious talks, as Nigeria insisted that full peace negotia-

tions must be under the OAU. As had happened before, there were reports that Biafra might not insist on full sovereignty, followed by confirmation that it still did, as a *West Africa* editorial noted on 8 November. On 1 November, at Biafra's Consultative Assembly meeting at Akokwa, Ojukwu said talks must be unconditional and not based on the terms of the OAU resolutions.[221]

Gowon told the *Daily Telegraph* in mid-November, "The end is very near."[222] Fighting intensified about then, having never ceased completely. There were reports of attacks between Onitsha and Awka and towards Nnewi, and in the south towards Owerri. Definite reports of federal advances came in mid-December, including some said to be possibly aimed at cutting the Biafran enclave in two; this, it turned out later, was the aim. Frederick Forsyth reported in *The Observer* of 7 December that the Biafrans were beating off a "final" federal attack. Some momentary federal defeats were reported, but overall the reports in several British papers showed the Biafrans in retreat, losing Okpuala on the Aba–Owerri road. Ordinary life in Biafra was said to be still going on—school certificate examinations were scheduled in schools still functioning[223]—and despite the war reports, I do not recall anyone saying or writing then that Biafra was close to the end. In the fighting, Uli was one important Nigerian objective, and the federal forces now had new Soviet 122-mm artillery which, it was thought, could hit the airstrip from a long distance. The various war reports[224] were not confirmed by the FMG, which imposed a complete news blackout.

On 11 December the Ethiopian government said there were preparations in hand for a meeting of Nigerians and Biafrans, and on the 15th a Biafran delegation headed by Okigbo arrived in Addis Ababa; Count von Rosen was said to be with them. But the Nigerian ambassador to Ethiopia said the peace moves were within the context of the OAU resolution.[225] In fact no negotiations took place; the Biafrans may have gone to Addis Ababa under false hopes. Christmas came soon afterwards with no truce; Akpan cancelled the Christmas holiday for civil servants. There remained no official news as the new year began, but on 2 January 1970 there was an unofficial report from Lagos that a federal advance to cut Biafran territory in two had succeeded, with men of the First and Third Divisions meeting between

Ikot Ekpene and Umuahia.[226] Still, at that moment, planes were landing at Uli every night, Biafra Radio was on the air, and few people
outside the war zone knew the true situation.

8

NIGERIAN VICTORY AND RECONCILIATION

Downfall and desolation

I recall that none of us on the *West Africa* staff knew, in late December 1969 and early January 1970, that Biafra was very near final and total defeat. The few reports about the military situation did not suggest this. Kaye Whiteman went to Cameroon for the celebrations of the tenth anniversary of the independence of ex-French Cameroun, which fell on 1 January 1970. David Williams, the editor, and I were in the office. On Sunday 11 January, the *Sunday Telegraph* published a long feature devoted to a report by Colonel Robert Scott, defence adviser to the British High Commission in Lagos, including considerable excerpts from the report itself. This report, which turned out to have been leaked, was an assessment not originally intended for publication, entitled "An Appreciation of the Nigerian Conflict". It caused a stir as it spoke very frankly about the weaknesses of the Nigerian armed forces. I read the article on the Sunday, and on arrival at the office on Monday morning, I spoke of it with the editor, who said it was authentic and truthful. But Williams gave no sign of having read the previous day's *Sunday Times*, which had a report from Richard Hall saying "Biafra Is Dying"; I had not seen this either.

During that Monday, 12 January, news came in thick and fast to confirm that Biafra had been totally defeated. In fact, the news had been coming in since the Saturday, but unfortunately we could miss news coming in at weekends. Early reports from people arriving in Gabon from Biafra were spread in Paris (where Raymond Offroy had just told Pompidou that it was time to recognise Biafra).[1] From the 12th, dozens of reports came in, confirming that the end had come suddenly from about 8 January onwards. From 12 to 15 January I worked at a hectic pace to collate and process the news now flowing in about the end of Biafra, for the news pages and a feature, "Relief: What Is Needed Now", in the issue of 17 January. It became clear that the Biafran troops had simply collapsed, and a new mass flight of civilians had begun. In the east, the Biafrans lost Arochukwu about 8 January. The Nigerian army advanced steadily, almost unresisted. The Biafrans lost their temporary capital, Owerri, on 9 January. There were still flights into and out of Uli during the night of 9–10 January, but on the 10th the Biafran cabinet met and decided that General Ojukwu must leave; he handed over to General Philip Effiong, chief of staff, who became the officer administering the government.

That night Ojukwu left, with Michael Okpara, General Madiebo and N.U. Akpan among others. The destination was not immediately known, but it turned out to be Ivory Coast, where Ojukwu was given asylum; Akpan returned to Nigeria soon afterwards. Ojukwu must have been very dazed by the sudden defeat, for he said he was going to explore some new arrangement with Nigeria and hoped to be back soon.[2] A JCA plane flew into Uli on that night of 10–11 January, and three aircraft the following night, but on 12 January Uli airstrip was captured. That same day Effiong announced the surrender of Biafra and said a delegation was ready to meet Nigerian representatives to negotiate peace "on the basis of the OAU resolutions".[3]

The defeat was complete; all the talk of guerrilla war came to nothing, and the Biafran Organisation of Freedom Fighters surrendered or went back to civilian life like the other troops. Very obviously the defeat was due above all to hunger and exhaustion. There was not enough space to record in detail in *West Africa*'s 17 January issue what was being told in many reports, about the starvation—already well known for months—getting ever worse and affecting soldiers and other adults as well as children. Before the end, starving soldiers had begun taking relief food meant for destitute civilians, while men barely able to stand still unloaded relief planes while they still came into Uli. A dreadful consequence of siege also occurred (as in Leningrad in the Second World War)—cannibalism, whose occurrence was to be confirmed by Akpan in his book published in 1971.[4] That book includes a valuable account of the last weeks and days of Biafra,[5] showing for example how the federal advances took the few remaining food-producing areas in parts of Aba, Annang, Arochukwu and Bende Provinces.[6] At the time this broad picture of collapse through hunger was already clear; *West Africa* of 31 January said former Biafran officers confirmed that this was the main cause of the surrender. Another cause, mentioned in *West Africa* of 24 January, was the spread of a Cherubim and Seraphim sect whose preaching was said to have encouraged demoralisation among the Biafrans. A church of that name had had a wide following among Yorubas for decades, but I did not learn how it (or another group of that name, perhaps) had spread among Igbos and how it had contributed to demoralisation.

In our space-restricted summary of the end of the war on 17 January we recorded that on 12 January General Gowon welcomed the surrender and ordered his troops to continue their advance peacefully and obey the Code of Conduct. On the night after the surrender, a plane flew to Uga airstrip and back, but by the 14th federal troops had taken Uga and the Biafra Radio station, and they were now told to return to camps and hand over to police; but this did not happen immediately.

A delegation of Biafrans and ex-Biafrans was flown by the federal forces to Lagos for an official surrender ceremony at Dodan Barracks on 15 January 1970 by Effiong, three other senior army officers, and the chief of Biafran police. They formally surrendered to Gowon and all members of the Supreme Military Council. Sir Louis Mbanefo and Professor Eni Njoku also went to Lagos, and joined Gowon and others after the surrender ceremony.[7] By then several journalists were flocking to Nigeria, including Kaye Whiteman and others who had been attending the ceremonies in Cameroon and had a short way to fly to Lagos. There he and two other journalists—Bridget Bloom, formerly of *West Africa* and now of the

Financial Times, and Hugh Neville of Agence France-Presse—witnessed the handshake between Gowon and Effiong which clinched the surrender and the end of Biafra, as Kaye recorded in his book about the city of Lagos much later.[8]

There was great friendly camaraderie at that ceremony and at countless places in the war zone. The amazing reconciliation began immediately, with Nigerian officers and soldiers greeting their adversaries of yesterday warmly, drinking together and swapping stories. The foreign press soon reported all this, for journalists were very soon allowed into the war zone.

For Biafrans living abroad, and their sympathisers, it was a most unhappy time of hopes dashed and worry mounting as they read the news of the defeat and wondered what would happen next. Some clung to hope as long as they could; I recall that there were forlorn hopes that the hero Colonel Joe Achuzia was still fighting on, until news quickly came that he too had surrendered. Probably few Biafrans abroad could get any direct news from their people for some days at least. Some may have hesitated before making friends with Nigerians again; I went to a Nigerian student meeting whose organisers had invited ex-Biafrans to come along and make peace like the people at home, but they did not come, and the Nigerian diplomat present said the idea had been stupid anyway. For British and other Western people who had followed the war there was relief at its end, as expressed by the secretary of the Africa Centre, Margaret Feeny, in her regular newsletter: "Thank God the war is over!" But there was also fear for what was happening to the people of the war zone.

In that region of Igboland, hundreds of thousands of utterly ruined and destitute people were moving around, most returning to their home villages. Great numbers of them had been receiving relief rations, scanty but making a difference, and now the entire relief distribution system had collapsed. That was what aroused a great deal of the world's attention in the days after the surrender. Headlines in Britain warned of huge numbers likely to die in a short time.

The panic, grief and pleas now voiced by people of genuine compassion in many countries were not without cause; they did not deserve the mockery some made. The reason was quite simply that hundreds of thousands of people had been living in refugee camps or attending feeding centres, or had been assisted in their home villages, because of the relief airlift and the distribution network within Biafra which had gone on until near the end. There was probably little left in any warehouses, and lorries would soon have run out of fuel. So all those people were left stranded, with no food or medicine coming in. It was natural to call urgently, as many did, for something like the Biafra airlift to go on, if possible without a break, after Biafra had collapsed.

Unfortunately it was also quite impracticable, because of the general collapse and the mass movement of people—great numbers were on the move, even though many sick people would have been unable to move, probably many would not have had people to carry them, and many could not have stood the journey. The Biafran authority which had protected distribution and prevented theft of relief goods until near the end was gone, no normal authority was immediately present, everything was breaking down. There can be no doubt that many thousands died of starvation and disease in the weeks following Biafra's defeat, adding to a total for the war that was certainly in the hundreds of thousands at least.

New relief operations were quickly begun by the Nigerian Red Cross, and some overseas aid was requested, but almost immediately the Federal Military Government announced that no aid would be accepted from France, Portugal, South Africa or Rhodesia, or from any relief agency which had sent relief to Biafra from those countries or from Ivory Coast or Gabon, or from Joint Church Aid, Caritas, Canairelief of Canada, the French Red Cross or the Nordic Red Cross.[9] This was clearly an act of vindictiveness in response to Nigerian public opinion. Another such act was the arrest and later deportation of 105 Catholic missionaries who had done so much to help relieve suffering and maintain morale in Biafra; they had also expressed sympathy for the Biafran cause, but they had above all concentrated on their normal priestly ministry and on efforts to save lives. Similarly, while France and Portugal had directly aided Biafra militarily, the relief organisations now barred from the war zone had not, but had simply wanted to save the lives of people who were now Nigerians again.

Many humanitarians in the West clamoured for a new and enormous airlift—their clamour filled the British media from the first days after the Biafran defeat—and often called for it to go to Uli once again. That was pointless, as Enugu and Port Harcourt airports could have been used, but a big new airlift could have helped save many people, and so could the Holy Ghost Fathers if they had been allowed to stay, as the Nigerian relief operation was initially very poorly organised.

This fact was clear to everyone in the former war zone, and was described in detail by Bridget Bloom in a report for the *Financial Times*, reproduced in *West Africa* of 24 January 1970. After visiting Aba, Owerri, Orlu, Uli and other places, she reported that there was "no evidence of mass starvation" but "many of the people are very hungry" because the "Nigerian relief machine is simply not geared to coping with feeding and caring for them". The worst situation was in Owerri.[10] The Nigerian Red Cross was short of money, and there was a critical lack of lorries for transport; Britain offered to give £5 million and some lorries.[11] This shocking situation was predictable. It would not have been so serious if the International Committee of the Red Cross (ICRC) had not been kicked out a few months before. The sudden collapse of Biafra had caught the Nigerian Red Cross totally unprepared. There were in fact 13,000 tons of emergency food already in Nigeria, but there was far too little transport to take it to those in need.[12] *West Africa* had highlighted this omission two months earlier, and there was no possible excuse for it.

Of course the Biafrans could have avoided this situation by accepting a negotiated surrender earlier; the surrender could have been carried out in stages, to ensure that relief distribution was not disrupted. But it was still the FMG's responsibility to ensure, when it was clear that the end was near, that enough food and medicine supplies were waiting, together with enough vehicles for transporting them, and that clearly did not happen. Bridget Bloom's report said, "The Federal Government's contingency plans all but collapsed on Biafra's sudden demise."[13] In view of its own dereliction, the government had no good reason to prevent a new airlift of food and medicine. It did not explicitly say no airlift by anyone would be allowed, but it excluded agencies with the most experience of aid to the former war zone, and in fact no major airlift occurred; the government had not banned aid from the ICRC but for some reason did not call on it.

While the distribution system for airlifted relief had collapsed, a new one could have been started with sufficient supplies brought to nearby places by a new airlift. So the renewed blame placed on the FMG was justified. But many agencies and governments now rushed to help the very inadequate Nigerian Red Cross effort.

While the federal military and civilian authorities did not do their duty to the war-stricken population well, they did not kill them either. Kaye Whiteman, reporting from Enugu, spoke of "the great non-story of the war: the complete absence of massacre, genocide and slaughter which many confidently predicted would happen when Biafra was overrun".[14] Not only was there not genocide, there was not a wave of violent reprisals either, which would have been a more likely outcome of a civil war but did not happen after this one. Nor was there violent action against the Igbo intelligentsia, which had been an alternative fear. The Nigerian propaganda against them was not followed by any serious punitive action. One of them was, however, killed by federal soldiers—Professor Kalu Ezera, who had been associate professor of government and dean of social sciences at the University of Nigeria before the war and had published *Constitutional Developments in Nigeria* in 1964; I never learned the circumstances of what was an unusual occurrence.

There was some violence by the victorious troops. Indiscipline was said to be worst in the Third Division. Some killings were reported, but the most common crime was rape, which happened often and was highlighted by the foreign press. Nigerians might think the foreign press was always against them, but they could not expect it not to notice anything wrong or unpleasant. Concern overseas continued about the plight of the ordinary population in the former war zone, and on its side the FMG remained cool towards the foreign press, besides making it very difficult at times for journalists to enter the country by its immigration bureaucracy. But in fact the world's press was generally full of praise for Gowon, who carried out in many ways his promise of "no victors, no vanquished".

There was a sweeping amnesty for people involved in any way with Biafra, no civilians being put on trial; Effiong was detained for a time in 1970, and Pius Okigbo, Joe Achuzia and some others later, but most leaders of Biafra did not face even that. As promised, Igbos were able to return to their former salaried jobs in much of the country. Very soon after the surrender, thousands of people were returning to Enugu to get their former white-collar jobs back; all members of the former Eastern Region public service who were of East Central State origin were to be regarded as reinstated members of that state's public service.[15] Thus the creation of a normal administration in the Igbos' state, already advanced, could now be completed under the direction of the administrator, Anthony Asika, and his commissioners, who included Mrs Flora Nwakuche (the famous novelist Flora Nwapa) and Samuel Ikoku. Reintegration of Igbos had already progressed even in the Mid-West. Igbos were soon returning to Lagos; the *Daily Times* had by mid-1970 reinstated most of its staff who left before the war. And great numbers of Igbos returned to the North, where they were welcomed and those with abandoned property got it back. Over most of the country there were heart-warming scenes as former friends and workmates greeted each other. To help the people searching for each other after two and a half years, the *Daily Times* had a regular "missing persons" column.

"No victors, no vanquished" did not apply 100 per cent. Eventually a number of officers who had fought for Biafra were dismissed from the armed forces. While ex-Biafrans resumed work in the civil service, a decree in August 1970 allowed dismissal by public service commissions of any public officer who was actively engaged "in any hostile or subversive act or rebellion".[16] But this may not have been applied widely, because the reconciliation was obviously popular. There were some disgruntled and unreconciled people in the North, where a loathsome anti-Igbo song in Hausa was played, but without stopping Igbos coming back to Kano, Kaduna and other Northern cities and being welcomed back. Some prominent people, I heard, mocked Gowon as "General Amnesty" and "the Saint from Wusasa". They could be ignored, as Gowon was popular for winning the war and encouraging the reconciliation.

What really spoiled the picture of general reconciliation was the vindictive attitude in Rivers State, on which Kaye Whiteman reported for *West Africa* after visiting there. Igbos were for a considerable time—I do not know how long—prevented from returning to the neighbouring state where they had dwelt for decades, Port Harcourt having been a largely Igbo city. In that city there was no reconciliation now. The governor, Lt Commander Alfred Diete-Spiff, showed his disregard for the suffering people of the former war zone (who in fact included Rivers people) by organising a sumptuous celebration of his wedding in Port Harcourt soon after the Biafran surrender, with champagne and other luxuries flown in (foreign correspondents were unimpressed, one headline saying "champagne in horror land"). He shared and presided over the Rivers people's unbending hostility to Igbos (no doubt there were some Rivers people with a better attitude, keeping quiet). So Igbos could return to the North, where so many of their people and Rivers people too had been murdered, but not to the nearby Rivers State.

This added to the problem of Igbos' recovery from the ruins of war, which were enormous anyway. They could repopulate the empty cities of Enugu and Onitsha, and were welcomed back over most of the country, but almost all were ruined and broke. A major problem was that the Biafran currency was now worthless; for a short time it was still used in trading, but before long the question of possibly exchanging it for Nigerian currency became acute. Eventually it was agreed that each person could exchange any amount of Biafran currency, big or small, for a flat sum of £20. It was very little, perhaps enough for someone to travel to another part of Nigeria to seek work, perhaps barely enough for a family to eat for a time. The situation was bleak for huge numbers of Igbo people, and it was probably their own efforts to restart trading, using their well-known skills, that got them gradually out of it. Cyprian Ekwensi's *Survive the Peace*, published in 1973, is fiction but is surely based closely on the facts of a ruined people and their efforts at recovery; while not evading any of the grim reality, it describes a slow return to normal with some help from soldiers, an early source of Nigerian currency, and relief workers, and gives a generally positive picture, which was justified, as the recovery was remarkable.

Looking back at the war

To those who saw Igbos living and working at ease among other Nigerians again, as I did in the 1970s, it might have looked as though nothing had happened. Of course plenty had, and bitter memories always remained. There was plenty of death for millions to remember, violent death and slow death from starvation. There had been no genocide, but too many war crimes. Those committed by the Biafrans must have been one cause of the bitter vindictiveness in Rivers State.

On the federal side it was right for the world to be told that there was no genocide. Pope Paul VI declared after the surrender, "there are even those who fear a kind of genocide. We wish to exclude such a hypothesis for the honour of the African people and of their leaders who have themselves excluded it with many specific assurances"; unfortunately, many of the world's media published only the first few words, but *West Africa* published a letter giving the full wording, to correct the bad impression[17] (the Pope or his advisers should have realised that it was better not to mention the word at all). It was obvious to everyone that nothing like genocide happened. In later decades, Chinua Achebe maintained that there had been genocide,[18] and some other ex-Biafrans have continued to say so. In 2018, in a scholarly work mentioned in the last chapter, *Post-colonial Conflict and the Question of Genocide: The Nigeria–Biafra War, 1967–1970*, edited by A. Dirk Moses and Lasse Heerten,[19] 18 experts recall aspects of the Biafran war, noting the importance of the genocide accusation in Biafra and in many Western countries where support for the Biafrans was high; and the editors, in the introduction, examine whether the accusation was justified. They say, "Serious questions confront the case for genocide", and list seven good questions, concluding, "More thinking remains to be done to relate genocide and the FMG campaign."[20] Not much more is needed, really. Those who repeat the allegation simply recall mass killings (all highly criminal) and wrongly say these amounted to an overall plan for extermination, that is, genocide.

The federal forces' war crimes should not be forgotten. On returning from Nigeria, Kaye Whiteman told me things he had heard about such war crimes in the Mid-West, but said that now was not the time to publish such things, as nothing should interfere with the reconciliation. If that attitude was justifiable in the immediate aftermath of the war, it did not remain so later. The truth about the most evil acts in the war came out only slowly and late. In 1982 Buchi Emecheta, the famous Igbo novelist who spent most of her life in Britain, published *Destination Biafra*, another novel but based on the facts about Biafra, especially the Mid-West; her foreword says, "I hail from Ibuza in the Mid-West, a little town near Asaba where the worst atrocities of the war took place, which is never given any prominence."[21] More was published later, but much still remains to be made public.

In Nigeria in 1970 there was a popular song saying, "Secession is over, rebellion is crushed … The enemies of Africa must all eat their words." There had been "enemies of Africa", such as Portugal backing Biafra, but the great numbers who had been concerned only to save the lives of Africans did not deserve that description. There must be millions of Nigerians living today who would not be alive if they, or their parents or grandparents, had not been saved by the Biafra airlift. But while there was unjust criticism of good people, it seems likely that Nigerians, after fighting on different sides, found it easier to forgive each other by blaming outsiders (much as a wronged wife may find it easier to forgive the erring husband by putting all the blame on the "other woman"). I heard later of an ex-Biafran working well alongside fellow Nigerians but still full of anger at one BBC World Service broadcaster accused of being pro-Nigerian in the war. So punishing humanitarians may have been a way to make peace with people those humanitarians had aided.

The only words that really needed to be eaten were those predicting genocide—not all words uttered against the Nigerian war effort and British support for it. Of course it would be absurd to think that every war in the world is justified until it is proved to be a war of extermination, and many people opposed Nigeria's war against secession without believing in the genocide allegation. There were very good reasons for opposing it because of the enormous human cost and because of the events that had driven Eastern Nigeria to rebel. Did the reconciliation prove that the criticism of Nigeria had been mistaken? Some people seemed to think so,[22] but it is doubtful. Reconciliation could not help the hundreds of thousands dead.

Soon after the end of the war the world's interest in it plummeted. Biafra was soon a half-forgotten story. This was predictable: worldwide feeling about Biafra had been humanitarian, not supporting Biafran independence. Those who had been aiding or defending the hungry people of the war zone, even when they heard that the relief efforts there after the surrender were very insufficient, no longer felt able to help; they could still donate to UNICEF, which was active in relief efforts, but the urgency of the airlift had gone (Joint Church Aid was wound up soon after the end of the war). And the reconciliation must have reassured many concerned people, even those who had not expected genocide.

In the coming years, some Western people may have begun to doubt some of the facts about starvation in Biafra; Sir David Hunt wrote, "In Britain serious-minded men are asking themselves how they or anyone ever came to believe the stories about genocide and starvation."[23] This was a quite unjustified jibe, lumping together genocide, which was just a contested interpretation of facts, and starvation, which was pure fact. Nobody who had donated money for Biafran relief or publicised the famine should ever have had any regrets. As explained in the last chapter, the supposition that aid for the airlift prolonged the war is contestable and, even if proved, would not mean aid should not have been sent.

As for the British government's role, the main focus of protests, the outcome of the war does not prove that Britain was right to provide arms for Nigeria. In truth, Britain should rather have acted to bring about peace. Some details about the British involvement were revealed when Jonathan Aitken, one of the international military observers (Colonel Douglas Cairns), and two others were tried under the Official Secrets Act over the leaking of Colonel Scott's report;[24] they were all acquitted, but by then the Biafran war no longer interested many people in Britain.

All the foreign criticisms of Nigeria aroused the reactions described in this book, which led to the media attacks on humanitarians, the expulsion of the ICRC, and the restrictions on relief aid from overseas after the end of the war (which would have been defensible if Nigeria was organising relief properly itself). None of this benefited Nigerians suffering from the war. In any case, Nigerians needed to accept—maybe they and others understood it better after this war—that the world was already a global village then (still more today) and that one cannot expect neighbours to say and do nothing when one's house is on fire.

The situation in the former war zone, which had aroused so much concern, improved only very slowly after the war ended. As Igbos gradually resumed paid employment or found new jobs and remitted money to their home communities, and many others started or continued trading over much of the country, money became more available—though a shortage of coins in East Central State was noted in *West Africa* of 9 May 1970—and normal life, including education, could resume. But relief was still urgently needed, and was distributed slowly and inefficiently. The Nigerian Red Cross was severely hampered by a lack of funds, as already noted, until it received a large grant after the end of the war, and then took some time to set up a large relief operation; but this eventually fed about 2.5 million people in areas of widespread starvation, aided by overseas relief teams, some from the Save the Children Fund.[25] The continued food problems affected the negotiations for the return of children evacuated to other countries from Biafra (estimated to number 3,033 in Gabon and 900 in Ivory Coast); eventually many were returned to their families, but possibly not all.[26] In the former war zone there was plenty of overseas aid coming, including protein food from UNICEF, generators, hurricane lamps and blankets from the US, and medical supplies and Land Rovers from Britain.

The British government contribution, handled by the Ministry of Overseas Development, also included the provision of cement for rebuilding in the former war zone. But when the editor of *West Africa* asked a ministry official, "So you send cement to East Central State?" he answered, "Well, we send cement to *Lagos*." It can be assumed, lamentably, that other aid, including food more urgently needed than cement, could easily vanish into the wrong hands before reaching the war-stricken population. The prevailing Nigerian ills had continued through the war and were to continue and expand until now.

The Nigerian Red Cross ceased its coordination of emergency relief operations and handed over to the state Rehabilitation Commissions on 30 June 1970. Relief teams of the Christian Council of Nigeria (CCN), the Catholic Secretariat of Nigeria and Quaker Relief Services had been doing most of the work under Nigerian Red Cross coordination and continued to do so. The CCN went back on a decision to withdraw its relief teams on 30 June, saying *kwashiorkor* was possibly spreading; there were other reports of a worsening food situation, and new pockets of severe suffering were still being found.[27] Soon afterwards, Flora Nwakuche appealed in a news conference to the East Central State Rehabilitation Commission to intensify food supplies to affected areas "now that general scarcity of food prevails in the state".[28] An unpublished survey by the Nigerian government with the help of American doctors and the US State Department found that about a million Eastern Nigerians were suffering from oedema, owing to starvation.[29] And this, it must be remembered, was in a region where severe nutrition problems had been on a small scale before the war.

Emergency relief was only the beginning. A huge amount of reconstruction was needed, and would require a good deal of spending from the proceeds of Nigeria's now booming oil production; it was estimated that £60 million would be needed to rebuild Onitsha alone. But another consequence of the war would be even more difficult to tackle: the large numbers of unemployed former soldiers of the Biafran army. As commonly happens after a war, some of them turned to crime, using their knowledge of firearms. From 1970 onwards the former war zone became an area of widespread armed robbery, which led to the public execution by firing squad of convicted robbers, a horrible practice that went on for another three decades over many parts of Nigeria but did not stop the robberies. The problem of unemployment among Igbos was worsened by the exclusion from Rivers State. However, the postwar economic expansion must have created more jobs for them as for other Nigerians.

From Biafra to 36-state Nigeria

The way in which Eastern Nigerians returned to life among other Nigerians was really extraordinary. I saw it constantly in the North for years. When I visited Igbo areas I found Enugu was a flourishing big city again, as if it had not lain empty and abandoned just a few years earlier. But in East Central State post-war rebuilding was slow and Asika was an unpopular administrator, not only because of memories of his wartime role. In 1971 his government decreed the takeover of all church schools. This led to a decline in standards at those greatly respected schools, and constant complaints from parents. Vindictiveness towards the churches for their sympathy for Biafra cannot be excluded as a reason for this measure, which was replicated in many other states of Nigeria. But the Catholic Church in Igboland recovered well from the expulsion of missionaries. Many Igbo seminarians were soon entering the priesthood, more were to follow, and the Church continued to flourish until today. Some of the former missionaries were later able to revisit the country and see this.

The big exception to the miracle of reconciliation was the Rivers State (which I did not visit). Eventually there were many Igbos in Port Harcourt again, but my information is that the issue of pre-war Igbo property in the city was still unresolved until recently. In other parts of Nigeria the reconciliation was remarkable under Gowon, and continued after the coup which overthrew him on 29 July 1975 and replaced him with General Murtala Muhammed—with one exception: the new regime reversed Gowon's admirable decision not to award campaign medals for officers who fought against their own people. The Igbos' return to life in Nigeria was unaffected by the seizure of power by the war criminal responsible for the Asaba massacre; I do not recall any mention of that atrocity anywhere at the time. Igbos were probably quite pleased when Gowon fell, as Asika fell with him. Around the country Murtala Muhammed's government was popular as it took strong action against corruption and other major failings in public service and, although headed by a Northerner, enforced this without any regional or ethnic favouritism. Almost all the former state governors, and Asika, were found by an inquiry to have amassed wealth illegally; they were not gaoled, but their corruption, which had become notorious when they were in power, was now exposed. Murtala announced the findings about the former governors on 3 February 1976, and also announced the creation of seven more states, to make 19. East Central was divided into Imo and Abambra States, and South-Eastern State was renamed Cross River State, the idea being to get away from the labels of North, West and East.

On 13 February 1976 Murtala was assassinated in Lagos in an attempted coup, whose authors did not succeed in taking power. The country was severely shaken but there was no serious violence, ethnic or otherwise. Murtala's second-in-command, the former Third Division commander General Olusegun Obasanjo, took over as head of state. In death, Murtala was given quite amazing adulation, revered as something like a saint. But for a time Gowon, now living in England, was accused of involvement in the coup attempt; it was never proved, but for great numbers of Nigerians it was an article of faith, as a chauvinistic spirit rather like that which spread during the war years. Britain, suspected of involvement in the coup attempt, was once again under suspicion, until the fury died down. Considerably later, Gowon was to return peacefully to live in Nigeria.

In the first years after the war the oil industry revived and expanded, and federal and state government revenue boomed. A good deal of the more plentiful money was diverted into various pockets or otherwise squandered; in 1975–6 vast quantities of cement, ordered from abroad under dubious contracts, filled up ships which stayed for months off Lagos harbour. But a good deal of money was better spent. Nigeria built several good major roads, besides rebuilding the Niger Bridge. In 1976 an ambitious programme was launched to achieve universal primary education (UPE). This required efforts mainly in the Northern States, although it could not bridge the gap in Western-style education between the North and the South, the root cause of the country's problems; while Northerners got more education, people of other parts of the country forged further ahead from their better starting point, with increasing numbers going to Nigeria's own universities (numbering 12 by the late 1970s) and others in Europe and North America.

Indeed, the North–South division continued, and still continues. All the confident assurances given during the war that Northern domination had ended meant only that the old Northern Region, which had covered 80 per cent of the country, could not return. A part of that former region—the Muslim Hausa–Fulani emirates plus the culturally similar emirates of Borno and Nupe—still had power in the country. Nigerians commonly talk of "the North" to this day, meaning that area, which is populous and a major food-producing region, and which contains great cities like Kano. It also has a strong collective determination to defend its interests in politics, and thus regularly arouses fear among other Nigerians. About the time when Gowon announced in September 1974 postponement of the programme to return to civilian rule, though that may or may not have been the cause, there were rumours in the North of preparations for new pogroms, this time directed against Yorubas. That did not happen, but the rumours reminded everyone of the dismal fact that the basic causes of the crisis and civil war remained. Obasanjo's administration resumed the civilian rule restoration programme and completed it, but when a new constitution was being debated in 1978, there was extreme North–South tension again when some representatives of the North (that is, the emirates in the North) demanded that Islamic sharia law should be given a place in the constitution; the slogan was "No sharia, no Nigeria".

The new constitution departed from the independence constitution by introducing American-style democracy with an executive president. Elections were held in 1979 for a president, the Senate, the House of Representatives, state governors, and state assemblies. They were peaceful, but I recall that it was a tense and worrying time, especially when Alhaji Shehu Shagari was declared winner of the presidential election after achieving the required number of votes by a narrow margin according to a Supreme Court ruling that was queried by many, especially supporters of Chief Obafemi Awolowo, the next most popular candidate. During the election campaigns, Awolowo had been strongly denounced in the Eastern States because of his calls for the denial of all emergency food relief to Biafran territory. This showed that the war was still a fresh and very painful memory. Obviously nobody could have expected otherwise, though for some years in the 1970s I recall that in conversation Igbos almost never mentioned the war, and I have heard that the subject was avoided in Igbo families, at least in the early post-war period. However, it was shown in 1979, and later, that the press was free to recall the war from a Biafran viewpoint. Books about the war were on sale in Nigeria, apparently unrestricted.

Shagari's party, the National Party of Nigeria (NPN), was seen as a party of his fellow Northerners, but it had support in many parts of the country. And in 1982 he granted a pardon to Ojukwu, who returned from Ivory Coast to a rousing welcome. He was active in the NPN for some years, while holding the traditional title of Ikemba of Nnewi. When he died on 26 November 2011 he was buried with full state honours.

Nigeria's history since 1979 need only be summarised briefly here. The military took power again at the end of 1983 and held it for ten years, first under General Muhammadu Buhari and then, from 1985, under General Ibrahim Babangida; both had held senior commands in the civil war, when Babangida also married a wife of Hausa and Igbo parentage, born in Asaba. In a strange period of political turmoil in 1993 a new presidential election was won by a leading Yoruba businessman, Moshood K.O. Abiola, but the election was annulled, and instead Babangida handed power to an unelected civilian, Ernest Shonekan, who a few weeks later was overthrown by another general, Sani Abacha. His particularly brutal and corrupt regime ended with his sudden death in 1998, and General Abdulsalami Abubakar handed over power in 1999 to an elected civilian regime with a new presidential constitution; this, however, was headed by the former military head of state, General Obasanjo.

For twenty years Nigeria has had a working elective government at the federal and state levels, the number of states having now risen to 36. Obasanjo was president for eight years and was succeeded by Musa Yar'Adua (2007–10), Goodluck Jonathan (2010–15) and then another former military ruler turned elected president, Muhammadu Buhari. While maintaining stability at the top government level, Nigeria has suffered widespread general problems affecting the lives of the population, now estimated at about 200 million. The gross inequality already blatant in the 1960s has increased; a minority of people are very wealthy, while a smaller minority including politicians have become notorious for staggering illicit fortunes splashed around Nigeria, Britain and the US. This self-enrichment and big spending were already notorious under Shagari's presidency, and investigations and trials exposed it after 1983—but without deterring other arch-profiteers in later years. Other African countries also have major corruption, like Kenya, Angola and South Africa, but Nigeria has special, deserved notoriety. The scandals have been described in many books, notably the recent work by the late Stephen Ellis, *This Present Darkness* (2015). While a small minority get very rich or stay rich, the majority live in everyday poverty or destitution, with men, women and children struggling to keep alive by all sorts of work and trade, both in the rural areas and in the towns and cities, where it is now estimated that about half of Nigeria's population lives, including the chaotic megacity of Lagos.

Because of the misgovernment and crime, the hopes expressed in 1970—that after the ordeal of civil war Nigeria had a bright future ahead with its oil wealth—have been long since dashed. While the oil flows, Nigeria's four refineries, which should provide most or all of the country's petrol and other oil products, have been largely idle or producing far below capacity for decades, owing to malpractice or negligence. Many of the other manufacturing industries have been run down in the same way. The road system is very inadequate and Nigeria Airways was kept going in a ruinous state before it was finally closed down. All these and other aspects of avoidable economic failure are well known and publicised by Nigerians, among others. Complaints of foreign reporters' hostility to Nigeria, as in the war years, are still heard, but what those reporters say, Nigerians also say continuously; talk to any Nigerian about the daily lives of ordinary people in their country and it is the same dismal story. But there are reports of improvements in many areas in the past few years.

There are some successes to record. The mammoth operation to move the federal capital from Lagos to Abuja was successfully completed in 1991. More important, Nigeria's agriculture and its internal trade in agricultural produce have continued to feed a big population now about half urban. This is one area where foreign criticisms have often gone astray. It has often been alleged that Nigerian agriculture has been declining rapidly, but that is only true of crops for export and industrial use. Food production and distribution have not declined. Trade statistics show that food imports are too high, accounting for more than half of the total—US$22 billion out of $36.5 billion in 2018—but this works out at only about $110 (or roughly 40,000 Nigerian naira) per head of population or about $220 (roughly 80,000 naira) per head of urban population per year. From this it is clear that most food consumed in the country is produced there, though it may be transported over long distances, especially from the North, which is the main food-producing area, to other parts. And recently the food import bill has been falling.

This agricultural achievement owes little to the government, which is only very marginally involved in agricultural marketing since the abolition of the marketing boards in 1986. In agriculture and much else, private enterprise rules Nigeria, and only a part, though too large a part, is criminal private enterprise. While administration has somehow always kept going, despite problems that have included staff owed salaries for months on end, generally Nigeria is kept afloat by the ordinary people's hard work and enterprise. It remains a devil-take-the-hindmost society; one consequence of the poverty of millions is prevalent crime including armed robbery—in a country with gigantic unemployment, many will try criminal means to stay alive. As in other parts of Africa, besides the truly destitute there are vast numbers of people with limited education and few or no opportunities, and only a minority of these can do what great numbers want to do, namely emigrate to the West.

All that is wrong with Nigeria affects the Eastern States as well as others. There are now ten states in the former Eastern Region declared independent as Biafra in 1967: Enugu State, Anambra State, Imo State, Ebonyi State and Abia State in the territory of former East Central State; Cross River State and Akwa Ibom State in the former South-Eastern State; and Rivers State and another state carved out from Rivers, Bayelsa State. The presence of oil under the soil of many of those states has not spared them a big share of Nigerian hardships; the protests of the Ogoni people of the oil-producing area, headed by Ken Saro-Wiwa until his execution under the Abacha regime in 1995, brought Nigeria briefly back into something like the Biafra war headlines around the world; and guerrilla attacks in other oil-producing parts of the Niger Delta continued for years. And besides the hostile environment for Igbos in Rivers State, there have been allegations that the general post-war reconciliation with the Igbos did not extend to equal economic opportunities for them. Chinua Achebe claims in *There Was a Country* that the application of the 1974 Indigenisation Decree (reserving large percentages of many sorts of business to Nigerian indigenes) was part of a process of limiting economic opportunities for Igbos. In fact, the Igbo people, predictably, have done well in business, for example Augustine Ilodibe, whose fine coach service, Ekene Dili Chukwu ("glory to God" in Igbo), I recall well from the 1970s. But the impression that Igbos have been denied full opportunities in business is supported by Ellis's book.

There is a large Igbo diaspora, especially in the US, where possibly hundreds of thousands live. Some of them keep the memory of Biafra alive, but it is not necessary to emigrate to do that. There is an Umuahia war museum in Ojukwu's underground shelter, with photographs of the war, and the wreck of an Ilyushin is preserved. There have been many books written about the war by people very closely involved. As early as 1971 N.U. Akpan published *The Struggle for Secession*, a most valuable account by someone close to the seat of power in Biafra but, as is clear, not among the top decision-makers. General Alexander Madiebo published *The Nigerian Revolution and the Biafran War* in 1980. Fictional accounts, all obviously based on the authors' or others' real experience, include *Survive the Peace*, by Cyprian Ekwensi, already mentioned; Chinua Achebe's *Girls at War and Other Stories* (1973); *Never Again* (1975), by Flora Nwapa; and *Behind the Rising Sun*, by S.O. Mezu (described in chapter 4).

There have also been books written from the Rivers vantage point: Elechi Amadi's factual *Sunset in Biafra* (1973) and Ken Saro-Wiwa's fictional *Sozaboy* (1985), which is oddly written in a combination of various sorts of English and Pidgin. On the factual side, General Obasanjo published *My Command* in 1980.[30] These books have well-known publishers and international sales, but there have also, most probably, been more local publications about the war that are little known outside Nigeria, though I have no information about them. The Internet has added a good deal more writing about the war.

The Oputa Commission appointed by President Obasanjo heard plenty of testimony about the crimes committed in the war, and although its report was never published officially, it is said to be available online. General Gowon has apologised for the Asaba crime, a memorial to the victims has been erected, and the book already cited, by Elizabeth Bird and Fraser Ottanelli, has given a full account of the atrocity; now there is at least some dissent from the prevailing hero worship of General Murtala Muhammed, though his picture is still on the 20 naira note and his name is still borne by Lagos International Airport.

Nigeria still has a president who commanded federal forces in the war, and it remains to be seen when the country will have an Igbo president, which would make the reintegration of ex-Biafrans and their descendants more complete (President Jonathan was from the former Eastern Region, but from Bayelsa State). The ethnic issues that led to the crisis are still very much present. In politics there always is and perhaps always will be a lurking fear that unless "the North" is given its desired share in government, it could be danger-ous. If the president is not a Northerner, the vice president must be one, and vice versa. The country is divided into six zones for calcula-tion of balance of ethnic representation in institutions. The fear of one section of the country making trouble by alleging discrimination or "domination" is always there. However, lessons were learned, as was shown when the great crisis of February 1976 did not lead to mass violence. All the four successful coups d'état since 1966 have been bloodless, though two unsuccessful ones, in 1976 and 1990, were not. The war left disturbing memories and not only among the defeated; among other Nigerians I more than once heard people say, "We're not going through that again."

But danger has remained because of the poverty and inequality in particular. These are probably one cause of the new religious phe-nomena in Nigeria, though any analysis of religious belief must always give priority to genuine conviction. While the churches origi-nating from missions have been flourishing and expanding—the Catholic Church, for example—there has been since the 1980s a mushrooming of new Pentecostalist churches, which have a huge following and abundant funds. Although headed by wealthy people, they seem to respond to the social needs of the less well-off, albeit in a peaceful way. The phenomenon of Muslim revival and militancy seen in the North since the late 1970s has been perceived also as based on the needs of the underprivileged. It too has sometimes been peaceful, but there have been sporadic deadly clashes between Muslims and Christians in some places in the Northern States, and in 1980 a new Maitatsine sect, or Yan Izala, fought police and troops in Kano for days. Later, after the final (it seems) return to civilian rule in 1999, Northern States decided to apply sharia law. And finally, most terribly, there has been the war waged in Borno State and other north-eastern areas of Nigeria by the ferocious Boko Haram sect, whose name means "Western education is sinful"; that is not normal Islamic doctrine, and this sect, like the Maitatsine sect before, is not truly Muslim at all. It attacks Muslims, accusing them of not being true Muslims, more than anybody else. Its hideously brutal campaign has included the notorious kidnapping of the "Chibok Girls" in 2014, as well as bombs in mosques and countless other crimes. The Nigerian army has found it more difficult to defeat than the Biafrans, as they are irregular fighters who are totally fanatical and will stop at nothing. With their campaign, Nigeria's forty years of general peace came to an end, and at the time of writing there is no end in sight. And besides this conflict there has for years been constant criminal violence around the country, including clashes between herdsmen and farmers over land use in many Middle Belt areas, creating permanent fear and tension.

Boko Haram does not demand a separate state, and there have been no secessionist movements in Nigeria since Biafra. It must be said again that Biafra's secession was not bound to encourage other secessionist movements either in Nigeria or in other African states, and its defeat was not bound to discourage them. The most prolonged and deadly secessionist wars in Africa—in southern Sudan and Eritrea—began before Biafra and continued regardless of its defeat, and were ultimately successful. The suffering in those wars exceeded even that in the Biafran war, and eventually neither Eritrea nor South Sudan provided a good advertisement for secession in Africa: in Eritrea, a harsh authoritarian regime fought a crazed war with Ethiopia over valueless territory (1998–2000); and in South Sudan, armed factions tore the country apart just as it finally got independence after decades of war.

Apart from Sudan and Ethiopia, only one African country has had a major war of secession since Biafra: Senegal, where fighters for the independence of the Casamance region waged a generally low-intensity war for decades, now apparently at an end. But now, since 2017, serious unrest in North-West and South-West provinces of Cameroon has turned into a guerrilla war, of low intensity so far, for independence of that area, former British Southern Cameroons; the "anglophone" population there has continued English-language education and has a feeling of separateness from the "francophone" Cameroonians, who are much more numerous, and has suffered from discrimination under the central and highly centralised government in Yaoundé. Refugees from the fighting have gone to the Eastern States of Nigeria, and there must be memories of Biafra among the anglophone Cameroonians who sympathised with the Biafrans fifty years ago.

In the area that was for a short time Biafra, a Movement for the Actualisation of the Sovereign State of Biafra (MASSOB) was founded in 1999. Another movement with a less cumbersome name, Indigenous People of Biafra (IPOB), was founded in 2012; its leader, Nnamdi Kanu (born in the year of secession, 1967), has operated a new Radio Biafra from London. These movements call openly for independence for Biafra. They are regarded with suspicion and hostility by the Federal Government, whose forces are said to have killed in 2016 many people in Anambra State celebrating the anniversary (30 May) of Biafra's declaration of independence. How many people support these movements? Nobody should. The situation today is quite unlike 1967, even if federal repression brings back memories. Certainly the Igbos still suffer today, especially from deprivation of many sorts, but so do most other Nigerians. There is no particular ill-treatment of the Igbos to compare with what happened fifty years ago.

Instead of adding more problems for a country with too much violence already, those who want to remember Biafra should do so by helping record the full true history of the secession and war, rejecting myths and facing the most unpleasant facts but not seeking to settle scores with other Nigerians. They should make a proper study of the extent and effects of starvation and disease which so cruelly struck Eastern Nigerians and so shocked the world. A large-scale historical project, perhaps organised by universities in the Eastern States, to produce a full objective record of Biafra, interviewing survivors while there is still time, would be the best way to commemorate Biafra. I end this book by calling for such a project.

NOTES

1. NIGERIA: BUILD-UP TO THE CRISIS

1. This is now the accepted spelling of the name which, at the time of the war and for some time later, was always spelt "Ibo". The first syllable is pronounced "ee" with an almost silent "g". In this book, quotes from the time under review retain the "Ibo" spelling.

2. "Sardauna" was an important traditional office under the Sultan of Sokoto, the senior of the Northern Nigeria emirs and spiritual leader of the region.

3. *West Africa*, 29 Jan. 1966.

4. For this episode and all others in the crisis and civil war, A.H.M. Kirk-Greene, *Crisis and Conflict in Nigeria: A Documentary Sourcebook 1966–1969*, 2 vols., Oxford: Oxford University Press, 1971, is valuable not only for its collection of original documents but also for its historical introduction. For the 15 January 1966 events, two general histories of the crisis and war, John de St Jorre, *The Nigerian Civil War*, London: Hodder & Stoughton, 1972, and Michael Gould, *The Struggle for Modern Nigeria: The Biafran War 1967–1970*, London: I.B. Tauris, 2012 are recommended; also N.J. Miners, *The Nigerian Army, 1956–1966*, London: Methuen, 1971 and Walter Schwarz, *Nigeria*, London: Pall Mall Press, 1968.

5. Text of broadcast in Kirk-Greene, *Crisis and Conflict*, vol. 1, pp. 125–7. *West Africa*, for reasons of space, seldom reproduced speeches of key personalities in full; for full texts, the Kirk-Greene work should be consulted. In this speech, "ten percent" refers to the proportion of a contract price demanded as a bribe to secure government contracts (as assumed by the public—no doubt some corrupt parties could demand less or more).

6. Elechi Amadi, *Sunset in Biafra: A Civil War Diary*, London: Heinemann, 1973, p. 10.

7. See the article by Onyekaba Nwankwo, "Why Easterners Migrated", *West Africa*, 29 Apr. 1967.

8. Long extracts (with some names removed) were published in Kirk-Greene, *Crisis and Conflict*, vol. 1, pp. 115–24. The report has been published again since then.

315

9. Kirk-Greene, *Crisis and Conflict*, vol. 1, pp. 125–7.

10. One of the core group, Ben Gbulie, wrote a book about the coup entitled *Nigeria's Five Majors: Coup d'État of 15th January 1966; First Inside Account*, Onitsha: Africana Educational Publishers, 1981, and that figure is used by other sources, but the Special Branch report lists seven majors and a captain as the "inner circle". Such details cannot be examined here.

2. 1966: THE YEAR OF SELF-DESTRUCTION

1. A *griot* is a traditional village chronicler by memory of oral history, in many societies of the Senegal–Gambia–Mali region.

2. *West Africa*, 24 Sept. 1966.

3. Which in fact President Mobutu nationalised in 1967 without difficulty; neo-colonial big business was not so strong as it seemed.

4. Frederick Forsyth, *Emeka*, Ibadan: Spectrum Books in association with Safari Books (Export), St Helier, 1982, pp. 50–9.

5. *West Africa*, 4 June 1966.

6. *West Africa*, 25 June 1966.

7. *West Africa*, editorial, 16 July 1966, "The Treaty of Lagos"; *West Africa*, 23 July 1966, report on the signing and a banquet at State House in Lagos.

8. That story about Fajuyi, reproduced in *West Africa*, was widely believed; but J. Isawa Eliagwu in *Gowon: The Biography of a Soldier-Statesman*, Ibadan: West Books Publisher, 1986 says the killing of Fajuyi had in fact been planned (p. 65).

9. Much less is known about the July coup than about the January one. But see the accounts by John de St Jorre, *The Nigerian Civil War*, London: Hodder & Stoughton, 1972, pp. 69–75, and Raph (Raphael) Uwechue, *Reflections on the Nigerian Civil War*, Paris: Jeune Afrique, 1971, pp. 36–44.

10. Frederick Forsyth, *The Biafra Story*, Harmondsworth: Penguin, 1969, pp. 210–11.

11. Walter Schwarz, *Nigeria*, London: Pall Mall Press, 1968, pp. 210–11.

12. It is reproduced in full in A.H.M. Kirk-Greene, *Crisis and Conflict in Nigeria: A Documentary Sourcebook 1966–1969*, Oxford: Oxford University Press, 1971, vol. 1, pp. 196–8.

13. For example, A. Waugh and S. Cronje, *Biafra: Britain's Shame*, London: Michael Joseph, 1969, p. 65.

14. Kaye Whiteman, *Lagos: A Cultural and Historical Companion*, Oxford: Signal Books, 2012, pp. 155–6.

15. Whiteman, *Lagos*, pp. 155–6.

16. Kirk-Greene, *Crisis and Conflict*, vol. 1, introductory section, p. 79.

17. N.J. Miners, *The Nigerian Army, 1956–1966*, London: Methuen, 1971, p. 174.

18. That reported plan by Bello and Akintola was widely suspected, and was mentioned, as fact, in *West Africa*'s first report on the January coup, on 22 January 1966; but it may not have been proved.

19. *West Africa*, 6 Aug. 1966.

20. Forsyth, *Emeka*, pp. 74–6.

21. *West Africa*, 3 Sept. 1966.

22. *West Africa*, 1 Oct. 1966.

23. *West Africa*, Portrait, 16 July 1966.

24. *West Africa*, 24 Sept. 1966.

25. *West Africa*, 1 and 8 Oct. 1966.

26. The story of the Radio Cotonou report has been constantly repeated, but is puzzling. If it was true, people in Northern Nigeria would have heard of the massacre by more direct means, quite soon. But it is generally said to have been false; so who caused it to be broadcast, and why?

27. Schwarz, *Nigeria*, pp. 215–19.

28. Forsyth, *The Biafra Story*, pp. 75–8.

29. De St Jorre, *The Nigerian Civil War*, pp. 84, 86.

30. Elizabeth Isichei, *A History of Nigeria*, Harlow: Longman, 1983, p. 473. She is the New Zealand-born wife of an eminent Igbo medical professor, Peter Isichei.

31. "Nigerian Attitudes", *West Africa*, 3 Dec. 1966.

32. James O'Connell, "Political Integration: The Nigerian Case", in Arthur Hazlewood (ed.), *African Integration and Disintegration*, Oxford: Oxford University Press, 1967, pp. 177, 178.

33. *West Africa*, 19 Nov. 1966, "Exodus from the North".

34. B.J. Dudley, *Parties and Politics in Northern Nigeria*, London: Frank Cass, 1966, p. 25, quoting the *Report on the Kano Disturbances*.

35. *West Africa*, 24 Dec. 1966.

36. It is not impossible that, as asserted in Arthur Nwankwo and Samuel Ifejika, *The Making of a Nation: Biafra*, London: C. Hurst & Co., 1969 (p. 150), some expatriate staff at ABU joined in what they expected to be peaceful student protests, before people turned to violence. If that happened, they deserved the sack.

37. Kirk-Greene, *Crisis and Conflict*, vol. 1, pp. 255–6. *West Africa* reported (8 Oct.) what seems to have been a separate special message from Gowon to the North, in English and Hausa.

38. Kirk-Greene, *Crisis and Conflict*, vol. 1, pp. 277–82.

39. "Portrait" in *West Africa*, 17 Sept. 1966.

40. *West Africa*, 26 Nov. and 3 Dec. 1966, "Settling the Refugees".

41. "Exodus from the North", *West Africa*, 12 and 19 Nov. 1966.

42. "Nigerian Attitudes", *West Africa*, 10 Dec. 1966.

43. *West Africa*, 24 Dec. 1966, editorial on the railway.

44. *West Africa*, 3 Dec. 1966.

45. *West Africa*, 10 Dec. 1966.

46. Christian Council of Nigeria, *Christian Concern in the Nigerian Civil War*, Ibadan: Daystar Press, 1969, p. 46.

47. *West Africa*, 20 Aug. 1966.

48. *West Africa*, 31 Dec. 1966.

3. THE BREAK-UP

1. Much of the transcript is reproduced in A.H.M. Kirk-Greene, *Crisis and Conflict in Nigeria: A Documentary Sourcebook 1966–1969*, Oxford: Oxford University Press, 1971, vol. 1, pp. 315–40. Some extracts were published in *West Africa*, 11 Mar. 1967.

2. *West Africa*, 14 Jan. 1967, editorial and news reports.

3. *West Africa*, 21 Jan. 1967.

4. *West Africa*, 4 Feb. 1967.

5. *West Africa*, 28 Jan. 1967.

6. Ibid.

7. The text of the "Top Secret" resolution, later obtained by the Easterners, is in Kirk-Greene, *Crisis and Conflict*, vol. 1, pp. 340–5.

8. *West Africa*, 14 Jan. 1967.

9. *West Africa*, 21 Jan. 1967.

10. *West Africa*, 4 Feb. 1967, interview "Ojukwu Speaks".

11. *West Africa*, 4 Feb. 1967, Matchet's Diary.

12. Jonathan Derrick, *Africa, Empire and Fleet Street: Albert Cartwright and the* West Africa *Magazine*, London: C. Hurst & Co., 2017.

13. *West Africa*, 4 Mar. 1967.

14. *West Africa*, 11 Mar. 1967.

15. *West Africa*, 25 Mar. 1967, editorial and news reports.

16. *West Africa*, 8, 15 and 22 Apr. 1967.

17. *West Africa*, 15 Apr. 1967.

18. *West Africa*, 29 Apr. 1967.

19. *West Africa*, 29 Apr. 1967.

20. *West Africa*, 6 May 1967; full text of speech in Kirk-Greene, *Crisis and Conflict*, vol. 1, pp. 415–18.

21. *West Africa*, 27 May 1967.

22. *West Africa*, 1 Apr. 1967.

23. *West Africa*, 25 Mar. 1967.

24. D.K. Fieldhouse, *Merchant Capital and Economic Decolonization: The United Africa Company*, Oxford: Oxford University Press, 1994, p. 471, quoting a letter from Pedler to Margaret M. Green on 5 June 1967.

25. *West Africa*, 21 and 28 Jan. 1967.

26. *West Africa*, 25 Mar. 1967, Matchet's Diary.

27. Raph Uwechue, *Reflections on the Nigerian Civil War*, Paris: Jeune Afrique, 1971, pp. 51–9.

28. N.U. Akpan, *The Struggle for Secession 1967–1970: A Personal Account of the Nigerian Civil War*, London: Frank Cass, 1972, pp. 78–9.

29. *Nigerian Guardian*, article by Dara Babarinsa, 16 Mar. 2016. Other Nigerian newspapers' accounts vary regarding some details.

30. *West Africa*, 13 May 1967.

31. *West Africa*, 20 May 1967.
32. *West Africa*, 3 June 1967.
33. Hence the title of the novel, set in the civil war, by Chimamanda Ngozi Adichie, *Half of a Yellow Sun*, New York: Alfred A. Knopf, 2006, and the film made from it.

4. THE FIRST SIX MONTHS OF WAR (JULY–DECEMBER 1967)

1. *West Africa*, 17 June 1967.
2. *West Africa*, 10 June 1967, editorial, Matchet's Diary and news items.
3. *West Africa*, 17 June 1967. Asiodu and some other permanent secretaries were prominent among the many senior representatives that Nigeria constantly sent to London and other foreign capitals during the war; these diplomatic efforts were begun very early by both sides.
4. *West Africa*, 8 July 1967.
5. *West Africa*, 24 June 1967.
6. Gowon presented a copy of the Code to Bridget Bloom in July (*West Africa*, 15 July 1967). The text is in A.H.M. Kirk-Greene, *Crisis and Conflict in Nigeria: A Documentary Sourcebook 1966–1969*, Oxford: Oxford University Press, 1971, vol. 1, pp. 455–6.
7. *West Africa*, 24 June 1967.
8. *West Africa*, 17 June 1967.
9. *West Africa*, 19 Aug. 1967.
10. Olusegun Obasanjo, *My Command: An Account of the Nigerian Civil War 1967–1970*, London: Heinemann, 1980, p. xi.
11. See long report by Griot, in *West Africa*, 5 Aug. 1967.
12. Obasanjo, *My Command*, p. xi.
13. These planes were mentioned in reports at the time and in later published sources; full details of them and their raids are in Al J. Venter, *Biafra's War 1967–70: A Tribal Conflict in Nigeria That Left a Million Dead*, Solihull: Helion & Co., 2015, pp. 139–57.
14. *West Africa*, 14 Oct. 1967.
15. Chinua Achebe, *There Was a Country: A Personal History of Biafra*, London: Penguin, 2012, pp. 184–5.
16. *West Africa*, 5 and 12 Aug. 1967.
17. Obasanjo, *My Command*, pp. 27–8.
18. The full text of the broadcast, as reproduced in Kirk-Greene, *Crisis and Conflict*, vol. 2 (pp. 155–9), does not include this exact phrase; where we got it from I cannot recall. But the full text has plenty conveying the same idea; for example, Banjo addressed "fellow Nigerians", and suggested that while the declaration of Biafra was justified, the Biafrans could rejoin a greatly reformed Nigeria.
19. Some details of the plotting are given in John de St Jorre, *The Nigerian Civil War*, London: Hodder & Stoughton, 1972, pp. 166–71.
20. Raph Uwechue, *Reflections on the Nigerian Civil War*, Paris: Jeune Afrique, 1971, pp. 56–7.

21. *West Africa*, 7 and 14 Oct. 1967. Frederick Forsyth in *The Biafra Story*, Harmondsworth: Penguin, 1969, gave a different account, of Banjo planning to kill Ojukwu (pp. 116–21), based on Biafran sources.

22. Obasanjo, *My Command*, p. 31.

23. Wole Soyinka, *The Man Died: Prison Notes of Wole Soyinka*, London: Rex Collings, 1972, pp. 19, 31, 174–81.

24. Michael Gould, *The Struggle for Modern Nigeria: The Biafran War 1967–1970*, London: I.B. Tauris, 2012, pp. 65–6.

25. *West Africa*, 26 Aug. 1967; Obasanjo, *My Command*, pp. 31–6.

26. *West Africa*, 19 Aug. 1967.

27. *West Africa*, 26 Aug. 1967.

28. *West Africa*, 12 and 19 Aug. 1967. The timing shows that the decision to authorise arms shipments had been taken before the invasion of the Mid-West.

29. See notably Suzanne Cronje, *The World and Nigeria: The Diplomatic History of the Biafran War 1967–1970*, London: Sidgwick & Jackson, 1972, especially chapters 2–8, 14.

30. This was revealed much later by Michael Leapman—who as the *Sun*'s correspondent had brought starvation in Biafra to the attention of the general British public on 12 June 1968—after examination of newly released government documents: *Independent on Sunday*, 4 Jan. 1998.

31. *West Africa*, 26 Aug. 1967.

32. File FCO 28/42/54, The National Archives, Kew.

33. It was reported that Sir Louis Mbanefo had done so, but later reports still called him Sir Louis.

34. *West Africa*, 26 Aug. 1967.

35. *West Africa*, 9 and 16 Sept. 1967.

36. *West Africa*, 2 Sept. 1967; the text of the White Paper is in Kirk-Greene, *Crisis and Conflict*, vol. 2, pp. 163–5.

37. *West Africa*, 30 Sept. 1967.

38. Ibid.

39. *West Africa*, 21 Oct., 28 and 1967; Obasanjo, *My Command*, pp. 41–3.

40. *West Africa*, 21 Oct. 1967.

41. *The Times*, 31 Oct. and 1 Nov. 1967.

42. At least, not officially; it is apparently available on the Internet.

43. Elizabeth Bird and Fraser M. Ottanelli, *The Asaba Massacre: Trauma, Memory and the Nigerian Civil War*, Cambridge: Cambridge University Press, 2017.

44. Bird and Ottanelli, *The Asaba Massacre*, pp. 36–54.

45. *West Africa*, 7 and 14 Oct. 1967.

46. *West Africa*, 28 Oct. 1967.

47. *West Africa*, 2 Mar. 1968; and see "The Man for Enugu", *West Africa*, 4 Nov. 1967.

48. *West Africa*, 18 Nov. 1967.

49. *West Africa* did not quote from the first of these speeches but quoted those words about Enugu from the second (10 Feb. 1968). The full texts are in Kirk-Greene, *Crisis and Conflict*, vol. 2, pp. 183–7 and 192–9.

50. *West Africa* had a report ("Oil and the Rivers") on the court in exile headed by the military governor of Rivers State, Lt Commander Alfred Diete-Spiff, in Lagos, on 14 Oct. 1967.
51. *West Africa*, 12 June 1967.
52. Quoted in *West Africa*, 14 Oct. 1967.
53. *West Africa*, 23 Sept. 1967.
54. *West Africa*, 16 Sept. 1967.
55. Ibid.
56. Frederick Forsyth, *The Outsider: My Life in Intrigue*, London: Bantam Press, 2015, pp. 177–97.
57. *West Africa*, 9 Dec. 1967.
58. *West Africa*, 11 Nov. 1967.
59. *West Africa*, 30 Dec. 1967.
60. *West Africa*, 10 Feb. 1967.
61. Apart from a brief report on 2 Mar. 1968, *West Africa*'s news pages generally did not report much on the mercenaries. Several books give details of them, e.g. de St Jorre, *The Nigerian Civil War*, pp. 323–7.
62. *West Africa*, 17 Feb. 1968.
63. S.O. Mezu, *Behind the Rising Sun*, London: Heinemann, 1971.
64. *West Africa*, 6 Jan. 1968.
65. *West Africa* examined the implications for West African countries of the UK devaluation in the issues of 25 Nov. and 2 Dec. 1967.
66. *West Africa*, 4 Nov. 1967.
67. *West Africa*, 9 Dec. 1967.
68. *West Africa*, 11 Nov. 1967.
69. Ibid.
70. *West Africa*, 10 Feb. 1968.
71. *West Africa*, 25 Nov. 1967.
72. *West Africa*, 25 Nov. 1967.
73. Editorial, *West Africa*, 11 Nov. 1967.
74. *West Africa*, 30 Dec. 1967.
75. *West Africa*, 13 Jan. 1968.

5. RETREAT AND RECOGNITION (JANUARY–JUNE 1968)

1. *West Africa*, 23 Dec. 1967; the review was headed "Behind Biafra".
2. Christian Council of Nigeria, *Christian Concern in the Nigerian Civil War*, Ibadan: Daystar Press, 1969, p. 80.
3. *Christian Concern in the Nigerian Civil War*, pp. 65–7. I deplore again the omission of dates from this collection of excerpts from the *Nigerian Christian*.
4. *West Africa*, 6, 13 and 20 Jan. 1968.
5. *West Africa*, 27 Jan. and 3 Feb. 1968.
6. *West Africa*, 20 July 1968.

7. Figures are given in A.O. Makozi and G.J. Afolabi Ojo (eds.), *The History of the Catholic Church in Nigeria*, Lagos: Macmillan Nigeria, 1982, but with a warning that they are not precise; total population figures are from the 1963 census, figures for Catholics are from 1979 (pp. 100–14).

8. Emmanuel Urhobo, *Relief Operations in the Nigerian Civil War*, Ibadan: Daystar Press, 1978, p. 13.

9. *90 Days: A Report on the First 90 Days Activities of the Joint Biafra Famine Appeal*, published later in 1968. This Irish initiative was to be dwarfed by others in many countries. It is mentioned here because of its date, well before the date when, according to a certain myth, the story of starvation in Biafra appeared from nowhere.

10. Urhobo, *Relief Operations*, p. 13. This book, written by the Mid-Westerner who became head of the Christian Council of Nigeria's Relief and Rehabilitation Commission, is impressively objective and impartial about relief operations on both sides. However, this source, like others, leaves the full picture of churches' humanitarian aid to the Biafran side unclear.

11. Tony Byrne, *Airlift to Biafra: Breaching the Blockade*, Dublin: The Columba Press, 1997.

12. Byrne, *Airlift to Biafra*, p. 74.

13. Interview with Achebe, *Transition* (Kampala) 7, no. 36 (1968), pp. 31–7.

14. Raph Uwechue, *Reflections on the Nigerian Civil War*, Paris: Jeune Afrique, 1971, p. 53.

15. N.U. Akpan, *The Struggle for Secession: A Personal Account of the Nigerian Civil War*, London: Frank Cass, 1972, p. 97.

16. The reporter Auberon Waugh (of whom more later) said the Biafra office was "a delightful villa by the Torre de Belem, just outside Lisbon": *Spectator*, 26 July 1968.

17. *West Africa*, 30 Mar. 1968 and long report ("Over the Bridge, from Our Correspondent, Onitsha"), 13 Apr. 1968.

18. Frederick Forsyth, *The Biafra Story*, Harmondsworth: Penguin, 1969, p. 126.

19. *West Africa*, 27 Apr. 1968.

20. Quoted in *West Africa*, 10 Feb. 1968.

21. This would have required public enactments and elaborate arrangements that would have filled the Nigerian newspapers. The *Daily Times* called for conscription at the end of 1968, and another Nigerian daily did the same sometime in 1969, which shows that it was not in fact introduced.

22. *West Africa*, 20 Jan. 1968.

23. Akpan, *The Struggle*, pp. 97–8.

24. Akpan, *The Struggle*, pp. 92–3, 156–7.

25. *West Africa*, 4 May 1968.

26. See A.H.M. Kirk-Greene, *Crisis and Conflict in Nigeria: A Documentary Sourcebook 1966–1969*, Oxford: Oxford University Press, 1971, vol. 2, p. 300.

27. See Jean Wolf and Claude Brovelli, *La guerre des rapaces: La vérité sur la guerre du Biafra*, Paris: Albin Michel, 1969, pp. 52–5. Neither this report nor Imkeme's was mentioned in *West Africa*.

28. Elechi Amadi, *Sunset in Biafra: A Civil War Diary*, London: Heinemann, 1973, pp. 54–70.

29. Vol. 1, no. 3 was dated 4 Nov. 1967. According to Kirk-Greene, *Crisis and Conflict* (vol. 2), this started on 20 October, succeeding an *African Monthly Review*, and went on until no. 30 of 22 June 1968 (Bibliography, pp. 499–500); other overseas Biafran publications are mentioned there.

30. Some accounts of the war write the name as "Mark Press", but a single word was normal usage at the time.

31. *West Africa*, 27 Jan. 1968.

32. *West Africa*, 1 June 1968.

33. *West Africa*, 2 Mar. 1968.

34. *West Africa*, 27 Apr. 1968.

35. Akpan, *The Struggle*, p. 107.

36. About the first half of April, according to Kirk-Greene, *Crisis and Conflict*, vol. 2, p. 35.

37. The full lyrics, in four verses, are in Arthur Nwankwo and Samuel Ifejika, *The Making of a Nation: Biafra*, London: C. Hurst & Co., 1969, p. 351.

38. *West Africa*, 30 Mar. and 6 Apr. 1968.

39. *West Africa*, 22 June 1968.

40. *West Africa*, 30 Mar. 1968.

41. For example, *West Africa* 2, 9 and 16 Dec. 1967, 3 Feb. 1968.

42. *West Africa*, 17 Feb. 1968.

43. *West Africa*, 17 Feb. and 24 Feb. 1968.

44. *West Africa*, 9 Mar. 1968.

45. Kirk-Greene, *Crisis and Conflict*, vol. 2, pp. 206–11.

46. *West Africa*, 27 Apr. and 4 May 1968.

47. F. Forsyth, *The Outsider: My Life in Intrigue*, London: Bantam Press, 2015, p. 202.

48. Paul Harrison and Robin Palmer, *News out of Africa: Biafra to Band Aid*, London: Hilary Shipman, 1986, p. 25.

49. *West Africa*, 20 Apr. 1968.

50. *West Africa*, 15 June 1968.

51. *West Africa*, 6 July 1968.

52. *West Africa*, 2 Sept. 1967.

53. Elizabeth Bird and Fraser M. Ottanelli, *The Asaba Massacre: Trauma, Memory and the Nigerian Civil War*, Cambridge: Cambridge University Press, 2017, pp. 92–4.

54. *West Africa*, 27 Apr., 4 May, 11 May 1968.

55. *West Africa*, 18 May 1968.

56. *West Africa*, 27 Apr. 1968.

57. *West Africa*, 18 May 1968.

58. *West Africa*, 11 May 1968.

59. *West Africa*, 18 May 1968.

60. *West Africa*, 11 May 1968.

61. *West Africa*, 2 Mar. 1968.

62. *West Africa*, 25 May 1968.

63. See the detailed account of the Rivers State battles in Forsyth, *The Biafra Story*, pp. 129–33.

64. *West Africa*, 25 May 1968.

65. Quoted in *West Africa*, 8 June 1968.

66. Akpan, *The Struggle*, p. 157.

67. *West Africa*, 25 May 1968.

68. *West Africa*, 6 July 1968.

69. *West Africa*, 18 May 1968.

70. *West Africa*, 25 May 1968.

71. Cecil King's long association with Nigeria was not forgotten; Alhaji Jose attended his funeral in Dublin in 1987.

72. *West Africa*, 1 and 8 June 1968.

73. *West Africa*, 22 June 1968.

74. *West Africa*, 25 May 1968.

75. *West Africa*, 25 May 1968.

76. *West Africa*, 8 June 1968.

77. *West Africa*, 15 June 1968.

78. Urhobo, *Relief Operations*, p. 10.

79. S. Elizabeth Bird and Rosina Umelo, *Surviving Biafra: A Nigerwife's Story*, London: C. Hurst & Co., 2018.

80. Bird and Umelo, *Surviving Biafra*, pp. 119–21.

81. *West Africa*, 11 May 1968.

82. *West Africa*, 6 July 1968.

83. *West Africa*, 15 June 1968.

84. Uwechue, *Reflections*, pp. 140–1.

85. *Observer*, 26 May 1968.

86. *West Africa*, 1 June 1968.

87. *West Africa*, 15 June 1968.

6. FAMINE AND RELIEF IN THE HEADLINES (JUNE–DECEMBER 1968)

1. He repeated this to me personally in April 2017.

2. *West Africa*, 6 July 1968.

3. Arua Oko Omaka, *The Biafran Humanitarian Crisis, 1967–1970: International Human Rights and Joint Church Aid*, Lanham, MD: Farleigh Dickinson University Press, 2016, pp. 98–9.

4. In Paul Harrison and Robin Palmer, *News out of Africa: Biafra to Band Aid*, London: Hilary Shipman, 1986, pp. 28–31; and at the launch of Michael Gould's book at the School of Oriental and African Studies in London in January 2012.

5. Omaka, *The Biafran Humanitarian Crisis*, pp. 68–70.

6. Harold Wilson, *The Labour Government 1964–1970: A Personal Record*, Harmondsworth: Penguin, 1974, pp. 703–4.

7. Michael Gould, *The Struggle for Modern Nigeria: The Biafran War 1967–1970*, London: I.B. Tauris, 2012, p. 194.

8. Graham Harrison, *The African Presence: Representations of Africa in the Construction of Britishness*, Manchester: Manchester University Press, 2013, p. 110. The pages on Biafra in this book are not very accurate.

9. Maggie Black, *A Cause for Our Times: Oxfam, the First 50 Years*, Oxford: Oxfam, 1992, p. 121.

10. See notably Suzanne Cronje, *The World and Nigeria: The Diplomatic History of the Biafran War 1967–1970*, London: Sidgwick & Jackson, 1972, especially chapters 2–8.

11. Notably by *Peace News* at the time and Suzanne Cronje in *The World and Nigeria*.

12. See Harrison and Palmer, *News out of Africa*. It is recorded there (pp. 28–9) that a *Daily Express* photographer took pictures of the famine some weeks before the *Sun* story, but the editor was not interested.

13. Black, *A Cause for Our Times*, pp. 63–7.

14. A.H.M. Kirk-Greene, *Crisis and Conflict in Nigeria: A Documentary Sourcebook 1966–1969*, Oxford: Oxford University Press, 1971, vol. 2, p. 224.

15. Raph Uwechue, *Reflections on the Nigerian Civil War*, Paris: Jeune Afrique, 1971, p. 64.

16. W.A. Ajibola, *Foreign Policy and Public Opinion: A Case Study of British Foreign Policy over the Nigerian Civil War*, Ibadan: Ibadan University Press, 1978, pp. 138–9.

17. Jean Wolf and Claude Brovelli, *La guerre des rapaces: La vérité sur la guerre du Biafra*, Paris: Albin Michel, 1969, p. 66.

18. A.B. Akinyemi, "The British Press and the Nigerian Civil War", *African Affairs* 71, no. 285 (October 1972), pp. 408–26; A.B. Akinyemi, *The British Press and the Nigerian Civil War: The Godfather Complex*, Nigerian Institute of International Affairs Monograph Series, Ibadan: University Press in association with OUP, 1979.

19. Akinyemi, "The British Press and the Nigerian Civil War", p. 418. We saw Walter Schwarz quite often during the war when he visited the office; he was mentally fit.

20. He was probably behind an editorial on 2 January 1968 saying the government should consider any request by Nigeria for naval assistance for the blockade; this caused shock and fear among the Biafrans, because of the myth that *The Times* is an organ of the British government.

21. Akinyemi, *The British Press and the Nigerian Civil War*, pp. 48–9. Similarly *The Observer* published an article by Conor Cruise O'Brien as well as regular articles by Colin Legum: Akinyemi, "The British Press and the Nigerian Civil War", pp. 419–20.

22. Akinyemi, "The British Press and the Nigerian Civil War", p. 423.

23. Ajibola, *Foreign Policy and Public Opinion*.

24. Ajibola, *Foreign Policy and Public Opinion*, pp. 91–100.

25. Some may have compared or even confused the Nigerian situation with that in Sudan, where there really was a war by a government of Northern Muslims against largely Christian Southern insurgents; there was great concern about that too among Catholics in the West.

26. The Vatican certainly did not recognise Biafra as a state, as stated by Graham Harrison (*The African Presence*, p. 127).

27. Quoted in *West Africa*, 25 May 1968.

28. *The Tablet*, 8 June 1968. *West Africa* mentioned the sermon briefly in Matchet's Diary on 8 June 1968.

29. *West Africa*, 27 Aug. 1968.

30. *West Africa*, 3 Aug. 1968.

31. *West Africa*, 17 Aug. 1968.

32. *West Africa*, 28 Dec. 1968.

33. https://api.parliament.uk/historic-hansard/commons/1970/jan/26/nigeria-relief-plans.

34. Akinyemi, "The British Press and the Nigerian Civil War", p. 425.

35. "Student Relief Team in the South Eastern State", in Christian Council of Nigeria, *Christian Concern in the Nigerian Civil War*, Ibadan: Daystar Press, 1969, pp. 118–23.

36. *West Africa*, 6 July 1968.

37. Emmanuel Urhobo, *Relief Operations in the Nigerian Civil War*, Ibadan: Daystar Press, 1978.

38. Omaka, *The Biafran Humanitarian Crisis, 1967–1970*.

39. Frederick Forsyth, *The Biafra Story*, Harmondsworth: Penguin, 1969, pp. 180–96.

40. Urhobo, *Relief Operations*, pp. 12–13.

41. The activities of various parties in this period, as noted earlier, remain unclear from Urhobo's account (*Relief Operations*, pp. 13–16). More details are given in Omaka, *The Biafran Humanitarian Crisis*, pp. 91–100. I regret that I cannot give a fuller account of the early months of the relief airlift here.

42. Omaka, *The Biafran Humanitarian Crisis*, pp. 93–4.

43. *West Africa*, 8 June 1968.

44. *West Africa*, 22 June 1968.

45. *West Africa*, 29 June 1968.

46. Black, *A Cause*, pp. 117–31. The account of Oxfam's role in the Biafran war by Ms Black, who worked for Oxfam later, is unfortunately short and full of inaccuracies, and its summary of the controversies over relief delivery is quite inadequate.

47. Black, *A Cause*, p. 124.

48. *West Africa*, 27 July 1968.

49. *West Africa*, 20 and 27 July, 3 Aug. 1968.

50. *West Africa*, 27 July 1968.

51. The text is in Kirk-Greene, *Crisis and Conflict*, vol. 2, pp. 247–72.

52. Text in Kirk-Greene, *Crisis and Conflict*, vol. 2, pp. 280–314.

53. *West Africa*, 10 and 17 Aug. 1968.

54. *West Africa*, 24 Aug. 1968, article "General Gowon Talks to the Editor", and "Dateline Africa" news.

55. Forsyth, *The Biafra Story*, pp. 191–2.

56. *West Africa*, 24 Aug. 1968.

57. Ibid.

58. *West Africa*, 7 Sept. 1968.

59. Forsyth, *The Biafra Story*, pp. 191–3.

60. *West Africa*, 14 Sept. 1968.

61. *West Africa*, 3 Aug. 1968.

62. *Foccart parle: Entretiens avec Philippe Gaillard*, vol. 1, Paris: Fayard and Jeune Afrique, 1995.

63. *Foccart parle*, p. 345.

64. *Foccart parle*, p. 342.

65. *Foccart parle*, pp. 342–3.

66. See article "The Whale and the Minnows", *West Africa*, 10 Aug. 1968.

67. There was a detailed report in *Time* magazine, 26 Dec. 1968.

68. *Foccart parle*, pp. 343, 344.

69. *Foccart parle*, pp. 344–5.

70. *Foccart parle*, p. 346.

71. *West Africa*, 30 Nov. 1968.

72. Wolf and Brovelli, *La guerre des rapaces*.

73. *West Africa*, 3 Aug. 1968.

74. *West Africa*, 14 Sept. 1968.

75. Ibid.

76. *West Africa*, 20 July 1968.

77. *West Africa*, 6 July 1968.

78. Chinua Achebe, *There Was a Country*, Harmondsworth: Penguin Books, 2013, pp. 228–39.

79. There can be debate about certain other cases of gigantic mass killing, in the same century, which were equally criminal but arguably (the debate can continue) did not aim to wipe out a distinct group: the murderous enforcement of Communist agricultural schemes causing huge famines in the Soviet Union in 1932–3 and China in 1958–62, and the nightmare slaughter in Cambodia under the Khmer Rouges in 1975–9.

80. *West Africa*, 7 Oct. 1967.

81. In 2009 the civil war in Sri Lanka was to end in the way some had mistakenly thought the Nigerian civil war would end.

82. Forsyth, *The Biafra Story*, pp. 210–13.

83. Forsyth, *The Biafra Story*, pp. 218–21.

84. *West Africa*, 20 July 1968.

85. *West Africa*, 3 Feb. 1968.

86. Sir David Hunt, *Memoirs Military and Diplomatic*, London: Trigraph, 2006, p. 255. Whatever Hunt thought, the Nigerian government initially expected a short war: Obasanjo recalled later that "The Federal side prepared and planned for an operation lasting days rather than weeks" (Olusegun Obasanjo, *My Command: An Account of the Nigerian Civil War 1967–1970*, London: Heinemann, 1980, p. xi).

87. Hunt, *Memoirs*, pp. 247–8.

88. Hunt, *Memoirs*, p. 246.

89. Wilson, *The Labour Government*, pp. 704–5.

90. *West Africa*, 20 July 1968, "Nigeria: The Crisis and the British".

91. John de St Jorre noted this (*The Nigerian Civil War*, London: Hodder & Stoughton,

1972, pp. 372–3), and speaking to federal POWs in Biafran hands in front of their guards, he heard them declare full loyalty to Nigeria (p. 376).

92. *West Africa*, 5 Oct. 1968.

93. *West Africa*, 20 July 1968.

94. *West Africa*, 27 July 1968.

95. https://api.parliament.uk/historic-hansard/commons/1968/aug/27/nigeria.

96. *West Africa*, 10 Aug. 1968, "Nigerian War Relief: The Hunt Plan".

97. *West Africa*, 20 July 1968.

98. *West Africa*, 3 Aug. 1968.

99. *West Africa*, 31 Aug. and 7 Sept. 1968.

100. *West Africa*, 31 Aug. 1968, Matchet's Diary and article "Is It the War's End?"

101. *West Africa* reported this episode briefly on 7 Sept. 1968. A fuller account was published the following year by Wolf and Brovelli, *La guerre des rapaces*, pp. 206–15.

102. *West Africa* did not quote from the FMG's official invitation to the observers, or any official statement outlining their duties. The word "genocide" may not have been used in any such official Nigerian document. But the observers clearly assumed that they had to answer that allegation.

103. This case is studied at length in Cronje, *The World and Nigeria*, pp. 100–9.

104. *West Africa*, 9 Mar. 1968.

105. Lagos Radio broadcast, 7 Sept. 1968, in Kirk-Greene, *Crisis and Conflict*, vol. 2, pp. 326–7.

106. *West Africa*, 14 Sept. 1968.

107. Interviewed, on a visit to London, in *West Africa*, 17 Aug. 1968.

108. *West Africa*, 24 Aug. 1968.

109. See article in *West Africa*, 14 Sept. 1968.

110. De St Jorre, *The Nigerian Civil War*, pp. 229–30.

111. Uwechue, *Reflections*, pp. xxiv–xxv.

112. Cronje, *The World and Nigeria*, pp. 112–13.

113. *West Africa*, 5 Oct. 1968.

114. N.U. Akpan, *The Struggle for Secession 1967–1970: A Personal Account of the Nigerian Civil War*, London: Frank Cass, 1972, p. 111.

115. *West Africa*, 28 Sept. 1968.

116. *West Africa*, 5 and 12 Oct. 1968.

117. *West Africa*, 19 Oct. and 16 Nov. 1968.

118. *West Africa*, 5 Oct. 1968.

119. *West Africa*, 21 Sept. 1968.

120. *West Africa*, 31 Aug. 1968.

121. *West Africa*, 26 Oct. 1968.

122. *West Africa*, 16 Nov. 1968.

123. *West Africa*, 16 and 23 Nov. 1968.

124. *West Africa*, 7 Dec. 1968.

125. *West Africa*, 19 Oct. 1968.

126. *West Africa*, 9 Nov. 1968.

127. *West Africa*, 2 Nov. 1968.

128. *West Africa*, 19 Oct. 1968.

129. Ibid.

130. Omaka, *The Biafran Humanitarian Crisis*, pp. 94–6. I do not recall hearing at the time what Omaka and others have mentioned since, that JCA was nicknamed "Jesus Christ Airline".

131. *West Africa*, 21 Sept. 1968.

132. *West Africa*, 28 Sept. 1968.

133. *West Africa*, 19 Oct. 1968.

134. Described by Omaka, *The Biafran Humanitarian Crisis*, p. 97.

135. *West Africa*, 2 Nov. 1968.

136. *West Africa*, 7 Dec. 1968.

137. *West Africa*, 21 Sept. 1968.

138. Rev. Canon J.A.I. Falope, "Visit to Calabar and Uyo", in Christian Council of Nigeria, *Christian Concern*, pp. 128–32.

139. *West Africa*, 19 Oct. and 9 Nov. 1968.

140. Urhobo, *Relief Operations*, pp. 16–18.

141. *West Africa*, 5 Oct. 1968.

142. Omaka, *The Biafran Humanitarian Crisis*, p. 100.

143. Christian Council of Nigeria, *Christian Concern*, p. 124.

144. Urhobo, *Relief Operations*, p. 16.

145. Gould, *The Struggle for Modern Nigeria*, p. 3.

146. Gould, *The Struggle for Modern Nigeria*, p. 135.

147. Gould, *The Struggle for Modern Nigeria*, p. 186. Gould's book has useful parts dealing with military and some political aspects, but is quite unreliable on relief operations and on the role of the press.

148. Gould's passage implying this (*The Struggle for Modern Nigeria*, p. 135) is not based on the facts at all.

149. *West Africa*, 5 Oct. 1968.

150. *West Africa*, 2 Nov. 1968.

151. *West Africa*, 18 Nov. 1968.

152. *West Africa*, 2 and 23 Nov., 14 Dec. 1968.

7. BIAFRA ON LIFE SUPPORT (DECEMBER 1968—NOVEMBER 1969)

1. Raph Uwechue, *Reflections on the Nigerian Civil War*, Paris: Jeune Afrique, 1971, p. xxv.

2. A.H.M. Kirk-Greene, *Crisis and Conflict in Nigeria: A Documentary Sourcebook 1966–1969*, vol. 2, Oxford: Oxford University Press, 1971, p. 85.

3. *West Africa*, 9 Nov. 1968.

4. *West Africa*, 21 and 28 Dec. 1968, 4 Jan. 1969.

5. *West Africa*, 22 Feb. and 8 Mar. 1969.

6. *West Africa*, 15 Feb. 1969.

7. *West Africa*, 15 Feb. 1969, quoting a report by Michael Leapman on a return trip for *The Sun*.

8. *West Africa*, 30 Nov. 1968, 4 and 11 Jan. 1969.

9. *West Africa*, 16 Nov. 1968.

10. *West Africa*, 12 Oct. 1968.

11. *West Africa*, 25 Jan. 1969.

12. *West Africa*, 15 Feb. 1969. Rosina Umelo recalls these efforts in her recent book, mentioning maize and cassava growing especially: S. Elizabeth Bird and Rosina Umelo, *Surviving Biafra: A Nigerwife's Story*, London: C. Hurst & Co., 2018, pp. 157–9.

13. *West Africa*, 16 Nov. 1968.

14. *West Africa*, 11 Jan. 1969.

15. *West Africa*, 1 Mar. 1969.

16. Harold Wilson, *The Labour Government 1964–1970: A Personal Record*, Harmondsworth: Penguin, 1974, p. 921.

17. *West Africa*, 14 Dec. 1968.

18. *West Africa*, 4 Jan. 1969.

19. *West Africa*, 11 and 18 Jan. 1969.

20. *West Africa*, 18 Jan. 1969.

21. *West Africa*, 1 Feb. 1969.

22. *West Africa*, 18 Jan. 1969, editorial.

23. *West Africa*, 7 Dec. 1968.

24. *West Africa*, 18 Jan. 1969.

25. *West Africa*, 11 Jan. and 1 Feb. 1969.

26. Mentioned in Matchet, *West Africa*, 4 Jan. 1969.

27. *West Africa*, 11 Jan. 1969.

28. Ibid.

29. *West Africa*, 11, 18 and 25 Jan. 1969.

30. *West Africa*, 1 Feb. 1969, article "Two Sides of War Relief".

31. *West Africa*, 5 Oct. 1968.

32. *West Africa*, 8 Feb. 1969.

33. *West Africa*, 8 and 15 Feb. 1969.

34. *West Africa*, 15 Mar. 1969 and (a long article) 22 Mar. 1969.

35. Al J. Venter, *Biafra's War, 1967–70: A Tribal Conflict in Nigeria That Left a Million Dead*, Solihull: Helion & Co., 2015.

36. Venter, *Biafra's War*, p. 62.

37. Venter, *Biafra's War*, pp. 62, 128; but he also cites a source suggesting they were the same (pp. 135–6).

38. Venter, *Biafra's War*, pp. 118–34.

39. De St Jorre offers evidence for at least some temporary tacit agreement (*The Nigerian Civil War*, London: Hodder & Stoughton, 1972, pp. 318–20); Michael Gould, *The Struggle for Modern Nigeria: The Biafran War 1967–1970*, London: I.B. Tauris, 2012, gives a more improbable account (pp. 135–6). Venter in *Biafra's War*, full of information about mercenary pilots, does not back this story.

40. *West Africa*, 15 Feb. and 1 Mar. 1969.

41. *West Africa*, 8 Mar. 1969.

42. *Daily Express*, 8 May 1969.

43. A.B. Akinyemi, "The British Press and the Nigerian Civil War", *African Affairs* 71, no. 285 (October 1972), p. 423.

44. *West Africa*, 15 Mar. 1969.

45. Ibid.

46. *West Africa*, 22 Mar. 1969.

47. *The Times*, 6 Mar. 1969.

48. Wilson, *The Labour Government*, p. 707.

49. *West Africa*, 22 Feb. 1969.

50. *West Africa*, 15 Mar. 1969, editorial "Harold Wilson's Arms".

51. *West Africa*, 5 Apr. 1969. The tour was very widely reported in the mainstream British press.

52. Wilson, *The Labour Government*, p. 794.

53. *West Africa*, 5 Apr. 1969.

54. *West Africa*, 12 Apr. 1969.

55. *West Africa*, 31 May 1969.

56. *West Africa*, 26 Apr. 1969.

57. *West Africa*, 31 May and 7 June 1969.

58. *West Africa*, 17 May 1969.

59. Mentioned in Frederick Forsyth, *The Biafra Story*, Harmondsworth: Penguin, 1969, p. 219.

60. As described by A.H.M. Kirk-Greene in *West Africa*, 17 and 24 May 1969.

61. *West Africa*, 25 Jan. 1969.

62. *West Africa*, 8 Feb. 1969.

63. *West Africa*, 8 Mar. 1969.

64. *Foccart parle: Entretiens avec Philippe Gaillard*, Paris: Fayard and Jeune Afrique, 1995, vol. 1, 1995, p. 348.

65. *West Africa*, 22 Mar. 1969.

66. *West Africa*, 26 Apr. 1969.

67. *West Africa*, 31 May 1969.

68. *West Africa*, 26 Apr. 1969.

69. *West Africa*, 18 Jan. 1969.

70. I wrote about this, as Griot, in *West Africa*, 4 Oct. 1969.

71. *West Africa*, 16 Aug. 1969.

72. June Milne, *Kwame Nkrumah: A Biography*, London: Panaf Books, 1999, pp. 221–3, 225.

73. Letter of Kwame Nkrumah to June Milne (his secretary), 17 June 1968, in June Milne (compiler), *Kwame Nkrumah: The Conakry Years, His Life and Letters*, London: Panaf (imprint of Zed Press), 1990, pp. 240–1.

74. This resentment was muted under Ahidjo, more vocal after a more democratic system was introduced under his successor, Paul Biya, in 1991, and eventually led to a secessionist movement and the beginnings of guerrilla activity from 2017.

75. *West Africa*, 4 Nov. 1967.

76. Forsyth, *The Biafra Story*, p. 127; Venter, *Biafra's War*, p. 215.

77. Uwechue, *Reflections*, pp. 67, 116–17, chapter 5 (Uwechue's italics).

78. A. Nwankwo and S. Ifejika, *The Making of a Nation: Biafra*, London: C. Hurst & Co., 1969. After the war, those authors set up the Nwankwo-Ifejika publishing company in Enugu.

79. Nwankwo and Ifejika, *The Making of a Nation*, p. 292.

80. Nwankwo and Ifejika, *The Making of a Nation*, p. 290.

81. N.U. Akpan, *The Struggle for Secession, 1966–1970: A Personal Account of the Nigerian Civil War*, London: Frank Cass, 1972, pp. 97–9.

82. *West Africa*, 2 Aug. 1969.

83. *West Africa*, 7 June 1969.

84. *West Africa*, 3 May 1969.

85. Chinua Achebe, *There was a Country: A Personal History of Biafra*, Harmondsworth: Penguin Books, 2012, pp. 143–9.

86. Briefly reported in *West Africa*, 7 and 21 June 1969. The full text is in Kirk-Greene, *Crisis and Conflict*, vol. 2, pp. 376–93.

87. Akpan, *The Struggle*, pp. 119–30.

88. *West Africa*, 19 July 1969.

89. *West Africa*, 3 Jan. 1970.

90. Frederick Forsyth, *The Dogs of War*, London: Hutchinson, 1974. It was turned into a television film, excessively far removed from the original. It became known later that Forsyth had been involved in a real but unsuccessful plot to overthrow President Macías.

91. Forsyth, *The Biafra Story*, p. 114.

92. Forsyth, *The Biafra Story*, pp. 130–9.

93. Frederick Forsyth, *The Outsider: My Life in Intrigue*, London: Bantam Press, 2015, pp. 242–3. Forsyth concluded that the SAS man had been on a deep penetration mission inside Biafra, but this can be doubted.

94. Jean Wolf and Claude Brovelli, *La guerre des rapaces: La vérité sur la guerre du Biafra*, Paris: Albin Michel, 1969, pp. 217–18.

95. Forsyth, *The Outsider*, pp. 252–3.

96. Forsyth, *The Outsider*, pp. 225–30.

97. Zdenek Červenka, *A History of the Nigerian War 1967–1970*, Frankfurt: Alfred Metzner, 1971; Ibadan: Onibonoje Press, 1972, p. 134.

98. *West Africa*, 14 Dec. 1968. However, Venter in *Biafra's War* (p. 251) says the Biafrans did buy two Meteors, but one was ditched at sea during its delivery flight and one was impounded by the Portuguese in Bissau.

99. He was John Christie, as he told me himself decades later.

100. "A Lisbon Diary", *Spectator*, 26 July 1968.

101. *West Africa*, 6 July 1968.

102. Venter, *Biafra's War*, pp. 242–3.

103. *West Africa*, 8 Mar. 1969.

104. *West Africa*, 1 Mar. 1969.

105. Quoted in *West Africa*, 22 Mar. 1969.

106. *West Africa*, 1 Mar. 1969.

107. *West Africa*, 22 Mar. 1969.

108. *West Africa*, 1 Mar. 1969.

109. *West Africa*, 26 Apr. 1969.

110. *West Africa*, 10 May 1969.

111. *West Africa*, 19 Apr. 1969.

112. *West Africa*, 21 June 1969. The magazine mentioned this belief but did not endorse it.

113. Emmanuel Urhobo, *Relief Operations in the Nigerian Civil War*, Ibadan: Daystar Press, 1978, pp. 44–5, 60–2.

114. *West Africa*, 26 Oct. 1968.

115. A. Waugh and S. Cronje, *Biafra: Britain's Shame*, London: Michael Joseph, 1969. It was reviewed in *West Africa*, 1 Nov. 1969.

116. Waugh and Cronje, *Biafra*, pp. 113–14.

117. S. Cronje, *The World and Nigeria: The Diplomatic History of the Biafran War 1967–1970*, London: Sidgwick & Jackson, 1972, pp. 277–8.

118. A. Dirk Moses and Lasse Heerten (eds.), *Post-colonial Conflict and the Question of Genocide: The Nigeria–Biafra War, 1967–1970*, New York: Routledge, 2018.

119. Douglas Anthony, "Irreconcilable Narratives: Biafra, Nigeria, and the Arguments about Genocide, 1966–1970", in Moses and Heerten, *Post-colonial Conflict*, p. 63.

120. W.A. Ajibola, *Foreign Policy and Public Opinion: A Case Study of British Foreign Policy over the Nigerian Civil War*, Ibadan: Ibadan University Press, 1978, pp. 154–5.

121. The UN Special Tribunals (for the former Yugoslavia and Rwanda) lay decades ahead, and the International Criminal Court even further ahead.

122. I have examined that committee only because it is mentioned at some length in a source published during the war; the facts about it are obscure, and the important fact that it apparently confirmed, about numerous war crimes, is beyond doubt anyway.

123. Sources seem to agree on this, but the correct name of the plane (or maybe a version of it) has been said to be Minicoin ("mini-counter-insurgency").

124. *West Africa*, 31 May, 7 June, 14 June 1969; see also later accounts in Cronje, *The World and Nigeria*, pp. 148–59, and Venter, *Biafra's War*, pp. 135–7, 257–64, 265–73.

125. *West Africa*, 31 May and 2 Aug. 1969.

126. *West Africa*, 21 June 1969.

127. *West Africa*, 5 July 1969.

128. *West Africa*, 12 July 1969.

129. Ibid.

130. Ibid.

131. As the end of the war approached, Father Anthony Byrne, who had done much to start the Caritas airlift, proposed that if it was stopped there should be para-

chute drops instead, but Caritas in Rome vetoed the idea. It was a wholly impracticable one: parachute drops often fall off target, and how could signals have been sent to tell pilots where to make the drops? But the reason for the Caritas superiors' veto is worth noting: Bayer said, "the Vatican regards parachutes as quasi-military equipment" (Tony Byrne, *Airlift to Biafra*, Dublin: Columba Press, 1997, pp. 15–16, 99–101).

132. *West Africa*, 12 July 1969.
133. *West Africa*, 21 June and 12 July 1969.
134. *West Africa*, 5 July 1969.
135. *West Africa*, 31 Aug. 1968.
136. *West Africa*, 26 July 1969.
137. *West Africa*, 23 Aug. 1969.
138. *West Africa*, 9 Aug. 1969.
139. *West Africa*, 23 Aug. 1969.
140. *West Africa*, 20 Sept. 1969.
141. Ibid.
142. *West Africa*, 26 July 1969.
143. *West Africa*, 27 Sept. 1969.
144. *West Africa*, 4 Oct. 1969.
145. *West Africa*, 3 May 1969.
146. *West Africa*, 5 Oct. 1968.
147. *West Africa*, 16 Aug. 1969, editorial.
148. *West Africa*, 23 Aug. 1969.
149. *West Africa*, 6 Sept. 1969.
150. *West Africa*, 15 Nov. 1969.
151. Bird and Umelo, *Surviving Biafra*; see especially chapter 10, "The Hunger".
152. Bird and Umelo, *Surviving Biafra*, pp. 169–73. The novelist Ogali A. Ogali wrote forcefully about church people involved in this, in a post-war pamphlet (quoted in Emmanuel Obiechina, *An African Popular Literature: A Study of Onitsha Market Pamphlets*, Cambridge: Cambridge University Press, 1973, p. 113).
153. *West Africa*, 19 July 1969, quoting *The Sun*.
154. Cronje, *The World and Nigeria*, pp. 189–91.
155. Venter, *Biafra's War*, pp. 225–38.
156. *West Africa*, 13 Dec. 1969.
157. *West Africa*, 3 Jan. 1970.
158. *Foccart parle*, p. 347.
159. Pierre Péan, *Affaires africaines*, Paris: Fayard, 1983 (see pp. 71–81 on Gabon and Biafra).
160. François-Xavier Verschave, *La Françafrique: Le plus long scandale de la République*, Paris: Stock, 1988 (see chapter 4 on Biafra).
161. Marcel Amondji [an assumed name], *Félix Houphouët et la Côte d'Ivoire: L'envers d'une légende*, Paris: Karthala, 1984.
162. Akpan, *The Struggle*, pp. 179–80.

163. Cronje, *The World and Nigeria*, pp. 197–8.

164. Jonathan Aitken, *Officially Secret*, London: Weidenfeld & Nicolson, 1971. This is an account of the trial of Aitken and three others over the leaking of the Scott Report on the Biafran war (see the next chapter).

165. Aitken, *Officially Secret*, pp. 90–6.

166. Sir David Hunt, *Memoirs Military and Diplomatic*, London: Trigraph, 2006, p. 256.

167. *West Africa*, 25 Jan. 1969.

168. Frederick Pedler letter to Margaret M. Green, 5 June 1967, quoted in D.K. Fieldhouse, *Merchant Capital and Economic Decolonization: The United Africa Company*, Oxford: Oxford University Press, 1994, p. 471. At the time, the *West Africa* staff were constantly in touch with UAC staff and often talking with them about the war, but I remember nothing significant that was said.

169. *West Africa*, 8 June 1968.

170. *West Africa*, 1 June 1968.

171. *West Africa*, 5 Oct. 1968, 19 April 1969.

172. Fieldhouse, *Merchant Capital*, p. 472.

173. Pedler to Gordon Wilson, date apparently 14 June 1968, quoted in Fieldhouse, *Merchant Capital*, p. 473.

174. Fieldhouse, *Merchant Capital*, p. 472.

175. Fieldhouse, *Merchant Capital*, cable Wilson to Pedler, 11 June 1968.

176. Described in *West Africa*, Commercial News, 10 Aug. 1968.

177. Ola Balogun, *The Tragic Years: Nigeria in Crisis 1966–1970*, Benin: Ethiope Publishing Corporation, p. 95.

178. Quoted in *West Africa*, 2 Aug. 1969.

179. Cronje, *The World and Nigeria*, p. 211.

180. Lasse Heerten, *The Biafran War and Postcolonial Humanitarianism: Spectacles of Suffering*, Cambridge: Cambridge University Press, 2017.

181. Heerten, *The Biafran War*, p. 266.

182. Heerten, *The Biafran War*, p. 10.

183. *West Africa*, 8 Mar. 1969.

184. *West Africa*, 5 July 1969.

185. Akpan, *The Struggle*, p. 161.

186. *West Africa*, 2 Aug. 1969.

187. Alex de Waal, *Famine Crimes: Politics and the Disaster Relief Industry in Africa*, London: African Rights and International African Institute in association with James Currey, Oxford, and Indiana University Press, Bloomington, 1997.

188. Zoë Marriage, *Not Breaking the Rules, Not Playing the Game: International Assistance to Countries at War*, London: C. Hurst & Co., 2006.

189. Suzanne Franks, *Reporting Disasters: Famine Aid Politics and the Media*, London: C. Hurst & Co., 2013.

190. Ian Smillie, *The Alms Bazaar: Altruism under Fire; Non-profit Organizations and International Development*, London: IT Publications, 1995, p. 104.

191. Smillie, *The Alms Bazaar*, p. 105.

192. De Waal, *Famine Crimes*, pp. 72–7.

193. Gould, *The Struggle*, pp. 133–5.

194. Maggie Black, *A Cause for Our Times: Oxfam, the First 50 Years*, Oxford: Oxfam, 1992, pp. 130–1.

195. All this was reported very briefly in *West Africa*, 13 Dec. 1969; there are more details in Urhobo, *Relief Operations*, pp. 31–5.

196. *West Africa*, 2 Aug. 1969.

197. *West Africa*, 2 Aug., 9 Aug., 16 Aug., 18 Oct., 8 Nov., 15 Nov., 22 Nov. 1969.

198. *West Africa*, 8 and 22 Nov. 1969. The pilot, Gil Pinto de Souza, was helped by villagers, who lent him a bicycle to go to a police station, and spent five years in prison, being eventually freed after the Portuguese revolution in 1974.

199. *West Africa*, 25 Oct. 1969.

200. *West Africa*, 4 Oct. 1969.

201. *West Africa*, 24 May 1969.

202. Matchet's Diary, *West Africa*, 2 Aug. 1969.

203. *West Africa*, 30 Aug. 1969.

204. *West Africa*, 12 July, 27 Sept., 4 Oct., 18 Oct., 25 Oct. 1969.

205. *West Africa*, 4 Oct. 1969.

206. *West Africa*, 11 Oct. 1969.

207. *West Africa*, 13 Dec. 1969.

208. Matchet's Diary, *West Africa*, 27 Sept. 1969.

209. *West Africa*, 22 and 29 Nov. 1969.

210. *West Africa*, 29 Nov. 1969.

211. *West Africa*, 6 Dec. 1969.

212. *West Africa*, 2 Aug. 1969.

213. *West Africa*, 21 Dec. 1968.

214. *West Africa*, 15 Nov. 1969.

215. *West Africa*, 18 Oct. 1969.

216. *West Africa*, 21 June 1969.

217. Interview, *West Africa*, 24 May 1969.

218. *West Africa*, 13 Sept. 1969.

219. *West Africa*, 8 Nov. 1969.

220. *West Africa*, 25 Oct. and 1 Nov. 1969.

221. *West Africa*, 8 Nov. 1969. There was a review in the same issue of Ojukwu's *Biafra: Selected Speeches and Random Thoughts*, published by Harper & Row.

222. *West Africa*, 22 Nov. 1969.

223. *West Africa*, 13 Dec. 1969.

224. *West Africa*, 6 Dec., 13 Dec., 20 Dec., 27 Dec. 1969.

225. *West Africa*, 20 and 27 Dec. 1969.

226. *West Africa*, 10 Jan. 1970.

8. NIGERIAN VICTORY AND RECONCILIATION

1. *West Africa*, 10 Jan. 1970.

2. There have been many accounts of the last days of Biafra and the last flights out. Frederick Forsyth's is inaccurate, saying Ojukwu left on 23 December (*The Outsider*, London: Bantam Press, 2015, pp. 257–60). N.U. Akpan's account is the best (*The Struggle for Secession 1967–1970: A Personal Account of the Nigerian Civil War*, London: Frank Cass, 1972, pp. 165–75).

3. The accounts published later of the final operations include notably the inside account by Obasanjo, *My Command: An Account of the Nigerian Civil War 1967–1970*, London: Heinemann, 1980, chapters X and XI.

4. Akpan, *The Struggle for Secession*, p. 195.

5. Akpan, *The Struggle*, chapters 14–17.

6. Akpan, *The Struggle*, pp. 193–4.

7. *West Africa*, 24 Jan. 1970.

8. Kaye Whiteman, *Lagos*, Oxford: Signal Books, 2012, pp. 157–8.

9. *West Africa*, 17 Jan. 1970.

10. "Report from Iboland", *West Africa*, 24 Jan. 1970.

11. *West Africa*, 17 Jan. 1970.

12. "Report from Iboland", *West Africa*, 24 Jan. 1970.

13. Ibid.

14. "Red Cross in the Field", *West Africa*, 31 Jan. 1970.

15. *West Africa*, 31 Jan. 1970.

16. *West Africa*, 22 Aug. 1970.

17. Letter from Father Joseph B. Schuyler, SJ, head of the Sociology Division of the University of Lagos, *West Africa*, 31 Jan. 1970.

18. In his book *There Was a Country: A Personal History of Biafra*, London: Penguin, 2012.

19. A. Dirk Moses and Lasse Heerten (eds.), *Post-colonial Conflict and the Question of Genocide: The Nigeria–Biafra War, 1967–1970*, New York: Routledge, 2018.

20. Lasse Heerten and A. Dirk Moses, "The Nigeria–Biafra War: Postcolonial Conflict and the Question of Genocide," in Moses and Heerten, *Post-colonial Conflict*, pp. 28–9.

21. Buchi Emecheta, *Destination Biafra*, London: Allison & Busby, 1982, p. vii.

22. Including, I think, my colleague the late Kaye Whiteman. During the war he had sympathy for the Biafrans, as I had, but later he said he had changed his views.

23. Sir David Hunt, *Memoirs Military and Diplomatic*, London: Trigraph, 2006, p. 243.

24. Aitken recalls the case in detail in *Officially Secret*, London: Weidenfeld & Nicolson, 1971.

25. *West Africa*, 9 May 1970.

26. Arua Oko Omaka, *The Biafran Humanitarian Crisis, 1967–1970. International Human Rights and Joint Church Aid*, Lanham, MD: Farleigh Dickinson University Press, 2016, pp. 104–6.

27. *West Africa*, 4 July 1970.

28. *West Africa*, 18 July 1970.

29. Ibid.

30. This list of books published by Nigerians about the war is not meant to be exhaustive.

BIBLIOGRAPHY

Achebe, Chinua, interview in *Transition* (Kampala) 7, no. 36 (1968), 31–7.

————, *There Was a Country: A Personal History of Biafra*, London: Allen Lane, 2012.

Adichie, Chimamanda Ngozi, *Half of a Yellow Sun*, New York: Alfred A. Knopf, 2006.

Aitken, Jonathan, *Officially Secret*, London: Weidenfeld & Nicolson, 1971.

Ajibola, W.A., *Foreign Policy and Public Opinion: A Case Study of British Foreign Policy over the Nigerian Civil War*, Ibadan: Ibadan University Press, 1978.

Akinyemi, A.B., "The British Press and the Nigerian Civil War", *African Affairs* 71, no. 285 (October 1972), 408–26.

————, *The British Press and the Nigerian Civil War: The Godfather Complex*, Nigerian Institute of International Affairs Monograph Series, Ibadan: University Press in association with Oxford University Press, 1979.

Akpan, N.U., *The Struggle for Secession 1967–1970: A Personal Account of the Nigerian Civil War*, London: Frank Cass, 1972.

Amadi, Elechi, *Sunset in Biafra: A Civil War Diary*, London: Heinemann, 1973.

Amondji, Marcel, *Félix Houphouët et la Côte d'Ivoire: L'envers d'une légende*, Paris: Karthala, 1984.

Balogun, Ola, *The Tragic Years: Nigeria in Crisis 1966–1970*, Benin City: Ethiope Publishing Corporation, 1973.

Bird, Elizabeth and Fraser M. Ottanelli, *The Asaba Massacre: Trauma, Memory and the Nigerian Civil War*, Cambridge: Cambridge University Press, 2017.

Bird, Elizabeth and Rosina Umelo, *Surviving Biafra: A Nigerwife's Story*, London: C. Hurst & Co., 2018.

Black, Maggie, *A Cause for Our Times: Oxfam, the First 50 Years*, Oxford: Oxfam, 1992.

Byrne, Tony, *Airlift to Biafra: Breaching the Blockade*, Dublin: The Columba Press, 1997.

BIBLIOGRAPHY

Červenka, Zdenek, *A History of the Nigerian War 1967–1970*, Frankfurt: Alfred Metzner, 1971; Ibadan: Onibonoje Press, 1972.

Christian Council of Nigeria, *Christian Concern in the Nigerian Civil War*, Ibadan: Daystar Press, 1969.

Cronje, Suzanne, *The World and Nigeria: The Diplomatic History of the Biafran War 1967–1970*, London: Sidgwick & Jackson, 1972.

De St Jorre, John, *The Nigerian Civil War*, London: Hodder & Stoughton, 1972.

De Waal, Alex, *Famine Crimes: Politics and the Disaster Relief Industry in Africa*, London: African Rights and International African Institute in association with James Currey, Oxford, and Indiana University Press, Bloomington, 1997.

Debré, François, *Biafra an II*, Paris: Julliard, 1968.

Derrick, Jonathan, *Africa, Empire and Fleet Street: Albert Cartwright and the West Africa Magazine*, London: C. Hurst & Co., 2017.

Dudley, B.J., *Parties and Politics in Northern Nigeria*, London: Frank Cass, 1966.

Egbuna, Obi, *The Murder of Nigeria*, London: Panaf, 1968.

Eliagwu, J. Isawa, *Gowon: The Biography of a Soldier-Statesman*, Ibadan: West Books Publisher, 1986.

Emecheta, Buchi, *Destination Biafra*, London: Allison & Busby, 1982.

Fieldhouse, D.K., *Merchant Capital and Economic Decolonization: The United Africa Company*, Oxford: Oxford University Press, 1994.

Foccart parle: Entretiens avec Philippe Gaillard, vol. 1, Paris: Fayard and Jeune Afrique, 1995.

Forsyth, Frederick, *Emeka*, Ibadan: Spectrum Books in association with Safari Books (Export), St Helier, 1982.

———, *The Biafra Story*, Harmondsworth: Penguin, 1969.

———, *The Dogs of War*, London: Hutchinson, 1974.

———, *The Outsider: My Life in Intrigue*, London: Bantam Press, 2015.

Franks, Suzanne, *Reporting Disasters: Famine Aid Politics and the Media*, London: C. Hurst & Co., 2013.

Gbulie, Ben, *Nigeria's Five Majors: Coup d'État of 15th January 1966; First Inside Account*, Onitsha: Africana Educational Publishers, 1981.

Gould, Michael, *The Struggle for Modern Nigeria: The Biafran War 1967–1970*, London: I.B. Tauris, 2012.

Harrison, Graham, *The African Presence: Representations of Africa in the Construction of Britishness*, Manchester: Manchester University Press, 2013.

Harrison, Paul and Robin Palmer, *News out of Africa: Biafra to Band Aid*, London: Hilary Shipman, 1986.

Heerten, Lasse, *The Biafran War and Postcolonial Humanitarianism: Spectacles of Suffering*, Cambridge: Cambridge University Press, 2017.

BIBLIOGRAPHY

Hunt, Sir David, *Memoirs Military and Diplomatic*, London: Trigraph, 2006 (first published as *On the Spot: An Ambassador Remembers*, London: Peter Davies, 1975).

Isichei, Elizabeth, *A History of Nigeria*, Harlow: Longman, 1983.

Joint Biafra Famine Appeal, *90 Days: A Report on the First 90 Days Activities of the Joint Biafra Famine Appeal*, Dublin: Joint Biafra Famine Appeal, 1968.

Kirk-Greene, A.H.M., *Crisis and Conflict in Nigeria: A Documentary Sourcebook 1966–1969*, 2 vols., Oxford: Oxford University Press, 1971.

Knapp, George, *Aspects of the Biafran Affair*, London: Britain–Biafra Association, 1969.

Madiebo, Alexander, *The Nigerian Revolution and the Biafran War*, Enugu: Fourth Dimension Publishing, 1980.

Makozi, A.O. and G.J. Afolabi Ojo (eds.), *The History of the Catholic Church in Nigeria*, Lagos: Macmillan Nigeria, 1982.

Marriage, Zoë, *Not Breaking the Rules, Not Playing the Game: International Assistance to Countries at War*, London: C. Hurst & Co., 2006.

Mezu, S.O., *Behind the Rising Sun*, London: Heinemann, 1971.

Milne, June (compiler), *Kwame Nkrumah: The Conakry Years; His Life and Letters*, London: Panaf (an imprint of Zed Press), 1990.

————, *Kwame Nkrumah: A Biography*, London: Panaf Books, 1999.

Miners, N.J., *The Nigerian Army, 1956–1966*, London: Methuen, 1971.

Moses, A. Dirk and Lasse Heerten (eds.), *Post-colonial Conflict and the Question of Genocide: The Nigeria–Biafra War, 1967–1970*, London: Routledge, 2018.

Nwankwo, Arthur and Samuel Ifejika, *The Making of a Nation: Biafra*, London: C. Hurst & Co., 1969.

Obasanjo, Olusegun, *My Command: An Account of the Nigerian Civil War 1967–1970*, London: Heinemann, 1980.

Obiechina, Emmanuel, *An African Popular Literature: A Study of Onitsha Market Pamphlets*, Cambridge: Cambridge University Press, 1973.

O'Connell, James, "Political Integration: The Nigerian Case", in Arthur Hazlewood (ed.), *African Integration and Disintegration*, 129–84, Oxford: Oxford University Press, 1967.

Ojukwu, Odumegwu, *Biafra: Selected Speeches and Random Thoughts*, New York: Harper & Row, 1969.

Omaka, Arua Oko, *The Biafran Humanitarian Crisis, 1967–1970: International Human Rights and Joint Church Aid*, Lanham, MD: Farleigh Dickinson University Press, 2016.

Péan, Pierre, *Affaires africaines*, Paris: Fayard, 1983.

Schwarz, Walter, *Nigeria*, London: Pall Mall Press, 1968.

Smillie, Ian, *The Alms Bazaar: Altruism under Fire; Non-profit Organizations and International Development*, London: IT Publications, 1995.

BIBLIOGRAPHY

Soyinka, Wole, *The Man Died: Prison Notes of Wole Soyinka*, London: Rex Collings, 1972; Penguin, 1975.

Urhobo, Emmanuel, *Relief Operations in the Nigerian Civil War*, Ibadan: Daystar Press, 1978.

Uwechue, Raph (Raphael), *Reflections on the Nigerian Civil War*, London: OITH International Publishers, 1969; rev. ed., Paris: Jeune Afrique, 1971.

Venter, Al J., *Biafra's War 1967–70: A Tribal Conflict in Nigeria That Left a Million Dead*, Solihull: Helion & Co., 2015.

Verschave, François-Xavier, *La Françafrique: Le plus long scandale de la République*, Paris: Stock, 1988.

Waugh, Auberon and Suzanne Cronje, *Biafra: Britain's Shame*, London: Michael Joseph, 1969.

Whiteman, Kaye, *Lagos: A Cultural and Historical Companion*, Oxford: Signal Books, 2012.

Wilson, Harold, *The Labour Government 1964–1970: A Personal Record*, Harmondsworth: Penguin, 1974.

Wolf, Jean and Claude Brovelli, *La guerre des rapaces: La vérité sur la guerre du Biafra*, Paris: Albin Michel, 1969.

Archival reference

FCO 28/42/54, The National Archives, Kew.

Online references

https://api.parliament.uk/historic-hansard/commons/1968/aug/27/nigeria

https://api.parliament.uk/historic-hansard/commons/1970/jan/26/nigeria-relief-plans

INDEX

INDEX

INDEX

INDEX